The Economics of Saving

Recent Economic Thought Series

Editor:
Warren G. Samuels
Michigan State University
East Lansing, Michigan, U.S.A.

Other books in the series:

Feiwel, G.: *Samuelson and Neoclassical Economics*
Wade, L.: *Political Economy: Modern Views*
Zimbalist, A.: *Comparative Economic Systems: Recent Views*
Darity, W.: *Labor Economics: Modern Views*
Jarsulic, M.: *Money and Macro Policy*
Samuelson, L.: *Microeconomic Theory*
Bromley, D.: *Natural Resource Economics: Policy Problems and Contemporary Analysis*
Mirowski, P.: *The Reconstruction of Economic Theory*
Field, A.: *The Future of Economic History*
Lowry, S.: *Pre-Classical Economic Thought*
Officer, L.: *International Economics*
Asimakopulos, A.: *Theories of Income Distribution*
Earl, P.: *Psychological Economics: Development, Tensions, Prospects*
Thweatt, W.: *Classical Political Economy*
Peterson, W.: *Market Power and the Economy*
DeGregori, T.: *Development Economics*
Nowotny, K.: *Public Utility Regulation*
Horowitz, I.: *Decision Theory*
Mercuro, N.: *Law and Economics*
Hennings, K. and Samuels, W.: *Neoclassical Economic Theory, 1870 to 1930*
Samuels, W.: *Economics as Discourse*
Lutz, M.: *Social Economics*
Weimer, D.: *Policy Analysis and Economics*
Bromley, D. and Segerson, K.: *The Social Response to Environmental Risk*
Roberts, B. and Feiner, S.: *Radical Economics*
Mercuro, N.: *Taking Property and Just Compensation*
de Marchi, N.: *Post-Popperian Methodology of Economics*

This series is devoted to works that present divergent views on the development, prospects, and tensions within some important research areas of international economic thought. Among the fields covered are macromonetary policy, public finance, labor and political economy. The emphasis of the series is on providing a critical, constructive view of each of these fields, as well as a forum through which leading scholars of international reputation may voice their perspectives on important related issues. Each volume in the series will be self-contained; together these volumes will provide dramatic evidence of the variety of economic thought within the scholarly community.

The Economics of Saving

edited by
James H. Gapinski
Florida State University

Kluwer Academic Publishers
Boston/Dordrecht/London

Distributors for North America:
Kluwer Academic Publishers
101 Philip Drive
Assinippi Park
Norwell, Massachusetts 02061 USA

Distributors for all other countries:
Kluwer Academic Publishers Group
Distribution Centre
Post Office Box 322
3300 AH Dordrecht, THE NETHERLANDS

Library of Congress Cataloging-in-Publication Data

The Economics of saving/edited by James H. Gapinski.
    p. cm.—(Recent economic thought series)
  Includes bibliographical references and index.
  ISBN 0-7923-9256-6
    1. Saving and investment—United States. 2. Saving and
investment. I. Gapinski, James H. II. Series.
HC110.S3E25 1992
332′.0415—dc20   92-18281
                                                                               CIP

Copyright © 1993 by Kluwer Academic Publishers

All rights reserved. No part of this publication may be reproduced, stored in a retrieval system or transmitted in any form or by any means, mechanical, photo-copying, recording, or otherwise, without the prior written permission of the publisher, Kluwer Academic Publishers, 101 Philip Drive, Assinippi Park, Norwell, Massachusetts 02061.

Printed on acid-free paper.

Printed in the United States of America

To Nancy
for enduring

Contents

List of Tables	xi
List of Figures	xiii
Contributing Authors	xv
Preface	xvii

1
Questions on the Economics of Saving   1
James H. Gapinski

1.	Principal Interrogatories	1
2.	Saving Profiles	1
3.	Explaining Saving	6
4.	Fiscal Deficits and Saving	8
5.	Ricardian Equivalence	11
	5.1. Theoretical Considerations	11
	5.2. Tests Based on Consumption	13
	5.3. Tests Based on Saving	21
6.	Stagflation, Supply-Side, and Saving	25
7.	Income Distribution	28
8.	Growth and Transition	32
9.	Economic Development	37
10.	Answers, Harmonies, and Tensions	39

2
Toward a Theory of Saving   47
David J. Smyth

1.	The Keynesian Saving Function	48
2.	Early Saving Function Estimates	50

	2.1. Cross-Sectional Estimates of the Keynesian Consumption Function	50
	2.2. Time Series Estimates of the Keynesian Consumption Function	51
3.	Short-Run and Long-Run Behavior	54
	3.1. The Kuznets and Goldsmith Evidence	54
	3.2. The Trend in the Saving Function Hypothesis	55
	3.3. Short-Run Variability in the Marginal Propensity to Save	55
	3.4. Saving Phenomena to be Explained	56
	3.5. The Measurement of Saving, Consumption, and Disposable Income	57
4.	The Relative Income Hypothesis	57
	4.1. Cross-Sectional Form of the Relative Income Theory	58
	4.2. Ratchet Models	59
5.	Saving as a Multiperiod Decision	60
6.	The Permanent Income Hypothesis	62
	6.1. Present Value, Consumption, and Saving	62
	6.2. Permanent and Transitory Income and Consumption	63
	6.3. A Hypothetical Example of the Permanent Income Model	64
	6.4. Friedman's Evidence on the Permanent Income Hypothesis	67
	6.5. Further Empirical Evidence on the Permanent Income Hypothesis	68
7.	The Life Cycle Hypothesis	70
	7.1. Income and Consumption over a Lifetime	71
	7.2. Evidence on the Life Cycle Theory: Cross Section	73
	7.3. Evidence on the Life Cycle Theory: Time Series	74
8.	A Wealth-Adjustment Model	76
9.	Saving Functions Using Quarterly Postwar National Income Accounts Data	77
	9.1. The Measurement of Consumption and Saving	77
	9.2. The Behavior of Saving, Quarterly Data, 1947IV to 1990IV	78
	9.3. Alternative Saving Functions, Quarterly Data, 1953I to 1990IV	80
10.	Error Correction Models	82
11.	Rational Expectations Models	83
12.	Inflation and the Saving Function	85
13.	Conclusions	88

Commentary by Marjorie Flavin   93

Commentary by Edward B. Montgomery   102

3
National Saving and the Twin Deficits: Myth and Reality   109
Robert Eisner and Paul J. Pieper

1.	The Measurement of Saving	109
2.	Deficits and the Saving–Investment Identity	112
3.	U.S. Investment in the Eighties—A Historical Perspective	116
4.	The Effect of Deficits on Investment—An Empirical Analysis	119

CONTENTS

5.	Conclusion	128
	Appendix: Data Sources	130

Commentary by Ali F. Darrat   134

Commentary by Dennis Placone and Holley Ulbrich   145

4
Reaganomics, Saving, and the Casino Effect   153
E. Ray Canterbery

1.	Reaganomics and the Supply-Siders	153
2.	Say's Law Embued with Entrepreneurial Spirit	154
3.	Truth in Taxes and in Lending	155
4.	The Measurement of Saving	159
5.	Keynes Redux	160
6.	A Business and Household Net Worth Approach	164
7.	The Casino Effect of T	169
8.	Conclusions	173

Commentary by Robert S. Chirinko   176

Commentary by R. Jeffery Green   187

5
Saving and Distribution   193
Gian S. Sahota

1.	Main Theories of Saving	194
	1.1. Recent Debate: Focus on Intertemporal Theories of Saving	194
	1.2. Early Postwar Debate: Intragenerational Theories	197
2.	Income Distribution Theories	198
	2.1. Functional Income Distribution Theories	198
	2.2. Personal Income Distribution Theories	201
3.	Relationship Between Saving and Income Distribution and the Impact of Policies	202
	3.1. Rival Theories of Saving and Distribution	203
	3.2. Impact of Policies	206
	3.3. Uncertainty, Taxation, and Saving and Distribution	210
	3.4. Relationship of LDC's Domestic Saving to the Inflow of Foreign Saving and Distribution	211
	3.5. Any Estimate of Net Causal Relationship Between Saving and Distribution?	213
4.	Conclusions	215

Commentary by William A. Darity, Jr.   232

Commentary by Paul J. Taubman   239

6
Increasing the Saving Rate: An Analysis of the Transition Path   241
Laurence S. Seidman and Kenneth A. Lewis

1.	The Sato Controversy Revisited	241
2.	Empirical Analysis: A Continuous Time Model	243
3.	Empirical Analysis: A Discrete Period Simulation Model	246
4.	The Impact on the Wage of Low-Educated Labor	248
5.	Conclusion	249

Commentary by Winston W. Chang   253

Commentary by John Conlisk   262

7
Saving in the Development Process   279
T. N. Srinivasan

1.	Introduction	279
2.	Savings and Income in Developing Countries: Data Problems	287
3.	Saving and Investment: Empirical Evidence on Trends and Determinants	292
4.	Informal Credit and Insurance Markets	302
5.	Conclusions and Policy Implications	306

Commentary by Mark Gersovitz   312

Commentary by Christina H. Paxson   315

About the Authors   321

Name Index   327

Subject Index   332

List of Tables

1–1.	Saving Rates in the United States	2
1–2.	Saving Rates in Various Developed Countries	3
1–3.	Consumption-Based Tests of Ricardian Equivalence for the United States	15
1–4.	Further Consumption-Based Tests of Ricardian Equivalence for the United States	18
1–5.	Consumption-Based Tests of Ricardian Equivalence for Various Developed Countries	20
1–6.	Effect of Public Saving on Private Saving in the United States	22
1–7.	Effect of Public Saving on Private Saving in Various Developed Countries	24
1–8.	Time When Adjustment to the New Growth Path Becomes Virtually Complete	35
2–1.	Average Propensities to Save	55
2–2.	Hypothetical Permanent Income Model	65
2–3.	Alternative Saving Functions, Quarterly Data, 1947IV to 1990IV	80
2–4.	Tests for "Excess Sensitivity": 1947IV to 1990IV	86
2–5.	Inflation in the Wealth Adjustment Model: 1947IV to 1990IV	88
3–1.	Net Saving and Investment Account, 1990	110
3–2.	Federal Government Investment by Type, 1989	111
3–3.	Net Foreign Investment, 1990	115
3–4.	Measures of Real Gross Investment, Mean Percentage of GNP	117
3–5.	Adjusted Deficit and Private Tangible Investment	120
3–6.	Adjusted Deficit, Change in Monetary Base, Real Exchange Rate, and Private Tangible Investment	123
3–7.	Adjusted Deficit and Public Investment	124
3–8.	Adjusted Deficit, Change in Monetary Base, and Public Investment	125
3–9.	Adjusted Deficit, Change in Monetary Base, Real Exchange Rate, and Domestic and Total Tangible Investment	127

3C−1.	System Log-Likelihood Ratio Tests of Multivariate VAR Granger-Causality Hypotheses (FIML Estimations)	140
4−1.	Percentage Point Changes in Effective Tax Rates by Population Income Decile, 1977−1988	156
4−2.	Changes, Share of Money Income Received by Quintile	158
4−3.	Real Consumption Expenditures, Average Annual Growth Rates	161
4−4.	Personal Saving and Investment Rates	162
4−5.	Marginal Propensities to Save by Income Interval, Selected Years	163
4−6.	Average Propensities to Save by Quintiles of Income	163
5−1.	Combinations of Saving Theories and Distribution Theories	203
5−2.	Regression of Saving on Income Distribution	214
7−1.	Trends in Investment and Savings in Selected Developing Countries	293

List of Figures

1–1.	Macroeconomic Effects of a Supply-Side Disturbance	26
1–2.	Consumption Growth and Transition Paths Given Increased Thrift	36
2–1.	Keynesian Consumption and Saving Functions	50
2–2.	Saving Function Estimated from Household Budget Data, 1888–1890	51
2–3.	Annual Saving and Disposable Income Data, 1923 to 1940, Available to Early Researchers	52
2–4.	Illustration of a Ratchet Model	60
2–5.	Linear Expansion Path with a Homogeneous Utility Function	61
2–6.	Relationship Between Saving and Income in a Hypothetical Permanent Income Model	66
2–7A.	Income, Consumption, and Saving by Age, 1960–1961	72
2–7B.	Average Propensity to Save by Age, 1960–1961	72
2–8.	Real per Capita Saving and Disposable Income: Quarterly 1947IV to 1990IV	79
2–9.	Average Propensity to Save: Quarterly 1947IV to 1990IV	79

Contributing Authors

E. Ray Canterbery
Department of Economics
475 Bellamy Building, R-128
Florida State University
Tallahassee, FL 32306-2045

Winston W. Chang
Department of Economics
John Lord O'Brian Hall
Amherst Campus
State University of New York
Buffalo, NY 14260

Robert S. Chirinko
The Irving B. Harris Graduate
  School of Public Policy Studies
University of Chicago
1155 East 60th Street
Chicago, IL 60637

John Conlisk
Department of Economics, D-008
University of California at San
  Diego
La Jolla, CA 92093

William A. Darity, Jr.
Department of Economics
University of North Carolina
Chapel Hill, NC 27514

Ali F. Darrat
Department of Economics and
  Finance
P.O. Box 10318, T.S.
Louisiana Tech University
Ruston, LA 71272-0046

Robert Eisner
Department of Economics
Northwestern University
2003 Sheridan Road
Evanston, IL 60208-2400

Marjorie Flavin
Department of Economics, 0508
University of California at
  San Diego
La Jolla, CA 92093

James H. Gapinski
Department of Economics
475 Bellamy Building, R-128
Florida State University
Tallahassee, FL 32306-2045

Mark Gersovitz
Department of Economics
Lorch Hall
University of Michigan
Ann Arbor, MI 48109-1220

R. Jeffery Green
Department of Economics
Ballantine Hall
Indiana University
Bloomington, IN 47405

Kenneth A. Lewis
Department of Economics
University of Delaware
Newark, DE 19716

Edward B. Montgomery
Department of Economics
3115H Tydings Hall
University of Maryland
College Park, MD 20704

Christina H. Paxson
Woodrow Wilson School of Public
 and International Affairs
Princeton University
Princeton, NJ 08544

Paul J. Pieper
Department of Economics
University of Illinois at Chicago
Box 4348
Chicago, IL 60680

Dennis Placone
Department of Economics
222 Sirrine Hall
Clemson University
Clemson, SC 29634-1309

Gian S. Sahota
Department of Economics
Vanderbilt University
Nashville, TN 37235

Laurence S. Seidman
Department of Economics
University of Delaware
Newark, DE 19716

David J. Smyth
Department of Economics
2107 CEBA
Louisiana State University
Baton Rouge, LA 70803

T. N. Srinivasan
Department of Economics
Yale University
1987 Yale Station
27 Hillhouse Avenue
New Haven, CT 06520

Paul J. Taubman
Department of Economics
3718 Locust Walk
University of Pennsylvania
Philadelphia, PA 19104-6297

Holley Ulbrich
Department of Economics
222 Sirrine Hall
Clemson University
Clemson, SC 29634-1309

Preface

This book began when a letter reached my desk in November 1989. Written by Warren Samuels, professor of economics at Michigan State University and editor for Kluwer Academic Publishers, the letter reviewed the philosophy behind Kluwer's series on recent economic thought and accordingly expressed interest in the controversies that surround contemporary topics in the discipline. It graciously went on to invite me to organize, consonant with that philosophy, a volume of chapters on saving. Soon thereafter I learned that the chapters were to be original compositions. I also learned that I would have substantial flexibility in structuring the volume and in recruiting contributors, who logically would be authorities in the field. Succinctly, Samuels was inviting me to work with leading scholars in exploring the current controversies in saving, one of my favorite subjects. That invitation was simply too tempting to refuse.

Preparation of the book's outline went smoothly. It was obvious that the statistics of saving should be covered along with the theories of saving. It was equally obvious that special issues must be addressed: Ricardian Equivalence, supply-side doctrine, and economic development among others. These themes should be handled so as to bring out the ideological tensions in the profession, and that criterion helped to shape the list of potential contributors. That is, both sides of a conflict should be represented, and both should be given the same treatment. Consequently, solicitation letters were mailed and telephone calls were placed to the rival camps until each essay was commissioned and each commentary was assigned. Prior commitments, parochial disinterest, nagging illnesses, or — perhaps more subtly — intellectual natural selection may have prevented ex post an exact compliance with the ex ante guideline. Yet in the end the contributors showed that controversy does flourish in the economics of saving.

The authors and commentators must be thanked for sharing their expertise, for their enthusiasm, and for their patience. Warren Samuels must be thanked for offering a truly rare academic opportunity. Zachary Rolnik, senior editor at Kluwer, kept administrative details from interfering with scholarly pursuits whereas Judy Pereira, the production editor, and Joyce Grandy, the copy editor, expedited the volume through its production cycle. They too deserve thanks. Debts of gratitude also are owed closer to home. William Laird, chairman of the Economics Department here at Florida State University, reallocated resources of various kinds to support the project. Andrea Mervar became immersed in data collection, Beth Anna Harris disappeared into reference checks, and Peter Krafft stopped drawing maps long enough to sketch graphs. Elizabeth Welsch took charge of correspondence as Carol Felton first and then Karen Hollen took charge of converting handscript into typescript. Michelle Liddon and Ben Shippen, Jr. helped during the hectic days of the page proofs. Still closer to home, special thanks go to Gerri, Missy, and Suzie for tolerating how one family member makes a living, to Helen and Henry for being there from the beginning, to Sally and Henry for being there along the way, and to Nancy, to whom the volume is dedicated.

J. H. G.

1 QUESTIONS ON THE ECONOMICS OF SAVING

James H. Gapinski
Florida State University

1. Principal Interrogatories

How has saving behaved in the United States, in other parts of the developed world, and in developing countries? What are the theories behind saving? Does a fiscal deficit affect saving unfavorably? Does private saving exactly offset public saving? Did macro policy of the 1980s stimulate saving and, with it, economic performance? How does saving influence the distribution of income? How does saving bear on economic growth and on the transition to growth? And how important is saving in the process of development?

Such questions are central to the contemporary discussion on the economics of saving. Some may have definite answers, whereas others may have definitely conflicting answers. Agreement, disagreement, harmony, and tension mark the discussion, and this chapter attempts to convey the richness of the debate. The chapter begins by looking at a few facts concerning saving.

2. Saving Profiles

Table 1−1 reviews the saving rates for the United States since the dawn of the 1970s. Personal saving, which registers 6.1 percent of real GNP

Table 1-1. Saving Rates in the United States

		Corporate		Private			National	
Years	Personal (1)	Gross (2)	Net (3)	Gross (4)	Net (5)	Public (6)	Gross (7)	Net (8)
1971–1975	6.1	11.5	2.3	17.6	8.5	−1.2	16.5	7.3
1976–1980	4.9	13.0	2.5	17.9	7.4	−0.8	17.1	6.7
1981–1985	4.3	13.2	1.8	17.5	6.1	−2.9	14.6	3.2
1986–1990	2.9	12.3	1.6	15.2	4.5	−2.4	12.8	2.1

Source: National Income and Product Accounts of the United States.

Notes: Each entry expresses real saving as a percent of real GNP. Data for 1990 include only the first-quarter figures. Gross rates reflect capital consumption allowances, whereas net rates subtract them. Column (4) equals column (1) plus column (2), and column (5) equals column (1) plus column (3). Similarly, column (7) sums columns (4) and (6), and column (8) sums (5) and (6).

from 1971 to 1975, diminishes continually to 2.9 percent in the half-decade 1986–1990.[1] By contrast, corporate saving inclusive of capital consumption allowances rises to a peak of 13.2 percent in 1981–1985 but then falls to 12.3 percent in closing out the decade. Net corporate saving, which excludes capital consumption allowances, parallels the gross figures in tracing an inverted-U pattern. It also demonstrates the enormous size of the depreciation component of corporate saving: More than 85 percent of gross corporate saving in 1986–1990 comes from depreciation.

Private saving is the sum of personal saving and corporate saving. Accordingly, its gross measure has an inverted-U shape and evidences a two-percentage-point drop between halves of the 1980s. Public saving represents the excess of tax collections over spending for all levels of government combined. The weight of the federal deficit clinches the sign of public saving, and the Reagan years stand out in bold relief. Public saving added to private saving yields national saving, which in net terms resolutely declines to 2.1 percent.

Table 1–2 compares the saving rates for the United States against those for other developed countries and in the process observes some similarities and some differences. For instance, most private saving rates slip between the early and late 1980s, but those for the United States lie at the lowest end of the scale. They are farthest from the Italian rates, which slide from 33.0 percent to 31.5 percent in gross terms and from 22.1 percent to 20.9 percent net; they are closest to the British rates,

Table 1-2. Saving Rates in Various Developed Countries

Years	Private			National			Private			National	
	Gross	Net	Public	Gross	Net		Gross	Net	Public	Gross	Net
			Belgium						Canada		
1971–1975	26.5	17.4	−3.5	23.0	13.9		25.8	16.3	−1.9	23.9	14.4
1976–1980	26.3	17.6	−6.7	19.6	10.9		28.2	18.3	−4.0	24.1	14.3
1981–1985	28.8	19.6	−12.2	16.6	7.4		30.0	19.7	−5.5	24.5	14.2
1986–1988	28.3	18.4	−9.2	19.1	9.2		25.5	14.8	−3.2	22.3	11.5
			Denmark						France		
1971–1975	20.8	12.8	1.5	22.3	14.3		25.8	14.9	−0.3	25.6	14.6
1976–1980	19.4	11.0	−1.0	18.4	10.0		24.0	11.6	−1.0	22.9	10.6
1981–1985	22.7	13.7	−5.1	17.6	8.6		23.0	10.4	−2.9	20.1	7.5
1986–1988	17.5	8.7	3.5	21.0	12.2		22.3	9.5	−2.3	20.0	7.3
			Germany						Italy		
1971–1975	26.6	16.5	−0.3	26.4	16.2		31.0	22.1	−8.3	22.7	13.8
1976–1980	24.9	14.2	−2.1	22.7	12.1		32.5	21.5	−10.4	22.1	11.1
1981–1985	24.9	13.1	−1.8	23.1	11.3		33.0	22.1	−13.3	19.7	8.8
1986–1988	26.3	14.7	−1.1	25.2	13.5		31.5	20.9	−11.8	19.7	9.1

Table 1–2. Continued

Years	Private		Public	National		Private		Public	National	
	Gross	Net		Gross	Net	Gross	Net		Gross	Net
	Netherlands					Sweden				
1971–1975	26.6	18.6	−0.9	25.8	17.8	24.5	15.9	−1.9	22.6	14.0
1976–1980	25.1	16.6	−3.6	21.5	13.1	23.8	14.0	−4.5	19.3	9.5
1981–1985	29.9	20.3	−6.9	23.0	13.4	27.9	17.6	−7.5	20.5	10.1
1986–1988	27.1	17.0	−3.1	24.0	14.0	20.5	10.3	0.4	20.9	10.7
	United Kingdom					United States				
1971–1975	21.7	13.0	−3.7	17.9	9.3	16.9	7.4	−1.7	15.2	5.7
1976–1980	24.1	13.9	−4.9	19.2	9.0	18.3	7.5	−2.7	15.6	4.8
1981–1985	21.5	10.7	−3.8	17.8	6.9	18.3	6.4	−4.5	13.8	1.9
1986–1988	16.4	5.0	−0.6	15.9	4.5	15.8	4.9	−3.8	11.9	1.1

Sources: *International Financial Statistics* of the International Monetary Fund and *National Accounts: Detailed Tables* of the Organization for Economic Cooperation and Development.

Notes: Each entry expresses real saving as a percentage of whichever activity variable appears in *International Financial Statistics*. For Belgium, Canada, Germany, the Netherlands, and the United States, it is gross national product; for the other five countries, it is gross domestic product. Deflation proceeds by the implicit price deflator that corresponds to the activity measure. As in table 1–1, gross rates include capital consumption allowances, and net rates subtract them. Tabulations end with 1988 because that year ends full data availability.

which decline from 21.5 percent to 16.4 percent gross and from 10.7 percent to 5.0 percent net. National saving, whose public component is now restricted by the data to the federal branch alone, yields the same type of profile: The U.S. rates, either gross or net, are again the smallest in the group. This ranking duplicates the ordering reported by Bosworth (1990, pp. 377–378) for the United States vis-à-vis Europe and Japan and carries over into a still broader context that includes developing countries. In table 7–1 Srinivasan shows that during the 1980s the *minimum* rate of gross national saving for selected developing nations registered 12.2 percent, a figure roughly equal to that for the United States.

The U.S. rates in tables 1–1 and 1–2 have roots in the National Income and Product Accounts (NIPA), which may not carry an automatic seal of approval. For one thing, the accounts derive saving in a residual manner by subtracting expenditures from income. Errors in either series thus become entangled in the saving numbers, and as Lipsey and Tice (1989, p. 11) note, the errors may be large. Moreover, NIPA means saving only from income associated with current production as reflected mainly in market transactions. Necessarily, then, it excludes capital gains and nonmarket activities. It likewise excludes saving in the form of consumer durables, an omission that Smyth, in chapter 2, finds annoying given the common theoretical interpretation of consumption as the volume of goods and services "used up." Furthermore, the NIPA algebra subtracts social security contributions by persons as it moves from national income to personal income. Consequently, NIPA implies that those contributions are not saving even though it simultaneously insists that household payments into private retirement plans do constitute thrift. Taubman, in his commentary on chapter 5, expresses concern along this line.

Problems with the NIPA have inspired considerable research. For instance, Holloway (1989, pp. 63–64) shows that including consumer durables in saving raises the saving rate by more than one percentage point, while Hendershott and Peek (1989, p. 218) put the increase between 1.5 and 4.5 points. Adding to that adjustment the purchases of government pension assets, including social security, and making other allowances, Hendershott and Peek (1989, pp. 186, 199–201, 206) determine the private saving rate to be seven percentage points greater on average than the official NIPA estimate. To illustrate, their rate, computed relative to net national product, is 13.5 percent for the years 1982–1985, whereas the NIPA rate, similarly computed, registers 6.9 percent. In other words, the corrected rate is twice the official rate.

Dissatisfaction with NIPA practices has led some scholars to treat saving as the change in net worth, thereby capturing capital gains. Canterbery takes that approach in chapter 4, and Sahota endorses it in chapter 5. For other researchers, however, dissatisfaction with NIPA rules has prompted the more drastic action of overhauling the ledgers. As examples, Ruggles and Ruggles (1982) offer their integrated economic accounts; Jorgenson and Fraumeni (1989) present their full accounts system; and Eisner (1989b), who in chapter 3 joins with Pieper in objecting to the NIPA framework, has his total incomes system of accounts. That the implications for saving can be monumental is demonstrated by Jorgenson and Fraumeni (1989, p. 260) as they calculate the recent rate of full saving inclusive of human capital to be roughly 45 percent of full expenditures. A 45 percent figure is a long way from the NIPA posting of seven percent.

The faults in the data on saving cannot be casually dismissed for developed countries. Yet they appear to pale when viewed against the mistakes for developing nations. In chapter 7 Srinivasan tells a disturbing tale whose chief moral is that the saving data are simply wrong. Incomplete imputations, residual calculations, deflator biases, export underinvoicing, import overinvoicing, smuggling activity, and black market trading distort the saving statistics, which may have been erroneous anyway given misunderstandings about basic concepts. Srinivasan is reminded of the subsistence farmer who, upon recognizing that expenditures equal receipts, might report income to be zero. He is also reminded of the artisan, the street vendor, and the cultivator who, by transacting business in kind rather than in cash, might have no idea about what the level of income is. Saving-related data for developing countries are suspect at best.

3. Explaining Saving

A question on a doctoral comprehensive examination in macro theory inquired about what macro economists knew for sure. Of course, the question had no fixed answer, but the student could draw from several preferred topic areas in shaping a response. One such area was consumption or its obverse, saving.

Ever since the Keynesian absolute income hypothesis proved to be flawed, scholars devoted much energy to discovering what was wrong or, perhaps more aptly, what was missing. Their thoughts proceeded down two different paths. Consonant with Keynes' (1936, pp. 96–97) own idea that household behavior was psychologically motivated, the habit persistence school insisted that consumption and saving were governed by habits associated with previous acts of consumption, and Duesenberry (1948), Modigliani (1949), Brown (1952), and Davis (1952) helped to elaborate the reasoning. By contrast, the wealth theoretic school based consumption and saving on utility maximization under a wealth constraint. The household might be longsighted as Friedman (1957) along with Modigliani and Brumberg (1954) and Ando and Modigliani (1963) contended, or it might be shortsighted as Ball and Drake (1964) maintained. In either case, optimization prevailed.

Plainly, wealth theoretics differed from habit persistence in terms of fundamentals; yet the two schools agreed that household conduct was subject to inertia, which in the end might be represented by lagged consumption or by lagged saving, as appropriate. Both intellectual paths led to the same conclusion, and both met at the missing piece to the Keynesian puzzle. Surely, economists knew consumption and saving.

Although Smyth concurs that considerable attention has been paid to consumption and saving for over a half-century, he asserts in chapter 2 that much remains to be learned. In his words, "Not only do we not have agreement on *the* saving function, our models have failed to provide us with adequate explanations of saving behavior."[2] Accordingly, he follows Harrod (1948) in entitling his contribution "Toward... ."

Smyth comprehensively reviews the theories of saving from the days of the classical economists to the present. After duly noting the Keynes offering, he strides down the twin paths of thinking to discuss the modern theories—namely, the relative income hypothesis, the permanent income hypothesis, the life cycle hypothesis, and the wealth adjustment hypothesis. Using new empirical analysis, he shows that the modern theories come up short: At minimum, they all fail stability tests.

Probing the permanent income hypothesis more deeply, Smyth cites the works of others to refute the hypothesis' corollary that the marginal propensity to consume transitory income is zero. Moreover, he challenges the support for the hypothesis given by the random walk models of the Hall (1978) sort. Again with new empirical exercises, Smyth establishes that, contrary to the implication of the permanent income paradigm, consumption (and hence saving) displays "excess sensitivity," where lagged variables inserted alongside lagged consumption significantly affect current consumption. In this regard Smyth joins Flavin (1981) in voicing displeasure over the hypothesis. At the same time, he agrees with Srinivasan, who in chapter 7 observes that the permanent income model often succumbed to empirical testing, but he disagrees with Sahota, who in chapter 5 holds that the model withstood such examination handily. With respect to the life cycle hypothesis, Smyth is displeased anew. On cross-sectional data the life cycle conception is markedly out-performed by a simple Keynesian function, and in the time series context, the distinguishing characteristics of the model disappear when the restrictions necessary to enable testing are imposed. The paradigm truly has data problems, and on that point Sahota wholeheartedly agrees.

In rounding out his discussion, Smyth calls on the profession to abandon the atheoretical approach of sophisticated time series techniques, as those methods are no substitute for insightful model building. Additionally, he urges researchers to include the inflation rate in their formulations because he finds that inflation exerts a strong, positive effect on saving.

Supplementing Smyth's survey, Flavin exudes enthusiasm about a saving model that generalizes the permanent income hypothesis, generalizes the capital asset pricing model of portfolio choice, and integrates the two. This comprehensive paradigm, known as the consumption-β model, has the attractive feature of combining the decision on saving level with the decision on saving composition. Flavin outlines its structure but laments that its empirical performance has been poor. One explanation for the weak showing is that the transactions costs involved in adjusting the stock of consumer durables invalidate a basic premise of the model. With this thought in mind, Flavin calls for further inquiry into durable goods consumption and thus joins Smyth in stressing the notion of "toward."

Montgomery, in his commentary, agrees with Smyth that research should be broadened to encompass inflation, but he goes further to recommend more study of risk, family structure, and market imperfections such as liquidity constraints. The saving effects of publicly provided pensions might be examined as well. He believes that the inquiries into the influence of government saving on private saving have led to ambiguous results, and he therefore advises additional work in that area. Section 5 of this chapter obliges. Although Montgomery is more conciliatory than Smyth in assessing the contemporary scholarship on saving, he reaches virtually the same conclusion, that "most of recent research ... points toward the need for better models ... to understand saving." Like Smyth and Flavin, Montgomery too underscores the notion of "toward."

Evidently, the theory of saving is still approaching; it has not yet arrived.

4. Fiscal Deficits and Saving

One important policy question regarding saving revolves around the fiscal deficit. Asked explicitly, How does the deficit affect saving? Eisner and Pieper study this question in chapter 3 by appealing to an identity relationship existing between saving and investment that may be derived as follows.

From familiar bookkeeping

$$Z = C + I + G + (X - R), \qquad (1-1)$$

where Z denotes real GNP and C signifies real consumption. Similarly, I represents real domestic investment; G, real government purchases; X, real exports; and R, real imports. Also familiar is the proposition that

$$Z = Y + T, \qquad (1-2)$$

with Y and T symbolizing real disposable income and real tax, respectively. Inserting expression (1–2) into (1–1) yields

$$S_p + S_f + S_{sl} = I + (X - R), \qquad (1-3)$$

whose S_p, S_f, and S_{sl}, respectively, designate saving by the private sector, by the federal government, and by state and local governments. Identity (1–3) explains that saving, which consists of private and public components, equals investment, which consists of domestic and net foreign elements.

Conventional wisdom holds that reducing a fiscal deficit bolsters national saving, and the left half of equation (1–3) appears to corroborate this view. That is, cutting the federal deficit raises S_f and hence the total of S_p, S_f, and S_{sl}. However, Eisner and Pieper challenge this conclusion for its unreasonable ceteris paribus presumption that S_{sl} and S_p remain constant. They establish econometrically that as the federal deficit falls, grants-in-aid to state and local governments decline and consequently S_{sl} might decline as S_f rises. Likewise, a contracted deficit means decreased disposable income and diminished private saving S_p. In short, S_p and S_{sl} may not remain fixed as S_f expands. Instead, they may fall, and given this possibility the logic behind convention begins to unravel.

Ambiguity on the saving side of identity (1–3) motivates Eisner and Pieper to explore the effect of deficits on saving by means of the investment side. Their intention is clear; for if it can be proven that deficits alter total investment $[I + (X - R)]$ in some particular way, then from the identity the inference can be drawn that deficits alter national saving in the same way. But again conventional wisdom must be dealt with, as it flatly asserts that deficits depress domestic investment I. According to a usual argument, the government is the borrower of first resort. Providing risk-averse savers with financial protection that cannot be obtained from private borrowers, upon enlarging its deficit the government absorbs additional credit, leaving less for the private sector at higher interest rates. Higher rates then translate into lower investment, completing the crowding-out sequence. A similar conclusion results if the deficit increase is pictured as a rightward shift in the bond supply curve. Bond price slumps, and because it is inversely connected to interest, the latter heads upward. As before, an increased deficit implies reduced investment.

Two things are wrong with this standard scenario, say Eisner and Pieper. First, it does not fit the facts. Econometric analysis covering recent years reveals that gross private domestic investment, expressed as a share of GNP, varies directly with the deficit, also written as a fraction of GNP. Moreover, gross investment, the entire right-hand side of expression (1–3), also moves directly with the deficit. These results are quite robust inasmuch as they persist from one regression specification to the next. The second shortcoming of standard reasoning is its myopia. Broadening the scope of investment to include the household's acquisition of durable items, the government's acquisition of capital goods, and the country's "acquisition" of intangibles is only natural, insist the authors, who then verify that each of these investment types exhibits a positive link to the deficit.

Because $I + (X - R)$ varies directly with the fiscal deficit, it follows that reducing the deficit must reduce national saving and that claims to the contrary, such as Sahota's in chapter 5, reflect more myth than reality. It also follows that to expand national saving, the deficit must be raised, not lowered.

Darrat disagrees. In his commentary to chapter 3 he reworks the empirical analysis of Eisner and Pieper to purge it of possible defects such as series nonstationarity, omitted variables, naive lag structures, and inappropriate policy measures. Appealing to Eisner and Pieper's own data set, Darrat attends to these matters and, in the end, estimates a pair of simultaneous vector-autoregressive models. With them, he too rejects the crowding out thesis, as a fiscal deficit is shown to exert a positive effect on domestic investment. However, he then shows that a deficit has a negative effect on gross investment and concludes therefore that to expand national saving, the deficit must be lowered, not raised. On that score, anyway, conventional wisdom may be right.

Siding with Darrat in championing orthodoxy, Placone and Ulbrich return to equation (1–3). They argue that even if a rise in S_f causes S_p and S_{sl} to decline, the declines would occur at less than a dollar-for-dollar rate. Consequently, national saving would increase when the deficit decreased. Investment too would increase, thereby admitting crowding out through the back door. In this regard Placone and Ulbrich part company not only with Eisner and Pieper but also with Darrat. They defend their position by relying on the proposition that deficits and interest rates move in the same direction. Actually, the latter assertion is somewhat surprising because it runs counter to their position a few years past (Placone, Ulbrich, and Wallace, 1985) when they established econometrically that higher deficits meant *lower* interest rates. Carried forward, that reasoning would reject crowding out and would make them allies of Eisner, Pieper, and Darrat, instead of adversaries.

5. Ricardian Equivalence

Eisner and Pieper avow that increasing the deficit increases national saving. Darrat, together with Placone and Ulbrich, asserts the opposite. A third point of view, which Eisner and Pieper (1984, p. 17) openly reject, contends that when the deficit increases, nothing happens to saving overall. How is this position justified?

5.1. Theoretical Considerations

Bailey (1962, pp. 75–77; 1971, pp. 156–158) argues that individuals perceive a fiscal deficit to mean higher future taxes. Consequently, they increase their saving now to prepare themselves for that higher tax bill. The interest earned on the extra saving enables them to cover the service charge of the deficit, and the saving principal enables them to satisfy the tax principal when it finally falls due. Should the individual die beforehand, the children would satisfy that obligation through the estate. According to Bailey, then, an increase in deficit causes private saving to increase by an equal amount, leaving total saving unchanged. The household saves the income it would have lost had the government opted for higher taxation rather than for bond issuance; as a corollary, consumption is the same for either method of finance.

Barro (1974, pp. 1101–1104) expresses a similar sentiment. In his view the household worries about its children and sees them as bearing the tax needed to redeem any current bond issue. Maximizing utility subject to a wealth constraint, the household determines the optimum net bequest—namely, the bequest level over and above the amount required to compensate the children for the government debt they must pay. Optimality insists that the net bequest be kept intact, and hence an increase in debt prompts a commensurate increase in gross bequest, leaving current consumption unchanged. Under discounting, today's bonds are tomorrow's taxes. Bonds are not perceived as wealth and therefore do not influence consumption.

The idea that debt is equivalent to taxation is actually very old. It dates back to Ricardo and, thanks to Buchanan (1976, p. 337), has come to be known as the Ricardian Equivalence Theorem. In an article entitled "Funding System," which he prepared for the 1820 *Encyclopedia Britannica*, Ricardo compared debt—or deficit—with taxation: "In point of economy, there is no real difference in either of the modes; for twenty millions in one payment, one million per annum for ever, or 1,200,000 l. for 45 years, are precisely of the same value;..." (Sraffa, 1951, p. 186).

That the validity of Ricardian Equivalence turns on several conditions, not all of them innocuous, should be apparent. For instance, the household must care about its offspring to the point of striving to leave an estate that holds them completely harmless from present debt. Likewise, the household must be inclined to make precise intergenerational calculations and to make them in the face of uncertainty. At bottom, of course, the household must believe in the equivalence of finance modes. Such assumptions, while common in contemporary theoretical work, may stretch reality more than a bit, and scholars besides Eisner and Pieper have campaigned against them. Bernheim (1987, pp. 3–20; 1989, pp. 63–67), for example, is exhaustive in his objections.

The critics draw attention to the possibility that Ricardian Equivalence may not be valid, and Ricardo himself expressed serious doubt. The concluding lines to the aforementioned passage make the case:

> In point of economy, there is no real difference in either of the modes; for twenty million in one payment, one million per annum for ever, or 1,200,000 l. for 45 years, are precisely of the same value; *but the people who pay the taxes never so estimate them, and therefore do not manage their private affairs accordingly.* [Sraffa, 1951, p. 186; italics added]

A few lines later Ricardo reiterated that view:

> It would be difficult to convince a man possessed of 20,000 l., or any other sum, that a perpetual payment of 50 l. per annum was equally burdensome with a single tax of 1000 l. He would have some vague notion that the 50 l. per annum would be paid by posterity, and would not be paid by him;... [Sraffa, 1951, p. 187]

As O'Driscoll (1977, pp. 208–209) confirmed, these excerpts transform the Equivalence Theorem into a nonequivalence theorem, for they hold that debt and taxes are not perceived as identical. Individuals see debt as net wealth, and hence consumption might rise with the deficit.

Whether Ricardian Equivalence is true happens to be something more than a challenging mind game. The theory has crucial practical content, which can be grasped by rewriting identity (1–3) as

$$X - R = S_p + S_g - I, \qquad (1-4)$$

where S_g denotes total government saving $S_f + S_{sl}$. If Ricardian Equivalence is true, then a decrease in public saving S_g brought about by deficit action prompts an exactly offsetting increase in private saving S_p.[3] As a result, the loanable funds being absorbed by the government are replaced and keep the interest rate stationary. No change occurs in domestic investment or, from equation (1–4), in the trade deficit. Yet if Ricardian Equivalence is false, then private saving does not increase to cancel a decrease in public saving. Furthermore, consonant with the consensus reasoning articulated by Sahota in chapter 5, interest rises, investment becomes crowded out, and the trade deficit worsens. The practical side of Equivalence cannot be taken lightly.

5.2. Tests Based on Consumption

Because it bears on consumption, Ricardian Equivalence may be tested by means of the consumption function. To sharpen the imagery, the government might be regarded as financing some programs entirely from tax revenue. However, it then decides to cut personal income taxes and to cover the newly created deficit by issuing securities. Because of the switch in financing, disposable income rises, and a consumption function having a standard formulation would imply that consumption rises as well. For the function to imply instead that consumption remains unaltered by the switch, it must include an "autonomous" component that reflects the deficit and cancels the "induced" effect.

One such formulation may be expressed as

$$C = \alpha_0 + \alpha_m m + \alpha_r r + \alpha_D D + \alpha_Y Y + \alpha_C C_{-1}. \qquad (1-5)$$

C now denotes real consumption expenditure per capita. Expenditure is used rather than service flow because it is expenditure that an equivalence-prone individual would manage under the deficit. m designates the growth rate of real $M1$ balances per person; it allows for a real balance effect. r represents the real Treasury bill rate and equals the nominal rate minus the actual rate of inflation. D stands for the deficit in real per capita terms. Work by Zahid (1988, pp. 726–730) suggests that different measures of deficit should be tried, and to that end six are checked. DEFRPC signifies the federal deficit in the income accounts. Its counterpart, TDEFRPC, refers to the deficit across the three levels of government: local, state, and federal. BORRPC represents total borrowing from the public. FDEBCRPC denotes the change in outstanding federal debt, whereas PDEBCRPC denotes the lion's share of that change: the change in public debt securities. Unlike the former, the latter excludes the change in security holdings by government agencies. Lastly, HOLDCRPC symbolizes the change in federal securities held by the public. All six deficit series are quantified in real per capita levels. Completing the notation is Y, real disposable income per capita. Deflation always proceeds by the implicit price deflator for consumption.

The conventional coefficients have the conventional signs, namely, $\alpha_m > 0$, $\alpha_r < 0$, $\alpha_Y > 0$, and $\alpha_C > 0$. Regarding the coefficient of primary concern, $\alpha_D = 0$ rejects the Equivalence Theorem. Furthermore, assuming that the induced factors, operating mainly through income and real balances, impact consumption positively, $\alpha_D > 0$ also rejects the theory and simultaneously implies that government bonds are perceived as net wealth. Quibble aside, $\alpha_D < 0$ accepts the theorem.[4]

Estimating equation (1-5) on U.S. quarterly data from 1969:1 to 1990:1 generates the numbers reported in table 1-3. Regression 1 gives the sans deficit version of the function. It performs well. The $\bar{R}^2$ registers almost one, the regression F of 8966.0 easily exceeds the critical value of roughly 3.0, and the DW statistic is gratifyingly close to 2.00. However, because the equation involves a lagged dependent variable, the DW statistic is biased toward that serial independence benchmark, and therefore the Durbin h statistic is given. It corroborates the absence of autocorrelation. As the first-order Markov coefficient ρ indicates, the fit is obtained by ordinary least squares.

With m being quantified as a proportionate rate on the order of 0.01, it can be converted into a percentage figure by moving its decimal point two positions to the right. Mentally doing so moves the coefficient's decimal two spaces to the left, leaving 26.32. That is, a one-percentage-point increase in the growth of per capita real balances increases consumption spending by $26.32 per person. Like m, Treasury bill rate r is expressed as a proportion, and thus its coefficient implies that a one-percentage-point increase in r causes consumption to fall by $4.92 per person. Although a $26 real balance effect might be seen as ample, a $5 interest rate effect probably cannot be. Evidently, consumption is only weakly responsive to interest rate adjustments.

The marginal propensity to consume disposable income equals 0.1414, hardly an atypical result. Lagged consumption displays an inertial coefficient of 0.8633, making A, the sum of the two coefficients, 1.0047. As indicated by the t-value for the A line of the table, 1.0047 is not statistically different from unity. This finding lends support to the previously cited shortsightedness hypothesis of Ball and Drake (1964, pp. 64-68), who stress that, owing to considerable uncertainty about the future, individuals

Table 1-3. Consumption-Based Tests of Ricardian Equivalence for the United States

Explanatory Variable	Consumption Regression Number						
	1	2	3	4	5	6	7
	Coefficients and [Student-t Values]						
CONSTANT	−98.55	−92.14	−109.79	−100.05	−28.57	−40.46	−69.93
	[−1.256]	[−1.005]	[−1.290]	[−1.170]	[−.321]	[−.470]	[−.809]
m	2632.3	2583.9	2726.5	2641.6	2066.7	2065.0	2357.1
	[5.592]	[4.378]	[5.012]	[5.122]	[3.550]	[3.495]	[4.037]
r	−492.47	−494.93	−493.49	−491.69	−500.20	−507.77	−510.84
	[−1.957]	[−1.950]	[−1.951]	[−1.938]	[−2.008]	[−2.035]	[−2.017]
DEFRPC		.0050					
		[.137]					
TDEFRPC			−.0122				
			[−.352]				
BORRPC				−.0116			
				[−.046]			
FDEBCRPC					.1616		
					[1.621]		
PDEBCRPC						.1578	
						[1.565]	

Table 1-3. Continued

Explanatory Variable	Consumption Regression Number						
	1	2	3	4	5	6	7
HOLDCRPC							.0805
							[.800]
Y	.1414	.1392	.1455	.1420	.1247	.1290	.1295
	[2.760]	[2.577]	[2.755]	[2.672]	[2.410]	[2.509]	[2.421]
C_{-1}	.8633	.8649	.8604	.8629	.8728	.8696	.8730
	[17.424]	[16.936]	[17.036]	[16.994]	[17.668]	[17.650]	[17.078]
Addendum							
$\bar{R}^2$	.9977	.9977	.9976	.9976	.9977	.9977	.9977
F	8966.0	7084.2	7094.2	7083.3	7319.2	7303.1	7140.6
ρ	0	0	0	0	0	0	0
DW	1.99	1.99	1.97	1.98	2.09	2.09	2.04
h	.072	.040	.148	.079	-.465	-.480	-.202
A	1.0047	1.0040	1.0059	1.0049	.9976	.9985	1.0025
	[.749]	[.483]	[.934]	[.692]	[-.312]	[-.206]	[.352]

Notes: Each equation postulates the dependent variable as C, which runs from 1969:1 to 1990:1, the last quarter of full data availability. The Student-t statistic for sum A takes the null value to be unity, whereas all other t-statistics take it to be zero.

gear their consumption decisions to optimally manage current wealth as opposed to lifetime wealth.

Regressions 2 through 7 of table 1–3 test the effect of the deficit on consumption. If Ricardian Equivalence is legitimate, then α_D should be statistically negative. According to the tests, however, it is not. Deficit measures DEFRPC, TDEFRPC, BORRPC, and HOLDCRPC have statistically weak coefficients that summarily reject the theorem. Measures FDEBCRPC and PDEBCRPC have stronger coefficients, but those coefficients are positive, not negative. If they suggest anything, they suggest that government bonds *are* net wealth. Bonds are similar to real balances in making households feel wealthier.[5]

Behind the regressions in table 1–3 rests the assumption that actual inflation appropriately models expected inflation in formulating the real rate of interest. As an alternative interpretation, expected inflation can be modeled as a distributed lag with declining weights; more exactly, as $\Sigma_{i=0}^{i=3}$ $[.10(4-i)] \Delta P_{-i}/P_{-i-1}$, where P_{-i} denotes the price level i quarters ago. Correspondingly, the real rate of interest may be denoted by ra. It should be clear from table 1–4 that not much changes under the adaptively rational rule, although the t-statistic for the interest coefficient is now slightly healthier across regressions. Importantly, however, the tests again consistently reject Ricardian Equivalence.

Taking the question of validity abroad requires an international data set, a convenient one being the *International Financial Statistics* (*IFS*) that underlies table 1–2. Its convenience comes at a price, however. Specifically, *IFS* does not report personal disposable income but rather gross national product or gross domestic product. Moreover, it provides only one definition of fiscal deficit. Nevertheless, *IFS* should say something about validity, and curiosity alone is sufficient to drive the inquiry forward.

The ten countries studied earlier comprise the international sample. This sample, annually formatted and covering the years 1962 to 1988, generates the regressions displayed in table 1–5. As before, currency magnitudes are expressed in real per capita terms. The host currency is used in each case, and no attempt is made to convert currencies into a common unit. Deflation now occurs by the implicit price deflator for gross national product or for gross domestic product, depending on the activity series extant. Consonantly, income is tracked either by real GNP per capita, GNPRPC, or by real GDP per capita, GDPRPC. Likewise, real money enters either as a per capita level M or as a change in that level ΔM. Because real interest never has a coefficient with proper sign on these data, it is dropped.[6] This deletion standard applies to all variables other than the deficit. Finally, because of autocorrelation the regressions are run by the Cochrane-Orcutt iterative procedure.

Table 1–4. Further Consumption-Based Tests of Ricardian Equivalence for the United States

Explanatory Variable	Consumption Regression Number						
	1	2	3	4	5	6	7
	Coefficients and [Student-*t* Values]						
CONSTANT	−100.51	−96.17	−114.08	−102.07	−33.36	−44.76	−73.63
	[−1.286]	[−1.052]	[−1.344]	[−1.198]	[−.375]	[−.520]	[−.854]
m	2600.6	2568.3	2711.7	2610.3	2069.8	2068.7	2346.7
	[5.529]	[4.372]	[5.009]	[5.069]	[3.572]	[3.519]	[4.039]
ra	−548.30	−549.36	−552.96	−547.55	−540.18	−548.00	−559.72
	[−2.129]	[−2.118]	[−2.135]	[−2.109]	[−2.116]	[−2.144]	[−2.164]
DEFRPC		.0034					
		[.093]					
TDEFRPC			−.0146				
			[−.421]				
BORRPC				−.0120			
				[−.048]			
FDEBCRPC					.1534		
					[1.543]		
PDEBCRPC						.1495	
						[1.488]	

HOLDCRPC

				Addendum			
Y	.1422 [2.789]	.1407 [2.615]	.1472 [2.799]	.1428 [2.700]	.1259 [2.438]	.1299 [2.534]	.0748 [.748] .1309 [2.456]
C_{-1}	.8631 [17.505]	.8641 [16.992]	.8595 [17.097]	.8626 [17.069]	.8724 [17.711]	.8693 [17.700]	.8722 [17.123]
$\bar{R}^2$	.9977	.9977	.9977	.9977	.9977	.9977	.9977
F	9041.4	7143.5	7158.8	7142.9	7358.4	7343.4	7193.4
ρ	0	0	0	0	0	0	0
DW	2.00	2.00	1.98	2.00	2.09	2.10	2.04
h	.017	−.005	.104	.024	−.484	−.497	−.234
A	1.0053 [.962]	1.0048 [.573]	1.0067 [.865]	1.0054 [.767]	.9983 [−.214]	.9993 [−.096]	1.0031 [.573]

Note: See the notes to table 1–3.

Table 1-5. Consumption-Based Tests of Ricardian Equivalence for Various Developed Countries

Explanatory Variable	Consumption Regression for										
	Belgium	Canada	Denmark	France	Germany	Italy	Netherlands	Sweden	U.K.	U.S.
	Coefficients and [Student-t Values]										
CONSTANT	12413.0 [2.522]	−72.13 [−.152]	8330.5 [1.402]	801.40 [.889]	477.61 [2.874]	524270. [.534]	−483.35 [−.672]	4448.4 [3.337]	117.64 [1.406]	−1408.6 [−3.617]
M		.3437 [3.390]		.0775 [.844]				.1090 [2.092]	.4370 [5.630]	.3288 [2.856]
ΔM							.3878 [1.799]			
DEFRPC	.2341 [2.335]	.0946 [.808]	−.0764 [−.867]	.0779 [.471]	.4843 [3.157]	−.0761 [−.232]	.0699 [.413]	−.0998 [−2.977]	.0006 [.006]	
GNPRPC	.2182 [4.620]	.4103 [5.912]			.2921 [5.051]		.5289 [4.176]			.3805 [6.702]
GDPRPC			.4722 [8.679]	.0725 [1.203]		.5374 [4.383]		.2477 [3.106]	.4105 [6.943]	
C_{-1}	.5975 [6.138]	.2238 [1.977]		.8403 [7.425]	.4437 [4.020]	.0748 [.329]	.1388 [.704]	.4372 [2.517]	.1789 [1.623]	.4510 [5.497]
	Addendum										
$\bar{R}^2$	.9981	.9485	.7810	.9984	.9973	.7059	.9618	.9955	.9901	.9898
F	4441.3	120.7	47.4	4049.2	3212.0	21.8	164.5	1435.4	649.5	633.9
ρ	−.070	.797	.831	−.310	.155	.709	.455	−.261	.332	.552
DW	2.02	2.09	1.74	2.03	1.87	2.18	1.72	2.08	1.69	2.13
h	−.422	5.121	na	−1.990	.981	nc	nc	−3.157	2.102	3.168

Notes: In each instance C serves as the dependent variable and spans the years 1962–1988 after allowing for the observation loss under Cochrane-Orcutt. *na* stands for not applicable; *nc*, for not computable.

According to table 1—5, the real balance effect operates in about half the countries examined. For example, in the United States a one-dollar increase in per capita real balances raises per capita consumption by 33 cents, a response echoing the reports in tables 1—3 and 1—4. For the United Kingdom a one-pound increase in per capita real balances boosts per capita consumption by 44 pence. At the low end of the response scale lie Sweden and France, with reactions of 0.11 kronor and 0.08 francs, respectively.

On the main issue of the Equivalence Theorem, table 1—5 essentially repeats the earlier rejection. Only for Sweden does the deficit variable exhibit a significantly negative coefficient. For six countries the deficit coefficient is insignificant, while for the remaining three it is significantly positive: Government bonds are net wealth in Belgium, Germany, and the United States.[7]

5.3. Tests Based on Saving

All the exercises summarized in tables 1—3 to 1—5 have a consumption orientation. Another way to look at Equivalence is through the eyes of saving. Private saving S_p may be viewed as composed of two parts. The first part is a counterpublic measure S_p^c; it adheres to Equivalence and offsets changes in public saving S_g. In equation language

$$S_p^c = \beta_0 + \beta_S S_g, \qquad (1-6)$$

where under the theorem $\beta_S = -1$. The second portion of private saving is driven by motives other than counterpublic, and this nonpublic component S_p^n may exhibit both cycle and trend movements; namely,

$$S_p^n = \gamma_0 + \gamma_C \text{ CYCLE} + \gamma_T \text{ TREND}. \qquad (1-7)$$

As a result, private saving becomes

$$S_p = (\beta_0 + \gamma_0) + \beta_S S_g + \gamma_C \text{ CYCLE} + \gamma_T \text{ TREND}. \qquad (1-8)$$

Table 1—6 reviews Cochrane-Orcutt fits of equation (1—8) for the United States over the quarters 1969:2 to 1990:1. Private saving and public saving are expressed in real terms relative to real GNP, and consequently both become proportionate rates. The private saving rate is treated alternatively as gross and net of capital consumption allowances, and the public rate is treated alternatively as inclusive (PUBSRATE) and exclusive (FEDSRATE) of saving by state and local governments. CYCLE takes the form of the proportionate rate of real GNP growth (RGNPGTH)

Table 1-6. Effect of Public Saving on Private Saving in the United States

Regressions for the Private Saving Rate

Explanatory Variable	Gross				Net			
	\multicolumn{8}{c}{Coefficients and [Student-t Values]}							
CONSTANT	.1513 [20.261]	.1693 [18.302]	.1523 [21.110]	.1668 [18.203]	.0819 [8.033]	.1059 [11.022]	.0824 [8.669]	.1028 [11.179]
DUM8290	-.0119 [-2.415]	-.0065 [-1.313]	-.0129 [-2.623]	-.0090 [-1.782]	-.0147 [-2.587]	-.0071 [-1.305]	-.0155 [-2.727]	-.0096 [-1.764]
PUBSRATE	-.4540 [-5.945]	-.7112 [-6.805]			-.3810 [-4.390]	-.7075 [-6.162]		
FEDSRATE			-.4616 [-5.918]	-.6609 [-6.528]			-.3805 [-4.311]	-.6503 [-5.841]
RGNPGTH	.1091 [2.080]		.0892 [1.704]		.1613 [2.793]		.1457 [2.520]	
U		-.6462 [-3.549]		-.4983 [-2.911]		-.8961 [-4.541]		-.7388 [-4.027]
TIME	.0011 [3.320]	.0023 [4.787]	.0009 [2.671]	.0017 [3.758]	-.0002 [-.346]	.0015 [3.000]	-.0003 [-.766]	.0009 [1.987]
TIME^2	-.00001 [-3.881]	-.00003 [-5.220]	-.00001 [-3.320]	-.00002 [-4.303]	-.000003 [-.607]	-.00002 [-3.939]	-.000001 [-.274]	-.00001 [-3.088]
\multicolumn{9}{c}{Addendum}								
$\overline{R}^2$	.4671	.5015	.4735	.4895	.4286	.5381	.4430	.5388
F	15.5	17.7	15.9	16.9	13.4	20.3	14.2	20.4
ρ	.679	.704	.669	.700	.729	.685	.713	.667
DW	1.83	1.83	1.81	1.82	1.77	1.81	1.80	1.84

Note: To allow for observation loss under Cochrane-Orcutt, all regressions cover the period 1969:2 to 1990:1.

or the proportionate rate of unemployment (U). In keeping with the inquiry by Summers and Carroll (1987, p. 616), TREND is posited as a quadratic function of time (TIME). Dummy variable DUM8290, which assumes units from 1982:1 to 1990:1 and zeros otherwise, anticipates the discussion on supply-side economics and may be ignored for now.

Like the earlier reports, the news from table 1–6 is bleak for Equivalence. Reducing public saving through deficit spending does promote private saving, but it does so at a pace substantially below the dollar-for-dollar standard of the Equivalence hypothesis $\beta_S = -1$. At best, a dollar drop in public parsimony leads to a 71-cent gain in its private counterpart, and that response could be as low as 38 cents. These findings are hardly glowing testimonials to Equivalence. In fact, they are much more supportive of the standard Keynesian response, where deficit action stimulates disposable income and then saving to a lesser extent. It may be worth noting that the failure of Equivalence is pervasive. Failure occurs regardless of whether private saving is postulated gross or net of depreciation, regardless of whether public saving is postulated inclusive or exclusive of state and local government finance, and regardless of whether saving is postulated as a level or as a rate.[8]

Turning attention to the situation abroad largely repeats the grim news for Equivalence, although a few favorable signs can be found. Table 1–7 has the details. The data sources for those drills are mainly the ones cited in table 1–2. Real public saving FEDSRATE refers to the federal component alone, and both saving measures are expressed as proportions of real GNP or real GDP, depending on availability. Variable YRGTH denotes the proportionate growth rate of either type of real gross product, and unemployment rate U is proportionate as well. Because the depreciation series for France and Italy exhibit permanent jumps in 1974, the regressions for those countries include dummy DUM74FF, which assumes units at and after 1974 but zeros before. DUM8288, consisting of units from 1982 to 1988 and zeros otherwise, parallels DUM8290 of table 1–6 and similarly anticipates a supply-side discussion. Cochrane-Orcutt steers the estimation over the annual data from 1962 to 1988.

According to table 1–7, seven of the ten countries have public saving coefficients that are significantly less than one in absolute value and that therefore deny the theorem. The German experience is particularly telling because there private saving rises barely at all when public saving falls. Of course, Canada, France, and Italy have FEDSRATE coefficients that can be construed as supporting Equivalence.

Champions of Equivalence might rally round these three points of light in celebrating the cheery statistical message of Barro (1989, p. 52). At the

Table 1–7. Effect of Public Saving on Private Saving in Various Developed Countries

Explanatory Variable	Regression for the Net Private Saving Rate in										
	Belgium	Canada	Denmark	France	Germany	Italy	Netherlands	Sweden	U.K.	U.S.
	Coefficients and [Student-t Values]									
CONSTANT	.1061 [14.288]	.1086 [4.748]	.1069 [10.095]	.1084 [5.258]	.2397 [9.964]	.1260 [6.914]	.2078 [2.485]	.1641 [4.534]	.0808 [4.185]	.0729 [7.880]
DUM74FF				−.0391 [−4.476]		−.0418 [−3.903]				
DUM8228	.0249 [2.612]	−.0137 [−.906]	.0279 [2.413]	−.0157 [−1.689]	−.0056 [−.522]	−.0198 [−1.591]	−.0018 [−.137]	−.0036 [−.238]	−.0041 [−.329]	−.0141 [−2.062]
FEDSRATE	−.6726 [−3.311]	−1.2613 [−5.106]	−.8252 [−4.878]	−1.1481 [−6.634]	−.1900 [−.752]	−1.1816 [−7.986]	−.9202 [−4.742]	−.8374 [−5.516]	−.8044 [−5.364]	−.8854 [−6.435]
YRGTH								.2018 [1.290]	.0494 [.539]	
U	−.6461 [−2.439]	−.5493 [−1.534]	−.7166 [−3.181]	−.5483 [−1.384]	−.0306 [−.095]	−.0474 [−.161]				−.2906 [−1.958]
TIME	.0068 [5.466]	.0084 [2.206]	.0064 [4.216]	.0059 [2.123]	−.0089 [−2.980]	.0012 [.429]	−.0042 [−.476]	−.0034 [−.719]	.5003 [1.739]	.0010 [.638]
TIME^2	−.0002 [−3.768]	−.0003 [−2.319]	−.0002 [−3.219]	−.0001 [−1.534]	.0002 [2.517]	−.00004 [−.386]	.00007 [.303]	.00004 [.309]	−.0002 [−2.443]	−.00006 [−1.320]
	Addendum									
$\bar{R}^2$	.8484	.7070	.7645	.7718	.3761	.8146	.4219	.6077	.7851	.6924
F	30.1	13.5	17.9	15.7	4.1	20.0	5.7	9.06	20.0	12.7
ρ	−.063	.585	−.191	.590	.678	.328	.805	.569	.424	.440
DW	2.02	1.57	1.81	1.51	2.21	1.91	1.78	1.96	1.88	1.65

Notes: The dependent variable always covers the period 1962–1988 due to the observation loss under Cochrane-Orcutt. The use of GNP versus GDP across countries can be inferred from the entries for gross product in table 1–5.

QUESTIONS ON THE ECONOMICS OF SAVING 25

same time, they might challenge the entire battery of tests offered here as being guilty of simultaneous equation bias, specification bias, errors in variables, and perhaps numerous other econometric sins. Yet as reasonable as the grumbles may seem, one must wonder why, if the theorem is indeed valid, supportive evidence emerges as the exception rather than the rule. The econometric inquiries by Bernheim (1987, pp. 64–73), Summers and Carroll (1987, pp. 613–617), and Eisner (1989a, pp. 73, 81–85) together with the empirical assessment by Srinivasan in chapter 7 only bolster the case against Equivalence. Further bolstering comes from Sahota, who in chapter 5 gives ten reasons for rejecting the theorem and asks the fundamental but insightful question of why private saving dropped in the United States during the 1980s when public saving plummeted. By Equivalence, private saving should have soared, especially because thrift incentives were operative and real interest rates were positive. To Sahota the influence of Ricardian Equivalence, and of its monetary counterpart known as the Rational Expectations Hypothesis, is waning as the academic pendulum swings back toward mainstream economics.

6. Stagflation, Supply Side, and Saving

To explain and treat stagflation, the simultaneously high rates of inflation and unemployment, various economists turned their attention away from the demand side of the market and directed their energies to the supply side. They claimed that stagflation was generated by supply shocks such as exploding energy prices, escalating wage costs, and climbing social security levies. Figure 1–1 demonstrates for the macro system. There P denotes price, Y signifies quantity, and Y_{FE} locates the full-employment benchmark. A supply-side perturbation shifts the supply curve upward from S to S' along demand curve D, causing price to rise, output to fall, and thus unemployment to worsen. Slaying the two-headed dragon calls for policy action to drive the supply schedule back to S, and that action consists of lowering the marginal tax rates on investment, employment, and saving. Unit production costs fall, and with them so falls the schedule.

Reducing the tax rates on saving increases thrift, thereby helping to finance capital acquisitions, which promote supply. However, because saving occurs mainly in the upper-income brackets, the tax cuts should favor the rich rather than the poorly saving poor, and hence supply-side doctrine collides head-on with egalitarian notions of income distribution.

In chapter 4 Canterbery expresses his disenchantment with supply-side thinking. He shows that the supply-side tax cuts secured by the Reagan

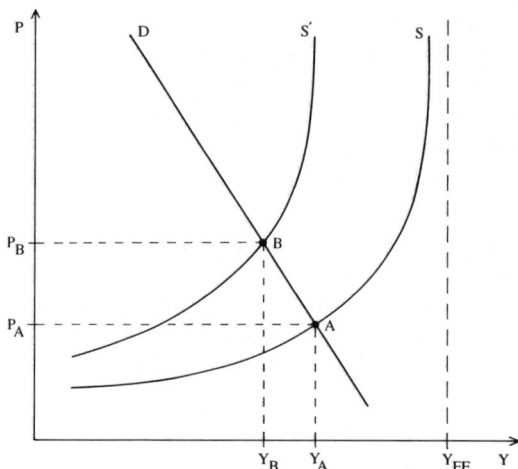

Figure 1−1. Macroeconomic effects of a supply-side disturbance.

administration in 1981 and superimposed onto the social security tax increases launched earlier by the Carter administration caused the tax rates for the top income groups to decline and those for low income earners to rise. This rotation in the rate structure had a predictable effect on income distribution, which became more congenial to the rich.[9] Specifically, the shares of income in the two high-income quintiles rose between 1969 and 1988, whereas they dropped for the lowest three quintiles. In this regard, anyway, supply-side action accomplished its purpose, writes Canterbery.

Did supply-side economics promote saving? Equation (1−8), augmented to allow for supply-side initiatives, answers the question skeptically. Dummy variable DUM8290 in table 1−6 isolates the effects on private saving of exogenous events that manifested themselves from 1982 to 1990. By its coefficients those events caused private saving, calculated from the income and product accounts, to decline rather than increase. Supply-side endeavors either had perverse effects on saving or were dominated by other developments. Whatever the case, supply-side philosophy failed to reverse the ebbing tide of saving in the United States. Evidence gathered from countries beyond the United States demonstrates that the philosophy, to the extent that it became part of national agendas, failed there too. Dummy DUM8288 in table 1−7 captures exogenous saving events from 1982 to 1988, but its coefficient is usually negative. Only Belgium and Denmark yield positive values.

Canterbery interprets the evidence more than skeptically. He argues that saving, measured as an increase in household net worth, *did* soar during the 1980s and concedes that saving *did* occur chiefly in the upper echelons of the income ranks. Yet he contends that a major reason for such responses was basic Keynes rather than advanced supply side: Preferential tax treatment of the well-to-do augmented their disposable income and, from it, their saving. A second principal explanation lay in the phenomenal appreciation of real estate. Curiously though, the expansion of saving came at a time when gross investment, expressed as a share of aggregate income, remained roughly constant and when net investment, expressed similarly as a share, actually fell. Contrary to supply-side logic, saving did not inspire investment. In fact, says Canterbery, the correct logic runs the other way as investment creates saving through its stimulating, or Keynesian, effect on income. What happened to saving if it did not finance investment? It fled into the Casino Economy, where it fueled speculative bubbles.

Thus in Canterbery's judgment, the true legacy of supply-side economics is that the rich became richer, the poor became poorer, and bubbles became commonplace.

In his commentary to this assessment, Green agrees that the supply-side tax cuts increased income inequality, but he doubts that supply-side policy caused speculative bubbles. Those excesses, he believes, were produced by financial deregulation and deposit insurance, both of which came into being before the Reagan administration came into office. By way of rejoinder, Canterbery concurs with Green's strict chronology of events, but he feels that President Reagan took deregulation to new heights, thereby giving speculative behavior new life. Turning to the marginal propensity to save, Green shares Canterbery's concern over the accuracy of the numbers though, after reviewing them, manages to conclude that the tax cuts did not expand national accounts saving greatly. This interpretation, of course, is consistent with the regression results presented in tables 1–6 and 1–7.

In other remarks, Green offers little sympathy for the supply-side proposition that a reduction in tax rates raises tax collections. The reason for his impatience is simply that the proposition can hold only in an extreme case. The United States has a tax structure that is roughly proportional, and hence tax collections T can be stated in terms of tax rate τ and income Y as $T = \tau Y(\tau)$. It naturally follows that $dT/d\tau = Y + \tau dY/d\tau$ and that $dT/d\tau = (1+\eta)Y$, where η denotes the elasticity of income with respect to the tax rate. For a rate cut to promote tax collections—that is, for $dT/d\tau < 0$—η must lie below -1.0, whereas empirically it lies somewhere around -0.5 for the United States. Therefore, $dT/d\tau > 0$: A rate cut *reduces* collections. In the same vein Green expresses his hesitancy about a second supply-side assertion, namely, that rate cuts stimulated productivity. Although the jury is still out, his hunch is that the consequent productivity gains were actually small.

In his chapter 4 commentary, Chirinko concurs with Green that the jury remains out, but he believes that it is deliberating the case of Reaganomics in toto and might return a Scotch verdict. Consonantly, he calls for more empirical testing of the relationships between the fiscal initiatives of the 1980s and the distribution of income, although the evidence that he himself provides regarding the incidence of corporate income taxes, the incidence of government expenditures, and the experience of the United Kingdom under Thatcher easily could be viewed as conclusively supporting Canterbery and renouncing Reagan. Chirinko finds the Casino Effect to be a novel and important concept, and he even traces its parentage back to the economics of Marx. Nevertheless, he again wants to see more empirical work. One exercise might quantify the impact of increased saving by the wealthy on real estate prices, whereas a companion effort might connect those speculative bubbles to key measures of economic performance.

Stressing fundamentals, Chirinko cites an early White House memorandum asserting that a primary objective of the 1980s economic program was to reduce the role of government in the marketplace rather than, as Canterbery suggests, to stimulate personal saving. Chirinko applauds the White House position for three reasons. First, tax incentives to encourage saving might have only modest success, a point that coincides with the findings in tables 1–6 and 1–7. Second, saving increases may have a minor effect on plant and equipment investment, a point that Canterbery enthusiastically endorses, and, third, investment may have little bearing on economic growth, a point that relies on a seminal study by Solow (1957). Going one step further, Chirinko questions why policy makers should care about the level of saving, and he remains unconvinced that the declining saving rates of the 1980s are a cause for major concern. He awaits proof beyond a reasonable doubt.

7. Income Distribution

One of the more popular theories of income distribution comes from the Cambridge school and emphasizes the way saving affects distribution. The saving schedule can be written in Kaldor (1956, pp. 95–96) style as

$$S = s_W W + s_C P, \qquad (1-9)$$

where S, W, and P denote real saving, real wage income, and real profit, respectively. The propensities to save s_W and s_C satisfy the restrictions $0 < s_W < s_C < 1$, which manifest the belief that the inclination to save is greater for capital owners than for laborers. Recognizing that total real income Y equals the sum of wages and profit, $Y = W + P$, and acknowledging that in equilibrium real investment I equals real saving, $I = S$, eventually imply for profit share P/Y that

$$\frac{P}{Y} = \frac{1}{s_C - s_W}\left(\frac{I}{Y}\right) - \frac{s_W}{s_C - s_W}. \qquad (1-10)$$

If s_W is set to zero as a simplifying approximation, then expression $(1-10)$ reduces to

$$\frac{P}{Y} = \left(\frac{1}{s_C}\right)\left(\frac{I}{Y}\right). \qquad (1-11)$$

Equations $(1-10)$ and $(1-11)$ have two favorable consequences for the capitalists. First, as investment increases, the profit share increases at the expense of the wage share W/Y, which is $1 - P/Y$. In other words, investment redistributes income from workers to capitalists. Second, diminished thrift by capitalists similarly enhances the profit share. That is, the more capitalists spend (the lower is s_C), the more they earn.[10] The widow's cruse never becomes empty, nor do the loaves and fishes ever become depleted. Religious connotations aside, however, laborers again lose in the bargain.

If workers receive a portion of the proceeds from capital and if they save that return at the rate s_W, then the saving schedule can be written in Pasinetti (1962, pp. 270–272) fashion as

$$S = s_W(W + P_W) + s_C P_C. \qquad (1-12)$$

Here P_C represents the amount of profit going to capitalists, whereas P_W indicates the amount channeled to workers given their claims against capital. Although schedule $(1-12)$ complicates the arithmetic, it nevertheless leads to formula $(1-11)$. In fact, it generates that expression without invoking the restriction that s_W equal zero. As before, judged in terms of income distribution, capitalist extravagance hurts labor.

Another popular conception of income distribution is neoclassical theory. Also known as the marginal productivity theory of income distribution, it supposes that production occurs under constant returns to scale, that competition prevails, and that factors are paid their marginal products. More specifically, a linear homogeneous production function

$$Y = f(L, K) \qquad (1-13)$$

connects output Y to labor L and capital K. Then from Euler's Theorem

$$Y = f_L L + f_K K, \qquad (1-14)$$

f_L and f_K signifying the respective marginal products of labor and capital. Equating marginal products to real unit labor price w and real unit capital price r under competition leaves

$$1 = wL/Y + rK/Y, \qquad (1-15)$$

a statement of income shares.

What determines the distribution of income under neoclassical conditions? This question can be answered by the relative capital share X; namely,

$$X = \left(\frac{f_K}{f_L}\right)\left(\frac{K}{L}\right). \qquad (1-16)$$

If the underlying technology imparts constancy to the elasticity of factor substitution σ, then function $(1-13)$ becomes

$$Y = \gamma(\alpha L^{-\rho} + \beta K^{-\rho})^{-1/\rho}, \qquad (1-17)$$

where the Greek letters identify parameters. Moreover, $\gamma > 0$, $\alpha > 0$ and $\beta > 0$ with $\alpha + \beta = 1$, and $\sigma = 1/(1 + \rho) \geq 0$. From schedule $(1-17)$, relative share X collapses to

$$X = \left(\frac{\beta}{\alpha}\right)\left(\frac{K}{L}\right)^{(\sigma-1)/\sigma}. \qquad (1-18)$$

Thus an increase in the factor proportion K/L raises capital's share relative to labor's when $\sigma > 1$ but lowers it when $\sigma < 1$. No change in relative shares happens when $\sigma = 1$, the Cobb-Douglas benchmark.[11]

By expression $(1-18)$ the distribution of income between capitalists and laborers is governed by properties of the production function. Yet, intuitively, saving must come into play because it influences investment and hence the capital stock. This intuitive sense can be sharpened by anticipating from section 8 that, in a neoclassical growth context, the capital–output ratio registers s/η, where parameter s designates the propensity to save S/Y and where parameter η symbolizes the growth rate of labor. As production function $(1-17)$ presumes for convenience, technical progress is absent. Then from that function, K/L can be restated in terms of K/Y, converting expression $(1-18)$ into

$$X = \beta[\gamma^\rho \, (\eta/s)^{(\sigma-1)/\sigma} - \beta]^{-1}. \qquad (1-19)$$

Consonant with the positive linkages that pass from saving to investment to capital, an increase in thrift s raises X when $\sigma > 1$, lowers it when $\sigma < 1$, and leaves it unchanged when $\sigma = 1$. Saving behavior combines with production characteristics to determine the distribution of income.

In chapter 5 Sahota advocates neoclassical theory over Cambridge theory, although he prefers both conceptions to three other views of functional distribution—income distribution that reflects payments to the factors of production. One member of the less-favored group is bargaining theory, which highlights the activity of pressure organizations such as unions and lobbies. A second member is the residual element theory, which treats the income of one factor as residual after obligations to some other factor are met. Rounding out the trio is monopolistic pricing theory, which focuses on the degree of monopoly power wielded by firms. To Sahota none of these three interpretations are terribly significant.

Personal income distribution strikes closer to home than does functional distribution because it pertains to the income of persons. Sahota lists seven perspectives on personal distribution, including inheritance theory and human capital theory. According to the inheritance camp, bequests, which are generated by saving, reinforce income inequalities, as the rich leave hefty estates and the poor leave nothing or even less. The human capitalists, however, feel that bequests actually may have an equalizing effect, as estates are granted unequally to compensate for unequal endowments among the next of kin. Nevertheless, evidence on equalization is mixed, and therefore the issue of whether saving—working through bequests—improves, worsens, or preserves personal income distribution remains open.

Turning to supply-side economics, Sahota agrees with Canterbery's assertion in chapter 4 that it intensified income inequality. Moreover, he adds econometric rigor to Canterbery's own empirical argument by showing from a cross section of 65 countries that increased income inequality, measured by the Gini coefficient,[12] stimulates saving. The distribution of income affects saving, and saving affects the distribution of income. Causation runs in both directions, completing the circle between the two concepts.

In reacting to Sahota, Darity compliments him for bringing together two seemingly disparate branches of literature—saving behavior and income distribution—and for covering them in detail from the standpoint of an applied microeconomist. That orientation is a strength of the chapter, declares Darity, but paradoxically it is also the central weakness because it rules out alternative perspectives. Particularly troubling to Darity is

Sahota's advocacy of neoclassical theory over Cambridge theory because it is Cambridge theory that offers the more general approach to saving and distribution. Moreover, Cambridge theory does not suffer from returns-to-scale restrictions and still reaches out to a set of interesting and relevant economic problems. For example, the restructuring of Eastern Europe, capital flight from developing countries, and North-South terms of trade all fall within the Cambridge ambit. Continuing his remarks, Darity observes that Sahota might have discussed how racial and ethnic inequalities in society affect income distribution. Those factors are critical and deserve treatment, he maintains.

8. Growth and Transition

Another area where saving leaves its mark is economic growth.[13] Output depends on capital, and hence output growth depends on capital expansion. In fact, investment is commonly regarded as the engine of growth. But, because investment depends on the finance provided by or, equivalently, the resources freed by saving, the link between saving and economic growth becomes closed.

One of the most celebrated models in macroeconomics highlights this linkage. Formulated by Harrod (1939), the paradigm posits a proportional saving schedule in keeping with the long-run nature of growth. Specifically,

$$S_t = sY_t, \qquad (1-20)$$

where S_t and Y_t denote, respectively, net saving and net output at time t and where the saving coefficient s satisfies the restriction $0 < s < 1$. Net investment I_t follows the simple accelerator; thus

$$I_t = v\dot{Y}_t. \qquad (1-21)$$

The dot signifies time differentiation. Parameter v is a constant that equals the ratio of capital K_t to output. Its constancy reflects the fixed factor proportions that underlie the simple accelerator. In equilibrium, investment equals saving, and therefore from equations (1–20) and (1–21)

$$\dot{Y}_t/Y_t = s/v. \qquad (1-22)$$

That is, output grows at the steady — constant — rate s/v, which Harrod calls the warranted rate. Obviously, increased thrift increases the rate of growth.

But not always. Solow (1956), relaxing the assumption of fixed factor proportions, reached an entirely different conclusion. Under variable proportions the production function may be written as

$$Y_t = F(K_t, A_t L_t). \tag{1-23}$$

L_t stands for the labor input, whose temporal motion follows an exponential rule. More precisely, $L_t = L_0 e^{\eta t}$, L_0 being the labor input at time zero. A_t represents an index of labor-augmenting technology: $A_t = A_0 e^{\psi t}$, ψ being the rate of disembodied progress. Exclusively time dependent, this technology is disembodied in the sense that technical advances enter the production process without the need of new capital. Function (1−23) is taken to be linear homogeneous, and therefore steady growth of K_t at the rate $\eta + \psi$ means steady growth of Y_t at the same rate; arithmetically,

$$\dot{Y}_t / Y_t = \eta + \psi. \tag{1-24}$$

Steady growth, which occurs at what in Harrodian parlance is termed the natural rate, no longer depends upon the saving coefficient.

The insensitivity of the steady growth rate to the saving parameter proves to be a general property. It holds for different formulations of the production function; it holds when technology is embodied — when technical advances must be carried into the production process on the backs of new capital; and it holds when capital is putty-clay — when factor proportions are variable during capital's design stage but not afterward. Still to conclude from this litany that saving has no bearing on growth magnitudes would be a mistake. For instance, the Solow model envisions equilibrium as $\dot{K}_t = sY_t$ in the spirit of equation (1−20). Dividing through by K_t and recalling that $\dot{K}_t / K_t = \dot{Y}_t / Y_t$ in steady growth leave

$$K_t / Y_t = s/(\eta + \psi). \tag{1-25}$$

Raising s raises investment and therefore raises the capital−output ratio on the steady growth path. Similarly, increasing s increases per capita output Y_t / L_t. From equation (1−23), $1 = F(K_t / Y_t, A_t L_t / Y_t)$, which implies $A_t L_t / Y_t = G(K_t / Y_t)$. Rearrangement of terms and substitution from equation (1−25) then yield $Y_t / L_t = A_t H[s/(\eta + \psi)]$, with $H' > 0$.

As already observed, economic growth has a long-run orientation. Shocks generating a new growth path often set into motion responses that eventually lead to that path, but the speed of such adjustment varies with many factors, one of them being saving. In other words, saving governs the transition path and thus influences the length of the short run and the arrival time of the long run.

Work on the speed of adjustment is properly associated with the Professors Sato. Ryuzo Sato (1963) demonstrated that transition to a new growth path was extremely slow, requiring a full century for adjustment to become 90 percent complete. The long run almost never arrived. At the heart of that inquiry rested a Cobb-Douglas production function and technical progress exclusively of the disembodied type. Several years later, another Sato, Kazuo Sato (1966), extended the analysis to include embodied progress inter alia.

In the synthesized Sato view, adjustment time can be written as

$$t_\varepsilon = \lambda\{\ln[1 - (1 - s_0/s_N)\varepsilon] - \ln(1 - \varepsilon)\}. \qquad (1-26)$$

t_ε denotes the length of time required for adjustment of the capital–output ratio to become 100ε percent complete. s_0 and s_N denote, respectively, the old and new values of the saving coefficient. Furthermore, λ is a positive scalar that reflects various growth agents including the rates of disembodied and embodied progress, the latter being symbolized by μ. From equation (1–26) it should be evident that a change in the saving coefficient disrupts the growth path and that adjustment time hinges on the direction of the change. In particular, the adjustment time for an increase in s should be shorter than for an equivalent decrease.

Table 1–8 presents in the first eight rows results derived from equation (1–26). The Satos, like Solow, suppose that factor proportions are variable to the same degree before and after the construction of capital. To them capital is putty ex ante and ex post, and those findings are prefaced accordingly. They show that adjustment caused by a saving increase is roughly twice as fast as one prompted by a saving decrease. They also show that the speed differential holds regardless of whether progress is disembodied or embodied. Moreover, for either s displacement, faster disembodiment quickens adjustment. Faster embodiment quickens it too, and for any given rate of progress, embodiment promotes faster adjustment than does disembodiment.

The putty-clay results, gauged by the adjustment in the number of operating capital vintages, are like those for putty-putty. That is, saving increases produce prompter responses than do saving decreases, and faster embodiment speeds reactions. However, consonant with the rigidity of capital ex post, adjustment under putty-clay tends to be slower than under putty-putty.

Depending on parameter magnitudes, convergence criteria, capital type, and disruptive force, adjustment time can vary greatly. With 90 percent convergence and with putty-putty capital, time ranges from a high of 163.6 years to a low of 27.0 years while 70 percent convergence ushers in a high of 96.4 and a low of 13.0. Even under the most favorable circumstances, adjustment to a growth shock takes a decade or more to work itself out, a time frame that might be a bit disquieting to policy makers. Raising the saving coefficient can have beneficial impacts. Yet policy that causes households to postpone current consumption may not be easy to

Table 1-8. Time When Adjustment to the New Growth Path Becomes Virtually Complete

		s Decreases from .20 to .10			s Increases from .20 to .30		
ψ	μ	$\varepsilon = .70$	$\varepsilon = .80$	$\varepsilon = .90$	$\varepsilon = .70$	$\varepsilon = .80$	$\varepsilon = .90$
				Putty-Putty Capital			
.01	0	96.4	122.1	163.6	52.1	72.2	108.1
.02	0	72.3	91.6	122.7	39.1	54.1	81.1
.03	0	57.8	73.2	98.1	31.3	43.3	64.9
.04	0	48.2	61.0	81.8	26.1	36.1	54.1
0	.01	64.2	81.4	109.1	34.8	48.1	72.1
0	.02	41.3	52.3	70.1	22.3	30.9	46.3
0	.03	30.4	38.5	51.7	16.5	22.8	34.1
0	.04	24.1	30.5	40.9	13.0	18.0	27.0
				Putty-Clay Capital			
0	.01	>10	>10	>10	1	7	>10
0	.02	6	7	9	1	4	6
0	.03	4	5	6	1	3	6
0	.04	4	4	5	1	1	3

Notes: For putty-putty capital, adjustment times are expressed in years; for putty-clay capital, in decades. Full details appear in Gapinski (1982, pp. 328–334, 350–356).

effect, and if the benefit of that sacrifice materializes only in a distant future, then it may not even be wise.

In chapter 6 Seidman and Lewis reach more optimistic conclusions. They charge that the gloomy prospect for thrift policy is the product of an incorrect focus. That is, convergence time, on which the conventional wisdom rests, focuses on the economy as it approaches the new steady growth path. Consequently, it misses altogether the possibility that after some point during transition, the economy may outperform behavior along the original steady growth path. Figure 1–2 illustrates the situation for the case of consumption. C_{Old} identifies the initial consumption trajectory under steady growth, and C_{New} indicates the steady growth trajectory that results from an increase in the saving coefficient at time t_0. Increased thrift first drops consumption below the original steady state levels, as the dashed transition line shows. However, the simultaneously higher investment levels stimulate income, which in turn drives consumption back to

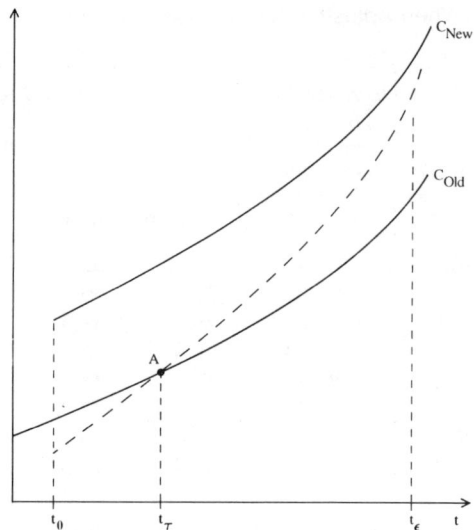

Figure 1-2. Consumption growth and transition paths given increased thrift.

the C_{Old} path and then propels it upward to C_{New}. Consumption is sacrificed only over the interval $t_\tau - t_0$. According to Seidman and Lewis, this sacrifice time equals roughly 6.5 years and falls substantially below convergence time $t_\varepsilon - t_0$. Moreover, it is rather insensitive to changes in underlying circumstances. For instance, stronger thrift policy shifts C_{New} upward, but it essentially rotates the transition path counterclockwise around point A. Although the "up front" consumption losses are greater, the later gains are greater as well. Do the discounted gains exceed the discounted losses? Indeed they do, conclude the authors after calculating a hefty positive rate of return on saving. Thus the adjustment to thrift policy occurs quickly, the benefits accrue early, and total discounted benefits swamp total discounted costs. A difference in focus makes a world of difference.

Chang, in his commentary, is not so sure. Although welcoming the new measures of the transitional path, he perceives some trouble with them. To illustrate, sacrifice time identifies the moment when consumption reaches the point where it would have been in the absence of the thrift increase, but it makes no allowance for the extent of forfeitures sustained en route or the degree of windfalls enjoyed afterward. A more informative measure, says Chang, is overtaking time, which he defines as the time when the discounted consumption losses are exactly offset by the discounted consumption gains. Overtaking time must vary directly with the discount rate. A greater rate implies a smaller weight for the later consumption gains, and as a result gains are required over a longer future if the initial consumption losses are to be neutralized. It is entirely possible for short sacrifice time to be associated with long overtaking time, and with that conclusion Chang nudges the wisdom on adjustment time back in the direction of Ryuzo Sato.

Continuing his probative remarks, Chang confirms that Seidman and Lewis suppose an infinite horizon for the rate of return on saving. To him a fixed finite horizon is more sensible from a policy standpoint; however, that reorientation would lop off the consumption gains occurring in the outer periods and therefore would lower the rate of return. In his commentary, on the other hand, Conlisk finds nothing wrong with a limitless range. What bothers him instead is that the rate of return measure is used by Seidman and Lewis under the assumption of exogenous technical progress. But progress may be endogenous, and, more to the point, it may vary directly with saving. In that circumstance increased thrift would exert a double impact on output: once through an expansion of capital and once through an improvement in progress. This double impact means that output rises more than it would in the exogenous case. Correspondingly, consumption rises more, and the saving rate of return becomes greater. By imposing exogeneity Seidman and Lewis actually understate the importance of increased thrift for transition, and the size of the understatement could be substantial, depending on how progress is made endogenous. Conlisk thus differs from Chang on the rate of return measure. Still, the two commentators share the same view of sacrifice time: They both see it as concealing more than it reveals.

9. Economic Development

Economic development concentrates on how to advance the economic base of a country, but its purview, unlike that of economic growth, is a country whose infrastructure is deficient. The communication network may be primitive, the road system may be fragmented, and airports and harbors may be scarce. Agriculture may be the main activity, and industry — or, more precisely, the lack thereof — may be the main concern. In that situation capital expansion is crucial, and hence so is saving. Srinivasan notes this traditional interpretation of saving in chapter 7, and he presents empirical evidence to show that saving in developing countries often increased significantly over the last several decades. The factors behind such behavior include the interest rate and various structural considerations.

Theory, says Srinivasan, is ambiguous about the sign governing the effect of interest on saving although quantitative studies typically report it to be positive. Nevertheless, the magnitude of that effect appears to be low. Complicating the picture is the rudimentary structure within which saving occurs. The absence of efficient credit markets means that individuals must save in advance of purchasing lumpy assets such as durables, and it likewise means that they must save to guard against emergencies, which can be common in an agricultural environment. The absence of private and public pension schemes implies that individuals must save to provide for their declining years; yet the fragility of the legal system cautions that contract enforcement may be sporadic, thereby inhibiting saving. Further complicating the picture is the existence of informal credit markets. To Srinivasan, those markets have been reproached unfairly. Rather than exploiting poor peasants, they channel credit to rural areas that would not be reached by a formal credit apparatus. Moreover, their rates are roughly competitive. In any event, informal credit markets are very popular, and they probably play a significant role in mobilizing saving.

Two other structural twists must be recognized. First, developing countries seek foreign financial capital to supplement domestic saving, but those inflows may work to displace domestic saving. Second, the uncertainties inherent in the development process may cause domestic finance to flee the nation. Plainly, all things considered, saving in the less developed countries is complicated business.

Perhaps equally complicated is the causation from saving to output growth in the developing context. According to Srinivasan, research confirms the anticipated positive relationship between the two series, but in his view the relationship turns out to be weaker than the usual story suggests. This finding may not bode well from the policy standpoint. Financial liberalization by interest rate adjustment may not generate much saving because of low interest elasticities, and whatever saving is generated may not have much impact on output. Besides, against this muted favorable response must be weighed the possible harm that liberalization may inflict on the informal credit markets. In other words, development policy too is complicated business.

Households in developing countries face low and variable incomes. If they are to avoid extreme hardship during lean times, it is essential that they smooth consumption by managing saving. But can they? Srinivasan takes up this issue, and both of his commentators join the discussion. Gersovitz volunteers that the record on smoothing is mixed: Some studies indicate that individuals can smooth consumption, and others conclude that they cannot. In an attempt to reconcile such conflicting information, Gersovitz reasons that income variations have different frequencies — high, medium, and low — and that only some frequencies lend themselves to smoothing. Paxson turns attention to the methodological matter of how one actually tests for smoothing. Citing problems that surround the standard use of instrumental variables, she advocates an alternative procedure that involves direct measurement of permanent and transitory incomes. She hastens to add, however, that the alternative has problems of its own. As regards empirical results proper, Paxson reports from her analysis of Thailand that households do smooth consumption through saving. She closes with the opinion that smoothing, at least in partial form, is common practice.

10. Answers, Harmonies, and Tensions

This chapter posed various questions related to the economics of saving, and in searching for answers it examined the following six chapters, commentaries on those chapters, and a few econometric results of its own.

The initial question posited regards the facts of saving: How has saving behaved in the United States, in other parts of the developed world, and in developing countries? At first blush the evidence is clear. Saving rates in the United States declined during the 1980s, a pattern that seems to hold for developed economies generally. For developing countries the rates often have increased since the middle 1960s, and correspondingly their recent values tend to exceed those for the West. Certainly they exceed the U.S. rates by a considerable margin.

Yet examined more deeply, the evidence becomes less clear. The saving statistics are usually based on national accounts data, and as such they are subject to both measurement error and tunnel vision. The first malady derives from the residual nature of the saving calculations, whereas the second arises from the orientation toward current productive activity. A broader interpretation is possible, as saving might be defined to include the acquisition of consumer durables or to reflect changes in total net worth. It is fair to say that the latter interpretation could drastically change the official picture of saving, and it is also fair to say that the consensus of authors in this volume supports a broadened scope for the measurement of saving.

What are the theories behind saving? Diverse. Some differ from one another merely as variations on the same theme, while others strike out in entirely different directions. The permanent income hypothesis and the life cycle hypothesis illustrate how similar the explanations can be, whereas the permanent income hypothesis and the relative income hypothesis demonstrate how discrepant they can be. Within the profession generally, the majority opinion champions the permanent income model and its variants as providing a faithful representation of saving behavior. The discussion here, however, challenges that sentiment. It maintains that the profession still has not established an adequate explanation of saving, and it lays much stress on the empirical failings of the permanent income paradigm. Nevertheless, not everyone here objects to that model, and their support serves to highlight a controversy that may have been less than widely known.

Does a fiscal deficit affect saving unfavorably? By traditional reckoning a fiscal deficit stimulates demand, income, and private saving. Because it combines with private saving to form national saving, however, it diminishes national saving and so can be viewed as unfavorable. Analogously, from the investment side of the saving-equals-investment identity, budgetary red ink stifles plant and equipment investment and promotes a negative foreign trade balance: A fiscal deficit crowds out investment while it creates a twin deficit in the international accounts. Though common, these beliefs are not shared by all theorists. Analysis in this volume shows that the fiscal deficit can lure in rather than crowd out capital goods investment. Additionally, some writers find that it boosts total investment, and from their vantage point the connection between the deficit and saving must be seen as favorable. Apparently, the relationships among saving components are rather intricate and by their nature prompt a companion question.

Does private saving exactly offset public saving? In other words, is the Ricardian Equivalence Theorem valid? This question is critical from the policy standpoint because if Equivalence prevails, then countercyclical fiscal maneuvering must be completely useless. In studying Equivalence this chapter returns to the original language of Ricardo, only to find Ricardo himself articulating the case for nonequivalence. Next it tests Equivalence through the consumption function and afterward through the saving function. Those tests are conducted for the United States and for other countries, but despite their number, they reject Equivalence almost without exception. As a corollary, those experiments suggest that government bonds are perceived by the private sector to be net wealth and that saving responds to deficit action more in Keynesian style than in Equivalence fashion. The other contributors who cite Equivalence likewise express doubt about its validity, their basis being either empirical or theoretical.

Succinctly, then, this volume observes substantial harmony among scholars in opposing Equivalence.

Did macro policy of the 1980s stimulate saving and economic performance? Probably not. The supply-side tax cuts of the early 1980s may have redistributed income toward those already wealthy, but the cuts seem to have had little beneficial effect on private saving as measured in the national accounts. Participants in the book report that saving actually fell during the tax-reduction years, and additional examination in this chapter leads to the judgment that supply-side policy either had a perverse effect on saving or became dominated by other events. The philosophy may fare better if saving is treated as the change in net worth. In that circumstance saving may have risen sharply, but rather than fuel investment in plant and equipment, it seems to have fueled speculative bubbles. Thus even if supply-side action did stimulate saving, it probably did not stimulate the economy generally. One commentator takes this last point further by showing that the rationale linking a tax rate cut to improved macro performance is flawed because the output response proves to be weak in practice.

How does saving influence the distribution of income? Income distribution can be defined at the functional level or at the personal level, but in either case saving is a decisive consideration. One popular theory of functional distribution comes from the Cambridge economists and postulates that income shares vary across productive factors, depending on their propensities to save. Another celebrated, albeit fundamentally different, functional paradigm has neoclassical roots and maintains that saving affects income shares by operating through the production process. Personal distribution theories may revolve around bequests, but one theory sees bequests as exacerbating income inequality, whereas a second views them as ameliorating inequality. Bequests, of course, are the result of saving, and hence saving can be regarded as providing a common denominator among disparate distribution theories.

How does saving bear on economic growth and on the transition to growth? To be sure, it bears heavily on growth. For instance, the thrift parameter influences the steady-state values of the capital–output ratio and the output–labor ratio, and, if factor proportions are fixed, it also influences the steady-state growth rate as greater thrift means faster growth. These properties are generally accepted within the profession and, now anyway, are not sources of tension. The same cannot be said of saving and the transition to growth. Although there is agreement that thrift constitutes a key determinant of adjustment time, there is no agreement about what measure to use in gauging convergence or about how long convergence takes. A quarter-century ago scholars were faced with the prospect that adjustment time could be enormously long. They responded by refining the problem, by developing more yardsticks, and by making additional calculations. But despite their efforts, or perhaps because of them, adjustment time estimates fell all over the map. Today the issue remains unresolved, and it simply may be unresolvable.

Finally, how important is saving in the process of development? Much needs to be done to improve the economic fortune of a less developed country, and saving, which represents a source of the requisite finance, should be urgent in that context. The statistics on saving rates support such a view, and the logic behind consumption smoothing strengthens it. Nevertheless, evidence concerning the relationship between saving rates and output growth casts doubt on it.

Saving is a fascinating concept. Households save, businesses save, governments save, and nations save. Everyone does it, and almost everyone has an opinion about it. Some opinions agree; others disagree. Consensus exists alongside controversy, harmony stands beside tension, and questions provoke answers that prompt new questions. Truly, the concept has vibrancy, and that vibrancy makes it fascinating.

Notes

1. A like pattern is displayed by Smyth in figure 2-9.
2. A similar sentiment is expressed by Sahota in the opening passage of chapter 5. Nevertheless, Darity, who comments on that discussion, appears to be unconvinced.
3. That a decrease in public saving associated with an increase in deficit prompts an exactly equal increase in private saving is clearly stated by Evans (1985, p. 85). Srinivasan also gives a clear statement in chapter 7.
4. The quibble arises because α_D might not be negative enough to offset the induced effects of the deficit. For present purposes, however, there seems to be little virtue in standing on quibbles.
5. The failure of Ricardian Equivalence in regressions 2 though 7 meshes nicely with the simultaneous finding that in each instance the sum of the coefficients of income and lagged consumption does not differ significantly from one. The latter property, a characteristic of the shortsightedness hypothesis, means that individuals do not try to make precise calculations about a distant, uncertain future. If they do not make such calculations, then they should not be inclined to make Equivalence calculations either. Apparently, they do not.
6. Working with similar international data, Bosworth (1990, p. 380) too has trouble with the real interest rate.
7. The coefficients of gross national (or domestic) product and lagged consumption sum to values that are uniformly less than one. Nonetheless, since the marginal propensity from "gross income" is less than that from disposable income, the behavior of the sum is not necessarily inconsistent with shortsightedness.
8. The exercises involving levels are withheld in the interest of space.

9. That the pro-rich redistribution of income stemmed from Carter-Reagan policies has its share of followers. Darity, for example, subscribes to it in his commentary on Sahota's chapter 5. His authority, however, is Bunting (1991), not Canterbery.

10. As equation (1–10) confirms, $\partial(P/Y)/\partial s_C < 0$ provided that $I/Y > s_W$, a reasonable condition that is necessarily satisfied by relation (1–11).

11. An excellent account of the Cambridge and neoclassical theories is presented by Hamberg (1971, pp. 38–42, 92–102).

12. In generic form the Gini coefficient expresses income inequality as a fraction ranging from zero for perfect equality to unity for perfect inequality.

13. Much of this section draws from the discussion by Gapinski (1982, chapters 9–11).

References

Ando, Albert, and Franco Modigliani. "The 'Life Cycle' Hypothesis of Saving: Aggregate Implications and Tests." *American Economic Review* 53, part I (March 1963): 55–84.

Bailey, Martin J. *National Income and the Price Level*. New York: McGraw-Hill, 1962.

———. *National Income and the Price Level*. 2nd ed. New York: McGraw-Hill, 1971.

Ball, R. J., and Pamela S. Drake. "The Relationship Between Aggregate Consumption and Wealth." *International Economic Review* 5 (January 1964): 63–81.

Barro, Robert J. "Are Government Bonds Net Wealth?" *Journal of Political Economy* 82 (November/December 1974): 1095–1117.

———. "The Ricardian Approach to Budget Deficits." *Journal of Economic Perspectives* 3 (Spring 1989): 37–54.

Bernheim, B. Douglas. "Ricardian Equivalence: An Evaluation of Theory and Evidence." Working paper No. 2330, National Bureau of Economic Research, Cambridge, Mass., July 1987.

———. "A Neoclassical Perspective on Budget Deficits." *Journal of Economic Perspectives* 3 (Spring 1989): 55–72.

Bosworth, Barry P. "International Differences in Saving." *American Economic Review* 80 (May 1990): 377–381.

Brown, T. M. "Habit Persistence and Lags in Consumer Behaviour." *Econometrica* 20 (July 1952): 355–371.

Buchanan, James M. "Barro on the Ricardian Equivalence Theorem." *Journal of Political Economy* 84 (April 1976): 337–342.

Bunting, David. "Savings and the Distribution of Income." *Journal of Post Keynesian Economics* 14 (Fall 1991): 3–22.

Davis, Tom E. "The Consumption Function as a Tool for Prediction." *Review of Economics and Statistics* 34 (August 1952): 270–277.

Duesenberry, James S. "Income-Consumption Relations and Their Implications." In *Income, Employment and Public Policy: Essays in Honor of Alvin H. Hansen*, pp. 54–81. New York: W. W. Norton, 1948.

Eisner, Robert. "Budget Deficits: Rhetoric and Reality." *Journal of Economic Perspectives* 3 (Spring 1989a): 73–93.

———. *The Total Incomes System of Accounts.* Chicago: University of Chicago Press, 1989b.

Eisner, Robert, and Paul J. Pieper. "A New View of the Federal Debt and Budget Deficits." *American Economic Review* 74 (March 1984): 11–29.

Evans, Paul. "Do Large Deficits Produce High Interest Rates?" *American Economic Review* 75 (March 1985): 68–87.

Flavin, Marjorie A. "The Adjustment of Consumption to Changing Expectations About Future Income." *Journal of Political Economy* 89 (October 1981): 974–1009.

Friedman, Milton. *A Theory of the Consumption Function.* Princeton: Princeton University Press, 1957.

Gapinski, James H. *Macroeconomic Theory: Statics, Dynamics, and Policy.* New York: McGraw-Hill, 1982.

Hall, Robert E. "Stochastic Implications of the Life Cycle—Permanent Income Hypothesis: Theory and Evidence." *Journal of Political Economy* 86 (December 1978): 971–987.

Hamberg, Daniel. *Models of Economic Growth.* New York: Harper and Row, 1971.

Harrod, R. F. "An Essay in Dynamic Theory." *Economic Journal* 49 (March 1939): 14–33.

———. *Towards a Dynamic Economics.* London: Macmillan, 1948.

Hendershott, Patric H., and Joe Peek. "Aggregate U.S. Private Saving: Conceptual Measures and Empirical Tests." In *The Measurement of Saving, Investment, and Wealth*, pp. 185–223. Studies in Income and Wealth, vol. 52, edited by Robert E. Lipsey and Helen Stone Tice. Chicago: University of Chicago Press, 1989.

Holloway, Thomas M. "Present NIPA Saving Measures: Their Characteristics and Limitations." In *The Measurement of Saving, Investment, and Wealth*, pp. 21–93. Studies in Income and Wealth, vol. 52, edited by Robert E. Lipsey and Helen Stone Tice. Chicago: University of Chicago Press, 1989.

Jorgenson, Dale W., and Barbara M. Fraumeni. "The Accumulation of Human and Nonhuman Capital, 1948–84." In *The Measurement of Saving, Investment, and Wealth*, pp. 227–282. Studies in Income and Wealth, vol. 52, edited by Robert E. Lipsey and Helen Stone Tice. Chicago: University of Chicago Press, 1989.

Kaldor, Nicholas. "Alternative Theories of Distribution." *Review of Economic Studies* 23 (March 1956): 83–100.

Keynes, John Maynard. *The General Theory of Employment, Interest, and Money.* New York: Harcourt, Brace and World, 1936.

Lipsey, Robert E., and Helen Stone Tice. "Introduction." In *The Measurement of Saving, Investment, and Wealth*, pp. 1–19. Studies in Income and Wealth, vol. 52, edited by Robert E. Lipsey and Helen Stone Tice. Chicago: University of Chicago Press, 1989.

Modigliani, Franco. "Fluctuations in the Saving–Income Ratio: A Problem in Economic Forecasting." In *Studies in Income and Wealth*, vol. 11, pp. 369–441. Conference on Research in Income and Wealth. New York: National Bureau of Economic Research, 1949.

Modigliani, Franco, and Richard Brumberg. "Utility Analysis and the Consumption Function: An Interpretation of Cross-Section Data." In *Post Keynesian Economics*, pp. 388–436, edited by K. K. Kurihara. New Brunswick: Rutgers University Press, 1954.

O'Driscoll, Gerald P., Jr. "The Ricardian Nonequivalence Theorem." *Journal of Political Economy* 85 (February 1977): 207–210.

Pasinetti, Luigi L. "Rate of Profit and Income Distribution in Relation to the Rate of Economic Growth." *Review of Economic Studies* 29 (October 1962): 267–279.

Placone, Dennis, Holley Ulbrich, and Myles Wallace. "The Crowding Out Debate: It's Over When It's Over and It Isn't Over Yet." *Journal of Post Keynesian Economics* 8 (Fall 1985): 91–96.

Ruggles, Richard, and Nancy D. Ruggles. "Integrated Economic Accounts for the United States, 1947–80." *Survey of Current Business* 62 (May 1982): 1–53.

Sato, K. "On the Adjustment Time in Neo-classical Growth Models." *Review of Economic Studies* 33 (July 1966): 263–268.

Sato, Ryuzo. "Fiscal Policy in a Neo-Classical Growth Model: An Analysis of Time Required for Equilibrating Adjustment." *Review of Economic Studies* 30 (February 1963): 16–23.

Solow, Robert M. "A Contribution to the Theory of Economic Growth." *Quarterly Journal of Economics* 70 (February 1956): 65–94.

———. "Technical Change and the Aggregate Production Function." *Review of Economics and Statistics* 39 (August 1957): 312–320.

Sraffa, Piero, ed. *The Works and Correspondence of David Ricardo*. Vol. IV: *Pamphlets and Papers, 1815–1823*. Cambridge: Cambridge University Press, 1951.

Summers, Lawrence, and Chris Carroll. "Why Is U.S. National Saving So Low?" *Brookings Papers on Economic Activity*, No. 2 (1987): 607–635.

Zahid, Khan H. "Government Budget Deficits and Interest Rates: The Evidence Since 1971, Using Alternative Deficit Measures." *Southern Economic Journal* 54 (January 1988): 725–731.

2 TOWARD A THEORY OF SAVING

David J. Smyth
Louisiana State University

Until the mid-1930s the theory of saving was simple. In classical economics, saving was an increasing function of the rate of interest. Investment was a decreasing function of the interest rate. Together the saving and investment functions gave the equilibrium level of saving (equal to capital formation) and the rate of interest. John Maynard Keynes's *General Theory* changed this. In the Keynesian model saving depended on disposable income. In the *IS–LM* model the saving function plays a crucial role in the determination of equilibrium output and expenditure. In the neo-classical synthesis, with prices variable, the *IS* and *LM* curves yield an aggregate demand curve, which, in conjunction with output determined by a perfectly inelastic aggregate supply curve, means the saving function is an important determinant of the price level. In recent years economists have analyzed the optimum consumption behavior of the representative household, where the rate of interest is again of importance in determining saving.

The chapter is structured as follows. Section 1 discusses the Keynesian saving function, and section 2 considers the early cross-section and time series estimates of saving functions. Economists soon observed a conflict between their observations of the saving–income relationship in the short and long runs; the dilemma they faced is outlined in section 3. Section 4 discusses an early attempt to resolve the conflict, the relative income theory. The basis for alternative approaches, saving as a multiperiod decision, is considered in section 5, and sections 6 and 7 consider two approaches that use a multiperiod model, the permanent income and life cycle models. Section 8 presents a simple wealth adjustment model. The results of fitting the alternative models to quarterly data from 1947 to 1990 are given in section 9.

The relative income, permanent income, life cycle, and wealth adjustment models are commonly called "modern" saving theories. However, they were all developed more than 30 years ago. Recent developments have been of two types. First, some economists have abandoned the attempt to develop theoretical models of macroeconomic aggregates and have used error correction models instead. Error correction models are considered in section 10. Second, in the permanent income model, adaptive expectations are replaced by rational expectations. Rational expectations models are discussed in section 11, and section 12 considers inflation and the saving function. Section 13 presents the chapter's conclusions.

1. The Keynesian Saving Function

Income received by households can be disposed of in three ways: It can be paid in taxes, consumed, or saved. Income after taxes is disposable income, so

$$Y = S + C, \qquad (2-1)$$

where Y is disposable income, S is saving, and C is consumption. Throughout, income, saving, and consumption are measured in real terms.

Some economists have analyzed the behavior of saving directly; the present chapter will follow this procedure as far as possible. However, many economists determine consumption behavior and leave saving to be determined as a residual. Accordingly, at times it will be necessary to develop arguments in terms of consumption and then convert the results into a relationship for saving.

Since Keynes's *General Theory*, disposable income has been taken to be the main, but not the only, determinant of saving and consumption. Keynes (1936) devoted book III of his *General Theory* to the propensity to consume. Most of his discussion dealt with the factors determining the slope and position of the function linking consumption (and hence saving) to disposable income, but he also specifically discussed factors that might cause shifts in the consumption function; he thought that these factors would be stable in the short run.

On the normal shape of the consumption function, Keynes (1936, pp. 97–99) argued as follows. "The fundamental psychological law, upon which we are entitled to depend with great confidence ... from our knowledge of human nature and from the detailed facts of experience, is that men are disposed, as a rule and on the average, to increase their consumption as their income increases, but not by as much as the increase in their income." This is the only assumption on the form of the consumption function that was necessary for the development of his model. Thus writing the consumption and saving function in general form, we have

$$C = C(Y), \quad 0 < C' < 1; \quad S = S(Y), \quad 0 < S' < 1. \quad (2-2)$$

The partial derivatives in equation (2–2), C' and S', are the marginal propensities to consume and save, respectively; Keynes's hypothesis is that they are both positive but less than one.

The ratio of consumption to disposable income, C/Y, is the average propensity to consume; the ratio of saving to disposable income, S/Y, is the average propensity to save. Keynes thought that because the average propensity to consume would be greater than the marginal propensity to consume, consumption may exceed income; that is, because the average propensity to save would be less than the marginal propensity to save, saving may be negative. These properties of consumption and saving are consistent with straight-line consumption and saving functions. They are also consistent with a consumption function that flattens out and a saving function that becomes steeper at high incomes.

A simple linear saving function that is consistent with Keynes's formulation is

$$S = S_0 + sY \quad S_0 < 0 \quad 0 < s < 1. \quad (2-3)$$

Using equation (2–1), this implies the consumption function

$$\begin{aligned} C &= Y - S \\ &= Y - (S_0 + sY) \\ &= -S_0 + (1 - s)Y \\ &= C_0 + cY \quad C_0 > 0 \quad 0 < c < 1 \end{aligned} \quad (2-4)$$

where $C_0 = -S_0$ and $c = 1 - s$. Figure 2–1 illustrates linear consumption and saving functions.

Various passages in the *General Theory* anticipate later consumption and saving function developments, in particular, dynamic adjustment processes and habit persistence.[1] It would be misleading to overestimate the importance of these with the benefit of hindsight. Still, it is erroneous to regard Keynes as thinking that disposable income was the only determinant of consumption and saving.

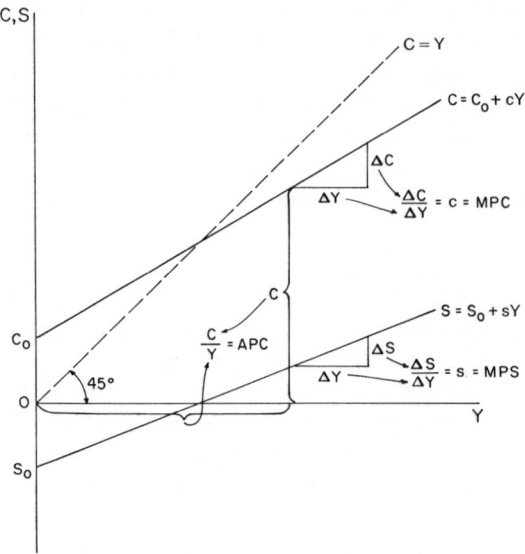

Figure 2-1. Keynesian consumption and saving functions.

2. Early Saving Function Estimates

The publication of Keynes's *General Theory* was soon followed by attempts to test and quantify his consumption and saving functions. Two types of data were available, cross-sectional data and time series data. Studies based on both sets of data found the marginal propensity to save to be positive and less than one, and the average propensity to save to be less than the marginal propensity to save.

2.1. Cross-Sectional Estimates of the Keynesian Consumption Function

Budget studies for U.S. households date back to the nineteenth century. The studies provide information on household income and expenditures of various types that may be aggregated to obtain total household expenditures; thus consumption and saving by households in different income classes may be obtained. To illustrate how cross-sectional studies were used, we analyze data from a budget study made in 1888–1890.[2]

Average income for income classes $0–$200, $200–$400, $400–$600, and so on up to $2000–$2200 and over $2200, with average expenditures for each income class are available. Figure 2–2 is a scatter plot of the data, together with the line estimated below.

The evidence supports Keynes's hypothesis: Saving rises as income rises, the marginal propensity to save is less than one, and the average propensity to save rises with income. For income up to the $1200–$1400 range, the points fall closely about a straight line with a negative intercept. At higher income levels the saving function becomes steeper. An equation that makes saving depend on a constant, income, and the square of income fits the data well. The estimated equation (using a heteroskedasticity-consistent covariance matrix) is

$$S = -75.2 + 0.073Y + 0.000155Y^2. \qquad \text{Adjusted } R^2 = 0.997. \quad (2\text{--}5)$$
$$(-4.44) \quad (2.35) \quad\quad (16.73)$$

This result is typical of those obtained in early budget studies. Thus the cross-sectional evidence supported a Keynesian saving function.

2.2. Time Series Estimates of the Keynesian Consumption Function

Time series data became available with the development of annual national income statistics in the United States and some other countries in the latter part of the 1930s. Figure 2–3 gives a scatter plot of annual U.S.

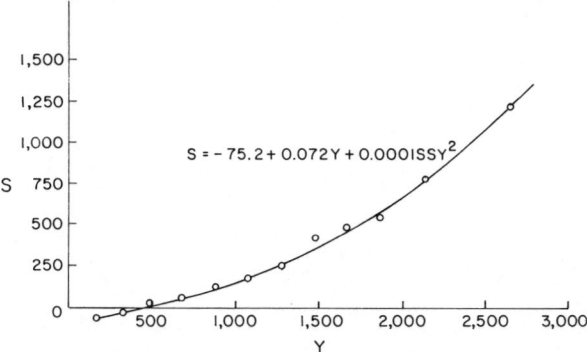

Figure 2–2. Saving function estimated from household budget data, 1888–1890. *Source*: Data are from Brady (1956, p. 182).

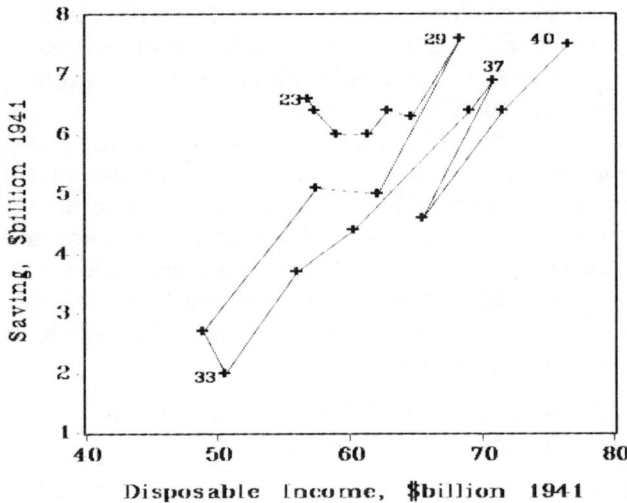

Figure 2–3. Annual saving and disposable income data, 1923 to 1940, available to early researchers.

saving and disposable income, using estimates made by the Commerce Department. The data, for the period 1923 to 1940, are representative of the data to which the early time series saving and consumption functions were fitted. They have been taken from Woytinski (1946, p. 4). Typical periods of analysis were 1923–1940 and 1929–1940, the shorter period often being used because the 1923–1928 national income estimates were regarded as less reliable than those for the later period; eventually the Commerce Department ceased to revise and publish the pre-1929 estimates.

Equations (2–6) and (2–7) report estimates of a simple Keynesian saving function using annual data for the periods 1923–1940 and 1929–1940, respectively.

$$S = -4.63 + 0.164Y \quad \text{Adjusted } R^2 = 0.972 \quad D-W = 0.60$$
$$(-2.14) \quad (4.74) \tag{2-6}$$

$$S = -7.11 + 0.195Y \quad \text{Adjusted } R^2 = 0.990 \quad D-W = 1.38$$
$$(-4.49) \quad (7.84) \tag{2-7}$$

Saving and disposable income are measured in billions of dollars at 1941 prices. The data used are those shown in Figure 2–3. The estimates are consistent with Keynes's hypothesis. The constant terms are negative. The marginal propensity to save is 0.164 for the 1923–1940 period and somewhat higher, at 0.195, for the shorter period. The estimated coefficients are significant at the 95 percent confidence level, and the correlation coefficients are high. But the Durbin-Watson statistics are low, especially for the 1923–1940 period, indicating serial correlation of the residuals; so the model is likely to be misspecified.

The results reported here are typical of those obtained in early time series studies made about the end of World War II. Such estimates caused some consternation among economists concerned with economic policy. Some, but not all, economists concluded that the estimated marginal propensities to save implied that, as incomes rose, the average propensity to save would rise to such levels that consumption would be insufficient to maintain the economy close to full employment. So, many economists expected a major depression to start shortly after the end of the war. Such a depression did not occur.

Reading later work on the saving and consumption functions, one can easily get the impression that the early researchers accepted their results uncritically. The failure of the early postwar forecasts of saving based on prewar regressions is one reason for this belief.[3] Still, a reading of the actual studies clearly shows that the early writers on the aggregate saving function were alive to many problems. They made continuous attempts to refine their analyses.[4] There was vigorous debate about whether estimates should be made using data in current or constant prices, whether the data should be expressed per capita, whether prosperity and depression periods should be distinguished, and whether additional variables should be added to income. The additional variables added in various studies included time trends, lagged income, change in income, quadratic terms, population, liquid assets, and a measure of income inequality.

The perceptive study by Wladimir Woytinski (1946) stimulated considerable comment. Woytinski stressed that projections beyond the range of actual observations require reservations for a considerable margin of error. Woytinski fitted functions in real terms and rejected those using data in current prices. A key contribution of Woytinski was to stress that the 1923–1940 period contained both a very deep depression and years of relative prosperity and that a simple regression equation fitted to these years would be inappropriate and yield unsatisfactory predictions outside the sample period if saving and consumption behavior differed in prosperity and depression. Woytinski argued that the marginal propensity to save was larger in depression than in prosperity and that a marginal propensity to save estimated over the whole period would lie between these values. Therefore, extrapolating to postwar prosperity, the level of saving would be overestimated and hence the level of investment needed to maintain high employment would be overestimated. This misestimation would be particularly marked if the shorter period, 1929–1940, were the database because it would then contain a lot of depression years.

Woytinski presented evidence showing that when the depression years were excluded, there was no tendency for the average propensity to save to vary with real disposable income. And he cogently argued that it was impossible for the simple saving function with a break-even point (at which saving was zero) as high as $45 billion (in 1941 prices) to represent "the" saving function, for at incomes lower than this saving would be negative. That is impossible, for it would have meant that before the early part of the twentieth century saving always would have been negative and we know that it was not.

3. Short-Run and Long-Run Saving Behavior

3.1. The Kuznets and Goldsmith Evidence

In 1942 Simon Kuznets, who was later to win the Nobel Prize in Economic Science, published estimates of U.S. national product and its major components by overlapping decades for the period 1879 to 1938. Kuznets later revised the estimates and carried them back to 1869. Subsequent estimates by Raymond Goldsmith confirmed Kuznets's findings. It soon became plain that the long-run and short-run consumption–income relationships were in conflict. Writing in 1945, Colin Clark pointed out:

> The savings–income relationship of the years 1929–40, a linear relationship with a marginal propensity to save of 0.24 is a short-period relationship, fully applicable within its own sphere. But when we are looking ahead into the postwar period, we must use the long-period relationship between income and savings, which is entirely different. *A priori* consideration will show that it is quite impossible that a marginal propensity to save of 0.24, or anything like it, can be maintained over a long period. This conclusion is confirmed by the data [based on Kuznets's 1942 estimates].

Table 2–1 gives Goldsmith's estimates of the average propensity to save for the 13 cycles between 1896 and 1949. There is no evidence of a rise in the average propensity to save as income has risen over time. The average propensity to save for each cycle is in the range 0.07 to 0.14 except for three cycles, those including the two world wars and that including the Great Depression. The average propensities to save are high during the wars (reflecting primarily rationing, shortages of goods,

Table 2-1. Average Propensities to Save

Cycle (trough to trough)	Ratio of Saving to Personal Disposable Income
1896–1900	.094
1900–1904	.105
1904–1908	.120
1908–1911	.105
1911–1914	.103
1914–1919	.161
1919–1921	.088
1921–1924	.110
1924–1927	.139
1927–1932	.074
1932–1938	.020
1938–1946	.194
1946–1949	.134

Source: Goldsmith (1955, vol. I, p. 76; calculated from Table VI, column 3).

and perhaps patriotic appeals for high saving), and the average propensity to save is low during the depressed 1930s.

3.2. The Trend in the Saving Function Hypothesis

An early attempt to reconcile the long-run and short-run evidence, made by Colin Clark (1945), Arthur Smithies (1945), and others, was simply to assume that the saving function shifted downward over time. Smithies suggested three possible causes of a downward trend in the saving function: migration from farms to cities, more equal income distribution, and the introduction of new goods making luxuries become necessities. A weakness of this hypothesis is that only by chance do the average saving and disposable income points give an average propensity to save that is constant over an extended period.

3.3. Short-Run Variability in the Marginal Propensity to Save

The discussion so far has implicitly assumed, and most of the early empirical studies explicitly assumed, that saving depends on disposable income in the same period. However, income received in any period may influence consumption and saving in more than one period. To confirm this proposition requires only that a household normally receive paychecks on just one day of the week or the month but make consumption expenditures daily. Suppose you are paid monthly. You probably will even out your stream of expenditures so that consumption is not much greater on payday than on other days. On most days you have some consumption but no income. On these days, the average propensity to consume will be something divided by zero, that is, infinity. Your saving will be negative, and with zero income the average propensity to save is negative. On payday, unless you take all your pay packet and spend it on a drunken orgy, your consumption will be much less than your income, so C/Y will be small and S/Y will be large. Thus if we relate saving to income for daily data, we do not get a meaningful saving function. Where does this averaging stop? An individual does not get a steady stream of income over his or her lifetime. Is a month, a quarter, a year, or a longer period appropriate to enable us to relate current S to current Y?

A simple way of looking at the short-run behavior of the marginal propensity to save is to calculate the ratio of the change in saving to the change in disposable income from one period to the next. When such calculations are made using annual per capita data from 1948 to 1990, the estimates are not clustered at all closely. Only 13 of the 43 estimates lie between 0 and 0.4. Thirteen are 0.41 or greater. Seventeen are negative. Quarterly marginal propensities to save are even more variable than the annual ones. We cannot predict the magnitude of changes in saving very accurately simply from changes in disposable income.

3.4. Saving Phenomena to Be Explained

The empirical evidence on saving behavior examined so far suggests that an adequate theory of the saving function had to explain the following phenomena:

- Short-run (cyclical) time series and cross-sectional budget study estimates that find the marginal propensity to save to be greater than the average propensity to save and the average propensity to save to rise as income rises.
- Secular constancy in the average propensity to save.
- Considerable variability in the marginal propensity to save calculated over successive time periods.

Consideration will now turn to some theories of saving behavior that try to explain these phenomena: in turn the relative income, permanent income, life cycle, and wealth adjustment models.

3.5. The Measurement of Saving, Consumption, and Disposable Income

Before considering the alternative theories, this section will briefly address the question of whether consumption expenditure and saving as measured in the national accounts are the appropriate measures to use. A distinction is sometimes made between consumption expenditure and consumption in the "use" sense. In the U.S. national accounts, consumption consists of expenditures on nondurable goods and services, on durable goods, and on house rental payments (imputed for owner-occupiers). However, automobiles, refrigerators, washing machines, and other consumer durables yield a flow of consumer services over a period of time. Should consumption be measured as in the national accounts, or should it be adjusted to exclude durable expenditures and to include an imputed flow of consumption from the stock of consumers' durables? Most of the theories were cast in terms of this more sophisticated use definition of consumption, but data limitations usually have caused them to be tested using the national income definition of consumption. Moreover, those studies that adopted a use measure of consumption did not adjust the definition of disposable income. Such an adjustment should be made because consumer durables not only provide consumption but also are a source of income beyond that measured in the national accounts.

To help evaluate alternative models, section 4 will report some results based on a time period and data set that has played an important role in the development of alternative consumption theories starting with Friedman (1957). This data set does measure the consumer durables component of total consumption as a flow of services rather than expenditures. All the data are expressed per capita. The estimates are made for the period 1909 to 1949, excluding the war years, using data from Goldsmith (1955). The estimates are reported in Smyth and Jackson (1977–78).

4. The Relative Income Hypothesis

The basic element of the relative income theory is that the consumption–income relationship is dependent on disposable income relative to some other disposable income. The theory has both cross-sectional and time series forms.

4.1. Cross-Sectional Form of the Relative Income Theory

The simple consumption function model assumes that a household's satisfaction depends on the amount of goods consumed. James Duesenberry (1949) suggested that people's preferences are interdependent, a household's satisfaction increasing only if its consumption increases relatively to that of other households in the community.

Duesenberry reasoned for a demonstration effect. People tend to emulate the other members of their community; therefore the consumption behavior of farmers will be influenced by that of other farmers, the consumption of city dwellers by that of other city dwellers, that of African Americans by other members of the African American community, that of college students by other college students, and so on.[5]

Households with incomes less than the average of their peers will have high average propensities to consume as they try to keep up with the community average and hence low average propensities to save. Households with above average income will correspondingly have a low C/Y ratio and a high S/Y ratio.

The relative income model can be specified in various ways. A simple linear formulation of saving by a household in a particular socioeconomic group is

$$S = s_1 Y^G + s_2(Y - Y^G)$$
$$= s_2 Y + (s_1 - s_2) Y^G, \qquad (2\text{--}8)$$

where Y^G is the average income of the household's socioeconomic group and $0 < s_2 < s_1 < 1$. The average propensity to save is then

$$\text{APS} = S/Y = s_2 + (s_1 - s_2) Y^G / Y. \qquad (2\text{--}9)$$

Consider a household with income equal to the group average. Then as $Y = Y^G$, $Y^G/Y = 1$, and the average propensity to save is s_1, the average propensity to save of the group. If the household's income is above the group average, $Y^G/Y < 1$ and, as $s_1 - s_2 > 0$, it follows that $S/Y > s_1$. Similarly, if $Y > Y^G$, then $S/Y < s_1$.

If a household's income increases (decreases) but the income of peer households is unchanged, the household's average propensity to save will rise (fall) because the partial derivative between the average propensity to save and Y is $-(s_1 - s_2)Y^G/Y^2$, which is negative. If the household's income and the group income change proportionately, which will be the tendency over the long-run, Y^G/Y is unchanged, so there is no change in the average propensity to save.

Thus in the short-run, where group income is given but individual household incomes differ, estimates of the average propensity to save will be higher than secularly when income changes are dominated by changes in group averages, not interhousehold differences. Duesenberry's cross-sectional relative income hypothesis was found to be consistent with a wide range of racial, geographic, occupational, and other differentials in consumption-saving behavior.

4.2. Ratchet Models

The time series form of the relative income hypothesis involves a ratchet in the relationship between saving and disposable income. Duesenberry argued that consumption expenditures will be influenced by recent living standards. It is more difficult for families to cut consumption when income falls than to expand consumption when income rises so households will attempt to maintain their previous living standards when income falls. What living standards? Duesenberry argues that the relevant standards are those associated with the highest living standards enjoyed in the past, those associated with previous peak income. Franco Modigliani (1949) also assigned a key role to previous peak income, taking the relationship between current and previous peak income as a cyclical index.

The saving function version of the ratchet model used by David Smyth and John Jackson (1977–78) is

$$S_t = s_1 \text{YPEAK}_t + s_2(Y_t - \text{YPEAK}_t), \qquad (2-10)$$

where t denotes the time period and YPEAK the highest value of Y achieved to date. If the current value of Y is the highest ever attained, then Y_t and YPEAK_t are equal. The constraints on the coefficients are the same as in equation (2–8). This ratchet model is simpler than that posited by Duesenberry and Modigliani: Their formulations involve asymmetrical time lags between upswings and downswings, and Duesenberry's formulation is nonlinear.

Figure 2–4 illustrates the ratchet model of equation (2–10). As disposable income rises from Y_0 to Y_1, saving follows a path along the continuous line to the right, rising from S_0 to S_1. Income now falls to Y_2. Saving falls but not along the same line as during the upswing. Instead it

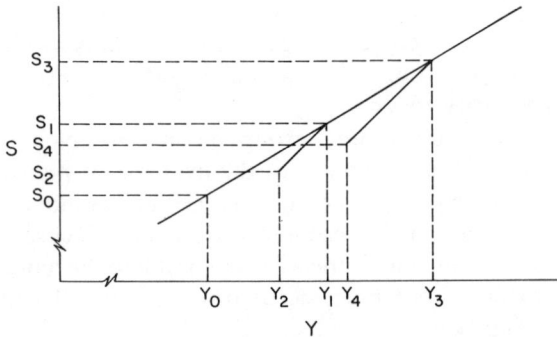

Figure 2-4. Illustration of a Ratchet model.

follows the ratchet path to S_2. As income rises again, the path followed in the downward direction is retraced until Y_1 is reached and then the growth line is followed until income Y_3, where saving is S_3. Income falls again to Y_4. The new downward path is to the right of the former ratchet path and parallel to it. Saving falls to S_4. From Y_4 the path is retraced until the previous peak at Y_3 is reached and the growth path is followed again. And so the process continues.

Smyth and Jackson fitted their ratchet model using the data set described at the end of section 3 that measures consumption of durable goods as a flow of services. Their model worked well and yielded estimates that imply that the marginal propensity to save when income is growing above its previous peak, $s_1 = 0.174$, is significantly less than the marginal propensity to save in recession and recovery, $s_2 = 0.490$.[6]

5. Saving as a Multiperiod Decision

Section 3 argued that saving is a multiperiod decision. Now this decision is treated in more formal fashion. We start by considering a representative consumer unit under perfect certainty faced with decisions for only two time periods, t and $t + 1$, and which consumes the total available receipts during the two periods so that it has zero assets at the end of period $t + 1$.

Our individual (or household) receives income Y_t and Y_{t+1} in periods t and $t + 1$ and consumes C_t and C_{t+1} in those periods. Assume the individual has a utility function

$$U = U(C_t, C_{t+1}) \qquad (2-11)$$

and can borrow or lend at the rate of interest R per period. He wants to maximize his utility subject to the constraints of his income flow and the rate of interest.

Our consumer can save all his income in period t and lend it out at the going rate of interest. Then in period $t+1$ he can consume $Y_{t+1} + (1+R)Y_t$. Another possibility open to the consumer is to spend income Y_t plus whatever he can borrow against the income of period $t+1$. In period $t+1$ he will have Y_{t+1} to repay his borrowings. Suppose he borrows x. Then $x + Rx = Y_{t+1}$ so $x = Y_{t+1}/(1+R)$. This is the maximum amount he can repay.

The extremes for the consumer's consumption are then: $C_t = 0$, $C_{t+1} = Y_{t+1} + (1+R)Y_t$; $C_t = Y_t + Y_{t+1}/(1+R)$, $C_{t+1} = 0$. These pairs are portrayed in figure 2–5. A straight line joining these two points defines the alternative combinations of consumption available in the periods. It is the consumer's budget line.

Figure 2–5 also contains a set of utility curves obtained from the utility function in equation (2–11). Each curve provides the combinations of C_t and C_{t+1} for which the consumer is indifferent. For the usual reasons the indifference curves are convex to the origin. The optimum combination of C_t and C_{t+1} is where the budget line is tangent to an indifference curve,

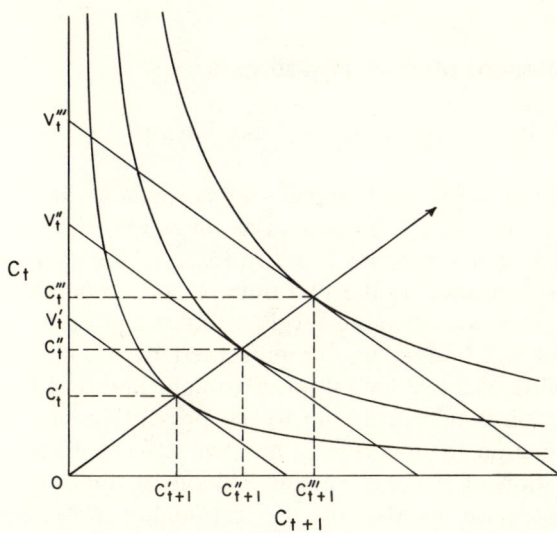

Figure 2–5. Linear expansion path with a homogeneous utility function.

point E in figure 2–5; this is the highest level of utility that the consumer can attain. The slope of the budget line depends only on R, as the slope is $-[Y_t + Y_{t+1}/(1+R)]/[(1+R)Y_t + Y_{t+1}] = -1/(1+R)$. The higher the rate of interest, the flatter the budget line. If $R=0$, it is a 135° line.

An increase in the consumer's income in any period shifts the budget line outward, and the consumer moves to point E' on a higher indifference curve in figure 2–5. The new budget line will be parallel to the old one for the interest rate, which is the rate at which present and future goods may be exchanged for each other, is unchanged. The rise in income in one period will normally cause consumption to rise in both periods.

This two-period analysis can be extended to n periods. The maximum amount that the consumer can consume in time period t may be regarded as the present value V_t of the future income stream. In the n period model

$$V_t = \sum_n [Y_{t+n}/(1+R)^n]. \qquad (2-12)$$

Two theories of consumption and saving, the permanent income and life cycle models, relate consumption, and hence saving, to the present value of the future income stream. To generate an operational theory some predictions have to be made about the form of the consumer's utility function. The permanent income and life cycle theories make different but related assumptions.

6. The Permanent Income Hypothesis

6.1. Present Value, Consumption, and Saving

Milton Friedman (1957) developed the permanent income hypothesis, sometimes just called PIH. Friedman assumes that the utility function is symmetrical and homogeneous in C_t and C_{t+1}. This means that the marginal rate of substitution in the two time periods depends on the ratio of C_t to C_{t+1}, not on the absolute levels of consumption. Consequently, in figure 2–5, as the budget line, represented by V_t, shifts outward, the successive points of tangency fall on a straight line through the origin so that consumption is proportionate to the present value.

The introduction of uncertainty has two effects. First, it complicates the interpretation of figure 2–5, but Friedman thinks that its presence should not systematically alter the proportionality relationship. Second, it introduces a reason for saving in addition to that of straightening out the income stream and earning interest, the provision of a reserve for future

TOWARD A THEORY OF SAVING

emergencies. The future flow of income used in the present value calculation consists partly of income from human wealth and partly from nonhuman wealth. Given that borrowing usually is easier when based on tangible physical assets than on one's human capital, the need for saving as a reserve to meet emergencies may be expected to be greater, given V, the smaller the proportion of V accounted for by nonhuman wealth; thus Friedman includes the ratio of nonhuman wealth to income as a variable determining the consumption–income and saving–income ratios.

6.2. Permanent and Transitory Income and Consumption

We might now expect Friedman to make consumption a function of this ratio and V. This is not the procedure he follows, however. Instead, Friedman makes use of the flow of income from V, which is RV. This he calls permanent income. Permanent income will normally differ from measured income. This permanent income is the discounted expected flow of income smoothed out. The permanent component of income reflects the effect of those factors that a consuming unit regards as determining the present value of its expected income stream and is analogous to the expected value of a probability distribution. Any difference between measured and permanent income is transitory income. Transitory income can be positive or negative.

Corresponding to permanent income is permanent consumption, consumption that is smoothed out, for the object of income smoothing is to smooth consumption. Permanent consumption will normally differ from measured consumption. Transitory consumption is the difference between measured and permanent consumption and may be positive or negative. The permanent part of consumption is the consumption that the household undertakes considering its permanent income. The transitory part of consumption reflects chance or unplanned components. Correspondingly, we can define permanent saving as the difference between permanent income and permanent consumption and transitory saving as the difference between measured saving and permanent saving.

Denoting permanent and transitory components by the superscripts P and T, respectively, and attaching no superscripts to measured or observed values, we have

$$Y = Y^P + Y^T \qquad (2\text{--}13)$$

$$C = C^P + C^T \qquad S = S^P + S^T \qquad (2\text{--}14)$$

$$C^P = C_P RV = C_P Y^P \qquad S^P = S_P RV = S_P Y^P \qquad (2\text{--}15)$$

where the proportionality factors C_P and S_P depend on the ratio of nonhuman wealth to income, the rate of interest, and the household's tastes and preferences.

Friedman assumes that the correlations between the following are all zero: permanent and transitory income, permanent and transitory consumption and hence permanent and transitory saving, and transitory income and transitory consumption. The most controversial assumption is that there is no connection between transitory income and consumption because this implies that the marginal propensity to consume out of transitory income is zero; that is, the marginal propensity to save out of transitory income is one.

It is these last assumptions that distinguish Friedman's theory from its precursors. Keynes (1936, pp. 57−58) and others recognized that consumption might be less responsive to temporary changes in income than to permanent changes. Colin Clark (1945) wrote:

> People's reactions to a change in real income largely depend upon whether they consider it temporary or permanent. In 1932−33, for instance, real income per head of the labour force was about at the 1900 level. Yet in 1900 people made substantial savings, in 1932−33 a substantial net dis-saving. If people in 1932 had believed that real income was likely to remain permanently at that level, they would have, in time, altered their habits of life and positive saving would have re-emerged. In the same way occasional years of sudden increase in income lead to savings above those expected from the normal relationship. This was the case in 1940 and 1941. If real income per head of the labour force is sustained for a few years at the 1941 level ... the general average of savings will once again be about at the level indicated by the long-period curve.

6.3. A Hypothetical Example of the Permanent Income Model

In table 2−2 the permanent income model is illustrated using hypothetical data for 9 households. Column 2 shows that three groups of households have permanent income of 80, 100, and 120. The marginal and average propensities to consume out of permanent income are 0.9, so the marginal and average propensities to save are 0.1. The resulting permanent consumption and permanent saving of each household are given in columns 3 and 4. Within each group one household has transitory income of 10, one 0, and one −10. Transitory income is listed in column 5. Column 6 gives measured income, $Y = Y^P + Y^T$. For simplicity, transitory consumption is

Table 2-2. Hypothetical Permanent Income Model

(1)	(2)	(3)	(4)	(5)	(6)	(7)	(8)	(9)
Household	Y^P	C^P	S^P	Y^T	Y	C	S	S^T
1	80	72	8	−10	70	72	−2	−10
2	80	72	8	0	80	72	8	0
3	80	72	8	10	90	72	18	10
4	100	90	10	−10	90	90	0	−10
5	100	90	10	0	100	90	10	0
6	100	90	10	10	110	90	20	10
7	120	108	12	−10	110	108	2	−10
8	120	108	12	0	120	108	12	0
9	120	108	12	10	130	108	22	10

zero so measured and permanent consumption are equal. Measured consumption is given in column 7 and measured saving, $S = Y - C$, in column 8. Finally, transitory saving, given by $S^T = S - S^P$, is reported in column 9. The correlation assumptions made by Friedman hold.

In figure 2-6 the broken line, line $S^P = 0.1Y^P$, gives the relationship between permanent saving and permanent income. However, only these of the nine points, those for households 2, 5, and 8 with zero transitory income, lie on this line. Households 1, 4, and 7 have negative transitory income and lie to the right of the $S^P = 0.1Y^P$ line; households 3, 6, and 9 have positive transitory income and lie to the left of this line.

A researcher estimating a saving function from the budget study data in table 2-2 will use the data on measured income and saving because the values of permanent income and permanent consumption are unknown. The ordinary least squares line fitted to the nine observations is

$$S = -18 + 0.28Y \quad \text{Adjusted } R^2 = 0.288.$$
$$(-1.30)\ (2.06) \tag{2-16}$$

This is the solid line in figure 2-6. The estimated marginal propensity to save is greater than that between permanent saving and permanent income, and the estimated constant term is negative instead of zero.

We obtain this result because we have used measured income in the regression. If we could use permanent income instead of measured income, we would estimate a marginal propensity to save between saving and permanent income of 0.1. In practice we cannot do this because we cannot observe permanent income. We can observe only measured income,

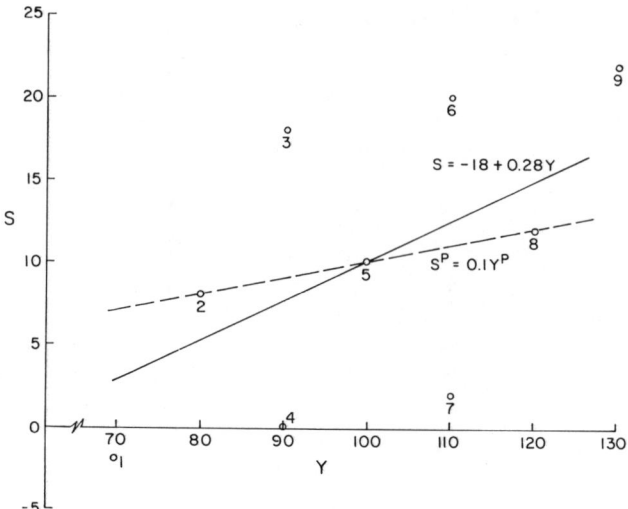

Figure 2-6. Relationship between saving and income in a hypothetical permanent income model.

which is a biased estimate of permanent income. A household has low measured income because its permanent income is low or because its transitory income is negative or both. Income classes with low measured income are likely to have more than their share of households with negative transitory income. For instance, in table 2-2 the income class with measured income below 95 contains one household with its measured income equal to its permanent income, one household with positive transitory income, and two households with negative transitory income. In figure 2-6 this pulls the lower part of the estimated line down and to the right of the broken line. Similarly, a household has high measured income because its permanent income is high or because its transitory income is positive or both. Income classes with high measured income are likely to have an above-average number of households with positive transitory income. This pulls the upper part of the estimated line up and to the left of the broken line. The result is that the estimated line is skewed about the broken line; it is steeper than the broken line and intersects the vertical axis with saving below zero.

Our conclusions are unchanged if we relax the assumption of zero transitory consumption. Also, if we group the observations and fit a line to data by classes, we will still get a line that is steeper than the line linking permanent saving to permanent income.

6.4. Friedman's Evidence on the Permanent Income Hypothesis

Friedman made both cross-sectional and time series tests of his hypothesis. However, they were not very rigorous. Friedman's tests amounted to no more than finding that a wide range of budget studies and time series data are consistent with the type of hypothetical examples given in the previous two sections. As we shall see shortly, Friedman did not directly test hypotheses about the marginal propensity to consume, and hence the marginal propensity to save, out of transitory income. Other economists have. We shall first examine Friedman's approach and then look at the more rigorous tests of the permanent income hypothesis.

Probably the best known of Friedman's tests of the permanent income hypothesis is that in which he related consumption to a constructed permanent income series. Friedman fitted this consumption function to annual per capita data for the period 1905 to 1951, excluding war years. In this time series analysis the consumption relationship that Friedman wishes to estimate, and the corresponding saving relationship, is

$$C_t^P = C_0 + C_P Y_t^P \qquad S_t^P = S_0 + S_P Y_t^P. \qquad (2-17)$$

Because permanent consumption is unobservable, Friedman makes use of the definition in equation $(2-14)$ to give

$$C_t = C_0 + C_P Y_t^P + C_t^T \qquad S_t^P = S_0 + S_P Y_t^P + S_t^T. \qquad (2-18)$$

Friedman approximates permanent income by a weighted average of past values of disposable income, assuming that the weights assigned to disposable income are smaller for more distant incomes than recent incomes. Specifically, he assumed that they declined geometrically. In addition, he made an allowance for an extraneously estimated growth rate in disposable income—if an allowance for growth in permanent income is not made, permanent income will be underestimated and so the marginal propensity to consume will be overestimated and the marginal propensity to save underestimated. Permanent income in period t may be defined as

$$\begin{aligned} Y_t^P &= (1 - \lambda)\,[Y_t + \lambda(1 + \mu)Y_{t-1} + \lambda^2(1 + \mu)^2 Y_{t-2} + \cdots] \\ &= \lambda(1 + \mu)Y_{t-1}^P + (1 - \lambda)Y_t \end{aligned} \qquad (2-19)$$

Here μ is the average rate of growth of real disposable income that Friedman took to be 2 percent, so $\mu = 0.02$. The income weights in periods $t,\ t-1,\ t-2,\ t-3,\ \ldots$ are $1,\ \lambda,\ \lambda^2,\ \lambda^3,\ \ldots$ where $0 < \lambda < 1$. Permanent income in period t is a weighted average of the current period's measured income and last period's permanent income adjusted for normal growth.

The relationship in equation (2–19) may be transformed into

$$Y_t^P - (1+\mu)\, Y_{t-1}^P = (1 - \lambda)\, [Y_t - (1 + \mu) Y_{t-1}^P]. \qquad (2-20)$$

As income changes, households revise their estimates of growth-adjusted permanent income. The revision is a proportion $1 - \lambda$ of the gap between measured income and the growth-adjusted permanent income of the previous period.

Two problems remain. First, transitory consumption is unobservable. Friedman resolves this issue by assuming that C_t^T is simply a random disturbance or error. Second, what value should be assigned to λ? Friedman fits equation (2–19) for alternative values of λ and chooses the value that results in the best-fitting equation. The value is 0.33. Friedman obtains a good fit between C_t and Y_t^P. His estimate of the marginal propensity to consume out of permanent income is $C_P = 0.88$. His estimate of C_0 is not significantly different from zero. This implies $S_0 = 0$ and $S_P = 0.12$.

A weakness of Friedman's procedure is that he does not test the hypothesis that the marginal propensity to consume out of transitory income is zero. Transitory income is not included in equation (2–18), and transitory consumption is just taken to behave randomly.

6.5. Further Empirical Evidence on the Permanent Income Hypothesis

Friedman's estimates fail to answer two key questions about the permanent income hypothesis. First, is Friedman's distinction between permanent and transitory income a useful one? For this to be the case, the marginal propensity to consume out of transitory income must be significantly different from the marginal propensity to consume out of permanent income. Second, if the answer to the first question is yes, is Friedman's assumption that the marginal propensity to consume out of transitory income is zero a valid one?

Abundant anecdotal evidence suggests that the marginal propensity to consume out of transitory income is positive but less than the marginal propensity to consume out of permanent income.[7] Such anecdotal evidence is supported by more rigorous econometric analysis.

James Holmes (1970) showed that a more complete time series test of the permanent income hypothesis is possible than that made by Friedman. Consider the model given by

$$C_t = C_t^P + C_t^T \qquad S_t = S_t^P + S_t^T. \qquad (2-21)$$

$$C_t^P = C_0 + C_P Y_t^P \qquad S_t^P = S_0 + S_P Y_t^P \qquad (2-22)$$

$$C_t^T = C_T Y_t^T + \epsilon_t \qquad S_t^T = S_T Y_t^T - \epsilon_t \qquad (2-23)$$

Equation (2–21) gives the definitions of measured consumption and measured saving. Equation (2–22) relates permanent consumption and permanent saving to permanent income with the addition of constant terms. Equation (2–23) allows for the marginal propensity to consume out of transitory income to be other than zero. ϵ_t is the error term in the transitory consumption equation; if $C_T = 0$, transitory consumption is simply a random term. Substituting from (2–22) and (2–23) in (2–21) gives

$$C_t = C_0 + C_P Y_t^P + C_T Y_t^T + \epsilon_t \qquad S_t = S_0 + S_P Y_t^P + S_T Y_t^T - \epsilon_t. \tag{2-24}$$

Using Holmes's model, the data set described in section 3, and Friedman's procedures to estimate permanent and transitory income, Smyth and Jackson (1977–78) obtained results that implied the following: $S_0 = 0$, $S_P = 0.11$, $S_T = 0.75$. The difference between the two marginal propensities to save was significant. Estimates such as these provide strong evidence against Friedman's formulation of the permanent income hypothesis that posits a marginal propensity to consume out of transitory income of zero.

Instead of searching over different values of λ in the expression for permanent income, it is possible to combine and transform the relationships in equations (2–21), (2–22), and (2–23) and make use of (2–20) to eliminate permanent and transitory income. The result is

$$\begin{aligned} C_t &= [1 - \lambda(1 + \mu)]C_0 + \lambda(1 + \mu)C_{t-1} + [(1 - \lambda)C_P + \lambda C_T]Y_t \\ &\quad - \lambda(1 + \mu)C_T Y_{t-1} + \epsilon_t - \lambda(1 + \mu)\epsilon_{t-1} \\ S_t &= [1 - \lambda(1 + \mu)]S_0 + \lambda(1 + \mu)S_{t-1} + [(1 - \lambda)S_P + \lambda S_T]Y_t \\ &\quad - \lambda(1 + \mu)S_T Y_{t-1} - \epsilon_t + \lambda(1 + \mu)\epsilon_{t-1} \end{aligned} \tag{2-25}$$

Then if μ is estimated extraneously, the values of the other parameters can be estimated.

Many studies have estimated a model like (2–25) with the Y_{t-1} term excluded. Such studies, like Friedman's, assume that C_T is zero so they fail to undertake a proper test of the permanent income hypothesis. When the Y_{t-1} term is included, again the evidence suggests that the marginal propensity to consume out of transitory income is positive but significantly less than the marginal propensity to consume out of permanent income.

When equations like (2–25) are estimated, one inconsistency with the permanent income hypothesis arises. Examination of equation (2–25) reveals that if the error term in equation (2–24), ϵ_t, is not serially correlated, equation (2–25) will contain a first-order moving average process, $\epsilon_t - \lambda(1 + \mu)\epsilon_{t-1}$, as well as the restriction that the moving average param̃ ẽr λ(1 + μ) should be equal to the coefficient of the lagged dependent variable.[8] A rigorous test of the model is provided by estimating an equation with a moving average error and restricting the moving average coefficient to be equal to the coefficient of the lagged dependent variables. Due to computational difficulties, this restriction was neglected until Baillie, McMahon, and Smyth (1980) made use of a computer program that enabled the estimation of a model with a constrained moving average process. Using quarterly data from 1953 to 1978, they found that the restriction on the model in equation (2−25) was violated. However, the dynamics of the unrestricted model were seen to be badly misspecified. They also investigated a model with a more general expectations scheme (Jorgenson's rational lag model). Once again, the restricted version is rejected but now the unrestricted version is satisfactory. Baillie, McMahon, and Smyth (1980, p. 42) concluded that "on the basis of these tests the permanent income hypothesis is rejected in all cases. The problem remains to determine what economic theory is generating the unrestricted parameter results."

We have been discussing tests of the assumption that consumption out of transitory income is zero when the data are in time series form. There have also been similar tests using cross-sectional data. An example of a transitory income receipt is a special life insurance payment made by the U.S. government to veterans in 1950. This payment provided economists with an experiment that could be used for a direct cross-sectional test of the permanent income hypothesis. Friedman proposed the use of this special payment to test his hypothesis. Tong Hun Lee (1975) fitted a consumption function to data for individual households using pre-insurance consumption to indicate permanent income. Lee found that the marginal propensity to consume out of the special payment was 0.55, much greater than zero, and much less than the marginal propensity to consume out of permanent income, about 0.9. Again the evidence does not support either the strong form of the permanent income hypothesis or the Keynesian consumption function.

7. The Life Cycle Hypothesis

The life cycle hypothesis makes use of the interaction between income, consumption, saving, wealth, and age. Early articles are by Franco Modigliani and Richard Brumberg (1954), Franco Modigliani and Albert Ando (1957), and Ando and Modigliani (1963). A review of the life cycle hypothesis is given by Modigliani (1986) in his Nobel Prize lecture.

7.1. Income and Consumption over a Lifetime

Figure 2-7A gives income, consumption, and saving by age from a 1960-61 budget study; the data are given in Nagatani (1972). In the early years after an individual becomes independent of his or her parents and forms a new household, saving is likely to be low. Consumption may well exceed income as the household goes into debt. Debt may be incurred to finance education or to generate a flow of services from a house, automobile, and other durables. The middle period of life is characterized by positive saving as previously incurred debts are paid back and the family accumulates resources for retirement and possibly to make bequests. The later stage of life, after retirement, may have some dissaving as some of the accumulated wealth is spent, but the average elderly family in figure 2-7A still saves. Thus the average propensity to save varies with age, first rising, then falling. Figure 2-7B shows the behavior of the average propensity to save over the life cycle.

With income and saving patterns like those in figures 2-7A and 2-7B, wealth initially declines. This is nonhuman wealth; investment in education should increase human wealth. Wealth eventually starts to rise as saving becomes positive and the interest or other returns are earned on the saving. After retirement, wealth grows at a slower rate.

The basic assumption of the life cycle hypothesis is that an individual attempts to maximize over his or her lifetime a utility function that is homogeneous with respect to consumption at different points of time. That is, the individual will allocate the marginal increments of resources to consumption in different time periods in the same proportion as total resources were allocated before the addition. In the simplest model, in which the individual does not expect to receive any inheritances and does not want to leave any bequests upon death, the total consumption of a person aged M years, C^M, will be proportional to the present value of total resources accruing to the individual over the rest of his or her life, V^M. If the individual expects to die at age N, so that $N - M$ is the expected number of years remaining, then in period t consumption and saving are given by

$$C_t^M = V_t^M/(N - M) \qquad S_t^M = Y_t - V_t^M/(N - M). \qquad (2-26)$$

The present value of resources at age M in period t has to be specified. Usually V_t^M is assumed to depend on wealth at the end of period $t-1$, W_{t-1}^M, the current disposable labor income in period t, YL_t^M, and the present value of expected disposable labor income, XYL_t^M. That is,

72   THE ECONOMICS OF SAVING

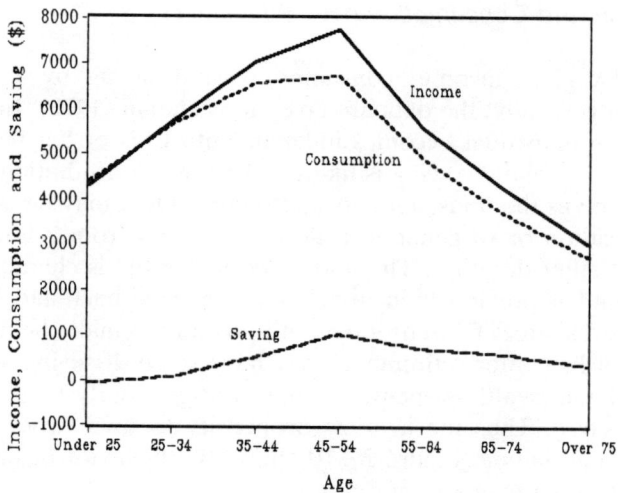

Figure 2—7A. Income, consumption, and saving by age, 1960—1961.

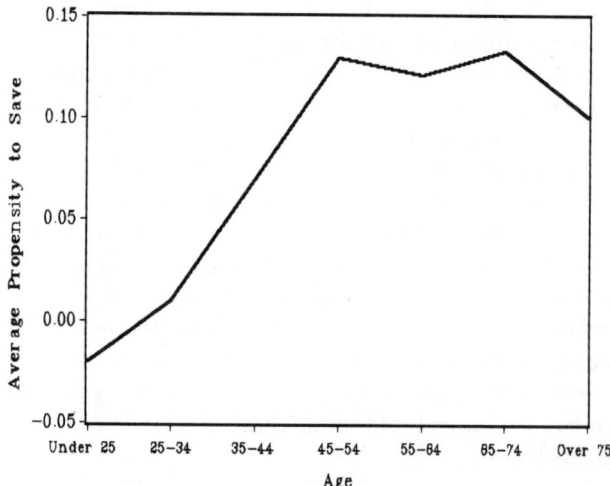

Figure 2—7B. Average propensity to save by age, 1960—1961.

$$V_t^M = W_{t-1}^M + YL_t^M + XYL_t^M. \quad (2-27)$$

Substituting from (2-27) in (2-26) gives

$$C_t^M = (W_{t-1}^M + YL_t^M + XYL_t^M)/(N - M)$$
$$S_t^M = Y_t - (W_{t-1}^M + YL_t^M + XYL_t^M)/(N - M) \quad (2-28)$$

Equation (2–28) implies that the marginal propensities to consume out of wealth, current labor disposable income, and expected future labor disposable income are the same and that the marginal propensities to save out of the various sources of income will be the same. This assumption immediately raises problems. First, there may be liquidity constraints — an individual may be unable to borrow against future income, especially future labor income. Second, there is the question of uncertainty and the assumption of no inheritances. Individuals are uncertain when they will die. They may have an expected age, but if they live longer than that, the total depletion of their resources by that age is likely to have unpleasant consequences. Accordingly, if individuals do indeed perform the sort of calculations implied by the life cycle hypothesis, they are likely to take account of uncertain life expectancy by using a higher age than N in their calculation so that expected bequests and inheritances will be positive. A further problem is the distinction between the individual and the household; for the typical family the household does not die when one individual dies. A major empirical problem is that we do not have data on expected labor income and it is necessary to use some proxy variable.

7.2. Evidence on the Life Cycle Theory: Cross Section

Both Cross-sectional and time series attempts have been made to test the life cycle hypothesis, and we shall briefly consider them both. If valid, the life cycle hypothesis will explain the tendency for the average propensity to save to rise with income, as high-income groups are likely to contain a high proportion of families in the middle-age groups and low-income groups to contain a high proportion of the young and the old. When saving and income are plotted against age, the U-shaped pattern similar to figure 2–7B is usually observed, and supporters of the life cycle theory regard such patterns as support for the theory.

There are two weaknesses with this simplistic approach. First, not just any U-shaped pattern of saving is consistent with the life cycle hypothesis. Equation (2–28) provides constraints to the pattern. Second, even if the resulting saving-to-income relationship by age looks satisfactory, it may not fare well against competing hypotheses. We need to know how well the theory performs against competing theories. A simple competing hypothesis is that saving is just determined by a Keynesian saving function.

As an illustration, consider a study by Keizo Nagatani (1972). In his theoretical analysis Nagatani extended the life cycle model to take account of an individual's uncertainty concerning future incomes and showed that a life cycle model leads to a consumption profile resembling the profile of labor income. Then he made use of the Bureau of Labor Statistics 1960–61 household budget data (given in Figures 2–7A and 2–7B) to generate predictions for consumption by age groups and found that they explained the actual consumption profile (and hence the actual saving profile) quite well. However, Smyth (1992) shows that Nagatani's analysis is inadequate. A simple Keynesian type function between consumption (and hence saving) and labor income markedly outperforms the life cycle model. Such results suggest that one should be very skeptical about the cross-sectional performance of the life cycle model.

7.3. Evidence on the Life Cycle Theory: Time Series

Aggregate consumption and saving are obtained by aggregating equation (2–28) over all age groups. As $N - M$ differs for different age groups, it follows that, given wealth, labor income, and expected labor income, aggregate consumption will depend on the age distribution of the population.

To test the life cycle theory against aggregate time series data, it is necessary to impose some restrictions on equation (2–28). Ando and Modigliani (1963) assume that every age group within the earning span has the same average income and the same expected income in any given year and that every household has the same expected and actual total life and earning spans. Together with the previous assumptions and the assumption that the rate of return on assets is constant and is expected to remain constant, summing over all age groups yields the aggregate relationships

$$C_t = a_1 YL_t + a_2 XYL_t + a_3 W_{t-1} \qquad S_t = Y_t - a_1 YL_t - a_2 XYL_t - a_3 W_{t-1}.$$
(2–29)

Constancy of the parameters in (2–29) will be ensured only by an appropriate set of conditions. One set is the constancy in time of the parameters of (2–28) for every age group, the age structure of the population and the relative distribution of income, of expected income and of wealth over the age groups. These are very restrictive conditions. Ando and Modigliani fit their model to data for the period 1929 to 1959, excluding the war years, and we know that the conditions are not fulfilled for this time period—there were marked changes in the age distribution of the population and changes in the distribution of income and wealth.

Ando and Modigliani suggest, on the basis of alternative assumptions, that reasonable values for the parameters in (2–29) would be between 0.61 and 0.73 for $a_1 + a_2$ and between 0.07 and 0.13 for a_3. If regression estimates were not close to these values, considerable doubt would be cast on the theory.

Because the expected income variable XYL_t is not directly observable, it is necessary to make some assumptions about it. Ando and Modigliani use two hypotheses: (1) that expected labor income is proportional to current labor income except for a scale factor, $XYL_t = a_4 YL_t$; and (2) that it depends on the unemployment rate, $XYL_t = a_5 YL_t/(1 - U_t)$. These assumptions yield

$$C_t = (a_1 + a_2 a_4) YL_t + a_3 W_{t-1}$$
$$S_t = Y_t - (a_1 + a_2 a_4) YL_t - a_3 W_{t-1} \qquad (2-30)$$

and

$$C_t = (a_1 + a_2 a_5/(1 - U_t)) YL_t + a_3 W_{t-1}$$
$$S_t = Y_t - (a_1 + a_2 a_5/(1 - U_t)) YL_t - a_3 W_{t-1} \qquad (2-31)$$

respectively. The estimated coefficients are fairly sensitive to the procedures used. Typically YL_t and W_{t-1} are significant but, perhaps because of multicollinearity, the unemployment adjusted income variable is not. When included, a constant term is positive and significant, which does not support proportionality.

Overall, time series results are fairly consistent with the life cycle hypothesis. This means that the results are consistent with the short-run and long-run behavior of saving. The short-run marginal propensity to save is given, holding wealth constant. In the long-run wealth rises, thus shifting the short-run saving function downward.

However, the time series tests of the life cycle hypothesis are weak tests. To get a model that can be estimated, the restrictions imposed are severe. They involve the destruction of the distinguishing and most interesting feature of the life cycle hypothesis. The novel part of the theory, that the age distribution of the population affects aggregate consumption and saving, vanishes from the model. All that is left is saving as a function of current income and wealth. This does not distinguish the life cycle hypothesis from other theories that yield similar predictions and alternative models. Alternative models, such as a wealth adjustment model, have a much simpler theoretical basis. In view of this, and the unsatisfactory performance of the life cycle hypothesis at the cross-sectional level, judgment on it must be unfavorable.

8. A Wealth-Adjustment Model

In the permanent income and life cycle hypotheses the role of wealth was essentially that of helping individuals smooth out their consumption stream over time. Wealth may be incorporated into the consumption function in an alternative and quite simple way. Suppose that households are "short-sighted" and do not have very precise expectations of the future. Thus they do not have a lifetime plan for consumption. They want wealth for what can be called a "precautionary motive." We shall assume that a household has some optimal or target level of wealth, W^*, that is proportional to its income so that

$$W_t^* = wY_t, \qquad (2-32)$$

where w is positive.

A household may not fully adjust its wealth to a desired level in any period. One reason is that the household may be subject to constraints that make such immediate adjustment impossible. A plausible assumption is one of partial adjustment. We thus assume that wealth adjusts by a constant proportion, β, of the divergence between desired wealth and the existing stock of wealth. Saving is the change in wealth from one period to the next so that

$$S_t = W_t - W_{t-1} = \beta(W_t^* - W_{t-1}) - \epsilon_t, \qquad (2-33)$$

where $0 < \beta \leq 1$ and ϵ_t is the error term. Substituting for W_t^* from (2-32) gives

$$\begin{aligned} S_t &= \beta(wY_t - W_{t-1}) - \epsilon_t \\ &= \beta wY_t - \beta W_{t-1} - \epsilon_t \end{aligned} \qquad (2-34)$$

A variant of the wealth adjustment hypothesis involves replacing disposable income by disposable labor income, resulting in a formulation similar to the life cycle hypothesis.

We may transform the wealth model and express it in a form with the wealth variable eliminated. To do this, write equation (2-32) for period $t-1$ and subtract it from (2-33); then make use of $W_{t-1} - W_{t-2} = S_{t-1}$ to get

TOWARD A THEORY OF SAVING 77

$$S_t = \beta w(Y_t - Y_{t-1}) + (1 - \beta)S_{t-1} - \epsilon_t + \epsilon_{t-1}. \quad (2-35)$$

Thus like one version of the permanent income model, that given in equation (2–25), saving depends on current disposable income and lagged income and lagged saving.

Estimates of (2–34) for a variety of countries (Lydall, 1963; McMahon and Smyth, 1971) yielded plausible parameter estimates. The estimates of the Smyth and Jackson (1977–78), using the data set described earlier, imply $\beta = 0.123$ and $w = 4.50$.[9] This gives a target wealth-to-income ratio of 4.5, with households adjusting about one-eighth of the way to the target level each year.

9. Saving Functions Using Quarterly Postwar National Income Accounts Data

9.1. The Measurement of Consumption and Saving

The relative income, permanent income, life cycle, and wealth adjustment theories are often called "modern" theories of the consumption function. Developed during the late 1940s and the 1950s, however, they are now more than 30 years old. They were originally tested on data dominated by the pre–World War II period. An important feature of the theories is that they do not view expenditures on consumer durables as consisting of consumption entirely within the expenditure period. Such expenditure is partly saving, as consumer durables have a life of several periods.

Most recent work (including some by the present writer) has failed to use data directly incorporating the flow of consumption services from durables. Instead, researchers analyze the relationship between real saving or consumption and real disposable income, using quarterly data from the U.S. National Income and Product Accounts. Consumption and disposable income are often expressed per capita. Various definitions of consumption, and hence of saving, have been used. The obvious approach is to use total consumption, the sum of consumer expenditures on durables, nondurables, and services. The weakness of this approach is that it assumes that durables are consumed entirely in the period of purchase. The advantage of this definition is that many researchers want to know the behavior of aggregate consumption and saving for use in dynamic macroeconomic models of the economy.

Following Hall (1978), many studies define consumption as the sum of nondurables and services. Hall (1978, p. 979) justifies this approach as follows. "All of the theoretical foundations of the aggregate consumption function apply to individual categories of consumption as well. Dropping durables altogether avoids the suspicion that the findings are an artifact of the procedure for imputing a service flow to the stock of durables." However, this approach has major theoretical inconsistencies. First, it assumes that, in any period, your expenditure on nondurables and services is independent of the flow of services that you are receiving from your stock of consumer durables and your current purchases of consumer durables. Thus, for instance, your expenditure on gasoline and automobile repairs is assumed to be independent of the number and age of the cars you own. Second, unless the utility function is separable between the consumption of durables and nondurables, this approach implies that all expenditure on durables is saving. Suppose your disposable income is $60,000 and you spend $45,000 on nondurables and services, leaving you with $15,000 to dispose of. You have the alternative of purchasing an automobile for $150,000 or putting the same amount into a certificate of deposit maturing in five years. Your wealth will be different in five years' time, but the definition of consumption that we are considering ignores this fact. Many automobile salespersons argue that the entire $15,000 spent on an automobile is saving, but to find economists taking this position is surprising.

Some economists go even further. Flavin (1981, pp. 997–998) uses expenditures on nondurable goods because she wants "to limit the consumption concept to a component which can be adjusted rapidly and smoothly to changes in permanent income." She excludes consumer durables from her consumption variable because "the existene of substantial transaction costs of adjusting stocks of durables suggests that the consumption of services of durable goods would exhibit lagged adjustment to changes in permanent income ... [and] ... data on consumption of services are subject to a similar objection, since services are defined to include the imputed service flow from housing."

One has to wonder just how useful such analyses are and whether they tell us much about macroeconomic behavior. Be that as it may, this is how recent work on consumption and saving has developed, and we must now consider it.

9.2. The Behavior of Saving, Quarterly Data, 1947IV to 1990IV

Figure 2–8 plots real per capita saving against real per capita disposable income, and figure 2–9 the average propensity to save. The data are quarterly covering the period 1947IV to 1990IV. The definition of saving

TOWARD A THEORY OF SAVING

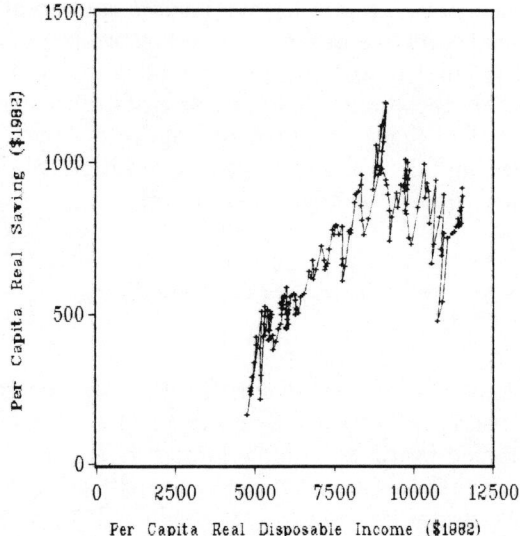

Figure 2-8. Real per capita saving and disposable income: Quarterly 1947IV to 1990IV.

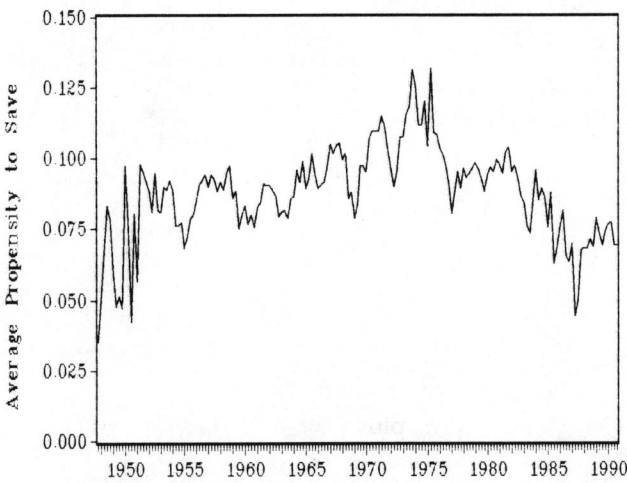

Figure 2-9. Average propensity to save: Quarterly 1947IV to 1990IV.

uses the difference between disposable income and total consumption (consumers' expenditures on durables, nondurables, and services). The pattern in the two figures is striking and rather disturbing. Until about the middle of the 1970s the points in figure 2−8 fall about a conventional saving function and in figure 2−9 the average propensity to save rises. Thereafter, the saving function appears to have shifted downward and the average propensity to save to have fallen.

9.3. Alternative Saving Functions, Quarterly Data, 1953I to 1990IV

Table 2−3 fits some alternative saving functions to the real per capita data used as the basis for figures 2−8 and 2−9. The results in the first five columns are discussed in this section; column 6 is discussed in section 12. All the models are fitted using a heteroskedasticity-consistent covariance matrix for calculating the t-statistics (see White, 1980).

Table 2−3. Alternative Saving Functions, Quarterly Data, 1947IV to 1990IV

	(1)	(2)	(3)	(4)	(5)	(6)
S_0	28.90	29.40				52.91
	(0.73)	(0.73)				(3.32)
S_{t-1}			0.932	0.938	0.964	0.821
			(29.93)	(28.68)	(127.28)	(26.70)
Y_t	0.085	−0.013	0.711	0.697		
	(15.40)	(−0.09)	(9.85)	(13.72)		
Y_{t-1}			−0.708	−0.694		
			(−9.62)	(−13.51)		
$Y_t - Y_{t-1}$					0.727	0.741
					(10.91)	(13.46)
YPEAK$_t$		0.096				
		(0.67)				
$MA(1)$				0.050		
				(−0.56)		
π_{t-1}						51.59
						(5.23)
Adjusted R^2	0.692	0.628	0.945	0.945	0.945	0.953
$D - W$	0.32	0.35	2.07	2.00	2.11	2.10

In the first column there is a simple Keynesian saving function. It is obviously unsatisfactory, as the Durbin-Watson coefficient shows marked serial correlation of the residuals.

Column 2 of table 2-3 gives the estimates for the ratchet model. It does not work well; the coefficient of Y_t is insignificant, and the residuals are serially correlated. YPEAK$_t$ and Y_t are closely correlated ($r = 0.999$), unlike in the shorter inter-war period when per capita disposable income fell markedly during the great depression.

Column 3 gives the model with income, lagged income, and lagged saving; the regression without a constant term is reported, as when a constant is included the t-statistic is negligible. In terms of the extended permanent income model, equation (2-25), and taking $\mu = 0.0053$, the average quarterly growth in Y, the model implies $S_P = 0.092$, $S_T = 0.760$, and $\lambda = 0.927$. Thus the marginal propensity to save out of transitory income is much larger than out of permanent income.

Column (4) adds a moving average error term, MA(1), to the regression. The coefficient of MA(1) is not significantly different from zero, whereas the model in equation (2-25) predicts that the moving average coefficient should be the same as that of lagged saving. The restriction that the two coefficients are equal is easily rejected. When more complicated lag processes are used again, the permanent income model restrictions are not met. The results confirm the findings of Baillie, McMahon, and Smyth (1980) that were based on a shorter data set with the variables not deflated by population. Hence it is necessary to conclude that either the permanent income model (modified to permit different propensities to save out of permanent and transitory income) is invalid, or that permanent income is not generated by a lag process, or both.

Column 5 in table 2-3 fits the simple wealth adjustment model, equation (2-35), which constrains the coefficients of Y_t and Y_{t-1} to be equal and opposite in sign. This restriction is not rejected. The estimates give $w = 20.589$ and $\beta = 0.0324$. Thus the ratio of target wealth to annual income is 5.1 compared to the estimate of 4.5 reported in section 8; annually households adjust approximately one-eighth of the way to the target level, the same as the earlier estimate in section 8. The short-run marginal propensity to save, obtained holding S_{t-1} and Y_{t-1} constant, is 0.727. If we assume that Y and S are growing at the rate $\mu = 0.0053$, we obtain 0.093 as the estimate of the long-run marginal and average propensities to save.

Standard tests of the stability of the relationships reported in columns 1 to 5 are not very encouraging. All easily fail the break-point and forecast versions of the Chow test at the 5 percent confidence level.

A break-point early in the 1980s is apparent. Recursive least squares estimates are equally discouraging. The recursive residuals, the one step-forecasts, and the n-step forecasts frequently fall outside the plus and minus two standard error bands. When the CUSUM of squares test is applied the CUSUM test statistic moves outside the critical 5 percent significance lines.

The modern theories of saving do not fare well on recent data, as the evidence presented in this section has shown. In response to such evidence, two approaches have become popular. One approach involves the abandonment of rigorous theoretical specification of saving behavior and uses instead error correction models. The second approach is to replace adaptive expectations in the permanent income and life cycle models with rational expectations. We consider these approaches in sections 10 and 11.

10. Error Correction Models

When using an error correction model, a researcher abandons the attempt to obtain a complete theoretical explanation of the relationship between macroeconomic aggregates such as consumption, saving, and income. Instead, an error correction modeler attempts to obtain robust empirical relationships. The researcher starts with simple stylized facts, such as saving depends on income, and then chooses a model using the principles of dynamic econometric modeling.

Consider a saving function in which saving in period t is related to saving in period $t-1$ and income in t and $t-1$, that is

$$S_t = \alpha_1 S_{t-1} + \alpha_2 Y_t + \alpha_3 Y_{t-1} - \epsilon_t, \tag{2-36}$$

which may be reparameterized as

$$\begin{aligned} S_t - S_{t-1} &= (\alpha_1 - 1)S_{t-1} + \alpha_2(Y_t - Y_{t-1}) + (\alpha_2 + \alpha_3)Y_{t-1} - \epsilon_t \\ &= \alpha_2 (Y_t - Y_{t-1}) + (1 - \alpha_1)(KY_{t-1} - S_{t-1}) - \epsilon_t \end{aligned} \tag{2-37}$$

where $K = (\alpha_2 + \alpha_3)/(1 - \alpha_1)$. Assume that S_t and Y_t are integrated of order one and S_t and Y_t are cointegrated. Then the parameters in (2-37) are interpreted as follows: α_2 is the impact effect, $1 - \alpha_1$ is the feedback effect, and K is the long-run response. Following Davidson and co-workers (1978), the name "error correction mechanism" is given to the term $KY_{t-1} - S_{t-1}$. This term reflects the deviation from the long-run equilibrium outcome with households removing $1 - \alpha_1$ of the disequilibrium each period. Various modeling strategies for error correction models have been suggested, but they have substantial econometric problems; see, for instance, Wickens and Breusch (1988) and Harvey (1990, section 8.5).

If $K = 1$, then (2-37) reduces to

$$S_t - S_{t-1} = \alpha_2(Y_t - Y_{t-1}) + (1 - \alpha_1)(Y_{t-1} - S_{t-1}) - \epsilon_t. \quad (2-38)$$

The case of $K = 1$ is of particular interest because it corresponds to long-run proportionality between saving and income. As Wickens and Breusch (1988, p. 193) note, an equation like (2-37) is "not a particularly convenient form for estimation—especially of ... [K] ...—hence the attraction of setting ... [K] ... equal to unity. Usually, however, this is not a price worth paying for the convenience of estimation."

It is a tempting and common procedure to test the assumption that $K = 1$ by simply adding Y_{t-1} as an explanatory variable and then rejecting proportionality if the t-statistic for the coefficient of Y_{t-1} is significant. However, Harvey (1990, p. 292) points out that a complication arises because the t-statistic for the coefficient of Y_{t-1} does not have an asymptotic normal distribution.

The equations reported in columns 3 and 5 of table 2-3 can be interpreted in terms of an error correction model. The column 3 estimates imply $K = 0.044$, the column 5 estimates that $K = 0$.

11. Rational Expectations Models

According to the permanent income model, as new information about future income becomes available individuals will revise their estimate of permanent income and hence change their consumption plans. Until the late 1970s the conventional way to model permanent income was to assume adaptive expectations. An alternative assumption is that expectations are developed rationally.

The theoretical basis for this approach is summarized by Hall (1989, p. 156) as follows: Hall (1978)

> ... neither tried to repair the traditional consumption function nor tried to estimate the deep parameters of utility. Rather, he formulated a simple empirical test of the idea that consumers maximize the expected value of lifetime utility subject to an unchanging real interest rate. The basic idea is to look at the Euler equation describing the optimal behavior of such a consumer. The Euler equation characterizes the equality of the marginal rate of substitution between consumption this year and consumption next year to the relative price of the two. The relative price is simply the present discounted cost of a unit of future consumption.

Denote the consumer's utility by U, rate of time preference by δ, disposable labor income by Y^L, end of period wealth apart from human capital by W, the after-tax real rate of interest by R, and the time period by t. Mathematically, the consumer wants to maximize discounted utility

$$\Sigma[1/(1 + \delta)]^t U(C_t), \qquad (2-39)$$

subject to the budget constraint

$$W_t = (1 + R)W_{t-1} + Y_t^L - C_t. \qquad (2-40)$$

The Euler equation (first-order condition) expressing the equality of the marginal rate of substitution to the price is

$$U'(C_{t-1}) = [(1 + R)/(1 + \delta)]U'(C_t). \qquad (2-41)$$

If the form of the utility function is log-linear as

$$U = \Sigma \ln C, \qquad (2-42)$$

then $U' = 1/C$ and the Euler equation is

$$C_t = [(1 + R)/(1 + \delta)]C_{t-1}. \qquad (2-43)$$

Like Friedman's version of the permanent income hypothesis, the rational expectations version assumes that consumption depends only on permanent income. If consumers form their expectations rationally, they take into account all the information available to them. In period $t-1$ consumers took into account all the information available to them in period $t-1$ and in earlier periods. So, when they are deciding on their consumption for period t, all the information about previous periods is already embodied in their consumption in period $t-1$. Thus

$$C_t = \alpha C_{t-1} + \epsilon_t, \qquad (2-44)$$

where $\alpha = [(1 + R)/(1 + \delta)]$ and ϵ_t is a random variable. Then to test the combined permanent income and rational expectations model, add variables dated $t-1$ or earlier to the right-hand side and compute a test for their exclusion. If such variables cannot be excluded, then either the permanent income model does not hold or expectations are not formed rationally, or both. In such a case, consumption is said to show "excess sensitivity" to income, in that consumption responds more than predicted by the model.

The initial study by Hall (1978) used per capita data on consumption of nondurables are services. Hall found that lagged real disposable income had little predictive power for consumption but that the Euler-equation restriction was rejected for the stock market. Flavin developed a structural model assuming that real income follows a stable stochastic process and concluded (Flavin, 1981, p. 1006) that her "tests reveal substantial evidence against the permanent income hypothesis. Using either nondurables consumption or consumption of nondurables and services as the dependent variable, the hypothesis that consumption exhibits no excess sensitivity to current income can be rejected at the 0.5 percent level." By now a number of studies have rejected the assumption that the excess sensitivity of consumption is zero (see Hall, 1989; Molana, 1991).

Excess sensitivity can be shown easily using U.S. quarterly data. Table 2−4 reports regressions for three measures of real per capita consumption: total consumption, nondurables plus services, and nondurables. For each consumption measure two regressions are fitted. In the first, consumption for quarter t is regressed on the previous quarter's consumption. In the second, four further variables dated $t-1$ or earlier are added. These variables are two lagged changes in income, $Y_{t-1} - Y_{t-2}$ and $Y_{t-2} - Y_{t-3}$, and two lagged inflation rates, π_{t-1} and π_{t-2}.[10] We want to test whether the four additional variables make a significant contribution to the explanation of the consumption variable. The F-statistics and likelihood ratio statistics obtained are so large that the null hypothesis that the additional variables have no explanatory power is rejected at the 99.99 confidence level. Thus either the permanent income model does not hold or expectations are not formed rationally, or both.

Various researchers have attempted to save the permanent income cum rational expectations model. These attempts deal with liquidity constraints; the special behavior of durable goods; intertemporal substitution; the behavior of transitory consumption and shifts in preferences; econometric respecifications; varying future prices and interest rates; the role of fiscal policy; substitution between consumption and leisure; and the temporal behavior of asset returns (see Hayashi, 1987; Hall, 1989; Molana, 1991). These extensions are often technically sophisticated. They have not been particularly successful, however, at increasing our knowledge of the determinants of saving.

12. Inflation and the Saving Function

The models estimated in the last section really provide no explanation for the changing pattern of the saving function and for the U-shaped path to the average propensity to save observed in figures 2−8 and 2−9. It is possible that saving is responsive to the rate of inflation. The role of inflation has largely been neglected in the U.S. literature, whereas

Table 2-4. Tests for "Excess Sensitivity": 1947IV to 1990IV

Variable	Total		Consumption Measure Services and Nondurables		Nondurables	
C_{t-1}	1.0047	1.0054	1.0042	1.0049	1.0023	1.0029
	(1726.23)	(755.13)	(2440.00)	(1043.53)	(1632.32)	(781.74)
$Y_{t-1} - Y_{t-2}$		0.137		0.071		0.064
		(3.09)		(2.32)		(3.51)
$Y_{t-2} - Y_{t-3}$		0.146		0.066		0.043
		(2.49)		(2.13)		(1.99)
π_{t-1}		-58.51		-48.65		-41.73
		(-2.98)		(-3.71)		(-4.97)
π_{t-2}		42.14		39.24		35.65
		(2.15)		(2.97)		(4.26)
Adjusted R^2	0.99911	0.99922	0.99947	0.99954	0.99711	0.99769
D-W	1.70	1.95	1.53	1.67	1.64	1.78
F-statistic		7.04		6.90		10.49
Likelihood ratio		26.81		26.33		38.56

TOWARD A THEORY OF SAVING

British studies have paid more attention to inflation (see, for instance, Gowland, 1990).

Column 6 of table 2–3 reports the regression obtained when lagged inflation is added to the column 5 model in which saving depends on the change in income and lagged saving. Inflation is the end of quarter to end of quarter rate calculated using the implicit price deflator for consumption.[11] The coefficient of lagged inflation π_{t-1} is positive, so inflation raises the household saving rate. Inflation is highly significant; the t-statistic is over 5. As a constant is significant, it is included in the reported regression.

What can account for the effect of inflation on saving? The Keynesian saving function ignored inflation because it simply posited a relationship between real saving and real disposable income. In the absence of money illusion, there was no reason to suppose that price changes would influence the saving–income relationship. Deaton (1977) has argued that consumers may be subject to money illusion, that they mistake inflation for a change in relative prices so that some purchases are delayed. However, as Gowland (1990, pp. 225–226) has noted, "It is implausible that it could be a significant explanation of a *large, prolonged* increase in saving ... as inflation may lead to relative price changes being mistaken for absolute ones ... [and] ... one might expect search activity to increase for goods (in practice durables) expensive enough to justify prolonged search rather than see purchases deferred."

A second reason that inflation may cause increased saving is that it increases uncertainty. Risk-averse households will react to increased uncertainty by increasing their saving. Thus in a permanent income model the propensity to save out of permanent income should be increased. In a wealth adjustment model, target wealth will be increased by inflation.

Third, inflation may affect real wealth. When prices change, the real value of wealth will change if the value of the assets does not change proportionately. Assets that are money-denominated will depreciate in value during inflationary periods. Money-denominated assets include cash, bank deposits, savings accounts, certificates of deposit, and bonds. Real assets, such as equities and houses, may appreciate with inflation, although the appreciation rate may be greater or less than the inflation rate.

If the saving function is estimated in a form that includes real wealth directly as an explanatory variable, changes in the prices of assets are incorporated in the wealth variable. If wealth is not directly included, then the effects of inflation on wealth may be directly incorporated into the model. To see this, again consider the wealth adjustment model. Repeating equation (2–34), we have

$$S_t = \beta(wY_t - W_{t-1}) - \epsilon_t. \qquad (2\text{–}45)$$

The impact of inflation on wealth can be modeled by

$$W_{t-1} - (1 + a\eta_{t-1})W_{t-2} = S_{t-1}, \qquad (2\text{-}46)$$

where $\eta = 0.01\pi$ and a measures the effect of inflation on wealth. If $a = 0$, then inflation has no effect on wealth; if the net effect of inflation on wealth (real and nominal) is negative, then $a < 0$.

Writing equation (2–45) for period $t - 1$, multiplying both sides of this by $(1 + a\eta_{t-1})$, subtracting the result from (2–45), substituting from (2–46), and rearranging give

$$S_t = (1 - \beta + a\eta_{t-1})S_{t-1} + \beta w(Y_t - Y_{t-1}) - \beta w a\eta_{t-1}Y_{t-1} - \epsilon_t + (1 + a\eta_{t-1})\epsilon_{t-1}. \qquad (2\text{-}47)$$

Nonlinear estimation of equation (2–47) using our data set gives the results reported in table 2–5.[12] Each percentage point increase in the inflation rate results in a reduction in the value of wealth by about half of one percentage point. The hypothesis that the inflation coefficient a is equal to zero is rejected at the 99.9 percent confidence level using a Wald test.

If, as in section 9, we assume that Y and S are growing at the rate $\mu = 0.0053$ per quarter, we can now calculate the steady state propensities for any rate of inflation. For quarterly rates of inflation of zero, 1, 2, and 3 percent, the long-run average (and marginal) propensities to save are 0.0481, 0.0865, 0.121, and 0.152, respectively. Saving is thus very sensitive to the rate of inflation.

13. Conclusions

Considerable talent has been lavished on the saving function over more than half a century. The results are disappointing. Not only do we not

Table 2–5. Inflation in the Wealth Adjustment Model: 1947IV to 1990IV

Coefficient	Estimate	t-statistic
β	0.079	6.74
w	9.688	7.18
a	−0.477	−4.28
Adjusted R^2	.950	
$D - W$	2.11	
$\varkappa^2$ for Wald test $a = 0$	18.29	

have agreement on *the* saving function, but our models have failed to provide us with adequate explanations of saving behavior.

Given the disarray on saving, the following suggestions for future work are made:

1. researchers should abandon the atheoretical approach of many recent studies—sophisticated time series techniques are not a substitute for intelligent model building.
2. the definition of saving and the structure of the theoretical models should specifically allow for the flow of consumption services from consumer durables. The more theoretically correct definition of saving should be used in empirical work.
3. the effect of fluctuations in the inflation rate should be incorporated in the models.

Notes

1. "For a man's habitual standard of life usually has the first claim on his income, and he is apt to save the difference between his actual income and the expense of his habitual standard; or, if he does adjust his expenditure to changes in his income, he will over short periods do so imperfectly. Thus a rising income will often be accompanied by increased saving, and a falling income by decreased saving, on a greater scale at first than subsequently" (Keynes, 1936, p. 97).

2. Dorothy Brady reported and discussed several budget studies for U.S. households. The data used here are taken from Brady (1956, p. 182).

3. James Gapinski (1982, pp. 123–125) gives some evidence on the extent of the forecasting errors that result from using prewar estimates to forecast the postwar economy.

4. A survey of the early work distinguishes 18 studies that appear to make original formulations (see Robert Ferber, 1953).

5. The demonstration effect was brought home to me the other day. Coming into the building housing the Department of Economics, I overheard the following conversation between a student and her father.

Student: "Daddy, Daddy, I've just got to have a new sports car. My high school graduation present is two years old. All my friends have new sports cars. I've just got to have one."

Father: "Darling, that can't be so. Look at the parking lot there. It's full of Honda Accords and Toyota Corollas."

Student: "Daddy, don't be so silly! That's the faculty parking lot."

6. A more complicated ratchet model also worked well. For a discussion of the specification of alternative ratchet models, see Smyth and Jackson (1977–78) and Jackson and Smyth (1985).

7. Recently I faced a clear test of the permanent income hypothesis. In the summer of 1990 I was invited to spend two months undertaking research on the New Zealand economy at the University of Canterbury in Christchurch, New Zealand, as an Erskine Fellow. The University of Canterbury undertook to provide me with a modest living allowance just adequate enough to cover the extra costs of living in Christchurch instead of in Baton Rouge (rental of an apartment, cost of meals, and the like). I arrived at Christchurch one Monday. When the head of the Department of Economics met me at the airport, he told me the good news that, on the previous Friday, the university had voted to raise the living allowance of Erskine Fellows by $1500 effective the day of my arrival. I immediately realized that this was positive transitory income. What did I do? Did I decide to invest this unexpected income so that my permanent income would rise by the annual return on $1500, say $125 per year, and this year and in all future years, increase my consumption (and that of my wife and children) accordingly? No way! It did not take me very long to decide that my standard of living in Christchurch could be rather better than I had anticipated. I drank better wine than I had planned, rented a larger television set than I had planned, and made more frequent phone calls home than I had planned. My marginal propensity to consume out of transitory income was definitely positive. However, I did save some of the extra income, more than I would have saved out of an increase in permanent income. So my marginal propensity to consume out of transitory income was positive but less than my marginal propensity to consume out of permanent income, and my marginal propensity to save out of transitory income was less than one but greater than my marginal propensity to save out of permanent income.

8. This problem also arises if it is assumed a priori that the marginal propensity to consume out of transitory income is zero.

9. These estimates are only approximations, as they are imputed from an unconstrained regression of S_t on Y_t, Y_{t-1}, and S_{t-1}, whereas there are only two coefficients to be estimated.

10. Inflation is the change in the implicit price deflator for total consumption, as described in footnote 11.

11. The inflation rate we want to use is the rate from the beginning of a period (which equals the end of the previous period) to the end of the period. Accordingly, we first calculate the end-of-period price level as the average of the current and succeeding periods and take the percentage change over the similarly constructed price level for the previous period. Thus the inflation rate is given by

$$\pi_t = 100\{\ln[0.5(P_t + P_{t+1})] - \ln[0.5(P_{t-1} + P_t)]\},$$

where P_t denotes the implicit price deflator for consumption in period t.

12. The disturbance term in equation (2-47) is $-\epsilon_t + (1 + a\eta_{t-1})\,\epsilon_{t-1}$, which is correlated with the rate of inflation. The procedure used to estimate the model does not take into account this constraint.

References

Ando, Albert, and Franco Modigliani. "The 'Life Cycle' Hypothesis of Saving: Aggregate Implications and Tests." *American Economic Review* 53 (March 1963): 55–84.

Baillie, Richard T., Patrick C. McMahon, and David J. Smyth. "Testing the Permanent Income Hypothesis Using a General Rational lag Formulation." *Economics Letters* 5 (1980): 39–43.
Brady, Dorothy S. "Family Saving 1888 to 1950." In *A Study of Saving in the United States*, vol. III, edited by Raymond W. Goldsmith, Dorothy S. Brady, and Horst Menderhausen. Princeton, N.J.: Princeton University Press, 1956, pp. 137–273.
Clark, Colin. "Post-War Savings in the U.S.A." *Bulletin of the Oxford University Institute of Statistics* 7 (May 19, 1945): 97–103.
Davidson, J. E. H., D. F. Hendry, F. Srba, and S. Yeo. "Econometric Modelling of the Aggregate Time Series Relation Between Consumption and Income in the U.K." *Economic Journal* 88 (December 1978): 661–692.
Deaton, Angus S. "Involuntary Saving Through Unanticipated Inflation." *American Economic Review* 67 (December 1977): 889–910.
Duesenberry, James S. *Income, Saving and the Theory of Consumer Behavior*. Cambridge, Mass: Harvard University Press, 1949.
Ferber, Robert. *A Study of Aggregate Consumption Functions*. New York: National Bureau of Economic Research, Technical Paper 8, 1953.
Flavin, Marjorie A. "The Adjustment of Consumption to Changing Expectations About Future Income." *Journal of Political Economy* 89 (October 1981): 974–1009.
Friedman, Milton. *A Theory of the Consumption Function*. Princeton, N.J.: National Bureau of Economic Research, 1957.
Gapinski, James H. *Macroeconomic Theory: Statics, Dynamics, and Policy*. New York: McGraw-Hill, 1982.
Goldsmith, Raymond W. *A Study of Saving in the United States, Volume I*. Princeton, N.J.: Princeton University Press, 1955.
Gowland, David. "Consumption, Borrowing and Saving." In *Understanding Macroeconomics*, edited by David Gowland. Aldershot, Hants: Edward Elgar Publishing, 1990, pp. 210–237.
Hall, Robert E. "Stochastic Implications of the Life Cycle–Permanent Income Hypothesis: Theory and Evidence." *Journal of Political Economy* 86 (December 1978): 971–987.
———. "Consumption." In *Modern Business Cycle Theory*, edited by Robert J. Barro. Cambridge, Mass: Harvard University Press, 1989, pp. 153–177.
Harvey, Andrew C. *The Econometric Analysis of Time Series*. 2nd. ed. Cambridge, Mass: MIT Press, 1990.
Hayashi, F. "Tests for Liquidity Constraints: A Critical Survey and Some New Observations. In *Advances in Econometrics, Fifth World Congress*, vol. 2, edited by T. Bewley. Cambridge: Cambridge University Press, 1987, pp. 91–120.
Holmes, James M. "A Direct Test of Friedman's Permanent Income Theory." *Journal of the American Statistical Association* 66 (September 1970): pp. 1159–1162.
Jackson, John D., and David J. Smyth. "Specifying Differential Response in Economic Time Series." *Economic Modelling* 2 (1985): 149–161.

Keynes, John Maynard. *The General Theory of Employment Interest and Money.* London: Macmillan, 1936.

Lee, Tong Hung. "More on Windfall Income and Consumption." *Journal of Political Economy* 83 (April 1975): 407–417.

Lydall, H. E. "Saving and Wealth." *Australian Economic Papers* 2 (December 1963): 228–250.

McMahon, Patrick C., and David J. Smyth. "Saving, Income and Wealth: A Reexamination of Stone's Post-War Expenditure Function." *Manchester School of Economic and Social Studies* 39 (March 1971): 37–44.

Modigliani, Franco. "Fluctuations in the Saving–Income Ratio: A Problem in Economic Forecasting." In Conference on Research in Income and Wealth, *Studies in Income and Wealth*, vol. 11. New York: National Bureau of Economic Research, 1949.

Modigliani, Franco. "Life Cycle, Individual Thrift, and the Wealth of Nations." *American Economic Review* 76 (June 1986): 297–313.

Modigliani, Franco, and Albert K. Ando. "Tests of the Life Cycle Hypothesis of Savings." *Bulletin of the Oxford University Institute of Statistics* 19 (May 1957): 99–124.

Modigliani, Franco, and Richard Brumberg. "Utility Analysis and the Consumption." In *Post-Keynesian Economics*, edited by Kenneth K. Kurihara. New Brunswick, N.J.: Rutgers University Press, 1954, pp. 388–436.

Molana, H. "The Time Series Consumption Function: Error Correction, Random Walk and the Steady-State." *Economic Journal* 101 (May 1991): 382–403.

Nagatani, Keizo. "Life Cycle Saving: Theory and Fact." *American Economic Review* 62 (June 1972): 344–353.

Smithies, Arthur. "Forecasting Postwar Demand: I." *Econometrica* 13 (January 1945): 1–14.

Smyth, David J. "On Testing the Life Cycle Model Using Cross-Section Data." *Atlantic Economic Journal* 20 (March 1992): 103.

Smyth, David J., and John D. Jackson. "A Theoretical and Empirical Analysis of Ratchet Models as Alternatives to Permanent Income and Continuous Habit Formation Consumption Functions." *Journal of Economics and Business* 30 (1977–78): 89–97.

White H. "A Heteroscedasticity-Consistent Covariance Matrix Estimator and a Direct Test for Heteroscedasticity." *Econometrica* 48 (May 1980): 817–838.

Wickens, M. R., and T. S. Breusch. "Dynamic Specification, the Long-Run and the Estimation of Transformed Regression Models." *Economic Journal* 98 (Supplement 1988): 189–205.

Woytinski, W. S. "Relationship Between Consumers' Expenditures, Savings and Disposable Income." *Review of Economics and Statistics* 28 (February 1946): 1–12; and "Five Views on the Consumption Function." *Review of Economics and Statistics* 28 (November 1946): 197–224.

Commentary by Marjorie Flavin
University of California at San Diego

David Smyth has provided an excellent overview of the evolution of thought on the saving/consumption decision from Keynes to the present. Instead of attempting to cover the same broad range of issues, this commentary will be devoted to extending a couple of the themes established by Smyth. After pursuing these themes to obtain the implications of a richer model of the saving decision, the discussion will close by using the model to identify points of agreement and points of disagreement with Smyth's chapter.

Two themes will be pursued: (1) Many of the models of saving behavior have been developed in terms of consumption behavior, with the implications for saving obtained by using the accounting identity; and (2) the decision to purchase durable goods, which has both a consumption and saving aspect, has not been adequately treated, especially in recent research.

With respect to the first point—that a model of the consumption decision is also a model of the saving decision—the standard approach has been to create an artificial dichotomy between the consumption decision and the portfolio choice (saving) decision, and only fairly recently has a model emerged that genuinely integrates the two decisions. To develop this point, the "standard approach" to the portfolio choice decision is defined to be represented by the traditional capital asset pricing model (CAPM), and the "standard approach" to the consumption decision to be represented by the permanent income or life cycle models. The consumption-β (or consumption-CAPM) is a single model that simultaneously generalizes both the CAPM and the permanent income model and, as such, stresses the interdependence of the consumption and portfolio choice decisions. According to the consumption-β model, the interdependence of the consumption and portfolio choice decisions is vastly more interesting than a simple accounting identity that says that what is left over after consumption is saved, or vice versa.

The traditional CAPM is based on a dichotomy of the two decisions in the sense that the model ignores nontradable assets, such as human wealth, and determines the risk premia attached to various assets by assuming that, for a given expected return, investors wish to minimize the variance of the return to the portfolio. An asset whose return is positively correlated with the market return carries a nondiversifiable risk and therefore requires a positive risk premium, whereas an asset whose return is negatively correlated with the market provides a hedge and therefore would be held with a negative risk premium. Using r_{jt} to denote the return to a single, risky asset, r_{mt} to denote the return to the market portfolio, and r_t to denote the riskless rate, the asset pricing implications of the CAPM are summarized by

$$E_t r_{jt+1} - r_{t+1} = \beta[E_t(r_{mt+1}) - r_{t+1}], \qquad (2C-1)$$

where

$$\beta = \frac{\text{cov}(r_{jt}, r_{mt})}{\text{var}(r_{mt})}.$$

Thus the basic message of the traditional CAPM is that asset premia are determined by the covariance of the asset's return with the return to the market portfolio. In principle, "the market" would include all tradable assets, including real estate, for example, but because of data limitations, the model is often empirically implemented by defining "the market" as those assets traded on the U.S. stock market.

For the purposes of this discussion, it is convenient to abstract from much of the detail of the life cycle and permanent income models and simply express the basic message of both models as saying that optimizing households will determine their consumption based on their lifetime resources rather than the resources that accrue during an arbitrary accounting period. Having characterized the permanent income and life cycle theories as modeling saving primarily as a device for "consumption smoothing," the crucial implication of these models will be summarized with the certainty version of the consumption Euler equation:

$$\left(\frac{1 + r_{t+1}}{1 + \delta}\right) U'(C_{t+1}) = U'(C_t), \qquad (2C-2)$$

where δ is the rate of time preference, and r_t is the riskless (although possibly time-varying) rate of return, as before. If we assume constant relative risk aversion utility, $U(C_t) = (C_t^{1-\gamma})/(1-\gamma)$, so that marginal utility is given by $U'(C_t) = C_t^{-\gamma}$, the Euler equation under certainty implies that the growth rate of consumption, $\Delta \ln C_{t+1}$, is given by

$$\Delta \ln C_{t+1} = \frac{1}{\gamma}[\ln(1 + r_{t+1}) - \ln(1 + \delta)] \approx \frac{1}{\gamma}(r_{t+1} - \delta). \quad (2C-3)$$

In equation (2C–3) the absence of a term involving the contemporaneous growth rate of income reflects the fact that, under certainty, lifetime consumption has a smooth profile unperturbed by transient fluctuations in current income. Whereas lifetime resources, or permanent income, affect the overall level of the path, the rate of growth of consumption from one period to the next is determined by the rate of return and the household's rate of time preference. Given the divergence between the rate of return and the rate of time preference, the growth rate of consumption also depends on the curvature parameter of the utility function; for greater values of the curvature parameter, γ, the household is more averse to substituting future consumption for current consumption, therefore the flatter the consumption profile.

As separate models of the consumption and portfolio decisions, the permanent income or life cycle model and the traditional CAPM were extremely successful models, both in terms of providing analytical structures that generated insights on a wide range of issues and in terms of explaining the data. As successful as these models were, however, each suffered from some important limitations. The permanent income–life cycle model incorporated consumption smoothing and investment motives for saving but did not integrate a precautionary motive. Although the life cycle model made predictions about the total level of saving held by the household, it was less useful in predicting the allocation of this saving among various assets. Behavior toward risk, obviously, is addressed by the CAPM. However, due to the focus of the model on asset pricing and to data limitations, the traditional CAPM emphasizes the risk arising from asset returns to the exclusion of other sources of risk—most notably, the riskiness of labor income. By integrating the two previous models, the consumption-β model addresses all of these limitations.

Next, the consumption-β model will be developed and an explanation given of the sense in which the model provides a generalization of both the traditional CAPM and the permanent income models.

Assume that the household's objective is to maximize expected lifetime utility:

$$\max V_t = \max E_t \sum_{\tau=0}^{T} \left(\frac{1}{1+\delta}\right)^\tau U(C_{t+\tau}), \quad (2C-4)$$

where the instantaneous utility function is of the constant relative risk aversion form:

$$U(C_t) = \frac{C_t^{1-\gamma}}{1-\gamma}. \tag{2C-5}$$

In deciding whether to devote the marginal dollar in period t to additional consumption or to investment in risky asset j, the household must satisfy the first-order condition:

$$E_t\left[\left(\frac{1+r_{jt+1}}{1+\delta}\right)C_{t+1}^{-\gamma}\right] = C_t^{-\gamma}, \tag{2C-6}$$

where r_{jt+1} is the return from holding asset j between periods t and $t+1$.

A convenient solution for the consumption path can be obtained if we assume that the asset return and the marginal utility of consumption are each log normally distributed, that is,

$$\ln(1+r_{jt+1}) \sim N(m_{r_j}, v_{r_j}) \tag{2C-7a}$$
$$\ln C_{t+1}^{-\gamma} \sim N(m_u, v_u), \tag{2C-7b}$$

where m_{r_j} and v_{r_j} are the conditional mean and variance, respectively, of the log of the asset return, and m_u and v_u are the conditional mean and variance, respectively, of the log of the marginal utility of consumption. The covariance of the asset return with the marginal utility of consumption plays a crucial role in this model; considering the log transformation of the variables, denote:

$$\text{cov}(\ln(1+r_{jt+1}), \ln C_{t+1}^{-\gamma}) = \text{cov}_{r_j u}. \tag{2C-8}$$

If the random variable x is log normally distributed, so that

$$\ln x \sim N(\mu, \sigma^2), \tag{2C-9}$$

then the mean of x is given by:

$$E(x) = \exp\left(\mu + \frac{\sigma^2}{2}\right). \tag{2C-10}$$

In the present context, this relationship between the moments of the log of x and the expectation of x itself implies that equation (2C-6) can be rewritten as

$$\frac{1}{1+\delta} \exp\left(m_{r_j} + m_u + (v_{r_j} + v_u)/2 + \text{cov}_{r_j u}\right) = C_t^{-\gamma}. \tag{2C-11}$$

Taking logs by using the definitions of the conditional means m_{r_j} and m_u and rearranging, equation (2C–11) becomes

$$E_t \Delta \ln C_{t+1} = \frac{1}{\gamma}[(v_{r_j} + v_u)/2 + \text{cov}_{r_j u} - \ln(1 + \delta)] \quad (2C\text{--}12)$$

$$+ \frac{1}{\gamma} E_t \ln(1 + r_{t+1})$$

or

$$E_t \Delta \ln C_{t+1} \approx \frac{1}{\gamma}[(v_{r_j} + v_u)/2 + \text{cov}_{r_j u}] + \frac{1}{\gamma}[E_t(r_{t+1}) - \delta]. \quad (2C\text{--}13)$$

Because equation (2C–13) has the same form as the consumption Euler equation under certainty (equation 2C–3), it seems sensible to start by discussing the sense in which the consumption-β model is a generalization of the permanent income and life cycle models. With uncertainty, the Euler equation now relates the expected growth rate of consumption to the expected rate of return. However, in addition to replacing the realizations of these variables with their corresponding conditional expectations, the introduction of uncertainty gives rise to a constant term that depends on the joint distribution of the asset return and the marginal utility of consumption.

To concentrate on the consumption decision for the moment, suppose that only a single asset is available to the household. Consider two households that differ in terms of the riskiness of their labor income streams. The household whose human wealth is inherently riskier will have a higher variance of consumption and therefore a higher variance of the marginal utility of consumption than the household with a more stable stream of labor income. According to equation (2C–13), the household with the riskier human wealth (and therefore the larger value of the variance of (the log of) the marginal utility of consumption) will have a steeper consumption profile. In making its consumption profile steeper, the household with relatively risky human capital is reducing current consumption in favor of future consumption, that is, undertaking more saving than the other household. Note that even if the asset were a riskless one, so that v_{r_j} and $\text{cov}_{r_j u}$ were both zero, uncertainty about future labor income implies a strictly positive value of the variance of the (log of the) marginal utility of consumption, v_u. Thus even apart from uncertainty arising from asset returns, the consumption-β model incorporates a precautionary motive for saving, in addition to the investment and consumption smoothing motives that appeared in the life cycle and permanent income versions of the model.

The asset pricing implications of the consumption-β model could also be discussed in terms of equation (2C–13). However, the comparison of the consumption-β, or consumption CAPM, with the traditional CAPM is more transparent if we go back to the more general Euler equation,

$$E_t\left[\frac{1 + r_{jt+1}}{1 + \delta} U'(C_{t+1})\right] = U'(C_t), \qquad (2C-14)$$

which is just the stochastic version of equation (2C–2). Equation (2C–14) must hold for all assets held by the household. Using r_t to denote the riskless rate of return, as before, the Euler equation for the riskless rate of return is

$$E_t\left[\frac{1 + r_{t+1}}{1 + \delta} U'(C_{t+1})\right] = U'(C_t). \qquad (2C-15)$$

Subtracting (2C–15) from (2C–14) and multiplying by $(1 + \delta)$, we get

$$E_t[(r_{jt+1} - r_{t+1}) U'(C_{t+1})] = 0, \qquad (2C-16)$$

which implies

$$E_t(r_{jt+1} - r_{t+1})E_t U'(C_{t+1}) + \text{cov}_t[r_{jt+1}, U'(C_{t+1})] = 0, \qquad (2C-17)$$

or

$$E_t r_{jt+1} - r_{t+1} = -\frac{\text{cov}_t[r_{jt+1}, U'(C_{t+1})]}{E_t U'(C_{t+1})}. \qquad (2C-18)$$

According to the consumption-β model, the risk premium associated with a given risky asset depends on the covariance of the asset's return with the marginal utility of consumption, rather than on the covariance of the asset's return with the market return. The intuition behind this result is simple. For an asset with a stochastic payoff, positive correlation between the return and the marginal utility of consumption means that on average, the asset pays off well in those states of nature or time periods when the payoff is particularly highly valued (i.e., when consumption is low and the marginal utility of consumption is high) and, conversely, tends to pay off poorly when the marginal utility of consumption is low. Compared to the riskless asset, an investment in an asset whose return is positively correlated with the marginal utility of consumption provides a form of insurance. The "premium" paid by households for the insurance provided by such assets takes the form of a negative risk premium, or an expected return less than the riskless rate. Conversely, an asset whose return is negatively correlated with the marginal utility of consumption — paying off well when the marginal utility of consumption is low and paying off poorly when the marginal utility of consumption is high — would require a positive risk premium.

The consumption-β model has the same basic form as the traditional CAPM, with the marginal utility of consumption replacing the return to the market portfolio as the crucial random variable that determines asset premiums. Because financial wealth is one component of the household's lifetime resources, the risk to asset returns will be one source of risk to the marginal utility of consumption; in many cases assets that would be predicted to carry positive risk premiums under the traditional CAPM because of positive correlation with the market return would also be predicted to carry positive risk premiums under the consumption-β model because of negative correlation with the marginal utility of consumption. However, in addition to reflecting the risk arising from asset returns, the marginal utility of consumption summarizes the risk impinging on the household's fortunes from all sources — human wealth as well as financial wealth. In contrast to the traditional CAPM, which relies on explicit measurements of asset values to obtain the crucial data series on the return to the market, the consumption-β model does not require explicit valuation of the household's stocks, real estate, and human wealth, relying instead on the household to reveal the stochastic evolution of its fortunes in the choice of its consumption level.

For a model that integrates and generalizes two of the most successful models in economics, the empirical performance of the consumption-β model is surprisingly poor, both in terms of the implications for consumption and the implications for asset pricing. In comparing the empirical failure of the consumption-β model with the empirical successes of the permanent income and life cycle models, I would argue that the recent rejections of the theory should not be interpreted as evidence in favor of the simpler versions of the model, but rather evidence that, with the advent of rational expectations and time series econometrics, in recent tests the null hypothesis is typically defined much more precisely than in the past.

In terms of its implications for asset pricing, the poor empirical performance of the consumption-β model is more troubling. On this question, the two competing models — traditional CAPM and consumption-β — are in agreement in saying that asset premiums are determined by the covariance of the asset's return with a crucial summary variable, the only disagreement lying in the specification of the crucial variable as the market return or the marginal utility of consumption. Despite the fact that the traditional CAPM seems to be a strongly restrictive special case of the more general consumption-β model, there is considerable empirical evidence that asset premiums are better explained by the covariance of the return with the market than by the covariance of the return with the marginal utility of consumption.

The conflict between theory and empirical evidence is convincingly resolved in an important paper by Grossman and Laroque (1990). In the idealized version of the consumption-β model, the level of consumption is costlessly adjustable. For such a consumption good, the marginal utility of observed consumption will always equal the marginal indirect utility of wealth. Grossman and Laroque point out that if, instead, the level of consumption is costly to adjust, an optimizing household will only infrequently incur the transactions costs required to maintain the equality of the marginal utility of consumption with the marginal indirect utility of wealth.

For illustrative purposes, Grossman and Laroque take the extreme case in which the household's consumption consists purely of the stream of services from a single durable (e.g., a house). For plausible values of the transactions costs involved in buying and selling the house (for example, a transactions cost that amounts to 6 percent of the value of the house for selling and no transactions cost for purchasing), the household will go for long periods with a constant level of consumption of housing services (and therefore of the marginal utility of consumption), despite continuing variation in the marginal indirect utility of wealth. Eventually, when the marginal utility of consumption is sufficiently out of line with the marginal utility of wealth to make it worthwhile to incur the transactions cost, the household will adjust its consumption level. However, for the substantial periods of time between the infrequent adjustments of consumption, the crucial link between the marginal utility of consumption and the marginal indirect utility of wealth is broken. If, unlike the costs incurred in buying and selling the durable consumption good, we assume that there are no transactions costs involved in buying and selling financial assets, the optimizing household will still want to hold a portfolio of financial assets that is mean-variance efficient. For this reason, asset premiums will be determined by the traditional CAPM. Admittedly, modeling consumption as the service flow from a single durable good is an extreme case. However, it seems extremely likely that the basic point that transactions costs will tend to break the link between the marginal utility of consumption and the marginal indirect utility of wealth would carry over to the more realistic case in which consumption consists of the service flows from different types of durables—houses, cars, appliances, clothes, and the like—as well as nondurable goods.

If transactions costs involved in adjusting the stock of durable goods are an important explanation of the empirical failure of the consumption-β model in terms of its implications for asset pricing, it seems likely that the same transactions costs would play an important role in the failure of the model in terms of its implications for consumption, as well. Having argued that the transactions costs involved in adjusting durable goods stocks are a key factor in understanding the otherwise paradoxical evidence on asset pricing, and suggested that the same factors are likely to be important in empirically successful models of consumption, I obviously very much agree with Smyth's assessment that the most important single deficiency in the current treatment of consumption and saving lies in the inadequate treatment of durable goods. However, developing an adequate treatment of durable goods will require more than merely translating data on expenditure on durable goods into the corresponding service flows. Even if the service flows associated with durable goods were observable and perfectly measured, the presence of transactions costs of adjusting durable good stocks introduces complicated dynamics to the model. Future research that succeeds in modeling the important aspects of durable goods—their hybrid nature as part consumption good and part asset and the transactions costs involved in adjusting the stock—should yield the next burst of important insights into the economics of saving.

Reference

Grossman, Sanford J., and Guy Laroque. "Asset Pricing and Optimal Portfolio Choice in the Presence of Illiquid Durable Consumption Goods." *Econometrica* 58, no. 1 (January 1990): pp. 24–51.

Commentary by
Edward B. Montgomery
University of Maryland

David Smyth has provided us with a useful survey of the evolution of neoclassical economic thought on the determinants of saving behavior. Starting with the Keynesian saving (consumption) function, he takes us through the life cycle and permanent income hypothesis, which are the received orthodoxy of modern analysis of saving behavior. Throughout Smyth's chronicle of the historical evolution of the saving function, he replicates old studies to illustrate the empirical regularities that shaped the debate on saving at each point in time. He also presents new time series estimates in order to judge the success or failure of attempts to provide theoretical underpinnings to the analysis of saving.

Smyth establishes some empirical regularities that any theory of saving or consumption must attempt to explain: that the marginal propensity to save is positive, less than one, volatile, and greater than the average propensity to save. The average propensity to save is constant over time but rises with income in cross section. This difference in long- and short-run behavior and the volatility of the short-run marginal propensity are inconsistent with the simple Keynesian model that emphasizes the contemporaneous correlation between income and saving. Smyth concludes, however, that the empirical evidence is not fully consistent with any of the current theories of saving and that the recent work on saving (although technically sophisticated) has done little to advance our knowledge of saving behavior.

By necessity, any survey must place greater emphasis on certain strands of the literature than on others. There are, however, two broad areas in the recent literature to which I wish Smyth had devoted more attention. The first can be broadly described as issues of measurement. That is, what should be the appropriate measure of saving or consumption to use in estimating consumption functions. The second area deals with the recent rational expectations challenges to the permanent income and life cycle models.

Smyth discusses the problems associated with the measurement of consumption of durable and housing services. Clearly, expenditures on these items reflect both consumption and saving so that it is conceptually inappropriate to use either nondurable consumption or consumption expenditures in estimating consumption functions. Although imputing a flow of services to durable expenditures introduces measurement error concerns, these will be present if either of the other two aforementioned constructs are used unless income or wealth have the same relationship to durable and nondurable spending. Work by Blinder and Deaton (1985) and others suggests that this is not the case, so this issue needs to be addressed. It should, of course, be noted that the fact that durables provide a service flow also alters the appropriate measure of income to use as an independent variable.

In a related vein there is the question of whether empirical studies should use saving measured as a residual from income, as in the National Income and Product Accounts (NIPA), or from wealth data. Although in theory these methods should yield the same measure, in practice they do not. As noted in Montgomery (1986) and elsewhere, household saving measured in the NIPA is substantially less than saving measured from asset data or the Flow-of-Funds. This issue may be important econometrically, as the ratio of these two measures is not time invariant as seen by the fact that it declined from 0.68 in 1975 to 0.32 in 1982. Bradford (1991) argues strongly that empirical saving functions might yield biased results unless a wealth-based saving concept is used. He points to the fact that in addition to the problem of durables previously mentioned, the NIPA saving series contains several other well-known "biases" due to inappropriate inflation accounting, the mismeasurement of government capital expenditures, the use of historical costs in calculating depreciation, and its failure to reflect capital gains on domestic and foreign assets.

The correct conceptualization of the saving function is also at the heart of the recent literature on the effects of social security and government debt on saving. In the case of social security the issue is to what degree consumers take account of the wealth accumulated in publicly provided pensions when making personal saving decisions.[1] A large literature has also developed around testing the Barro or Ricardian Equivalence notion that consumers take into account government saving (dissaving) when making their intertemporal consumption decisions. Although the empirical literature has attempted to sort out the relevance of these propositions, the evidence on both scores is still inconclusive.

Of course, when discussing the issue of empirical estimation of saving functions, one cannot ignore the issues raised in the Lucas critique (1976). Lucas questions the existence of a structural relationship between consumption and income in a world with rational expectations. In both the life cycle and permanent income models, saving depends on expected lifetime or permanent income, which may be functions of current and past values of income. Thus, there could well be a statistical relationship between income and consumption, but its form is dependent on the macroeconomic process generating income. Taken literally this critique has been interpreted to suggest that economists need to use VAR-type methods to analyze the income- and consumption-generating process simultaneously with those generating the other determinants of the evolution of the macro economy. Alternatively, recent work suggests that the structural parameters of the saving relationship can be uncovered through estimating Euler equations or the parameters of consumers' time-invariant utility function. These are the directions that much of the analysis of saving has gone over the past decade.

The permanent income and life cycle models were developed to provide microeconomic foundations to models of consumption behavior and remedy the empirical deficiencies of the simple Keynesian model. These two theories have similar analytic roots in that they exploit the notion that consumption decisions are the result of a dynamic utility-maximizing process. They predict that saving and hence consumption are no longer determined by contemporaneous income, as in the Keynesian model, but are related to the present value of lifetime or permanent income. Given this long-run focus, saving is seen as taking place to allow individuals to achieve a smooth intertemporal consumption path. These theories are analytically rigorous and until recently were thought to be consistent with the data.

Smyth recognizes the challenges to the rational expectations versions of these theories posed by the seminal work of Hall (1978) and Flavin (1981). Two important results emerge from these papers and have driven much of the work on consumption over the last decade. First, when interest rates are constant, the optimal intertemporal path for consumption should be a martingale. That is, once past consumption is controlled for, no other variable known at time t should help predict future consumption. Because this prediction has been consistently rejected by the data, a whole new body of work has attempted to develop rational expectations optimizing models of consumption consistent with this notion of "excess sensitivity" in consumption.

Second, changes in consumption should mirror changes in permanent income, or the ratio of the variance of changes in consumption to the variance of innovations in permanent income should be one. A ratio less than one implies excess smoothness, whereas a ratio greater than one implies excess sensitivity. In general, consumption is observed to be relatively smooth, but there is widespread debate about the process generating permanent income and hence whether the permanent income model holds. Work by Deaton (1987) suggests that given the finding that income has a unit root, consumption exhibits "excess smoothness" relative to the predictions of the permanent income model.

Smyth feels that this work on estimating rational expectation models of saving has taught us little about the determinants of saving. Although I am sympathetic to the notion that one of the goals of economic research is to allow us to "explain" or predict the real world, this does not mean that research geared toward developing and testing our theoretical models is of no value. The ability to win model "horse races" is not the sole or even best criterion for evaluating a body of research. The value added of recent saving research lies in illustrating what conditions or restrictions on the underlying process governing the macro economy need to hold if consumers do make decisions in the Fisherian intertemporal-optimizing way.

Along those lines some researchers have focused on the implications of stochastic interest rates and intertemporal substitution. With stochastic interest rates, labor income and interest rates may be co-integrated. Consequently, with a sufficiently elastic intertemporal substitution, observed consumption could be dampened enough by the co-movements of income and interest rates so that the observed movement of consumption is consistent with the permanent income theory. Although the magnitude of the intertemporal elasticity of substitution is still open to debate, the preliminary evidence suggests that the elasticity is small, so this channel of investigation is unlikely to be fruitful.

An alternative path of research has focused on the notion that consumers may not always be at interior solutions to their intertemporal allocation decisions. That is, they may face borrowing or liquidity constraints that restrict their ability to borrow to finance consumption. This hypothesis yields an intermediate case between the simple Keynesian model, where consumers neither borrow nor save to smooth consumption, and the simple permanent income model, where they are free to borrow or save. If there are constraints on borrowing, excess sensitivity of consumption to current income would exist even in a rational expectations permanent income model. The empirical work on this issue suggests that models in which consumers cannot borrow freely, either the simple Keynesian model or ones with formal liquidity constraints, tend to outperform the permanent income model analog. Clearly, more work needs to be done on how to incorporate these market imperfections into econometric analyses of saving behavior.

Finally, work by Gali (1991), West (1988), and others has attempted to measure or test for excess sensitivity or smoothness in consumption relative to permanent income. This work is quite sophisticated econometrically and is often tied to the large body of research in macroeconomics testing for the existence of unit roots in economic data series. Deaton's paradox illustrates that the question of whether there is a unit root in income is not simply a statistical curiosa but may matter for our understanding of the underlying process generating saving behavior. Quah (1990) has shown than the presence of a unit root in income need not automatically imply than consumption is too smooth to be consistent with the permanent income model. If permanent shocks to income are sufficiently small relative to the temporary shock, then the data on consumption and income might still be consistent with the permanent income model. Overall, however, most of recent research appears to support a finding of "excess smoothness" in consumption and points toward the need for better models of habit formation or liquidity constraints to understand saving.

Overall, I would like to commend David Smyth for a comprehensive and informative analysis of the literature on the determinants of saving and consumption. I would like to second his suggestions that more attention needs to be paid to the measurement and conceptualization of the appropriate saving measure. Further, econometric analysis of the stochastic properties of the consumption and income time series should be viewed as complements rather than substitutes for better models. Finally, I would encourage more work on the role of risk, family structure, inflation, and market imperfections.

Note

1. In a related fashion there is the issue of whether agents take into account their private pensions and to what degree they see through the corporate veil and treat retained earnings as saving. Research in this area points away from the use of personal saving as the appropriate saving concept.

References

Blinder, Alan, and Angus Deaton. "The Time Series Consumption Function Revisited." *Brookings Papers on Economic Activity* 2 (1985): 465–522.
Bradford, David. "Market Value Versus Financial Accounting Measures of National Saving." In *National Saving and Economic Performance*, edited by B. Douglas Bernheim and John Shoven; National Bureau of Economic Research. University of Chicago Press, 1991.
Deaton, Angus. "Life-Cycle Models of Consumption: Is the Evidence Consistent with Theory?" In *Advances in Econometrics, Fifth World Congress*, vol. 2, edited by T. Bewley. Cambridge: Cambridge University Press, 1987.
Flavin, Marjorie. "The Adjustment of Consumption to Changing Expectations about Future Income." *Journal of Political Economy* 89 (October 1981): 974–1009.
Gali, Jordi. "Budget Constraints and Time Series Evidence on Consumption," *American Economic Review* 81, no. 5 (December 1991): 1238–1253.
Hall, Robert. "Stochastic Implications of the Life Cycle-Permanent Income Hypothesis: Theory and Evidence." *Journal of Political Economy* 86 (December 1978): 971–987.
Lucas, Robert. "Econometric Policy Evaluation: A Critique." In *The Phillips Curve and Labor Markets*, edited by Karl Brunner and Allan Meltzer. Carnegie-Rochester Conference Series on Public Policy, vol. 1, Suppl., *Journal of Monetary Economics*, 1976.
Montgomery, Edward. "Where Did All the Saving Go? A Look at the Recent Decline Personal Saving Rate." *Economic Inquiry* 24 (October 1986): 681–697.
Quah, Danny. "Permanent and Transitory Movements in Labor Income: An Explanation for Excess Smoothness in Consumption." *Journal of Political Economy* 98 (June 1990): 449–475.
West, Kenneth. "The Insensitivity of Consumption to News about Income." *Journal of Monetary Economics* 21 (January 1988): 17–34.
Zeldes, Stephen. "Consumption and Liquidity Constraints: An Empirical Investigation." *Journal of Political Economy* 97 (April 1989): 305–346.

3 NATIONAL SAVING AND THE TWIN DEFICITS: MYTH AND REALITY

Robert Eisner and Paul J. Pieper

Northwestern University and University of Illinois at Chicago

Reality: National saving in the United States went down in the last decade, at least during the 1982–83 recession, budget deficits went up, and the trade and current accounts moved to deficit.

Myth: Eliminating or reducing budget deficits will **both** eliminate or reduce the current account deficit *and* increase national saving.

That our budget and trade deficits have reduced national saving has been argued widely. But much discussion of saving and deficits is careless of definitions and irrelevant to the economic variables that should concern us. Net foreign investment, the other side of the coin of the trade deficit—or more properly, the current account deficit—is not what it appears to be. And the budget deficit may actually contribute to more national saving, rather than less.

1. The Measurement of Saving

The conventional or official measure of gross saving in the United States is produced by the Bureau of Economic Analysis (BEA) of the Department of Commerce as part of the National Income and Product Accounts (NIPA). As shown in table 3–1, NIPA is equal to the sum of personal saving—personal income minus personal taxes and personal outlays for consumption expenditures, interest, and transfer payments—corporate

Table 3–1. Net Saving and Investment Account, 1990* (billions of dollars)

Gross private domestic investment	745.0	Personal income	4,645.6
		Less: Personal tax and nontax payments	699.8
Less: Capital consumption allowances with capital consumption adjustment	575.7	Less: Personal outlays Personal consumption expenditures	3,766.8 3,658.1
Net private domestic investment	169.3	Interest paid by consumers to business	107.8
Net foreign investment	−90.1	Personal transfer payments to foreigners	0.9
		Personal saving	179.1
		Undistributed corporate profits with inventory valuation and capital consumption adjustment	29.1
		Government surplus or deficit (−), national income and product accounts	−126.0
		Federal	−161.3
		State and local	35.4
		Net saving	82.2
		Statistical discrepancy	−3.1
Net Investment	79.2	Net Saving and Statistical Discrepancy	79.2

* Adapted from *Survey of Current Business*, January 1991, tables 1.1, 1.9, 2.1 and 5.1, pp. 6, 8, 10 and 13.

saving (undistributed profits), and what is sometimes called "government saving." This last measure comprises the sum of the federal, state, and local government surpluses. Gross saving is equal, except for a statistical discrepancy, to gross investment, the sum of gross private domestic investment and net foreign investment. Net national saving plus the statistical discrepancy is then equal to net private domestic investment — gross private domestic investment minus capital consumption allowances — and net foreign investment. Because gross private domestic investment includes only the acquisition of reproducible tangible capital by business, fixed capital by nonprofit institutions, and residential housing by households, national saving is thus restricted to a part of private investment in tangible assets and the acquisition of assets in the rest of the world, net of foreign acquisitions in the United States.

This NIPA measure of saving and investment is quite narrow. From an economic perspective, investment may be defined simply as any type of activity that will yield future benefits. The BEA is now committed to some broadening by moving our accounts into conformity with the UN-recommended System of National Accounts, which explicitly includes public investment along with private investment and which may also advise taking into account investment in R&D and other intellectual property. The current NIPA measure of investment, however, excludes (1) all investment by government, at all levels; (2) all investment by government enterprises; (3) all investment by households except that in new housing; (4) all investment in the intangible capital of education and

Table 3-2. Federal Government Investment by Type, 1989

Investment	Expenditure (billions of dollars)	Percent of Federal Expenditures
Tangible capital	124.4	10.5
Direct	99.6	8.4
Structures	13.4	1.1
Equipment	86.2	7.3
Grants-in-aid	24.8	2.1
Education and training	25.8	2.2
Direct	3.7	0.3
Grants-in-aid	13.8	1.2
Transfer payments	8.3	0.7
Research and development	61.7	5.2
Total	211.9	17.8
Addendum:		
Health expenditures	164.9	13.9
Direct	23.3	2.0
Grants-in-aid	40.2	3.4
Transfer payments	101.4	8.5

Sources: *National Income and Product Accounts of the United States*, tables 3.7 and 3.15; and *Special Analyses: Budget of the United States Government*, Table D-8.

training, research, and health; (5) most increases in the real value of existing assets, including assets held in the rest of the world; and (6) most investment in land and natural resources. Clearly, from the extent of these exclusions, this most widely used or conventional measure of national saving relates to only a small part of the capital that we provide for the future, in the order of some 15 to 20 percent (see Eisner, 1989, 1991a). An account of just the federal government component of these exclusions is shown in table 3−2. Whatever the effect of these exclusions on the narrow, conventional measure of national saving, reduction of budget deficits would seem almost certainly to reduce the full, relevant measure by curtailing household or consumer investment and government tangible and intangible investment.

2. Deficits and the Saving−Investment Identity

We take as the starting point for our analysis, ignoring the statistical discrepancy, the following national income accounting identity:

$$S^P - D^F + S^{S\&L} = I + \text{NFI}, \qquad (3-1)$$

where S^P is private saving, D^F is the federal deficit, $S^{S\&L}$ is the composite state and local government surplus, I is gross private domestic investment, and NFI is net foreign investment. The left-hand side of the equation is of course equal to gross saving.

The saving−investment identity is a useful foundation for economic analysis. It is not a substitute for it. Because national saving is the sum of public saving and private saving, many assert, with little argumentation, that increasing public saving or reducing public dissaving in the form of federal budget deficits will increase national saving. But this is assuredly true only if other public saving (state and local government surpluses) and private saving are not reduced or, looking at the other side of the coin, if the sum of net private domestic investment and net foreign investment is increased. This is unlikely to be the case, however, for three major reasons.

First, as another look at table 3−1 will show, one frequently ignored first effect of reducing the federal budget deficit may be to reduce the composite state and local surplus. This reduction would occur quite directly if the federal government reduced its deficit by cutting grants-in-aid to states and localities, currently running over $130 billion per year, more than 17 percent of total state and local government expenditures. Empirical confirmation that this may be so is found in the following

AR(1) regression between federal grants-in-aid to state and local governments, GIA, and the price-adjusted high-employment deficit, PAHED, both expressed as a percent of GNP:

$$\Delta GIA_t = 0.138 X1 - 0.059 X2 + 0.086 \Delta PAHED_t, \quad t = 1956-1989,$$
$$\quad (0.052) \quad\ \ (0.049) \quad\ \ (0.027) \quad\quad\quad\quad\quad\quad (3-2)$$

$R^2 = .397$, $D - W = 2.21$, $\rho = 0.298$. Equation (3-2) was estimated with a first-order correction for serial correlation. $X1$ is a constant term for the 1956-1972 period, and $X2$ is a constant for the 1973-1989 period. The estimates indicate that each dollar more of the inflation-and-cyclically-adjusted federal surplus was accompanied by 8.6 cents less in federal grants-in-aid to state and local governments.

The federal deficit can also affect state and local government saving indirectly by increasing the burden on state and local services or by encroaching on state and local sources of revenue. A proposal floated in Washington in the summer of 1990 to limit federal tax deductibility of state and local taxes offers another example of a measure to reduce the federal deficit at the expense of state and local budgets. These latter budgets would be plagued by great resistance to the taxes necessary to maintain *their* surpluses or lower *their* deficits.

Second, identity (3-1) has in practice been applied to conventional measures of the deficit and saving. However, the conventional deficit measure includes many types of investment expenditures, such as expenditures on infrastructure, education, and R&D.[1] Even if the deficit did reduce private investment dollar for dollar, its effect on total investment would be less if the deficit were partly a result of increased expenditures on government investment. As may be seen in table 3-2, about 18 percent of federal government spending is in the form of investment in tangible capital, education and training, and research and development. Another 14 percent of federal spending is devoted to health care, some portion of which represents investment in human capital. In addition, because some items of federal spending such as interest payments on the debt are relatively fixed, government investment is likely to be more than proportionally affected by cuts in the budget deficit.

Third, looking to the behavior of private agents, we must recognize first that any change in the federal deficit is likely to change personal income and/or personal tax and nontax payments, thus affecting disposable personal income (DPI). If the deficit is reduced—either by cutting spending or raising income taxes—DPI will be reduced. Since personal saving is the difference between DPI and personal outlays, unless the latter change dollar for dollar with DPI, personal saving will decline.

Increases in excise or sales taxes will generally raise the cost or value of personal consumption expenditures, thus also reducing personal saving. Increases in corporate taxes (or reductions in government payments to corporations) will similarly reduce undistributed corporate profits, a component of national saving.

Simply enough then, we cannot tell, in terms of the saving identity itself, whether increases in the budget deficit will reduce national saving or whether reductions will raise it. We can, of course, state that a reduction in the federal deficit will increase national saving *if* all other components of saving remain the same, but this result is hardly to be expected and is indeed almost impossible, given the further identities between federal net payments to other sectors and their receipts from the federal government.

The effect of the federal deficit on saving may be better understood by examining its effect on the other side of the saving—investment identity: private domestic investment and net foreign investment. What will a reduction in the federal deficit do to either measure?

Some conventional wisdom suggests that a reduction of the federal deficit will increase private domestic investment by freeing funds and resources otherwise used for lending to the government or for financing consumption expenditures. But the reduction in the flow of private funds to finance the deficit is, in the first instance, exactly matched by a reduction in the funds available because the Treasury has either reduced what it is paying out or increased what it is taking in taxes. And if consumption is reduced, can we be sure that business will find it more profitable to invest? If consumers do not buy that new U.S. car, will that make GM or Chrysler more likely to invest? Or less?

We may go all the way back to Lange (1938) for the classic argument that there is a rate of consumption that will maximize investment, given the dual effects of increased consumption in raising the demand for capital to facilitate greater output and its effect in reducing the demand for capital by raising interest rates. If consumption is initially at or below this maximization point, reductions in consumption are likely to lower investment, not increase it. In fact, throughout the last several decades, changes in consumption have been positively correlated with changes in domestic investment. And, as we have reported in other work, budget deficits themselves have been positively related to increases in gross private domestic investment (Eisner 1986; Eisner and Pieper, 1988).

But what about net foreign investment? Here we may anticipate a different scenario. Net foreign investment is equal to exports, plus the usually zero or trivial item of net capital grants received by the United

States, minus imports, transfer payments to foreigners from persons and government, and interest paid by government to foreigners, as shown in Table 3–3. But then, just as an increase in taxes or a reduction of income receipts from the federal government may lead us not to buy a Ford or a Chrysler, it may lead some of us not to buy a Toyota or a Mazda. Any reduction in imports, other things equal, must reduce foreign accumulation of dollars. It thus reduces foreign investment in the United States and hence U.S. net foreign investment. And in this case, a number of the other items in the net foreign investment identity are likely to move in the direction of reinforcing the negative correlation between deficits and net foreign investment.

This scenario is clear, for example, if a reduction in the deficit entails reductions of government transfer payments to foreigners or, with the decline in DPI, if personal transfer payments to foreigners are reduced. And in the long run, reduction of the deficit, to the extent that it holds down the federal debt, may lower interest paid by government to foreigners. (More to the point, if budget deficits do contribute to negative U.S. foreign investment, they add to foreign claims on the United States. Higher claims result in higher business interest, dividend, and profit payments to foreigners, thus raising imports, and to higher government interest payments to foreigners to the extent the claims are on government debt.)

Thus we have what should be an obvious way by which a reduction in the federal deficit can reduce the current account deficit and raise foreign investment: by bringing on a recession. Lower income and output will certainly reduce imports. Unless the exchange rates can and are allowed to adjust sufficiently and/or unless the rest of the world moves as deeply into recession as the United States, exports will not fall as much as

Table 3–3. Net Foreign Investment, 1990* (billions of dollars)

Exports of goods and services	672.8
Plus: Capital grants received by the United States (net)	0
Less: Imports of goods and services	704.0
Transfer payments to foreigners (net)	15.5
From persons (net)	0.9
From government (net)	14.6
Interest paid by government to foreigners	38.8
Net foreign investment	−85.5

* Adapted from *Survey of Current Business*, April 1991, Account 4.1, p. 14.

imports, if at all. It is rarely put this way, but it is precisely by causing a recession that reducing the budget deficit will reduce the trade deficit. And it is precisely because budget deficits have stimulated the U.S. economy, and some of the relative prosperity has spilled into greater purchases of foreign goods, that budget deficits have contributed to the trade deficit.

Whether reductions in the structural or cyclically adjusted deficit will do more to increase net foreign investment than they do to reduce net private domestic investment, however, is extremely doubtful. If they do not, they obviously will not increase national saving.

We shall undertake a look at the historical record and then a more rigorous analysis of the empirical relation between budget deficits and current account deficits or its negative; net foreign investment, and between budget deficits and gross private domestic investment, the other component of the conventional measure of gross and net national saving. This will entail exploration as well of the role of the monetary regime and exchange rates. We shall devote attention, as we proceed, to appropriate measures of budget deficits, net foreign investment, and national saving and note the relations involving these broader and generally economically more relevant variables.

3. U.S. Investment in the Eighties — A Historical Perspective

Conventional wisdom holds that the rate of U.S. saving, and investment with it, fell during the decade of the eighties. Because the eighties were also a period of large government budget deficits, this condition has, in turn, fostered a belief that government deficits have reduced investment and that the way to increase investment is to reduce the deficit.

The conclusion that U.S. investment fell during the eighties is usually based on the NIPA measure of gross investment, which is included in table 3–4. The major component of gross private domestic investment has in fact fallen only slightly from its level in the seventies and is actually higher than its level in the fifties and sixties. Net foreign investment, though, has swung sharply negative. As a result, NIPA gross investment in the eighties has fallen by about 2 percent of GNP compared to the sixties and seventies. Even worse, this measure did not rebound during the latter part of the decade, when the economy rebounded, but instead fell further, with a precipitous decline in net foreign investment.

As we have pointed out, however, the NIPA measure of investment is quite narrow. The more comprehensive measures of investment in table

Table 3–4. Measures of Real Gross Investment, Mean Percentage of GNP

Investment Measure	(1) 1953–1959	(2) 1960–1969	(3) 1970–1979	(4) 1980–1989	(5) 1984–1989
Gross private domestic	15.86	16.50	17.15	16.87	17.73
Net foreign	0.21	0.62	0.24	−1.64	−2.70
Gross (BEA)	16.07	17.12	17.40	15.23	15.03
Consumer durables	5.92	6.24	7.85	9.23	10.04
Federal tangible	4.83	2.92	1.56	2.44	2.61
S&L tangible	2.84	3.30	2.54	1.92	1.95
Total tangible (including net foreign)	29.66	29.57	29.35	28.83	29.64
R&D	1.91	2.76	2.27	2.55	2.62
Education & training	4.24	5.41	6.37	5.91	5.81
Intangible[1]	6.15	8.17	8.64	8.44	8.43
Total tangible and intangible	35.81	37.74	37.99	37.27	38.06

See appendix for data sources.
[1] R&D plus education and training.

3–4 show that investment in consumer durables has increased throughout the postwar period, with a particularly large increase occurring during the eighties. Government tangible investment was largely unchanged from the seventies to the eighties, with a decline in state and local investment offset by an increase in federal investment. However, government tangible investment as a percent of GNP has fallen significantly from its level in the fifties and sixties.

The portion of GNP devoted to total tangible investment was only 0.5 percent to 0.8 percent less than the portion invested during the previous three decades. The large drop in net foreign investment has been offset to a large extent by increased investment in consumer durables. Further, all of the drop in investment in the eighties occurred during the first part of the decade. Expressed as a fraction of GNP, tangible investment in the 1984–1989 period was as large or larger than its value in the previous three decades.

Table 3–4 also offers measures of intangible investment. We define intangible investment narrowly to include only expenditures on research and development, education, and government-financed training. Intangible investment as a fraction of GNP has been roughly constant over the past three decades. During the eighties, the fraction of GNP spent on education fell, but this decrease was largely offset by an increase in R&D expenditures.

Looking at the comprehensive investment measures in table 3–4, it may be seen that the BEA NIPA investment is only about 40 percent of the total of tangible, including net foreign, and intangible investment. Our total investment measure, which includes all types of tangible investment and some types of intangible investment, tells a story different from that suggested by the NIPA measure. Total investment in the eighties was about the same as the U.S. postwar average and only slightly below the level of the sixties and seventies. Declines in net foreign investment have been offset largely by increases in investment in consumer durables.

To the extent this occurred is not to be dismissed glibly as a "consumption binge." Households buying automobiles are, after all, providing for their future transportation services just as are Avis and Hertz or as private companies might be doing in buying new busses. Most of the small decline in total investment that did occur took place in the deep recession in the first part of the decade. Gross investment in the latter part of the decade, when concern about deficits was greatest, was actually a higher proportion of GNP than average.

We can therefore dismiss the simple argument that large deficits in the eighties caused a reduction in investment.[2] This argument is based on the false premise that investment fell during the eighties. Further, the measures of investment presented so far have been expressed as a percentage of GNP. This practice will understate the effect of deficits on investment if deficits have a stimulatory effect on GNP. Deficits may very well increase total investment even if the fraction of GNP that is invested remains the same.

All this is not to argue that total saving and investment are necessarily adequate or well focused to provide optimally for our future. But this may relate more to the distribution between public and private and tangible and intangible investment. A third of a generation growing up functionally illiterate and millions of our more advantaged youth woefully behind their foreign counterparts in math and science may reflect our most important, real deficits.

4. The Effect of Deficits on Investment— An Empirical Analysis

The effect of deficits on saving may be better understood by examining the investment side of the saving−investment identity. Obviously, deficits cannot reduce saving unless they reduce one or more components of investment.

We hypothesize first the following relationship between investment and the deficit:

$$I_{j,t}/\text{GNP6}_t = b_{0j} + b_{1j}\text{PAHES6}_{t-1} + u_{j,t}, \qquad t = 1957 \text{ to } 1990, (3\text{−}3)$$

where I_j is real investment of type j, GNP6 is an estimate of the GNP associated with a 6 percent unemployment rate, and PAHES6 is the price-adjusted 6 percent high-employment surplus as a percent of actual GNP, taken from the BEA for the years 1970 to 1990 and extrapolated backward on the basis of the BEA middle expansion trend deficit for the earlier years.

Equation (3−3) differs in three respects from the usual formulation of the deficit−investment relationship. First, we express investment as a fraction of potential GNP rather than actual GNP. Using actual GNP in the denominator would result in an understatement of the effect of deficits on investment if deficits have an expansionary effect on output.

Second, our deficit measure is cyclically adjusted to remove the reverse causation of the economy on the deficit. In addition, our deficit measure is "price-adjusted," which means it in effect includes only *real* interest among federal outlays, or counts as an "inflation tax" the loss in the value of government debt due to inflation. This correction is approximately equal to the rate of inflation times the net federal government debt (financial liabilities less financial assets). A reduction in the real value of government debt would be expected to reduce the private sector's wealth, thereby decreasing consumption and increasing or decreasing investment, depending on whether the output effect is greater or less than the substitution effect of possible lower real interest rates. And finally, the deficit variable is lagged, to permit its hypothesized stimulatory effects to operate on investment in accordance with widely shared views of the investment function. To control for serial correlation, equation (3–3) was estimated by AR(1) (Cochrane-Orcutt) regressions.

Table 3–5. Adjusted Deficit and Private Tangible Investment ($I_{j,t} = b_0 + b_1 PAHED6_{t-1}$)

I_j	Regression Coefficients[1]					
	\$PAHED6_{t-1}\$					
	b_0	b_1	R^2	$D-W$	ρ	n
Gross private domestic	16.488 (0.527)	0.769 (0.297)	0.315	1.63	0.513 (0.181)	34
Net foreign	−0.250 (0.749)	−0.407 (0.086)	0.882	2.05	0.891 (0.088)	34
Gross	16.072 (1.134)	0.473 (0.309)	0.443	1.73	0.762 (0.129)	34
Consumer durables	16.052 (45.080)	0.299 (0.072)	0.931	1.57	0.989 (0.059)	34
Private domestic tangible	24.030 (0.618)	1.335 (0.317)	0.613	1.54	0.539 (0.159)	34
Private tangible	24.064 (0.784)	0.785 (0.355)	0.393	1.60	0.616 (0.159)	34

[1] Ordinary least squares with a first-order correction for serial correlation. Standard errors are shown in parentheses. Sample period is 1957–1990.

Variable definitions:

PAHED6 = price-adjusted 6 percent high-employment deficit, as estimated by the BEA for the years 1970–1990 and extrapolated backward by the Holloway method on the basis of the BEA middle expansion trend deficit for the earlier years, as percent of GNP.

I_j = real investment of type j — GPDI, NFI, gross, and consumer durables from the BEA — taken as a percentage of GNP. Private domestic tangible is the sum of gross private domestic investment and consumer durables. Private tangible is the sum of gross investment and consumer durables.

Estimates for private investment are shown in table 3–5. We may note first that the lagged price-adjusted high employment deficit, PAHED6, clearly is related *positively* to gross private domestic investment. Each percentage point of deficit was associated with 0.769 percentage point *more* of subsequent investment as a ratio of potential GNP.

However, the lagged deficit showed a significant negative relation with subsequent net foreign investment, reflecting the stimulatory effect of deficits on imports. On balance, the positive effect on domestic investment appeared larger than the negative effect on foreign investment so that the total effect on the BEA measure of gross investment was positive, although not significantly so in this regression.[3]

As we have pointed out though, private investment properly includes all acquisitions of assets that contribute future returns. An automobile purchased by a household contributes to transportation services as does an automobile the household rents from Hertz. Our lagged deficit variable shows a highly significant positive relationship with investment in consumer durables, which is excluded from the official measures of investment. Each additional dollar of deficit was associated with an additional 30 cents of consumer durables expenditures in the following year.

The relation between our deficit variable and private tangible investment (excluding investment in land and household investment in semidurables and inventories, however) is substantially and significantly positive, with a coefficient of +1.335 for the lagged deficit variable in the regression of domestic capital tangible investment. Although the adjusted structural budget deficit does appear to relate negatively to net foreign investment, there is certainly no evidence that it reduces even the narrow BEA total of gross private investment, domestic and foreign, let alone a broader total that would include household investment in consumer durables. Here, the coefficient for the deficit variable is a highly significant +.785.

Of course, the price-adjusted high employment deficit does not fully, or perhaps even accurately, define the exogenous fiscal parameters affecting investment, let alone all of the parameters, including specifically those relating to monetary policy. As in previous work, therefore, we have introduced as a regressor the real change in the monetary base — defined here as the mean monetary base in the month of December as reported by the Federal Reserve Board of Governors, deflated by the fourth-quarter GNP implicit price deflator. This variable was taken as a percentage of GNP, but a consistent series was available only from 1960 on, thus reducing our sample period, because of the lags introduced, to one beginning in 1962.

The results of regressions including this monetary variable, shown in table 3–6, point to a strong and significant positive role for increases in the monetary base in affecting domestic investment and a negative role in net foreign investment, as might have been expected. Easier money, as it stimulates the economy, will again encourage imports. If it also brings about a lowering of the exchange rate, moreover, it will have a further effect of encouraging exports and discouraging imports.[4] The signs of coefficients of the deficit variable remain as before, but the magnitude and significance of the coefficients in the case of gross private investment and the BEA's gross investment are reduced. Apparently, some of the presumed impact of inflation in reducing the real deficit was captured by its effect in reducing the real increase in the monetary base. Nevertheless, its coefficient in the gross investment equation, though not manifesting a high level of statistical significance, suggested that the lagged, appropriately adjusted deficit increased, rather than decreased, the conventional measure of investment and saving.

We still see, however, a significant, positive role for the deficit variable with regard to investment in consumer durables and private domestic tangible investment as a whole. Each percentage point of the deficit–GNP ratio was associated with 1.2 percentage points *more* of the latter and .682 percentage point more even of total private tangible investment, including the negative component of net foreign investment.

Getting further away from the narrow BEA, NIPA measure of private investment, however, to include tangible public investment sharpens the picture considerably. Whatever its effect on private investment, one should expect an immediate impact of reductions in budget deficits on government expenditures, whereas increase in deficits should be associated with greater expenditures. One should further expect that at least some of this impact on government expenditures should be felt in public investment. That effect is precisely what is shown in table 3–7.

The impact of the federal deficit on federal investment is, not surprisingly, the clearest and most substantial. Most of the impact is in the same year; the regression coefficient indicates that each additional dollar of deficit was associated with an additional 12.1 cents of federal tangible investment expenditures in that year and another 4.6 cents the following year, a total then of 16.7 cents over the two years. The impact on state and local government investment, perhaps directly or indirectly through grants-in-aid or contributions to jointly financed programs, was considerably less, but still positive, coming to 6.3 cents over the two years.

Introducing the monetary variable, as shown in table 3–8, sharpens the relation considerably. We now see that the sum of the coefficients of

Table 3–6. Adjusted Deficit, Change in Monetary Base, Real Exchange Rate, and Private Tangible Investment ($I_{j,t} = b_0 + b_1\text{PAHED6}_{t-1} + b_2\text{DMB}_{t-1} + b_3\text{ERR}_{t-2}$)

I_j	Regression Coefficients[1]				R^2	D–W	ρ
	b_0	PAHED6_{t-1} b_1	DMB_{t-1} b_2	ERR_{t-2} b_3			
Gross private domestic	20.846 (3.738)	0.507 (0.373)	5.578 (2.270)	−0.045 (0.039)	0.364	1.83	0.489 (0.213)
Net foreign	2.028 (2.044)	−0.267 (0.111)	−0.322 (0.642)	−0.032 (0.013)	0.897	2.26	0.931 (0.089)
Gross	22.730 (3.941)	0.485 (0.341)	5.132 (1.935)	−0.074 (0.038)	0.603	2.02	0.847 (0.129)
Consumer durables	13.026 (11.129)	0.282 (0.085)	1.157 (0.496)	−0.009 (0.001)	0.936	1.51	0.971 (0.061)
Private domestic tangible	30.320 (4.326)	1.119 (0.389)	5.759 (2.592)	−0.062 (0.045)	0.603	1.67	0.535 (0.190)
Private tangible	32.665 (4.229)	0.682 (0.395)	6.321 (2.350)	−0.087 (0.044)	0.460	1.76	0.646 (0.183)

[1] Ordinary least squares with a first-order correction for serial correlation. Standard errors are shown in parentheses. Sample period is 1962–1990; there are 29 observations.

Variable definitions:

PAHED6 = price-adjusted 6 percent high-employment deficit as percent of GNP.
DMB = change in the real monetary base as a percent of GNP (December figures divided by 4th quarter GNP implicit price deflator).
ERR = trade weighted real exchange rate (1972–100).
I_j = real investment of type j — GPDI, NFI, gross, and consumer durables, from the BEA, taken as a percent of potential GNP. Private domestic tangible is the sum of gross private domestic investment and consumer durables. Private tangible is the sum of gross investment and consumer durables

Table 3–7. Adjusted Deficit and Public Investment ($I_{k,t} = b_0 + b_1\text{PAHED6}_t + b_2\text{PAHED6}_{t-1}$)

I_k		Regression Coefficients[1]						
	b_0	PAHED6_t b_1	PAHED6_{t-1} b_2	ΣPAHED6 b_1+b_2	R^2	$D-W$	ρ	n
Federal tangible	1.829 (0.372)	0.121 (0.037)	0.046 (0.036)	0.167 (0.051)	0.938	1.14	0.891 (0.031)	34
S&L tangible	0.148 (3.609)	0.025 (0.030)	0.038 (0.030)	0.063 (0.042)	0.904	1.14	0.981 (0.040)	34
Total government tangible	3.591 (1.256)	0.140 (0.058)	0.080 (0.057)	0.220 (0.081)	0.943	1.12	0.938 (0.038)	34
Education & training[2]	0.036 (0.057)	0.041 (0.014)	−0.003 (0.014)	0.038 (0.022)	0.516	1.93	0.729 (0.129)	32
Government R&D[2]	−0.016 (0.025)	0.001 (0.009)	0.013 (0.009)	0.014 (0.015)	0.464	2.19	0.592 (0.122)	32
Total government	8.258 (6.335)	0.183 (0.066)	0.102 (0.065)	0.285 (0.093)	0.934	1.08	0.977 (0.043)	33

[1] Ordinary least squares with a first-order correction for serial correlation. Standard errors are shown in parentheses. Sample period is 1957–1990 for federal tangible, S&L tangible, and total government tangible. Sample period is 1957–1989 for education and training, government R&D, and total government.
[2] Estimated as first differences.

Variable definitions:
PAHED6 = price-adjusted 6 percent high-employment deficit as percent of GNP.
I_k = real investment of type k — federal tangible, S & L tangible, education & training, government R&D, and total government — generally from the BEA, taken as percentage of potential GNP.

Table 3–8. Adjusted Deficit, Change in Monetary Base, and Public Investment ($I_{k,t} = b_0 + b_1\text{PAHED6}_t + b_2\text{PAHED6}_{t-1} + b_3\text{DMB}_t + b_4\text{DMB}_{t-1}$)

I_k	Regression Coefficients[1]										
	b_0	PAHED6$_t$ b_1	PAHED6$_{t-1}$ b_2	DMB$_t$ b_3	DMB$_{t-1}$ b_4	ΣPAHED6 b_1+b_2	ΣDMB b_3+b_4	R^2	D–W	ρ	n
Federal tangible	1.836 (0.333)	0.121 (0.049)	0.079 (0.054)	−0.346 (0.333)	−0.119 (0.329)	0.200 (0.080)	−0.465 (0.572)	0.845	1.42	0.873 (0.059)	29
S&L tangible	0.857 (3.279)	0.036 (0.038)	0.099 (0.043)	−0.436 (0.263)	−0.418 (0.260)	0.135 (0.064)	−0.854 (0.452)	0.948	1.20	0.974 (0.040)	29
Total government tangible	3.581 (1.136)	0.152 (0.074)	0.173 (0.083)	−0.780 (0.512)	−0.541 (0.505)	0.325 (0.124)	−1.321 (0.879)	0.929	1.25	0.928 (0.046)	29
Education & training[2]	0.008 (0.082)	0.033 (0.016)	−0.004 (0.017)	0.007 (0.110)	0.027 (0.105)	0.029 (0.029)	0.034 (0.197)	0.596	1.63	0.810 (0.127)	27
Government R&D[2]	−0.018 (0.032)	−0.001 (0.011)	0.002 (0.012)	0.112 (0.076)	0.093 (0.073)	0.001 (0.020)	0.205 (0.136)	0.557	2.04	0.680 (0.162)	27
Total government	7.931 (5.084)	0.204 (0.088)	0.190 (0.097)	−0.906 (0.629)	−0.388 (0.587)	0.394 (0.148)	−1.294 (1.041)	0.936	1.16	0.968 (0.045)	28

[1] Ordinary least squares with a first-order correction for serial correlation. Standard errors are shown in parentheses. Sample period is 1962–1990 for federal tangible, S&L tangible, and total government. Sample period is 1962–1989 for education and training and government R&D.
[2] Estimated as first differences.

Variable definitions:
PAHED6 = price-adjusted 6 percent high-employment deficit as percent of GNP.
DMB = change in the real monetary base as a percent of GNP. (December figures divided by 4th quarter GNP implicit price deflator)
I_k = real investment of type k taken as percentage of potential GNP. See appendix for data sources.

the current and lagged deficit variable is +.200 for federal tangible investment and +.135 for state and local tangible investment. For government as a whole, therefore, the coefficients suggest that each additional dollar of deficit was associated with an *additional* 32.5 cents of tangible investment. If we include government intangible investment in education and training and in R&D, the total impact of each additional dollar of deficit would appear to be an additional 39.4 cents in investment.

We are led finally to table 3−9, in which we present regression results for all domestic tangible investment and for total tangible investment, including net foreign investment, both as measured and adjusted. First, the simple regression of total domestic tangible investment on the lagged, price-adjusted 6 percent unemployment budget deficit yields a highly significant positive coefficient of 1.325 over the years 1957 to 1990. Introducing the lagged change in the monetary base brings a significant positive coefficient for that variable as well, while still leaving a highly significant, though reduced, positive coefficient of .971 for the deficit.

Considering the role of the current deficit blurs matters some, however. Although a larger adjusted deficit is associated with more current public investment, it is also associated with less private investment. Notice, however, that the coefficient of the current deficit will be biased downward if policy makers follow a countercyclical fiscal policy. The sign of the current change in the monetary base is also negative, suggesting that a coefficient bias due to stabilization policy exists. The sum of coefficients of the current and lagged deficit variables is still a substantially positive .748 but has a large standard error of .546.

Turning to total tangible investment, despite the negative relation with the net foreign investment component included in the total, the coefficient of the lagged deficit variable remains significantly positive when standing alone in the regression. Introducing the monetary base variable, however, again reduces the coefficient of the deficit variable. With both current and lagged deficits in the regression, we find the sum of the coefficients further reduced, but still positive, although not significantly so.

One last adjustment may be undertaken, to correct net foreign investment for the official measure's exclusion of much of the changes in dollar market value of international assets, particularly direct investment (see Eisner and Pieper, 1990). We now see a significant positive coefficient of 1.211 for the lagged deficit variable and still a substantial positive coefficient of .935 in a regression including both the lagged change in the monetary base and the real exchange rate lagged two years.

We have also regressed measures of net national saving, working from changes in stocks of durable goods—in business, households, and government—thus in effect subtracting out capital consumption allowances. We

Table 3-9. Adjusted Deficit, Change in Monetary Base, Real Exchange Rate, and Domestic and Total Tangible Investment
($I_{k,t} = b_0 + b_1 PAHED6_t + b_2 PAHED6_{t-1} + b_3 DMB_t + b_4 DMB_{t-1} + b_5 ERR_{t-2}$)

Regression Coefficients[1]

I_k	b_0	$PAHED6_t$ b_1	$PAHED6_{t-1}$ b_2	DMB_t b_3	DMB_{t-1} b_4	ERR_{t-2} b_5	$\Sigma PAHED6$ b_1+b_2	ΣDMB b_3+b_4	R^2	D-W	ρ	n
Total domestic tangible	29.092 (0.639)		1.325 (0.321)						.584	1.55	0.562 (0.153)	34
Total domestic tangible	29.031 (0.756)		0.971 (0.388)		5.261 (2.459)				.627	1.58	0.605 (0.187)	29
Total domestic tangible	29.519 (0.736)	−0.481 (0.364)	1.229 (0.395)	−1.803 (2.613)	4.493 (2.571)		0.748 (0.546)	2.690 (4.355)	.656	1.51	0.581 (0.184)	29
Total tangible	28.934 (1.012)		0.871 (0.344)						.468	1.62	0.706 (0.131)	34
Total tangible	28.881 (1.321)		0.601 (0.387)		5.135 (2.283)				.572	1.61	0.783 (0.139)	29
Total tangible	29.580 (1.141)	−0.525 (0.364)	0.795 (0.394)	−2.078 (2.476)	4.244 (2.432)		0.270 (0.562)	2.167 (3.855)	.624	1.54	0.758 (0.150)	29
Total adjusted tangible	27.999 (1.582)		1.211 (0.602)						.508	1.51	0.676 (0.214)	18
Total adjusted tangible	34.865 (6.030)		0.935 (0.639)		9.511 (4.003)	−0.077 (0.061)			.605	1.77	0.718 (0.201)	18

[1] Ordinary least squares with a first-order correction for serial correlation. Standard errors are shown in parentheses. Sample period is 1957–1990 for total tangible. Sample period is 1957–1989 for private tangible plus total government.
[2] Estimated as first differences.

Variable definitions:
PAHED6 = price-adjusted 6 percent high-employment deficit, as estimated by the BEA for the years 1970–1990 and extrapolated backward by the Holloway method on the basis of the BEA middle expansion trend deficit for the earlier years, as percent of GNP.
DMB = change in the real monetary base as a percent of GNP (December figures divided by 4th quarter GNP implicit price deflator).
ERR = Trade weighted real exchange rate (value of the dollar, March 1973 = 100).
I_k = real investment of type k, taken as percent of potential GNP.

have some reason to question the appropriateness of measures of capital consumption and net capital stocks and do not report these results. They do not, however, differ significantly (see Eisner, 1991*b*) from those for the gross investment series that we have reported.

5. Conclusion

The ultimate concern of many, appropriately, is the total of national saving. A major, probably *the* major, argument against budget deficits is that they have depressed national saving, by crowding out private domestic investment and by turning net foreign investment negative, thus increasing our debt to the rest of the world. They have thus, it is argued, put an undue burden on the future. A full response to that contention would take us beyond the scope of this chapter to the critical issues of investment in human and intangible capital.[5] What may most be jeopardizing the lives of those living in the future, as we have suggested, are the developing inadequacies of millions of a generation growing up semiliterate, the inferior education of millions more of our more advantaged students compared to their counterparts in other advanced and advancing nations, our slippage in basic research and investment in advanced technology, and our inability to eliminate the scourges of crime and drugs.

None of our empirical results should be taken as definitive. Estimation of this kind is treacherous. Unrecognized spurious correlations or transient peculiarities of data may well mislead. But our results should give pause to those who see in recent budget deficits, certainly as they are usually measured, harbingers of doom, as the national saving that they view as inadequate is all the more depressed. Our results should give all the more pause because they are particularly consistent with the body of macroeconomic theory that recognizes our economy as it is, one subject to recurrent if not persistent departures from full employment and potential output. In such an economy, real structural budget deficits may be expected to have precisely the outcomes indicated in this chapter.

By increasing aggregate demand, these deficits raise employment and output. With or without the further impact of increases in exchange rates, they thus contribute to greater imports and a trade deficit and hence less foreign investment, thus depressing national saving. With room for increases in national income and output (or, conversely, the reality of declines where real, structural deficits are reduced), budget deficits may, and apparently do, contribute more to national saving by stimulating domestic private investment. They do so all the more if we go beyond the narrow BEA measure of private investment and include household investment in consumer durables. And the effect is magnified still more when we add public investment, as federal deficits seem clearly related to contemporaneous federal tangible investment.

For those concerned with the rate of national saving the lesson would seem to be: Either work to *in*crease real, structural deficits, particularly for worthwhile public investment, or look elsewhere for solutions to our saving problems.

Acknowledgments

Maurice Ewing, Oliver Haberstroh, Satish Reddy, Craig Safir, and Marc Sokol have been of invaluable research assistance. The authors are indebted to the National Science Foundation (grants SES-8707979 and SES-8913660) for financial support.

Notes

1. See Aschauer (1989) and various of the works of Edwin Mansfield, Gary Becker, and many others for arguments and findings that the productivity of tangible public infrastructure, R&D, and human capital in general are at least as high if not considerably higher than that of conventionally measured gross private domestic investment.

2. Measures of net saving have declined from their levels of the fifties and sixties. The measures of the decline and their interpretation are likely, however, to be misleading for several reasons. First, the BEA's measure of depreciation is uncertain. The BEA measures depreciation essentially as a weighted average of past investment, using weights assumed to be constant over time. Our knowledge is limited regarding actual depreciation rates for different types of capital and how these rates may change with changing economic and technological conditions and changing productivity of new investment. The last should be taken into account in any measure of net saving and investment. Second, the conventional measure of net foreign investment ignores revaluations of existing assets on the U.S. net international investment position. These revaluations are often sizable and in recent years have generally been in favor of the United States (see Eisner and Pieper, 1990). Third, net saving measures reflect the rate of growth of capital, which in turn reflects the rate of growth of output, rather than saving propensities per se. A decline in GNP growth, such as that which occurred with the post-1973 productivity slowdown, will result in an increase in the ratio of depreciation allowances to GNP and a reduction in net saving (see Pieper 1989).

3. It is arguable that the social return to domestic investment is greater than the return to foreign investment, so that even if the deficit caused an offsetting change in these two items, the net return might still be positive. In addition to providing a return to the owners of capital, greater domestic investment will raise the level of productivity and real wages of the labor force by increasing the capital–labor ratio. The comparable externality for net foreign investment will accrue to foreign labor forces. The real rate of return to foreign

investors in the United States has appeared to be quite low; we estimated it in the neighborhood of 4 percent in 1989.

4. The real exchange rate merits inclusion as an independent variable both because its value is clearly not determined entirely by the fiscal and monetary variables and because it may be expected to have its effects with some considerable lag. Unfortunately, data on its value prior to 1973 are not available. The exchange rate variable was assumed, in the regressions that included such observations, to have a value of 100 for those earlier years. The base for the underlying trade-weighted index was March 1973 = 100.

5. Measures of investment in intangible capital for the years 1946 to 1981 may be found in Eisner (1988, 1989). Their contributions to national saving are discussed further in Eisner (1991), and their relation to budget deficits is considered in Eisner (1992).

Appendix: Data Sources

1. High-Employment Surplus and High-Employment GNP

The high-employment surplus is defined for a 6.0 percent rate of unemployment. The sources for both series for the years beginning with 1970 are the issues of the *Survey of Current Business* of December 1983, May 1985, August 1989, and August 1990. For the years from 1955 to 1969, the high-employment surplus is estimated by taking the Department of Commerce "mid-expansion trend" cyclically adjusted series and using Holloway's (1989) estimation procedure to convert it to a 6 percent basis. The Holloway procedure is in fact now used by the Commerce Department to estimate the 6 percent unemployment surplus.

High-employment GNP for the years from 1970 on is taken from the already mentioned *Survey of Current Business*. For the years prior to 1970, high-employment GNP is estimated as GNP6 = GNPME*[1 + .02 (UME − 6)], where GNPME is the Commerce Department of "mid-expansion trend GNP" and UME is the percentage point unemployment rate associated with mid-expansion trend GNP. (The BEA estimates that in the post-1970 period each percentage point of unemployment is associated with 1.9 percent less of cyclically adjusted output. With productivity probably greater prior to 1970, it has seemed reasonable to round the 1.9 percent up to .02 in our formulation.) The mid-expansion trend GNP, unemployment rate, and cyclically adjusted deficit are published in the December 1983 *Survey of Current Business*.

2. Price-Adjusted Surplus (and Deficit)

The price-adjusted surplus is equal to the 6 percent high-employment surplus already defined plus price effects on the federal net debt. Price effects on the federal debt are in turn estimated as

$$PE_t = [(A - 1) D_{t-1} + (B - 1) (D_t - D_{t-1})]/B,$$

where

PE = price effects
D = net federal debt at market value
$A = P^e_t/P^e_{t-1}$
$B = P^e_t/P_t$
P^e = end-of-year GNP deflator (taken as the mean of the fourth quarter deflator and the deflator for the first quarter of the subsequent year) and
P = annual GNP deflator.

The deficit is of course simply the negative of the surplus.

3. Monetary Base

The nominal monetary base is taken from the *Economic Report of the President*. The figures are averages for the month of December. The monetary variable used in the regression is defined as the change in end-of-period real stocks divided by real GNP. Algebraically, this may be written as

$$MBCH_t = 100 [(MB82_t - MB82_{t-1})/GNP82_{t-1}],$$

where MB82 is the real monetary base and GNP82 is real GNP. The fourth quarter implicit GNP deflator is used to deflate the monetary base.

4. Real Exchange Rate

The real exchange rate is a trade-weighted index of ten major trading partners of the United States. The series is constructed by the Federal Reserve Board and published in the *Economic Report of the President*. The index is available for 1973 onward. The index is assumed to be constant prior to 1973.

5. Investment Measures

NIPA refers to the *National Income and Product Accounts of the United States*. The number of following the NIPA designation refers to the table and line number.

Consumer Durables	NIPA 1.2.3
Gross Private Domestic	NIPA 1.2.6
Net Foreign Investment	NIPA 4.1.22 deflated by GNP implicit price deflator
Net Foreign, Adjusted	Net foreign investment (NIPA 4.1.22) plus difference between changes in adjusted international investment position of the United States at market value and changes in official international investment position, from Eisner and Pieper (1990), columns 7 and 2 of table 3–8, deflated by the GNP implicit price deflator
Federal Tangible	NIPA 3.8.4 + 3.8.11 + 3.8.13 + 3.8.30
State & Local Tangible	NIPA 3.8.22 + 3.8.27.
Research & Development	NSF (1987), appendix table B.5, and for later years, *U.S. Statistical Abstract*, deflated by GNP implicit price deflator.
Education	
Federal	NIPA 3.15.20 + 3.15.48 + 3.15.78, deflated by deflator for nondefense government purchases constructed by dividing nominal by constant dollar purchases reported in NIPA 3.7 and 3.8
State and Local	NIPA 3.16.9 + 3.16.40 − 5.5.47, deflated as for federal
Private	NIPA 2.5.85

References

Aschauer, David. "Is Public Expenditure Productive?" *Journal of Monetary Economics* (March 1989): 177–200.

Eisner, Robert. *How Real Is the Federal Deficit?* New York: The Free Press, 1986.

———. "Extended Measures of National Income and Product." *Journal of Economic Literature* (December 1988) 26: 1611–1684.

———. *The Total Incomes System of Accounts*. Chicago: University of Chicago Press, 1989.

———. "The Real Rate of U.S. National Saving." *Review of Income and Wealth*, Series 37, no. 1 (March 1991): 13–32.

———. "U.S. National Saving and Budget Deficits." For *The Political Economy of Investment, Saving and Finance: A Global Perspective*, Gerald Epstein and

Herbert Gintis, eds., A Project of the World Institute for Development and Economic Research (WIDER), The United Nations University, Helsinki, Finland, manuscript copy, 6/20/92.

Eisner, Robert and Pieper, Paul J. "A New View of the Federal Debt and Budget Deficits." *American Economic Review* 74 (March 1984): 11–29.

———. "Deficits, Monetary Policy and Real Economic Activity." In Kenneth J. Arrow and Michael J. Boskin, eds., *The Economics of Public Debt*.Macmillan Press in association with the International Economic Association, 1988, London, pp. 3–40.

———. "'The World's Greatest Debtor Nation'?" *The Review of Economics and Finance* 1 (1) (1990): pp. 9–32.

Holloway, Thomas M. "Measuring the Cyclical Sensitivity of Federal Receipts and Expenditures: Simplified Estimation Procedures." *International Journal of Forecasting* 5 (1989): 347–360.

Lange, Oscar. "The Rate of Interest and the Optimal Propensity to Consume." *Economica* (New Series) 5 (February 1938): 12–32. Reprinted in American Economic Association, *Readings in Business Cycle Theory*. Philadelphia: Blakiston, 1944, pp. 169–192.

Pieper, Paul. "Why Net Investment Has Fallen." Paper presented at Western Economic Association meeting, June 1989.

Commentary by Ali F. Darrat
Louisiana Tech University

For the United States the 1980s have been years of large and unprecedented federal budget deficits, massive trade deficits, as well as low and declining national saving (as a share of GNP). The low and declining U.S. saving rate has generated a lot of concern in view of its deleterious impact on capital formation, productivity, and long-term economic growth. That the three phenomena are somehow related has been frequently asserted. More specifically, many analysts have argued that the escalating federal budget deficit is the culprit behind the other two problems and that reducing federal deficits will mitigate the trade deficit and, at the same time, promote national saving.[1] In the words of Michael Boskin (1990, p. 13), the Chairman of the President's Council of Economic Advisers, "The reduction of the federal budget deficit ... is the surest and safest way to raise national saving, so long as it is accomplished in a manner that does not decrease private saving," a view equally shared by Manuel Johnson, a former vice Chairman and a current member of the Board of Governors of the Federal Reserve System (see Johnson, 1990).

The main purpose of Eisner and Pieper's contribution is to explore this so-called conventional wisdom and to cast doubt on its validity, primarily from the empirical standpoint. The authors argue, quite convincingly, that one cannot conclude from looking at the saving side of the saving–investment identity that higher federal deficits have contributed to the falling off of U.S. national saving. The difficulty essentially arises from the interrelationships among federal deficits and the other components of national—namely, private saving and other public (state and local government) saving. Consequently, a more fruitful inquiry into the impact of federal deficits on national saving would instead focus on the impact of federal deficits on the investment side of the identity, that is, on private domestic investment (I), and on net foreign investment (NFI), the latter being the negative of the current account deficit.

Eisner and Pieper hypothesize, based on earlier work, a positive relationship between federal deficits and private domestic investment and a negative relationship between federal deficits and net foreign investment. If reductions in the federal budget could increase net foreign investment by more than they would reduce private domestic investment, then one may assert that federal budget cuts can contribute to promoting national saving. Using annual data over 1957–1990, Eisner and Pieper report regression evidence that appears to be inconsistent with their contention: The coefficient of the federal deficit variable in the private domestic investment equation is positive *and* large, whereas that in the net foreign investment equation is negative *and* small. Taken together, and contrary to the conventional wisdom, the federal deficit is shown to exhibit a positive relationship with national saving. According to Eisner and Pieper's results, curtailing federal deficits would then worsen, rather than improve, the U.S. saving problem.

1. Some Issues

Although novel and interesting, Eisner and Pieper's empirical evidence can be discredited for a number of reasons. First, none of the variables employed in the model were tested for stationarity. Yet, recent work (e.g., Stock and Watson, 1989) has shown that if nonstationarity exists in the data, the usual test statistics would not exhibit standard distributions, perhaps leading to misleading inferences.

Second, the basic (bivariate) models estimated by Eisner and Pieper are conceptually misspecified, for they ignore several other exogenous variables that could potentially impact investment. Among others, inflation and long-term interest rates appear likely candidates. In fact, Fackler (1985) has provided empirical evidence indicating that interest rates represent the main channel linking policy variables (federal deficits and base money) with the real side of the economy. Clearly, omitting such variables can lead to serious estimation biases only if they are highly correlated with the policy variables included in the estimated equations (see Batten and Hafer, 1983). Because inflation and interest rates are typically considered by policy makers as key policy goals, this omission-of-variables problem could have biased Eisner and Pieper's results (see also Lutkepohl, 1982).

Another problem with Eisner and Pieper's estimated equations is that they lack a richer lag structure beyond the restrictive contemporaneous and one-year lag scheme. In fact, this one-year lag scheme was arbitrarily imposed without any testing. Nevertheless, employing an inappropriate lag structure can seriously bias the results. Still another cause for concern stems from using potentially inappropriate policy measures. Both theory and evidence have shown that the correct measure of fiscal policy is the change (not the level) of the federal deficit and that the correct indicator of monetary policy is the change in the nominal (not real) monetary base. Indeed, the restrictive lag scheme and inappropriate measures of policy variables were the main criticism leveled by Haan and Zelhorst (1988) against the earlier empirical work of Eisner (1986). When corrected for both problem, Haan and Zelhorst reported results inconsistent with Eisner's main findings.

Finally, Eisner and Pieper's models have also overlooked any potential feedback from investment to federal deficits and/or the monetary base. However, changes in the investment outlook could induce significant policy responses in view of the importance of investment behavior to capital formation and economic growth. Put differently, the two policy variables may not be totally exogenous (in the statistical sense) to investment changes.[2] With endogenous variables, single-equation estimates are known to be both biased and inconsistent. Indeed, at issue is not necessarily whether federal deficits and investment components (domestic and foreign) are correlated. Rather, the debate is about whether reductions in federal deficits can *cause* positive changes in gross investment (saving). Regressions like those reported by Eisner and Pieper, however, cannot distinguish between cause and effect. Indeed, although policy variables are expected to induce changes in investment components (the conventional view), investment components themselves could also feed back and induce changes in the stance of fiscal and/or monetary policy.

2. Alternative Tests

One could reasonably argue, then, that Eisner and Pieper's empirical evidence regarding the impact of federal deficits on national saving requires adjustment for the problems already discussed. This, in fact, is the main purpose of this comment.

Specifically, before estimating the model, each variable is converted to a stationary process through testing for unit roots using the Dickey-Fuller

(1979) procedure. The results show that the variables in levels (as used by Eisner and Pieper) are nonstationary. First-differences (and sometimes even second-differences) are required to induce stationarity in the data. To avoid the omission-of-variables phenomenon, inflation and long-term interest rates are introduced into the estimated model.[3] Economic theorizing suggests the potential importance of these two variables for determining investment as well as for shaping the stance of fiscal and monetary policy. Furthermore, the lag structure of each explanatory variable is selected on the basis of minimizing the final predicting error (FPE) of Akaike (1969), which has become quite popular in recent applied econometrics. Both policy variables (the price-adjusted high-employment deficit and the monetary base) are measured in changes rather than in levels. In addition, monetary base is measured in nominal (not real) terms to reflect more closely monetary policy actions.

Finally, to allow for possible endogeneity of all variables included in the analysis, two alternative six-variable vector autoregressive (VAR) systems are constructed and estimated (one VAR model for private domestic investment and another VAR model for net foreign investment). This VAR modeling technique has been recommended by some notable researchers (e.g., Sims, 1982) as a reliable alternative to the more conventional "structural" model, which may a priori impose spurious restrictions on the dynamic linkages in the model. Although many remain skeptical (e.g., Cooley and LeRoy, 1985), the VAR procedure has nevertheless received a lot of empirical support (e.g., Webb, 1984; Lupoletti and Webb, 1986; Genberg, Salemi, and Swoboda, 1987). In addition, combined with the FPE criterion, the VAR modeling technique is useful for revealing causal relationships among the variables included in the system. Under fairly general conditions, Hsiao (1981) has demonstrated that the inclusion of a variable in an equation based on the FPE criterion could be taken as evidence that a Granger-type causal ordering exists, at least in the weak form. If the variable is further found to exert a statistically significant effect within the system of equations, then the causal impact can be considered of the strong form (see Kawai, 1980). If, on the other hand, a variable is excluded by the FPE criterion, then no causal ordering is present.

After each of the six equations is individually specified by the FPE procedure, the six equations are pooled and estimated as a simultaneous system using the full information maximum likelihood (FIML) procedure. In addition to fostering statistical efficiency, another rationale for using the FIML estimation technique is to incorporate the contemporaneous relationship among the variables, which the single-equation estimation ignores due to the sole use of lagged variables. As Hsiao (1981) pointed out, such contemporaneous relationships could be reflected in the correlation of the contemporaneous error terms across equations that are taken into account by the FIML procedure.

The general form of the VAR model is given by the following unrestricted system:

$$Z_t = \Omega(L)Z_t + \alpha + \varepsilon_t,$$

where Z_t is a 6×1 column vector of the six endogenous variables, α is a 6×1 vector of constants, ε_t is a 6×1 vector of white-noise disturbance terms, and $\Omega(L)$ is a 6×6 matrix of lagged polynomial coefficients. The (i,j)th element of $\Omega(L)$ is defind in terms of the lag operator L, such that $\Omega_{ijm}(L) = (\Omega_{ij1}L + \Omega_{ij2}L^2 + \ldots + \Omega_{ijm}L^m)$. The six endogenous variables in the first VAR model (A) are private domestic investment (I), the deficit measure (F), monetary base (M), the exchange rates (E), long-term interest rates (R), and inflation (N). In the alternative VAR model (B), net foreign investment (V) is substituted for private domestic investment.

3. Empirical Results

Applying the FPE procedure (searching for up to 4 annual lags) over a similar sample period (1957–1990) like that of Eisner and Pieper's, the following VAR model (A) was obtained for the private domestic investment (I):

$$\begin{bmatrix} I_T \\ DF_t \\ DM_t \\ DE_t \\ DR_t \\ DN_t \end{bmatrix} = \begin{bmatrix} \Omega_{11}^2(L) & \Omega_{12}^1(L) & \Omega_{13}^3(L) & \Omega_{14}^2(L) & \Omega_{15}^1(L) & \Omega_{16}^4(L) \\ 0 & \Omega_{22}^1(L) & \Omega_{23}^1(L) & \Omega_{24}^3(L) & 0 & \Omega_{26}^3(L) \\ 0 & 0 & \Omega_{33}^3(L) & \Omega_{34}^3(L) & 0 & 0 \\ \Omega_{41}^3(L) & 0 & 0 & \Omega_{44}^1(L) & \Omega_{45}^1(L) & \Omega_{46}^2(L) \\ \Omega_{51}^3(L) & \Omega_{52}^3(L) & \Omega_{53}^3(L) & \Omega_{54}^3(L) & \Omega_{55}^3(L) & 0 \\ \Omega_{61}^1(L) & \Omega_{62}^2(L) & \Omega_{63}^3(L) & \Omega_{64}^1(L) & \Omega_{65}^1(L) & \Omega_{66}^1(L) \end{bmatrix} \begin{bmatrix} I_t \\ DF_t \\ DM_t \\ DE_t \\ DR_t \\ DN_t \end{bmatrix} + \begin{bmatrix} \alpha_1 \\ \alpha_2 \\ \alpha_3 \\ \alpha_4 \\ \alpha_5 \\ \alpha_6 \end{bmatrix} + \begin{bmatrix} \varepsilon_{1t} \\ \varepsilon_{2t} \\ \varepsilon_{3t} \\ \varepsilon_{4t} \\ \varepsilon_{5t} \\ \varepsilon_{6t} \end{bmatrix} \quad (A)$$

and the following VAR model (B) was obtained for the net foreign investment (V):

$$\begin{bmatrix} DV_T \\ DF_t \\ DM_t \\ DE_t \\ DR_t \\ DN_t \end{bmatrix} = \begin{bmatrix} \phi_{11}^1(L) & \phi_{12}^4(L) & 0 & \phi_{14}^3(L) & 0 & \phi_{16}^3(L) \\ 0 & \phi_{22}^1(L) & 0 & \phi_{24}^4(L) & 0 & 0 \\ 0 & 0 & \phi_{33}^3(L) & 0 & 0 & 0 \\ 0 & 0 & \phi_{43}^4(L) & \phi_{44}^1(L) & \phi_{45}^1(L) & 0 \\ 0 & \phi_{52}^1(L) & 0 & \phi_{54}^1(L) & \phi_{55}^3(L) & 0 \\ 0 & \phi_{62}^1(L) & 0 & \phi_{64}^1(L) & 0 & \phi_{66}^1(L) \end{bmatrix} \begin{bmatrix} DV_t \\ DF_t \\ DM_t \\ DE_t \\ DR_t \\ DN_t \end{bmatrix} + \begin{bmatrix} \beta_1 \\ \beta_2 \\ \beta_3 \\ \beta_4 \\ \beta_5 \\ \beta_6 \end{bmatrix} + \begin{bmatrix} \mu_{1t} \\ \mu_{2t} \\ \mu_{3t} \\ \mu_{4t} \\ \mu_{5t} \\ \mu_{6t} \end{bmatrix} \quad (B)$$

where L is the lag operator; the superscript in the lag polynomial refers to the appropriate (FPE-based) lag order; I_t = real domestic private investment as a percent of potential GNP; $DF_t = (1 - L)F_t$, F is the price-adjusted 6 percent high-employment deficit as a percent of GNP; $DM_t = (1 - L)B_t$, B is the nominal base money as a percent of GNP; $DE_t = (1 - L)E_t$, E is the trade-weighted real exchange rate (1973 = 100); $DR_t = (1 - L)\log R_t$, R is the long-term (10-year) government bond yield; $DN_t = (1 - L)^2 \log P_t$, P is the implicit GNP deflator; and $DV_t = (1 - L)FI_t$, FI is net foreign investment as a percent of potential GNP. Except for the two additional variables (DR and DN), all raw variables are defined analogously to Eisner and Pieper's work. They differ, however, in that they are expressed in differences (instead of levels) to satisfy the stationarity requirement. Tests of serial correlation evidenced no problem of significant serial correlation among the residuals in any equation. Furthermore, the Chow test could not reject the hypothesis of structural stability in any equation.

The full account of the coefficient estimates from both VAR models is not reported here to economize space, but it is available on request. Table 3C-1 reports the system log likelihood ratio statistics obtained for VAR models (A) and (B).[4] These (chi-squared) statistics form the basis of the implied Granger-causality inferences.

The most striking finding is that the budget deficit measure appears to have caused significant changes in both private domestic investment and net foreign investment. Such causal impacts of the budget deficit on the two variables, moreover, are of the strong form.[5] The reason is the deficit measure qualifies for inclusion in both investment equations according to the FPE criterion, and, furthermore, the deficit coefficients in both equations proved highly significant at better than the 5 percent level. Of further interest is the finding that the causal impact of the deficit variable on both investment measures is unidirectional, that is, without significant

Table 3C-1. System Log-Likelihood Ratio Tests of Multivariate VAR Granger-Causality Hypotheses (FIML Estimations)

	Model A (Private Domestic Investment, I)			Model B (Net Foreign Investment, V)		
Hypotheses	χ^2-Statistics (d.f.)		Inferences (at 5% level)	Hypotheses	χ^2-Statistics (d.f.)	Inferences (at 5% level)
$F \not\to I$	8.75 (1)		Reject	$F \not\to V$	13.65 (4)	Reject
$M \not\to I$	2.53 (3)		Do not reject	$E \not\to V$	12.40 (3)	Reject
$E \not\to I$	7.53 (2)		Reject	$N \not\to V$	10.75 (3)	Reject
$R \not\to I$	1.88 (1)		Do not reject	$E \not\to F$	13.43 (4)	Reject
$N \not\to I$	10.02 (4)		Reject	$M \not\to E$	12.77 (4)	Reject
$M \not\to F$	3.15 (1)		Do not reject	$R \not\to E$	11.47 (1)	Reject
$E \not\to F$	16.73 (3)		Reject	$F \not\to R$	12.96 (1)	Reject
$N \not\to F$	7.08 (3)		Do not reject	$E \not\to R$	3.13 (1)	Do not reject
$E \not\to M$	2.49 (3)		Do not reject	$F \not\to N$	4.42 (1)	Reject
$I \not\to E$	12.93 (3)		Reject	$E \not\to N$	2.53 (1)	Do not reject
$R \not\to E$	13.08 (1)		Reject			
$N \not\to E$	4.83 (2)		Do not reject			
$I \not\to R$	21.13 (3)		Reject			
$F \not\to R$	17.33 (3)		Reject			
$M \not\to R$	11.62 (3)		Reject			
$E \not\to R$	7.62 (3)		Do not reject			
$I \not\to N$	12.36 (1)		Reject			
$F \not\to N$	4.26 (2)		Do not reject			
$M \not\to N$	3.37 (3)		Do not reject			
$E \not\to N$	0.16 (1)		Do not reject			
$R \not\to N$	1.74 (1)		Do not reject			

Note: The signal $\not\to$ should read "does not Granger-cause." As to the variables, F refers to budget deficits; I refers to private domestic investment; M referss to base money; E refers to exchange rates; R refers to long-term interest rates; N refers to inflation; and V refers to net foreign investment. Each variable entered the model in the stationary format as dictated by unit root testing.

feedback [both investment measures appear with zero elements in the deficit equations in models (A) and (B)].

These empirical results, then, provide some support for Eisner and Pieper's use of the deficit measure as an exogenous variable in both investment equations. The results also support their finding that budget deficits play an important role in determining private domestic investment as well as net foreign investment (and consequently, gross saving). The model lag structures further suggest that private domestic investment responds rather quickly (within one year) to changes in budget deficits, whereas net foreign investment (the negative of trade deficits) requires about four years to adjust fully to changes in budget deficits.

As mentioned earlier, Eisner and Pieper further hypothesized that budget deficits exert a positive *and* stronger effect on private domestic investment, whereas the deficit effect on net foreign investment is negative *and* smaller. Only under these circumstances would one assert, as Eisner and Pieper did, that budget cuts will hamper (rather than promote) national saving. These latter implications of Eisner and Pieper's thesis, however, do not receive strong empirical support from the VAR models estimated here. According to these VAR results, the one-year lag coefficient of the deficit variable in the private domestic investment equation, $\Omega_{12}^{1}(L)$, is positive as hypothesized and equal to 0.37. As to the (four-year lag) sum coefficient $\phi_{12}^{4}(L)$ of the deficit variable in the net foreign investment equation of model B, it is negative as hypothesized, but larger and equal to -0.74.

Contrary to Eisner and Pieper's contention, these latter VAR results lend some support to the conventional wisdom that *reductions in the federal budget deficit can promote national saving* since the resultant enhancement of net foreign investment (improvement in the trade account) would more than offset the consequent reduction in private domestic investment.[6]

4. Concluding Remarks

In view of the paramount importance of the low national saving and its deleterious economic effects, contributions such as Eisner and Pieper's are timely and useful for academic and policy purposes alike. Also interesting is their framework of empirically analyzing the role of federal budget deficits in the determination of national saving. Based on single-equation estimates, Eisner and Pieper argued that higher federal deficits, if any, promote (rather than hamper) national saving. Clearly, such a contention runs contrary to the conventional view held by most analysts and policy makers who have proposed budget cuts as one key solution to the U.S. saving problem.

In this comment, I argued that Eisner and Pieper's empirical evidence appears weak on several grounds. After correcting for some of the estimation problems, and using a simultaneous-equation (VAR) modeling technique, the results appear inconsistent with Eisner and Pieper's work. In particular, although federal deficits do exert a positive causal effect on private domestic investment, and a negative causal effect on net foreign investment as they hypothesized, the former effect is however smaller than the latter. Taken together, such a finding supports the conventional wisdom and implies that federal deficits have a negative causal effect on national saving. As Eisner and Pieper pointed out, any empirical evidence can only be suggestive, particularly in veiw of the several problems plaguing VAR models and their interpretations, a problem compounded with the brevity of the sample period studied. At the very least, though, these VAR results do suggest that curtailing federal deficits should not be completely dismissed as a saving-promoting policy option.

Notes

1. Of course, curtailing the federal budget deficit is not the only suggested solution to the U.S. national saving problem. Other saving–promoting policy proposals advanced by analysts and observers include consumption-based taxes, reductions in income tax rates, reduction in capital gains taxes, expansion in individual retirement accounts, and investment tax credit, to name just a few. For more on this, see Walker, Bloomfield, and Thorning (1990).

2. Both the deficit and base money measures may be exogenous in the sense they are policy controllable. However, policy controllability of the two policy variables does not necessarily assure their *statistical* exogeneity with respect to the investment variables.

3. Long-term, rather than short-term, interest rates appear more relevant to investment decisions. Several interest-sensitive components of private investment, such as business plant and equipment and home construction, are particularly sensitive to changes in long-term interest rates.

4. The log-likelihood ratio statistic is defined in each of the VAR models as $6T[\log(SSR^c) - \log(SSR^u)]$, where SSR^c and SSR^u are the sums of squared residuals of the constrained and unconstrained systems, respectively, and T is the number of observations in each of the six equations. The test statistic is distributed asymptotically as $\chi^2(q)$, where q is the number of restrictions.

5. In a different context, Darrat (1988) has reported similar evidence for the impact of federal budget on the trade deficit.

6. The empirical results displayed in models (A) and (B) and in table 3C−1 reveal several other implications regarding the causal linkages among the remaining variables of the models. For space constraints, these implications are omitted here.

References

Akaike, H. "Fitting Autoregressions for Predictions." *Annals of the Institute of Statistical Mathematics* 21 (1969): 243–247.
Baskin, M. J. "Policy Prescriptions for Raising U.S. Saving." in *The U.S. Savings Challenge: Policy Options for Productivity & Growth*, edited by C. E. Walker, M. A. Bloomfield, and M. Thorning. Boulder, Colo.: Westview Press, 1990.
Batten, D. S., and R. W. Hafer. "The Relative Impact of Monetary and Fiscal Actions on Economic Activity: A Cross-County Comparison." Federal Reserve Bank of St. Louis, *Review* 65 (January 1983): 5–12.
Cooley, T. F., and S. F. LeRoy. "Atheoretical Macroeconometrics: A Critique." *Journal of Monetary Economics* 16 (November 1985): 283–308.
Darrat, A. F. "Have Large Budget Deficits Caused Rising Trade Deficits?" *Southern Economic Journal* 54 (April 1988): 879–887.
Dickey, D. A., and W. A. Fuller. "Distribution of the Estimators for Autoregressive Time Series with a Unit Root." *Journal of American Statistical Association* 74 (June 1979): 427–431.
Eisner, R. *How Real Is the Federal Deficit?* New York: Free Press, 1986.
Fackler, J. S. "An Empirical Analysis of the Markets for Goods, Money, and Credit." *Journal of Money, Credit, and Banking* 17 (February 1985): 28–42.
Genberg, J., M. K. Salemi, and A. Swoboda. "The Relative Importance of Foreign and Domestic Disturbances for Aggregate Fluctuations in the Open Economy: Switzerland, 1964–1981." *Journal of Monetary Economics* 18 (January 1987): 45–67.
Haan, J. de, and H. D. Zelhorst. "The Relationship Between Real Deficits and Real Growth: A Critique." *Journal of Post Keynesian Economics* 11 (Fall 1988): 148–160.
Hsiao, C. "Autoregressive Modelling and Money-Income Causality Detection." *Journal of Monetary Economics* 11 (January 1981): 85–106.
Johnson, M. H. "U.S. Fiscal Policy and Saving." In *The U.S. Savings Challenge: Policy Options for Productivity & Growth*, edited by B. E. Walker, M. A. Bloomfield, and M. Thorning. Boulder, Colo.: Westview Press, 1990.
Kawai, M. "Exchange Rate–Price Causality in the Recent Floating Period." In *The Functioning of Floating Exchange Rates: Theory, Evidence and Policy Implications*, edited by Bigman and Taya. Cambridge, Mass.: Ballinger Publications, 1980.
Lupoletti, W., and R. H. Webb. "Defining and Improving the Accuracy of Macroeconomic Forecasts: Contributions from a VAR Model." *Journal of Business* 59 (April 1986): 263–285.
Lutkepohl, J. "Non-Causality Due to Omitted Variables." *Journal of Econometrics* 19 (August 1982): 367–378.
Sims, C. A. "Policy Analysis with Econometric Models." *Brookings Papers on Economic Activity* (1982): 107–152.
Stock, J., and M. Watson. "Interpreting the Evidence on Money-Income Causality." *Journal of Econometrics* 40 (January 1989): 161–182.

Walker, C. E., M. A. Bloomfield, and M. Thorning. *The U.S. Savings Challenge: Policy Options for Productivity & Growth*. Boulder, Colo.: Westview Press, 1990.

Webb, R. H. "Vector Autoregressions on a Tool for Forecast Evaluations." Federal Reserve Bank of Richmond, *Economic Review* 70 (January/February 1984): 3–11.

Commentary by Dennis Placone and Holley Ulbrich

Clemson University

The issue of saving is an important one for the 1990s as the United States attempts to restore investment and economic growth to the rates of earlier periods. Saving is a multifaceted issue. In their chapter, Eisner and Pieper offer some provocative observations on the link between saving and the deficit by looking at the various individual linkages. In the process they also make some partinent observations about the relationship among saving, investment, and growth. In both cases, they take careful note of the fact that these relationships must be explored in an economy that is now much more open to trade and investment than in earlier decades. Finally, Eisner and Pieper attempt to develop a formal model of these relationships and to test it empirically. We will focus our comments on (1) the saving/growth link, (2) the disaggregated effects of the deficit on saving, (3) the implications of foreign versus domestic investment, and (4) the model and empirical tests.

1. The Relationship Among Saving, Investment, and Economic Growth

The debate over changes in the level of saving and investment in the United States is often taken out of its natural context of overall macroeconomic performance. Saving and investment are not, after all, ends in themselves but rather means to an end. That end is economic growth and a higher standard of living. If those objectives could be attained without much saving and investment, there would be little interest in what happens to saving and investment.

Investment contributes to economic growth by expanding the stock of productive resources, improving labor productivity, and embodying new technology. What is the role of saving? The standard view, in the classical/monetarist tradition, is that saving makes investment possible by supplying funds. Ceteris paribus, when saving is low, real interest rates will be high enough to discourage private sector investment. In this view, a government deficit can be viewed as negative saving, that is, as absorbing saving that might otherwise have gone into private investment, assuming no inflows of funds from other sources. The depression Keynesian view, cited by Eisner and Pieper, is that saving is at best irrelevant and at worst harmful because high saving means low consumption, low consumption means low expected sales, and investment depends on sales expectations.

In the messy intermediate world we occupy, there is some truth to both positions, but we cannot have it both ways. If growth is the goal, encouraging private investment is always good. Depending on circumstances, saving may be good or bad. In a recessionary situation, it may actually be desirable to discourage saving. Government kindly takes it on itself to reduce saving by running deficits. In the long term, however, saving is good. It frees resources for investment without either high real interest rates or inflation. Because the focus of the saving and investment debate is on the long term, the classical/monetarist long-term perspective is probably the more relevant one here; that is, that saving that makes low interest rates possible is good for investment and that the government deficit, by soaking up saving and driving up interest rates, discourages investment.

2. Deficits and Saving: Disaggregated Effects

Eisner and Pieper make a particularly useful contribution to the deficit/saving debate by calling attention to some of the potential disaggregated effects of deficit reduction on saving and/or investment. Consider, for example, the effect of deficit reduction on the state and local surplus, an important form of saving in the mid-1980s. (The actual state and local surplus disappeared with the 1990–1992 recession.) Eisner and Pieper argue that deficit reduction will cut grants to state and local governments, resulting in increased taxes or reduced spending at the state and local levels. This observation is a valid one. However, not all of any state or local tax increase will come out of saving and not all of the state and local spending cuts will fall on state and local investment. Thus the net effect of deficit reduction by cutting grants to state and local governments on saving and investment is likely to be positive, albeit less than one for one.

This same kind of impact applies to other kinds of spending cuts associated with deficit reduction. Some of the deficit reduction will come at the expense of the 18 percent of the budget that Eisner and Pieper identify as investment in infrastructure and human capital, but at least some part will come from government consumption. Defense cuts in particular are a form of government consumption inasmuch as they do not lead to increased future production of goods and services. Thus the so-called peace dividend, if and when it should materialize, is one way that government spending can be cut and government saving can be increased without any direct reduction in either public investment or private saving.

The third type of disaggregated effect of deficit reduction that Eisner and Pieper observe is the impact on personal income and disposable personal income. They argue that any reduction in government spending or any increase in taxes will shift aggregate demand to the left, depressing economic activity and with it saving and investment (particularly if investment is driven by changes in final demand). This view is a valid but short-run new Keynesian perspective. A tax increase will impact on both consumption and saving, so the reduction in saving is much less than dollar for dollar. The indirect impact on investment via reduced consumption is much harder to estimate, depending as it does on general economic conditions.

Left out of these relationships is the effect of reduced federal borrowing on interest rates, which should surely decline as a major borrower reduces its participation in the market. Thus the total impact of deficit reduction on private borrowing, whether for state and local projects, business investments, housing, or consumer durables, is difficult to predict but is probably more positive than Eisner and Pieper would predict.

Finally, there is the issue of how the budget deficit impacts on net foreign investment. Two forces are at work here, in that the budget deficit impacts on both current account and capital account. To the extent that a reduced deficit depresses economic activity, the trade balance will improve by way of reduced imports, and net foreign investment will increase on the investment side of the equation. To the extent that a reduced deficit depresses interest rates, the trade balance's mirror image, the capital account balance, must also decline. The result would be a reduced flow of funds into the United States (the foreign component of saving). The net effect of these various forces on the savings and investment equation is indeed a reduction, but because the U.S. foreign sector is still relatively small, the magnitude of the impact is probably quite modest. At most, a $1 change in GNP results in a $.10 change in net exports in the opposite direction, ceteris paribus; in most years it is less.

Eisner and Pieper state that easier money (measured by an increase in the monetary base) will lower the price of the dollar, thus encouraging exports and discouraging imports. Although this effect is more likely to be true in the long run if domestic inflation is higher than in the rest of the world, it is also likely that U.S. interest rates will rise relative to those abroad, putting upward pressure on the price of the dollar. If the dollar's price should rise instead of fall, the result would be the opposite of what Eisner and Pieper describe.

Even if we add all these effects, a dollar of decline in the deficit does not result in a dollar decline in private saving (and investment) to offset the increased government saving. All the effects listed are modest. To use the old Keynesian terms, the marginal propensities to save and to import are quite small. It would take heroic estimates of the relevant elasticities to agree with their statement that "we cannot tell, in terms of the saving identity itself, whether increases in the budget deficit will reduce national savings or whether reductions will raise it." For deficit reductions to increase saving, it is not necessary (as they suggest) that all other components of the saving and investment identity remain unchanged, only that they change by less than the amount of deficit reduction. Thus the net effect of deficit reduction is unequivocally positive for saving and, by extension, for investment.

3. Deficit Reduction in a Global Economy: The Who and Where of Foreign Investment

Another issue implied but not fully developed by Eisner and Pieper is that of who owns the investment asset and in which country it is located — a very different question from that of whether the investment occurs at all. This issue is too important to be neglected and may, in fact, lie at the heart of the controversy over the relationship between budget deficits, trade deficits, net foreign investment, and sluggish growth of GNP. In fact, the recent switch by the Commerce Department from GNP to GDP accounting reflects the fact that an increasing share of the economic activity within U.S. borders is under the management and ownership of foreign nationals.

Eisner and Pieper are correct in observing that investment has held up reasonably well in the past decade, except for the recession. However, with an increased share of the saving to finance that investment coming from abroad, a larger share of both productive and financial assets is owned by foreign nationals, who also have a claim on future earnings through those assets. If the objective of the economic game plan is to maximize the well-being of U.S. residents, this strategy is not necessarily the best one for doing so over the long term.

Jingoism aside, a flow of foreign saving into in the United States must be viewed as a mixed blessing in other ways. A deficit reduction that leads to a decline in the flow will depress the price of the dollar, drive up exports, and reduce imports. According to Lange via Eisner and Pieper, the result should be a stimulus to investment by domestic firms in exporting and import-competing industries. If the United States runs a trade deficit and a capital account surplus, in part the result of a deficit that stimulates income (and imports) and raises interest rates (and capital inflow), foreigners accumulate dollars that they recycle to the United States as net foreign saving. These funds are used to acquire investment assets, both existing assets and new investments. If the deficit is reduced, one might reasonably expect lower incomes, lower interest rates, and a resulting reduction in imports and in the flow of net foreign saving into the country. On the other hand, the reduction in the deficit will increase the government component of saving. Whether total saving and investment is greater or less under these conditions is an empirical question, but the domestically owned share of investment will be larger.

Returning to the fundamental objective of long-run economic growth, we also have to consider the long-run consequences of (in the words of Benjamin Friedman) "financing our consumption by selling our assets." With the recent levels of capital inflow, the purchase of interest-bearing assets by foreigners commits the United States to a future flow of interest payments and repayment of principal. A significant amount of those foreign savings went into U.S. Treasury obligations. Foreign nonofficial holdings of Treasuries rose more than fivefold between 1983 and 1989, from $26 billion to $135 billion, whereas foreign holdings of other bonds (including corporate) rose from $17 billion to $230 billion, an increase of 1352 percent. At the same time, direct investment and investments in common stock by foreigners in the United States showed a much smaller percentage increase of 328 percent, from $201 billion to $661 billion. If the inflow of funds were being used to invest in productive ways that enhance future income, then U.S. citizens would benefit. If, however, these funds are being used to finance government consumption and other activities not enhancing future growth, then current patterns of saving and investing are indeed mortgaging the future.

4. Empirical Issues

Turning to the model and empirical tests, Eisner and Pieper are again innovative but also vulnerable to some questions about their methodology and interpretation. First, the model used in the chapter is incomplete because the interest rate does not enter into it explicitly. To talk about investment and saving and ignore the interest rate is impossible. Deficit reduction may lead to lower interest rates, which, in turn, would decrease the government's interest expense (now 25 percent of total federal government expenditures). These funds may then be shifted to government investment.

Second, there are several problems with the way that variables are defined and measured. The use of investment as a fraction of potential GNP is arbitrary. All the other variables are divided by actual GNP. No cogent explanation is offered why investment is divided by potential GNP. Why is potential GNP not used for all the variables? Even if the use of potential GNP is conceptually sound, its measurement is difficult, and measurement errors may bias the results.

Another problem that relates both to model specification and variable definition arises in those equations that include the monetary base as an explanatory variable. This variable was used to account for the effects of monetary policy on investment. The base was entered as a percent of GNP from 1962 onward. Included in the same equation is the price-adjusted 6 percent high-employment deficit as a percentage of GNP. There is a close relationship between these two explanatory variables. An increased quantity of government bonds can force the Fed to hold more bonds than it might otherwise wish, thus increasing the monetary base. Therefore, exactly what the monetary base variable is measuring is not clear: it may, in fact, partially reflect changes in the deficit. Possibly the monetary effects of the deficit are being observed and the fiscal effects are very small, or vice versa.

Finally, the use of the real deficit concept has not been widely accepted in the profession. Real deficits, like the briefly popular real money supply, can understate the expansionary nature of policy when the policy-induced inflation reduces the deficit or money supply policy variable. Furthermore, the actual deficit may better reflect the degree of crowding out because it is the actual deficit that affects the bond markets and money supply.

5. Summary

Eisner and Pieper are, as always, provocative and somewhat iconoclastic in their approach to the age-old question of deficits, saving, and investment.

COMMENTARY

This chapter should stimulate further thinking about the consequences of deficit reduction in the 1990s. Although there is ample room to dispute their reasoning, their model, and their conclusions, they have pointed to some genuine reservations about the potential positive impact of deficit reduction on saving, investment, and economic growth. Hopefully, if the U.S. economy moves beyond the recession, reduces defense spending, and brings the deficit down to a more traditional ratio to GNP, we will be presented with a real-world experiment in deficit reduction that can test some of the ideas explored here.

4 REAGANOMICS, SAVING, AND THE CASINO EFFECT

E. Ray Canterbery
Florida State University

1. Reaganomics and the Supply-Siders

During the 1980s the theory of "supply-side economics" became identified with the set of policies known as "Reaganomics," policies aimed at ending inflation without reducing output and employment and thus escaping the stagnation that afflicted the U.S. economy during the 1970s. Tight monetary policy would curb inflation, while supply-side incentives would expand employment and production. Most of all, personal saving would be expanded through the incentives of tax cuts for the highest income earners. Supply-side economics thus became the Holy Grail of savers. Reaganomics, by whatever name or design, culminated in what I call the "Casino Economy."

In retrospect, the fact that Reaganomics even gained social acceptability, much less the status of holy writ, is a revealing commentary on the state of the public psyche. Reaganomics exploited widespread disillusionment with received principles of wealth redistribution and turned them on their heads. The poor were to be disgorged from federal welfare rolls because — receiving so much on the dole — they had disincentives to work. The rich were to receive the greatest tax cuts, for their tax burden was so great they had meager incentive to save. In the name of incentives, Robin-Hood-in-reverse implied that the poor had *too much* after-tax income and the rich *too little*. This frail piece of logic had such immediate appeal that it alone was nearly sufficient to support the Reagan Revolution. But it got lots of help.

Supply-side economics was a media event begun by Wall Street journalist Jude Wanniski, writer Bruce Bartlett, and pop sociologist George Gilder. All three writers made devoted reference to the second-generation Austrian economists—von Hayek, von Mises, Schumpeter, Frank Knight—and the neo-Austrians Kirzner and Rothbard. The Laffer curve, the Rosetta Stone of Reaganomics, drawn for Wanniski on a napkin in a Washington, D.C., "insiders'" hotel bar by Arthur Laffer, was given celebrity status in Wanniski's book *The Way the World Works*.

George Gilder gave a further boost to Lafferism even while embracing neo-Austrian entrepreneurship in his *Wealth and Poverty*, required reading for the 1981 White House staff. (David Stockman distributed 30 copies immediately upon its publication.) Gilder, the chief evangelist for Reaganomics, argued that personal income tax cuts for the rich would stimulate their output; eventually, the resulting expanded production and added tax revenue would allow further tax cuts for low- and middle-income families. But Gilder went further. The welfare state that America had become, he said, motivated the poor to choose leisure over work. Because only the rich could acquire enough savings to induce capital formation, their reduced tax rates would stimulate economic growth.

Thus the neo-Austrian spirit of entrepreneurship continued to blitz the White House long after the planned tax cut had been drafted. That is, although the initial impetus for Reaganomics came from Laffer's version of neoclassical economics, Gilder's fervor kept the ball rolling. His faith in God and enterprise apparently reassured the president, even after OMB director David Stockman had become convinced otherwise, that Reaganomics would stimulate output and employment.

In short, although it stressed those elements crucial to the supply of labor and productive capacity, the full Reaganomics program went beyond tax cuts to slashes in government welfare spending and decreases in regulation. The unique proclamation of supply-side economics is its dual promise of stimulating economic growth and retarding inflation. The next section will discuss the bricks and mortar of the supply-side economics archway.

2. Say's Law Embued with Entrepreneurial Spirit

The first canon of supply-side economics was Say's law, resurrected from its presumed entombment at the hands of the Great Depression and John Maynard Keynes. Say's law connects supply-side economics to economic growth. Saving is the starter key for the growth engine because of the guaranteed transmission of saving into investment. The engine always starts, no matter how chilly the investment climate, because every dollar saved is predestined to become a dollar of investment.

Because Reaganomics viewed the upper-income class (over $50,000 a year in 1980 dollars) as the dominant personal savers, the central economic purpose of the wealthy was to save. This perspective rationalized lowering marginal tax rates for the well-to-do as an incentive to increase personal saving, which would end up as new plant and equipment. As a failsafe, special tax benefits to corporations (larger credits, lower rates, and faster depreciation) would provide still more incentives for investment. No doubt this faith was buttressed by the neo-Austrian optimism regarding the alertness of the entrepreneur in responding to changed profit opportunities.

Thus, even though the various tax cuts would increase disposable income, their presumed effectiveness did not stem from their effects on Keynesian aggregate demand, which were thought to be nil. Rather, with neoclassical immaculateness, the effectiveness of tax reductions would come from their changing of relative prices. A reduction in tax rates would induce decision makers to substitute productive activity (investment, work, and exchange) for leisure and idleness, causing output to rise. Moreover, entrepreneurs, freed from the constraints of taxation, would play a role here. The shift from nonproduction (and consumption) toward production would enlarge total supply, causing real income to expand rapidly. The market supply of goods and services — that is, aggregate supply and hence economic growth — would be enhanced.

3. Truth in Taxes and in Lending

The 1981 Economic Recovery Tax Act cut taxes across the board for individuals: 5 percent in 1981, 10 percent in 1982, and another 10 percent in 1983. The most beloved policy slashed the top bracket from 70 percent to 50 percent. Although taxation of earned income had topped out at 50 percent in 1972, the same cap was placed on *unearned* income, providing great gains to the small set of households living off interest and rents; the top rate on capital gains was cut from 28 to 20 percent.

At the same time social security tax rates were allowed to climb from 6.05 percent in 1978 to 6.70 percent in 1982–83, 7.05 percent in 1985, and 7.51 percent in 1988–89, on a path blazed by the Carter administration in 1977. The share of federal tax receipts from this source rose from 31 percent in 1980 to 36 percent in 1988, even while the working class's share of the national income declined. The share of tax revenue contributed by the top 1 percent of taxpayers also rose, but only in step with their share of the national income; their ability to pay had been equally enhanced. According to the Congressional Budget Office, which has calibrated the effect of federal taxes by population decile for 1977–1984 and 1977–1988, the highest income households paid lower effective rates because of the tax cuts on income from interest, dividends, rents, and capital gains (table 4–1).

We pause, for practice seldom makes perfect theory. Did Reagan's advisers really believe that workers were so sensitive to small real-wage increments that meager marginal tax reductions would so energize work effort? If so, the effective federal marginal tax *increases* should cause labor productivity to nosedive!

The answer was provided by Stockman in his Christmastime 1981 "confessions" to the *Atlantic Monthly*. "The hard part of the supply-side tax cut is dropping the top rate from 70 to 50 percent—the rest of it is a secondary matter," he explained. "The original argument was that the top bracket was too high, and that's having the most devastating effect on the economy. Then, the general argument was that, in order to make this palatable as a political matter, you had to bring down all the brackets. But, I mean, Kemp-Roth (the name of the original supply-side tax bill) was always a Trojan Horse to bring down the top rate."[1]

Table 4–1. Percentage Point Changes in Effective Tax Rates by Population Income Decile, 1977–1988

Decile	1977–1984	1977–1988
1	+2.5	+1.6
2	−0.2	−0.4
3	+1.2	+1.3
4	+0.1	+0.6
5	−0.6	+0.1
6	−0.9	−0.1
7	−1.5	−0.7
8	−0.6	0.0
9	−0.7	+0.2
10	−3.1	−1.7
top 5%	−4.2	−2.6
top 1%	−7.8	−6.0

Source: Congressional Budget Office, *The Changing Distribution of Federal Taxes: 1975–1990*, October, 1987, Table 8, p. 48.

A Trojan horse? Supply-side economics was rolled into the enemy camp of labor with a horseload of entrepreneurs. For the stimulation of output the Reagan administration was counting not really on a Calvinistic response by workers but rather on Say's law. Stockman conceded as much: The supply-side theory was really new clothes for the naked doctrine of the old "trickle-down theory."[2] The main effect on the highest income quintile was to greatly increase after-tax income in the expressed belief that personal savings (and para passu private *real* investment) would rise.

Part of the plan was to give *direct* assistance to real capital formation. With reductions in corporate tax rates and liberalization of depreciation benefits, the share of federal tax receipts represented by corporate income tax revenues dropped to an all-time low of 6.2 percent in 1983, down from 12.5 percent in 1980.

The spending side of the federal fiscal ledger also became an instrument for redistribution. Reagan was elected on the platform that "government is the problem." Republicans claimed that a gigantic public sector had ended innovation and stifled creativity even as the welfare state destroyed the family. The Reagan solution was massive increases in defense spending that shifted federal funds out of human resources. Between 1980 and 1987 defense climbed from 23 percent to 28 percent of federal outlays, whereas human resources descended from 28 percent to 22 percent.

Federal deficits far beyond the lively imagination of John Maynard Keynes were the consequence. The 1981 tax bill married them to higher interest rates. The rise in federal debt interest from $96 billion in 1981 to $216 billion in 1988 virtually guaranteed that nonearned income from holding paper would rise faster than the wages of workers. The top quintile of households were receiving 80 percent of the federal interest payments made to individuals, even as the top tax rate on such receipts fell steadily (to 28 percent in 1988).

Finally, Reaganomics jumped on the deregulation bandwagon that the Carter administration had started rolling. Forces already in motion were sustained or accelerated in telecommunications, transportation, financial services, and many other industries. Removal by Congress in 1980 of deposit and loan interest ceilings had already awarded the greatest benefits to the 10 percent of families owning 86 percent of the net financial wealth.

The Wall Street raiders of the 1980s were encouraged — even cheered — as they used greenmail in the merger frenzy of the era. Between FY1980 and FY1988 merger filings soared more than 320 percent while the work-years allocated to antitrust enforcement plunged 40 percent. Raiders like

Carl Icahn, Boone Pickens, and Ivan Boesky, as well as LBO masters such as Henry Kravis, built a large, profitable infrastructure that assured huge fees from questionable ventures and an unrealistic upward spin to stock market prices.

The intent in word and deed was to redistribute income and wealth from the working class to the upper 10 percent, increasing both income and wealth concentration. Economists can defer to the Kitty Kellys to address the hypocrisy related to family values, but Reaganomics left no room for hypocrisy regarding income and wealth redistribution. President Reagan achieved what he had said he wanted. Even before the lopsided tax cuts, money income by quintile shows growing income inequality during the Reagan years (see table 4-2).

The wealth distribution is always less equal than the income distribution. The Joint Economic Committee of Congress compiled data on the total wealth held by the top 0.5 percent of U.S. households from date furnished by the Federal Reserve Board. By 1983 the share of wealth held by the super-rich had risen sharply (to 26.9 percent) after falling for 40 years. Further increases in income inequality since then, plus other evidence, suggest that this trend continues.

Average total corporate CEO compensation increased from $900,000 in 1983 to $2,025,000 in 1988 (93 times the earnings of the average factory worker). In 1988 Michael Milken of Drexel, the innovator of junk bonds, received between $180 and $199 *million*, up from a meager $60 million in 1987 and around $80 million in 1986. The net worth of the Forbes 400 (the wealthest 400 persons in the United States as estimated by *Forbes* magazine) went from $92 *billion* to some $270 *billion* between 1982 and 1989, a gain of 293 percent. In 1981 there were 600,000 millionaires. But by 1988 there were some 1,500,000 millionaires, 100,000 decamillionaires,

Table 4-2. Changes, Share of Money Income Received by Quintile

Year	1	2	3	4	5
1969	5.6%	12.4%	17.7%	23.7%	40.6%
1980	5.1	11.6	17.5	24.3	41.6
1983	4.7	11.1	17.1	24.3	42.8
1985	4.6	10.9	16.9	24.2	43.5
1988	4.6	10.7	16.7	24.0	44.0

Source: U.S. Census Bureau.

Notes: The 1988 income range for each quintile is 1 = Under $15,102; 2 = $15,102-$26,182; 3 = $26,182-$38,500; 4 = $38,500-$55,906; and 5 = Over $55,906.

1200 centimillionaires, and 51 billionaires. Many of these fortunes were made in finance and real estate.

To be sure, by this test supply-side economics worked. But did the income/wealth expansion and redistribution increase real saving and real investment? If so, did such increases come from supply-side tax "incentives"? Before addressing these questions, we need to ponder whether we have a correct measure of saving.

4. The Measurement of Saving

The difficulty of understanding saving at conception is exceeded only by data problems. The identity of saving and investment in the National Income and Product Accounts (NIPA) applies to *real* saving—real in the sense of a withholding of current income from consumption. It does not capture the additions in financial wealth that may result from increases in the value of existing and tangible assets. And it does not reflect creation of new credit, of which the Fed and the commercial banking system are usually capable. Having stated this caveat, we note that the NIPA show that personal savings as a percentage of disposable personal income dropped from 7.5 percent in 1981 to a low of 3.2 percent in 1987. If the truth be known, the U.S. Department of Commerce does not measure personal savings to generate its savings data. Instead, the Commerce Department measures disposable income and consumption and then subtracts consumption from disposable income to determine savings. This economists consider *real*.

Such a measure surely understates personal money savings during the 1980s, a fact that has brought tears of joy to many a supply-sider. Quite simply, the Commerce Department fails to account for changes in net worth, including that created by new credit. If an individual owns an asset that appreciates in value, such as a stock, bond, or house, are those new savings any less real to the person than savings accumulated by thrift? Not all increases in one's store of wealth are spent lavishly: That depends upon one's income class and tastes. By the same token, would not a depreciation of such assets diminish personal saving? Such personal money savings do go somewhere and influence the macroeconomy, but economists generally have been unable to determine their destination.

The Federal Reserve System also measures individual savings—indirectly, using a flow-of-funds approach. It is a much closer approximation of changes in net worth. The Federal Reserve measure adds increases in financial assets to net investment in consumer durables (such as a house purchase), and then subtracts the net increase in debts to arrive at savings. The Fed's number-crunchers attribute to households those flows not accounted for by banks, insurance companies, pension funds, and other funds handlers. Periodically, a Fed survey of consumer finance provides a direct check of some household financial behavior.

If one considers personal saving to be the increase in household net worth, the Commerce Department clearly undercounts personal savings, a discrepancy that greatly widened after 1981. The similarity in the two data series during 1961–1981 suggests that they had once been measuring the same thing. Nonetheless, during 1986, 1987, and 1988 the Fed's measure of personal saving was 30.2, 45.0, and 34.6 percent higher, respectively, than that of the Commerce Department. Still another alternative measure of savings has been provided by Block,[3] who focuses on the ability of households to supply a financial surplus to the business sector for investment.

Are then the supply-siders correct? Did the supply-side tax incentives greatly swell personal savings? This chapter shall argue otherwise. It is likely that personal money savings did soar during the 1980s, but for reasons quite apart from supply-side incentives. What happened to net business savings is the rest of the story.

5. Keynes Redux

The stimulative fiscal policy of the Reagan administration came into full effect as the 1981–1982 recession was ending and an aggregate demand stimulus was needed. Because personal income rose and was being redistributed to the highest income intervals, it would be surprising if personal money saving failed to soar along with consumption, especially by the upper classes. Tables 4–3 and 4–4 reveal those consequences: These data are "real" only in the sense that they are adjusted by price indices.

Price-adjusted consumption increased at an annual rate of only .03 percent between 1972–73 and 1980–81 but soared .46 percent between 1980–81 and 1986–87 (see table 4–3). Even so, the important story is found in the distribution of these growth rates by quintile. Most of the increased rate of consumption during the 1980s can be attributed to the two highest consuming quintiles. The 1980s' increases in household money net worth as a share of slow-growing money disposable income were higher than during the 1960s but lower than during the 1970s. However, given that the inflation in *goods* prices slowed during the 1980s, the increase in price-adjusted household net worth as a share of disposable income was phenomenal, especially during 1985–1988 (see table 4–4).

Table 4–3. Real Consumption Expenditures, Average Annual Growth Rates (in percent)

	1972–73 to 1980–81	1980–81 to 1986–87
All consumer units	0.03	0.46
By quintile		
Lowest fifth	1.49	0.23
Second fifth	0.28	−0.45
Third fifth	−0.33	0.01
Fourth fifth	−0.17	0.32
Highest fifth	−0.08	1.59

Sources: U.S. Department of Labor, Bureau of Labor Statistics; *Survey of Consumer Expenditures*; and *Consumer Price Index*.

Notes: As the same households are not necessarily in the same income quintiles in each period, the growth rates in consumption should be used with caution. The relative growth rates of the various income groups nonetheless can be meaningly compared across the two eras. A detailed discussion of these data appear in Robert Blecker, *Are Americans on a Consumption Binge?* (Washington D.C.: Economic Policy Institute, 1990).

A Keynesian explanation for rising money and price-adjusted household saving is provided in tables 4–5 and 4–6 by estimates of the marginal and average propensities to save. Because these propensities are based on before-tax income, the MPSs for the lowest income interval are misleading. Those MPSs would be much lower when measured against after-tax income. In any case, the average propensities to save by quintile of income are the most revealing. On the average the lowest two-fifths of the consumer units during the 1980s and the lowest three-fifths during 1987 and 1989 had *negative* average saving rates. As Keynesians and the average person on the assembly line would expect, the two highest quintiles did the positive saving.

No self-respecting Keynesian would be surprised that both consumption and saving rose with incomes, nor surprised that a redistribution of income toward the highest income interval would raise the personal money savings rate. The main effect of Reaganomics was to raise the incomes of those in the higher quintiles and increase their ability to spend *and* save. Moreover, as the highest income groups increased their rates of spending, even supply-siders would not be surprised to see soaring tourism in Europe or higher sales of luxury durables, including imported luxury cars.

In conventional macroeconomics, *real* saving is measured as the value of *real* investment—private business investment in plant, equipment, and

Table 4-4. Personal Saving and Investment Rates

	1960–1969	1970–1979	1980–1988	1985–1988
Shares				
Increase, household net worth/DI	27.0	38.9	33.9	32.1
Increase, real household net worth/DI[a]	14.0	8.4	11.2	28.5
Net fixed investment/NNP	6.6	6.7	4.8	4.9
Gross fixed investment/GNP	14.5	15.6	15.4	15.2
Growth Rates				
Growth rate, capital services, private business sector[b]	4.2	4.0	3.2	1.3
Growth rate, capital services, manufacturing sector[b]	4.7	3.7	2.2	1.5

Sources: Federal Reserve, *Balance Sheets for the U.S. Economy*; BEA, National Income and Product Accounts; and BLS, *Multifactor Productivity Measures*.

[a] Nominal household net worth is deflated by the GNP deflator.

[b] The BLS capital input series measures the services derived from the stock of physical assets. The assets included are fixed business equipment, structures, inventories, and land. Structures include nonresidential structures and residential capital that is rented out by profit-making firms or persons. Financial assets are *excluded* as are owner-occupied residential structures. The aggregate capital measures are obtained by weighting the capital stocks for each asset type within each industry using the respective rental prices. Rental prices are the sum of the real rate of return to all assets within the industry and rate of depreciation of the specific asset, adjusted for the effect of taxes. Data on physical assets and the gross product originating by industry used in measuring the rental prices are obtained from the BEA.

new inventories. If saving does not end up as such investment, it plays no further role in the economy. Table 4–4 notes that gross fixed investment as a share of GNP has remained steady for four decades. *Net* fixed investment (the really *real* part of investment) declined to less than 5 percent during the 1980s. Most importantly, the growth rates of capital services in the private business and manufacturing sectors had almost fallen through the factory floor by 1985–1988. During the 1980s the one

Table 4-5. Marginal Propensities to Save by Income Interval, Selected Years

Year	Income Interval						
	1	2	3	4	5	6	7
1982–							
1983	0.81	0.32	0.44	0.36	0.47	0.48	
1984	1.02	0.38	0.39	0.32	0.46	0.29	
1987	0.80	0.06	0.36	0.36	0.38	0.28	0.56
1989	0.83	0.13	0.36	0.28	0.26	0.52	0.24

Source: BLS, U.S. Department of Labor, *Consumer Expenditure Survey*, 1982–83, 1984, 1987, 1989.

Notes: The income intervals for 1982–83 and 1984 are: less than $5000, $5000–$9999, $10,000–$14,999, $15,000–$19,999, $20,000–$29,999, $30,000–$39,999, and $40,000 and over in income *before* taxes. The 1987 and 1989 surveys include an interval of $40,000–49,999 and a new highest interval of $50,000 and over. Moreover, the surveys beginning in 1987 integrate the results of a diary and interview portions of the Bureau's Consumer Expenditure Survey and are, therefore, more complete. The MPSs are calculated from changes in average incomes and expenditures between the income intervals. The data should be interpreted with care. The interview sample is selected on a rotating panel basis, targeted at 5000 consumer units each quarter in 109 areas of the country. The diary survey yields about 10,000 diaries a year (each for 2 one-week periods). Total expenditures or consumption are the transaction costs, including excise and sales taxes, of goods and services acquired during the interview period.

Table 4-6. Average Propensities to Save by Quintiles of Income

Year	Quintile of Consumer Units				
	1	2	3	4	5
1982–83	−1.03	−0.14	0.08	0.21	0.33
1984	−2.17	−0.28	0.02	0.16	0.30
1987	−1.25	−0.31	−0.04	0.11	0.29
1989	−1.12	−0.27	−0.03	0.09	0.30

Source: BLS, U.S. Department of Labor, *Consumer Expenditures Survey*, 1982–83, 1984, 1987, 1989.

Notes: See Notes to table 4–4.

thing private business did best was depreciate—lose capital to wear, tear, obsolescence, and destruction. In this view, real saving stagnated. Why—in the Gildered Age when the idolatry of capital was peaking and personal money saving was on the ascent—did so many machines commit suicide?

To solve the mystery of where personal money savings go when they die (in economic theory), we turn to a theory less conventional than Keynes's expenditures model. We need to examine the composition of savings in firms and households.

6. A Business and Household Net Worth Approach

This section follows the Fed's approach and considers the economy as a series of balance sheets. In this respect, often one household's or organization's asset is another's liability. Thus, when we speak of changes in assets, we often speak as well of co-movements in liabilities. Sometimes the co-movements occur within the same balance sheet. Banks and S&Ls that used high-interest-rate CDs and junk bonds (their liabilities) during the early 1980s to finance mortgages that began to depreciate by 1988 (their assets) have learned dearly this latter connection. There are at least three sources of change in assets. First, value appreciation or depreciation occurs as the prices of the items go up or down. Second, physical depreciation can happen as machines and buildings wear out or become obsolete. Third, exchange (which presumes a change in ownership of the asset) can increase or decrease holdings.[4]

The aggregate net worth of the private business sector (G_b) is equal to its money and money market asset holdings (M_b), plus its value of goods holdings that include inventories of finished goods, goods in process, raw materials, buildings and equipment, and land (Q_b), plus the net household indebtedness to business ($K_h - K'_h$), where K_h is total debts (such as installment credit) due to businesses from households and K'_h is the total debts due from businesses to households plus government bond holdings (B_b). The K'_h consists mostly of corporate bonds held by households. Business firms hold debt of other business firms but, in the aggregate, business-to-business debt cancels. New issues of equities increase the money and market asset holdings of the firm. Change in aggregate business net worth during any accounting period is

$$dG_b = dM_b + dQ_b + dK_h - dK'_h + dB_b = S_b \qquad (4\text{--}1)$$

Because the quantity dG_b is that part of profits not distributed in dividends, it comprises business saving or dissaving.

Net worth (saving) increases through the revaluation of assets above costs, normally at the moment of sale. Despite ritualistic chanting against inflation by business, inflation in goods prices is a reliable route to greater increases in net worth (and business saving). Money and money market assets ideally provide firms only with liquidity. Physical depreciation or value depreciation decrease net savings. Of course, an increase in debts due from households increases business saving even as it decreases household saving.

In a Keynesian-Kaleckian style model, the increased retained earnings of businesses is not only a source of investment funds but an incentive for *more* investment. A price markup is used to increase the value of the goods that businesses sell, adding to the funds flowing from household spending. Retained earnings from sales revenue becomes corporate savings, some of which will be invested. In turn, rising sales revenue nudging full capacity is an impetus to expand. These internal funds so generated by the firm can be levered by debt to finance still more capital assets. The more that is invested, the greater will be the sales of capital goods and the profits' share in the national income. In this regard it is the hope of firms that households will not be spendthrifts. Because of low transactions costs, retained earnings are a preferred source of funds to new issues of preferred or common stock or, in a tax-neutral world, to increased corporate debt (dK_h). Indeed, increases in corporate debt to households reduce business saving. In the *aggregate*, nonetheless, investment requires *external* funds.

And so, equation (4-1) illustrates how easily one can slip into the supply-side error whereby saving "causes" investment. Household saving is a source of corporate debt, an indebtedness no doubt incurred solely for *real* business investment purposes. However, these household savings only enter the firm when *new* corporate bonds are issued. Otherwise, households are merely exchanging ownership of corporate (and no doubt government) bonds with each other. In that process the value of financial assets may be bid up and the wealth and income distribution may be altered. A redistribution toward those of highest marginal and average propensities to save will diminish corporate sales revenue and the impetus for *real* investment. Moreover, there is no guarantee that any particular corporation will use retained earnings to enhance real investment.

Because real investment, when it does happen, raises the retained earnings of the capital goods industry, its employment, and the incomes of those it employs, the more believable parable is that investment "causes" saving. This view too, no doubt, is an oversimplification, but at least the *direction* of causality is clear. Moreover, for the 1980s, it is a relationship whose pattern—as we have seen—is found in the data.

A little noted component of declining saving is the slump in *business* saving. Business saving is conventionally measured in the national accounts by retained earnings of corporations. As a percentage of GNP, it fell from around 4.5 percent in the mid-1960s to 2.75 percent in the late 1970s, and to 1 percent during the late 1980s. Alternatively, the Federal Reserve balance sheet measure of corporate saving (which includes stock dividends and nondividend cash payments) suggests that corporate saving actually turned *negative* during the late 1980s. This event is related to the outbreak of leveraged buyouts and stock repurchases to fight them.

Now we turn to the ledger sheets of the household. Surely it is so that household saving equals household income less household consumption, properly measured. It is equally so that household saving is the change in household net worth. The household equation for saving comparable to that for the corporation is

$$dG_h = dM_h + dQ_h + dK'_h - dK_h + dB_h + dE_h = S_h, \qquad (4-2)$$

where dB_h is the increase in the value of government bond holdings of households and dE_h is the increase in the value of equities. Any increase in goods holdings would be in durables and would include the increase (or decrease) in the value of housing.

A reminder to the unwary reader: As long as these items are expressed in nominal terms, they can rise and fall from changes in either units or prices. In fact, a positive dQ_b in a business firm's balance sheet can be seen as a price increase *only*, given that firms attempt to sell products above cost. Even though the act of exchange is merely a change in asset ownership, those holding assets rising in price enjoy increased net worth.

We now move to the national income and its distribution. Aggregate profits of business (V) is the gross increase in net worth (i.e., gross business saving), out of which interest and dividends are paid (D), or

$$V = S_b + D. \qquad (4-3)$$

Substituting the components of business saving from equation (4-1),

$$V = dQ_b + (dM_b + dK_h - dK'_h + dB_b + D). \qquad (4-4)$$

Since household income is comprised of wages (W) and dividends and interest paid (D), we can write

$$S_h = (W + D) - C_h, \qquad (4-5)$$

where C_h is household consumption. Substitute the values from equation (4-2) for S_h and

$$W = C_h + dQ_h - (-dM_h + dK_h - dK'_h - dB_h - dE_h + D). \qquad (4-6)$$

If we ignore the direct transfers to and from governments and assume the inventory of government bonds to be constant for the period, there are transfer items that flow between the business and the household sectors comprised of changes in money holdings (the M's), changes in debt (the K's), changes in government bond holdings (the B's), increases in equity holdings (the E), and dividend and interest payments (D). The transfer item (T) defined in equation (4–4) as

$$T = dM_b + dK_h - dK'_h + dB_b + D. \qquad (4-7)$$

has the lightness of being highly liquid assets and liabilities. Without denoting exact ownership shares, T can be written as

$$T = dM + dK - dK' + dB + D. \qquad (4-7a)$$

The "T" for the household differs from the "T" for the business firm by the value dE_h, or the change in equity holdings. This complication requires some elaboration. An increase in household equity holdings can come from new stock issues, existing stock in the secondary market, or a rise in stock market prices. *Only* when a positive dE_h comes from *new* issues (about 1 percent of the value of all such transactions) does the corporation experience an increase in money offsetting the decrease in household money holdings (i.e., $dM_b = -dM_h$). Otherwise, the change in equity holdings merely shifts the ownership of equity and liquidity among households. The implications of this complication can begin to be understood by defining the household "T" as XT from equation (4–6) or

$$XT = -dM_h + dK_h - dK'_h - dB_h - dE_h + D. \qquad (4-8)$$

Now, we can simplify equations (4–4) and (4–6) to read

$$V = dQ_b + T \quad \text{and} \quad W = C + dQ_h - XT.$$

Aggregate wages and profits exhaust the value of aggregate output so that national income is

$$Y = W + V = C + dQ_h + dQ_b - (XT - T). \qquad (4-9)$$

Only when $T = XT$ would nominal saving be $dQ_h + dQ_b$ and national income be

$$Y = C + dQ_h + dQ_b. \qquad (4-9a)$$

The value "T" then would simply disappear as transfers between firms and households cancel.

Anyone who has struggled to understand T and who by now associates T with "torture" no doubt must be disappointed greatly to see it disappear! The nature of equation (4–9a) and, to a slightly lesser extent, equation (4–9) as identities tends to hide everything that went on in the economy in the determination of national income and its division, including the strategic role of T. In particular, we note that a net positive value of T transfers financial resources from households to businesses.

If net savings are determined independently from dividends, then business dividends are a "widow's cruse and Danaid jar": The more business distributes in interest and dividends, the more will return in profits to be distributed.[5] By the same token, the more business *pays* in interest, the lower its profits will go. Whereas the corporation can increase its cash from equities only with new issues (which were rare during the 1980s), the household can enjoy secondary-market appreciation in its equities holdings (via XT) without sharing such benefits with business.

Because XT and T differ only by dE_h in equation (4–9), the nominal national income is

$$Y = C + dQ_h + dQ_b + dE_h. \qquad (4\text{–}10)$$

National saving then is bolstered by an increase in household equity holdings, even by a rising stock market. Nominal national income would rise without a matching increment of *real* investment. A supply-siders' cut in the capital gains tax rate would add to nominal national income without altering plant capacity.

Thus far, it has been assumed that the central bank and private banks are not creating any new money nor is the federal government issuing new debt. It is important to relax both assumptions. When we do, equation (4–10) becomes

$$Y = C + dQ_h + dQ_b + (dM_h + dM_b + dB_h + dB_b + dE_h). \qquad (4\text{–}10a)$$

Now the *nominal* national income can increase as a direct result of credit and money creation. An increase in real national income is by no means guaranteed because real investment may not increase.

The various components of T and XT swirl about their own axes without necessarily intersecting with *real* investment and saving. Financial transactions in existing assets are not real output and not included in real national income. Still, they do exist. The values can expand and contract due simply to financial speculation—speculative real estate or corporate junk bond ventures. In turn, such appreciation or depreciation and compounding of interest can alter the wealth and income distributions. Moreover, the entire financial services industry—which greatly expanded between 1981 and 1987, only to begin a monumental collapse thereafter—revolves around T.

Banking, savings and loan, and brokerage firms are unique among businesses in holding demand deposit liabilities that are assets of other businesses and of households (M_b and M_h). During the 1980s, a period when new financial instruments such as junk bonds streamed out of Wall Street, the behavior of such accounts was the basis for what I call the "Casino Effect."

7. The Casino Effect of T

Financial fragility did not begin with Reaganomics; rather, the Reagan—congressional deficits and deregulation of the financial industry simply took an already fragile system and tempted its collapse. Since the late 1960s, credit or finance has become increasingly important in the United States and in the global economy. The financial disturbances of 1972—1973, 1974—1975, 1979, and 1981—1982 left the peak rate of inflation and the lowest rate of unemployment ever higher. This high-flying era was characterized by a volatile but generally upward movement in nominal interest rates, wild gyrations in exchange rates, and a general decline in the growth of consumption.

By the mid-1980s interest payments as a share of net national income had risen from only 1 percent to 10 percent. A major shift toward debt finance occurred in the aforementioned business balances sheets. Whereas in 1983 equity and debt issuance were $4.8 billion and $4.0 billion, respectively, in every year of the eighties since, net new equity issuance has been negative while corporate net bond issues have soared (to about $30 billion in 1989). The irresistible combination of a fast-rising U.S. private and public debt and soaring U.S. interest rates is responsible for skyrocketing net monetary interest. By 1991 federal government interest payments to bondholders were exhausting half of all personal income tax revenue.

During the Reagan years the entrepreneur's share of national income declined drastically even as the rentier's (unearned) income share has soared. All of the increase in disposable income during the 1980s is more than accounted for by the rise in the share of interest income, while the shares of labor and other income sources declined. Surely this is not the way the Golden Age of Entrepreneurship was supposed to unfold.

Of course, an economy can never reach a state in which 100 percent of its national income is net interest, because the sum of employee compensation, proprietor's income, and corporate profits would be zero! Even so, the interest part of D has been eating away at manufacturers' net worth. We can begin to picture an economy whose main industries would be printing (for credit instruments and money), financial firms, and retail outlets and in which all manufactured goods and services would be imported. The central function of businesspeople in such an environment would be speculation. The society would be a giant money market fund in which households and businesses would spend each day shifting financial assets about in their gigantic portfolios. The United States would implode into Las Vegas or Trump's Taj Mahal in Atlantic City—hence, what I have called the "Casino Economy." During economic expansion such an economy can operate almost independently of real production, but its downward spiral during a recession is dangerous.

The ownership of most interest-bearing assets is highly concentrated. Some 10 percent of families own 51 percent of liquid assets, 86 percent of tax-exempt municipal bonds, and 70 percent of other bonds. The richest 10 percent hold 57 percent of household net worth and 86 percent of net financial assets. The top 10 percent also own 72 percent of corporate stock, with the top 2 percent alone owning half.

Although the monetary system is at the core of the debt creation and repayment process, its stability depends on profit flows to borrowers sufficient to service their loans. The central problems of present-day capitalism are connected to the ownership, creation, and financing of capital assets whose distribution, in turn, has contributed to speculation in financial assets. Credit has become notoriously unstable.

What comprises net worth (or worthlessness) in the casino economy? In the financial system, we are interested in the value of net worth because such institutions are intermediaries for the savings in the economy. Consider the simplest possible balance sheet for the financial industry in which net worth (G_f) is, for the accounting period,

$$G_f = dCR_f + dK_{fh} + dK_{fb} - dDD_f - dCD_f, \qquad (4-11)$$

where dCR_f is the change in cash reserves, dK_{fh} and dK_{fb} are the changes in the values of loans to households and businesses, respectively, dDD_f is the change in demand deposit liabilities, and dCD_f is the change in value of long-term certificates of deposit. We will assume that most of the loans to the household sector are to keep it housed and most to the business sector are for commercial real estate, whereas long-term CDs are used as the primary source of funds for such mortgages. (Of course, such institutions also play a role in the creation of money to finance stock market purchases.)

The link between this financial industry and the real economy is the value of real estate. During 1983–1988 the appreciation of houses (as well as the building of more luxurious houses) was a major source of household personal savings. (The *increase* in the value of housing had nearly doubled in five years—from $158.3 billion in 1983 to $313.1 billion in 1988. The value of new corporate bond issues during this time pales alongside this huge figure.) Apparently expecting real estate to appreciate forever, the financial industry scurried to provide high-cost mortgage money financed from high-yielding CDs. (The S&Ls, of course, also placed heavy reliance on junk bonds.) The increased concentration of wealth or savings during this era is linked to the demand for real estate and the supply of funds for CDs.

Let RE be the value of real estate, K_f be the value of total mortgages held by the financial industry at any point in time (that change at the rate dK_f/dt), and W be the real value of wealth ("real" = deflated by goods prices) of the upper quintile of the distribution. This wealth is created by the dynamics of T and XT. These values are connected in a circular way even though the circle can expand or contract in space. In the simplest model the circles do not intersect, so that

$$[RE(t) - W(t)]^2 + [K_f(t) - W(t)]^2 = [W(t)]^2, \qquad (4-12)$$

a system of curves or circles whose position depends on the value of real wealth (W) at any point in time. The center of the circle is (W, W) and its radius is W. The following constraints define the curves: $0 \le RE \le W$, $0 \le K_f \le W$, and $RE + K_f \le W$. As W gets larger, the center of the circle moves away from the origin along a line bisecting the angle between the axes (45° line), and the radius of the circle increases. Imagine tossing different-sized units of gold bullion (W) into a smooth-surfaced lake; the larger the volume of bullion, the greater the circle made from the ripples. (Hopefully, I will not be accused of making a circular argument.)[6]

This simple model says that an increase in real wealth in the upper reaches will increase the potential values of RE and K_f. Because the values of mortgages as financial assets are also colinear with the value of real estate, RE and K_f most likely will follow the 45° line. If the real wealth of the top quintile declines, so too will the value of real estate and mortgages. If much of the real wealth is tied to real estate and the prices of real estate drop, this event can shrink the circle. This happens if real estate prices drop faster than goods prices in the economy. The supply-siders are correct about the importance of relative prices; but it is the relative price of real estate and goods rather than the relative price of leisure that is critical in the Casino Economy.

Now we arrive at the Casino Effect. Although RE and K_f may move together with respect to real wealth, their time path need not be (and has not been) linear. Rather, with respect to time the pattern would be exponential or

$$RE(t) = a_1 e^{k_1 W(t)} \qquad K_f(t) = a_2 e^{k_2 W(t)}, \qquad (4-13)$$

where the a's are positive integers and the k's are positive fractions. The k's, provisionally constant, are velocities at which wealth is trundled into its real estate and mortgage incarnations. The velocities, combined with the exponential nature of the function, give the Casino Effect.

Of course, as real estate values fall, the exponents will become negative. There is not a satisfactory way to model this sudden shift from asset appreciation to asset depreciation except to say that the initial state and conditions have changed. Indeed, the exponential pattern — up or down — did not characterize the era before the late 1960s. Events changed the initial state and conditions beginning at that time. First, income and wealth distributions became much more concentrated during the 1980s. Second, the Carter and Reagan administrations turned dramatically toward the deregulation of the financial industry. Third, the deposit insurance systems and the lender of last resort stance of the Fed — which had provided needed confidence to depositors after the Great Depression — now seemed to take the risk out of overexpansion by the financial industry.

Historically, speculative episodes have been preceded by rapid shifts of wealth toward smaller and smaller numbers. Why does this movement cause speculative bubbles? Why does T spin out of control and create larger and larger circles? One reason relates to ability to pay; the household needs wealth in excess of basic needs in order to "afford" to speculate. Moreover, such high-risk finance pays off during economic expansions, especially when there is a wealthier "greater fool" to bid assets still higher. Even generally cautious persons tend to jump onto the bandwagon. (No less a cynic than Thorstein Veblen took an uncharacteristic dive into the stock market during the 1920s but mercifully died a few months before the Great Crash.) Finally, in an environment of cutthroat competition in the financial industry, firms offer higher and higher interest rates to attract funds that in turn must be lent at still higher rates, requiring higher-risk loans. The compounding of the values of these assets and liabilities gives the exponential path.

We call such financial episodes "speculative bubbles" for their tendency to burst. Real estate values have slumped about 20 percent since their peaks in 1988. By historical standards this decline is huge. Just as sharp rises in real estate values relative to goods prices led the parade of high-yielding mortgages, CDs, and junk bonds, the decline in real estate values relative to modest inflation in goods prices has produced nonperforming loans nearly to the point of extinction of the S&L industry and to the point of grave threat to the banking industry. Even the insurance industry is threatened with a possible run, as it has about twice the share of junk-bond assets than was originally reported. Meanwhile, the prolonged recession beginning in July 1990 has led to sharp increases in bankruptcies throughout other industries as sales revenue growth has been insufficient to service heavy, existing debt. (Business failures per week have risen from 900 at the beginning of 1990 to more than 1700 by April 1991.) This contagion has spread to households, which also are filing record numbers of bankruptcies. The values of assets and liabilities in T indeed are connected in a nearly unbroken circle. The widening of the circle has now been reversed.

8. Conclusions

Every 40 to 50 years the policies of free enterprise's most devoted disciples bring American capitalism to its knees. The ideology renews itself as soon as the wounded generation has died or slid into a forgetful senility. Capitalism's survival—in newly directed and regulated form— speaks well of its strength. Each time it has survived the best efforts of its friends.

Properly measured, personal money *and* personal real savings soared during the 1980s. The main effect of supply-side "incentives" was to increase the disposable income of the highest-income families and in this way bolster personal savings. The other main source of personal savings is found in the speculative bubble in real estate. The explanation, however, is not Reaganometric but Keynesian.

We arrive at a dichotomy inexplicable in conventional thought: Real business saving and investment slumped. The dichotomy is explained by the Kaleckian-Keynesian tendencies within the economy. It takes rising sales from households having high average and marginal propensities to consume in order to motivate more investment, even as they provide internal funds to leverage debt that becomes *real* investment. During the 1980s retained earnings were damaged by income and wealth redistributions that shunted luxury spending toward foreign nations, by skyrocketing debt service costs, and by real investment's displacement by massive federal borrowing. Only when business is making real investments does personal saving become real saving.

With the slowdown in real net business investment, high levels of personal savings were diverted into the Casino Economy, creating speculative bubbles that have been exploding with an eerie regularity since October 1987. The American economy has shifted its focus from using money to produce goods to using money for speculative profits. Shifting tax policy to favor highest-income savers is part of the problem, not the solution. In fact, the use of public policy to encourage personal saving is based on mistaken notions regarding the true incentives for business investment.

For the first time since the Great Depression, the economy is in a downturn that has financial causes. Financial fragility has led to failing S&Ls, banks, and insurance companies. Thus far, the government has decided that it must rescue those financial institutions "too large to fail." However, the public is increasingly aware of their contingent liabilities in these bailouts. We know that the loans made by the U.S. Treasury will someday have to be paid. This awareness is coming at a time when state and local governments (having inherited the social welfare role partly abdicated by the Reagan administration) are raising taxes for mandated budget balancing. If taxpayers revolt against these continued bailouts, the failing institutions will become "too big to save."

The growing tax burden for the average household is coming at the worst of times. The 1990 recession is not an ordinary downturn. There is a danger that a rising tax burden and shrinking liquidity in an increasingly risky business environment could keep our economy in a troubled state for many years. That would be the most tragic legacy of Reaganomics. It made the rich so much richer that their speculative excesses have led to demands for their rescue. If we have so little compassion for the working poor, how can we find it in our hearts to bail out the bondholders?

Notes

1. Quoted by William Greider, "The Education of David Stockman," *Atlantic Monthly*, December 1981, p. 46. Stockman's confessions had been made to journalist-friend Greider.
2. Ibid., p. 47.
3. Fred Block, "Bad Data Drive Out Good: The Decline of Personal Savings Reexamined," *Journal of Post Keynesian Economics* 13, no. 1 (Fall 1990): 3–19. Robert Blecker also favors the use of the Federal Reserve's measure of net worth. See Robert Blecker, *Are Americans On a Consumption Binge?* (Washington, D.C.: Economic Policy Institute, 1990).
4. In this section I am following the lead—in spirit if not in detail—of Boulding (1950, pp. 243–302). Using a net worth approach, Boulding was able to integrate the income distribution into macroeconomic theory. Unfortunately, as he latter became aware, he made several errors. In this account I have attempted to correct those mistakes as well as introduce additional variables. Moreover, I express values in money rather than in real terms, whereas Boulding is using the traditional definitions of real saving and investment. In Boulding's update of his theory of distribution, he corrects his 1950 effort. See Kenneth Boulding, "Puzzles Over Distribution," *Challenge* (November/December 1985): 4–10.
5. Kenneth Boulding correctly disclosed this relationship even though he made some missteps along the way in Kenneth Boulding, *A Reconstruction of Economics* (New York: John Wiley, 1950), pp. 255–258.

6. There are other candidate equations, the most promising of which relate to the wave equation. Poisson developed a formula for the propagation of a wave with specified initial conditions that satisfied a second-order partial differential equation. A quite different method was used by Riemann in the course of his work on the propagation of sound waves of finite amplitude. Riemann considers a second-order linear differential equation that defines a curve and space. His method depends on finding a Riemann or characteristic function that satisfies an adjoint equation. The Reimann method is useful only for hyperbolic equations in two independent variables. Later the Helmholtz equation was used to represent all harmonic, acoustic, elastic, and electromagnetic waves. The work of Helmholtz was used by Kirchhoff to obtain another solution of the initial-value problem for the wave equation. These equations have since been generalized.

Commentary by Robert S. Chirinko
University of Chicago

Most policy discussions concerning saving focus on aggregates, and debates rage over the adequacy of national saving and the extent to which private saving is affected by public dissaving. The provocative chapter by Ray Canterbery encourages us to take a different approach, and suggests that a much more disaggregate focus is needed. Interactions between the income distribution and fiscal policies are highlighted, and these interactions bear critically on the ultimate success of public policies aimed at stimulating saving.

Canterbery is specifically concerned with the supply-side policies adopted by the Reagan administration, and his analysis proceeds in three steps. The chapter begins by identifying the intended macroeconomic effects of Reagan's economic program. The impact of the fiscal part of this program is noted with specific reference to its favorable effects for the upper segment of the income distribution. Coupled with the large amount of saving undertaken by the rich, this increase in income leads to Canterbery's Casino Effect—the tendency for those with substantial wealth to engage in speculation that forces asset values to spiral away from and then suddenly revert to their fundamental values. Although such speculative bubbles have been noted previously, what distinguishes the present analysis is linking their inevitable emergence to Reagan's fiscal policies. Canterbery's view of Reaganomics is largely negative, as the opening of the Casino has deleterious effects on the level of saving and the stability of the macroeconomy.

This creative piece brings together standard issues in public finance and current topics in macro/monetary economics (as well as Marxian analysis) in an insightful fashion. However, there are some serious difficulties in substantiating the existence and quantitative importance of these novel ideas. This comment follows in sequence the preceding three-point discussion—from supply-side policies to the income distribution to the Casino Effect and macroeconomic consequences. A Scotch verdict is reached, as the case against Reaganomics by way of the Casino Effect remains "not proven." This comment concludes by arguing that the saving rate is appropriately viewed as an intermediate policy target affected by a number of perplexing forces. The substantial complexities and prevailing uncertainties that make saving a challenging scholarly topic are precisely the reasons that make saving a poor intermediate target. From a policy perspective, the concern with the saving rate is largely misplaced, and policy discussions would be more informative if they focused on the market failures and unexploited opportunities amenable to policy actions.

1. Supply-Side Prescriptions and Reaganomics

The chapter begins with a list of the prominent precepts of supply-side economics—raise incentives to work, save, and invest with lower tax rates; reduce government expenditures; tighten monetary policy to control inflation; and remove those regulations that create unnecessary impediments. However, the discussion in the chapter does not provide an appropriate treatment of the Reagan economic program on two counts. First, some aspects of the program that had measurable effects on the income distribution reversed direction over Reagan's eight-year term: for example, business tax cuts, tax shelters, and restrictions on IRAs. Given these reversals, it is not at all clear that Reaganomics can be characterized as homogeneously as is done in the chapter. Second, insufficient distinction is made between the general supply-side prescriptions that became part of Reaganomics and the strident claims made by some prominent supply-siders, only some of whom were associated directly with the Reagan administration. Their sanguine conclusions concerning the self-financing nature of tax cuts and the rapid increase in economic growth should not affect the verdict one reaches concerning the Reagan economic program.[1]

A potentially important "free lunch" was being pursued by Reaganomics. It is well established that, in a large number of circumstances, government tax and regulatory policies *may* be distortionary and that removing these distortions can lead to an improved allocation of resources. This standard analysis is conducted with respect to markets that have adjusted to their long-run equilibrium, and hence the focus on Say's law with no distinction between supply and demand is quite appropriate in this context. Claims to the contrary notwithstanding, the theoretical foundations of

Reaganomics were quite sound, though it remains debatable whether the policy goals were attainable as an empirical proposition. Canterbery then correctly notes that this long-run focus may miss an important element, as movement to this new equilibrium may be interrupted by, among other impediments, the Casino Effect (more of that later). However, that the macroeconomy may be plagued by multiple equilibria and may get "stuck" in an inferior position is not to deny the possible welfare enhancements from removing allocative distortions.

The chapter contains a somewhat misleading suggestion that stimulating personal saving through tax incentives was a primary goal of the Reagan economic program. Two of the most prominent documents underlying Reaganomics — Martin Anderson's Policy Memorandum No. 1 dated August 1979 and the White House's *A Program of Economic Recovery* circulated in February 1981 — do not support this interpretation. Rather than focusing on the individual components of the program (including saving incentives), the latter document (pp. 2–3) emphasized that

> the ultimate importance of this program for sustained economic growth will arise not only from the positive effects of the individual components, important as they are. Rather, it will be the dramatic improvement in the underlying economic environment and outlook that will set a new and more positive direction to economic decisions throughout the economy.

According to this view, reducing the role of government was the primary means for improving the economic environment.

Any economic program would not want to rely too heavily on saving incentives for at least three good reasons. First, the response of saving to tax changes is ambiguous theoretically and usually rather modest empirically. Second, insofar as capital is sufficiently free to flow across national borders, increased domestic saving will have no direct impact on capital formation. Third, even if a substantial amount of new saving is forthcoming, the effect on growth is limited because a portion will flow into residential capital, the resulting impact on the nonresidential capital stock (which is approximately twice as large as GNP) is small, and capital plays only a small role in the Solow growth framework. This view of a limited role for capital is not meant to deny the possibility of stimulating growth due to other factors that fall outside of the standard framework, such as removing distortions that may impede efficient resource allocation or exploiting the substantial externalities that may exist in human and non-human capital formation.

COMMENTARY   179

2. Impact on the Distribution of Income

A key element in Canterbery's analysis is that Reaganomics led to a sharp redirection of resources to the rich and, because the marginal propensity to save by this group is quite high, there was the potential for substantial increases in the level of aggregate saving. Tables 4–1 and 4–2 present the changes over time of the distribution of effective tax rates and money income over the population, but the conclusion that these figures support the regressive tilt of the income distribution invites scrutiny.

For at least three reasons, focusing on personal tax rates or money income provides an incomplete assessment of fiscal policies. First, the effective tax rate calculations are sensitive to the assumption about the incidence of the corporate income tax. The results reported in table 4–1 are based on the assumption that the corporate tax is shifted to labor. More dramatic results are evident with the alternative assumption that the corporate tax is shifted to capital. For all but the top decile, changes between 1977–1988 are somewhat higher than reported in table 4–1.[2] However, for the top income group, the fall in tax rates is much larger than reported in the chapter; for the top 5 percent and 1 percent of the population, effective tax rates fell by −5.1 percent and −9.9 percent, respectively (in contrast to the −2.6 percent and −6.0 percent presented in table 4–1). Thus the preconditions for the Casino Effect may be even more substantial than reported by Canterbery.

Second, although much less studied than the incidence of taxation, the incidence of expenditures may be particularly important in assessing Reaganomics' effect on the distribution of resources, especially with changes in social security and welfare programs. These considerations would likely give a further regressive tilt to the Reagan fiscal policies.[3]

Third, even if the reported numbers are correctly adjusted for the effects of changes in tax and expenditure policies, difficulties remain because of the possibility of significant nonpolicy effects on the distribution of income. In the case of the 1980s, some suspect that other factors have been at work. Murphy and Welch (1989) found that the evolving pattern of international trade was an important contributor to movements in wage differentials, and Borjas, Freeman, and Katz (1991) concluded that the increased flow of less-skilled immigrants was also a contributing factor. Krueger (1991) reported that occupational wage growth and the return to education are both positively related to computer usage. However, consistent with Canterbery's argument, Bean and Symons (1989) reported that the income distributions for the United Kingdom and the

United States moved similarly during the 1980s and that these changes differed from those in the European OECD countries. Insofar as the economic policies pursued by Reagan and Thatcher were similar and the critical differentiating factor, this pattern provides some evidence that fiscal policies played an important role in widening the income distribution. This brief review of evidence is not meant to imply that the income distribution did not change in accord with Canterbery's hypothesis, but rather that much more work is needed before we can be comfortable with the conclusion that changes in the income distribution were linked to the economic policies of the 1980s.

3. The Casino Effect

The Casino Effect and the instability of the credit process are the most novel and important parts of the analysis, bringing together strands from the public finance, macro/monetary, and Marxian literatures. Financial fragility is an important topic in understanding economic fluctuations. The collapse of banks and the credit intermediation process in the 1930s were arguably the key factor in the severity and duration of the U.S. Great Depression. Much recent work in aggregate fluctuations focuses on the information problems that exist between borrowers and lenders and on the ways in which financial intermediaries solve these problems. Owing to the structure of their liabilities, intermediaries are both fragile and critical to the economic system, which thus becomes particularly susceptible to shocks.[4]

Canterbery relates these concerns to the analysis of Reagan's fiscal policies and argues persuasively that the increased concentration of wealth in the hands of the rich led to an increased demand for speculative financial assets. Real estate values and other assets of particular attraction to the rich thus depart sharply for some time from their fundamental values.[5] Speculative bubbles will not last, and ultimately asset values drop rapidly. These reevaluations will not be without consequence to the stability of the system. The important conclusion to be drawn from the Casino Effect is that the standard welfare analysis of fiscal policies will not suffice, and the interactions among the income distribution, financial system, and aggregate economy must be given serious consideration.

As with any good idea, Canterbery's Casino Effect raises a number of questions. Before considering them further, it should be noted that the preceding analysis of class distinctions, system instability, and wealth redistribution to the rich is very much in the spirit of Marx's analysis of capitalist crises. In discussing Say's law and the notion that commodities are always sold with the intention of immediately buying other commodities, Marx (1978, p. 446) noted:

> What a cozy description of bourgeois conditions! Ricardo even forgets that a person may *sell* in order to *pay*, and that these forced sales play a very significant role in the crises. The capitalist's immediate object in selling, is to turn his commodity, or rather his commodity capital, back into *money capital*, and thereby to *realize* his profit. Consumption ... is by no means the guiding motive in this process, although it is for the person who only sells *commodities* in order to transform them into means of subsistence. [*Emphasis in the original.*]

The Casino Effect brings back in a forceful way the role of the income distribution on aggregate activity and further reminds us of the value of the original Marxian analysis for understanding dynamic economic phenomenon.

Although the Casino Effect is persuasive theoretically, the question arises, as with a number of other issues in the chapter, whether it is plausible empirically. Three points need to be considered further. First, the chapter reports the substantial concentration of wealth and net financial assets in the top decile of the population. However, for the Casino Effect to be relevant, it is important to show that this distribution changed in an important way during the 1980s. Second, for whatever change exists, it is then important to know how much is needed to affect financial markets. If the top decile has increased its share of net financial assets by a given amount, how do we know that these funds have an appreciable influence on the real estate market? In the aggregate, this is a huge market. Can fiscally induced changes have a measurable impact? Is some portion of that market (e.g., second homes, a geographic region) the primary driver of the Casino Effect? Third, even if speculative bubbles exist, there is no necessary guarantee that they affect real economic activity. Such a link needs to be documented. When investigated with respect to business fixed investment, stock market bubbles do not appear to have substantial effects on real activity.[6]

At the beginning of the concluding section, there is a tantalizing suggestion that financial fragility is a recurring phenomenon in capitalist societies. Evidence from the historical record would be very welcome in support of this conjecture and its relation to changes in the income distribution. The experience of other countries in more recent times should also be informative, and the United Kingdom offers a particularly inviting comparison. My imprecise impression is that the fluctuations in U.K. real estate values might well confirm the presence of a Casino Effect.

4. Conclusion on Reaganomics and Thoughts on the Irrelevance of the Saving Rate

Evaluating the effects of Reaganomics on saving is a very difficult matter. As Canterbery rightly points out, the definition of saving provided by the National Income and Product Accounts is not adequate to the task in the face of fluctuating asset values.[7] However, some of these fluctuations reflect fundamental changes in the value of assets, while another, perhaps sizable, part is driven by the Casino Effect. Unfortunately, the chapter is not too helpful in quantifying these changes in asset values. Skinner (1990) has found that, when the gains from stocks and housing are included, the average household saving rate was only somewhat less than that prevailing in the 1970s. Insofar as some of these capital gains are merely speculative, the "real" saving rate has fallen in the 1980s. Of course, these results do not tell us what would have happened without changes in fiscal policy or other policy and nonpolicy stimuli, and hence reaching a final verdict on Reaganomics is very difficult.

As indicated by Canterbery and a number of others in this volume, understanding the measures and determinants of saving is a very difficult matter. My opinion is that these difficulties can and should be avoided because the concern with saving is largely misplaced.

Why should policy makers care about the level of saving? The extensive attention is presumably due to saving's role as an accurate proxy for the arguments that enter individual or aggregate welfare functions. Difficult issues in the measurement and interpretation of saving lead me to doubt the usefulness of this proxy. The justification for focusing on saving is because it serves an intermediate target for public policy. However, as Friedman (1977) emphasized in discussing monetary targets, a series is valuable as an intermediate target insofar as it reduces the uncertainty associated with observing the variables of ultimate interest. It is far from clear what informational advantages follow from focusing on saving instead of on the actual and sustainable levels of consumption and output.

Saving is of academic interest because it is at the core of a number of interesting aspects of economic behavior that are not fully understood. In surveying the saving literature, Kotlikoff (1989) lists eight principal determinants of saving: the theory of the consumption function, shape of the age–consumption profile, shape of the age–earnings profile, real interest rates, intergenerational transfers, uncertainty, demographics, and fiscal policy. The latter includes distortionary taxation, inter- and intragenerational redistributions, and government consumption. Understanding and quantifying the impact of these determinants result in fascinating scholarship. However, the substantial complexities and prevailing uncertainties that make saving a challenging, scholarly topic are precisely the reasons that make saving a poor intermediate target. Saving is buffeted by a number of perplexing forces and is thus very difficult to interpret. Rather than informing the policy process, the focus on saving adds additional noise; the saving rate should be abandoned as an intermediate target of policy.

Policy discussions would be much better guided if they focused on the market failures and unexploited opportunities amenable to policy actions. Social and private returns from investment in nonresidential fixed capital may diverge for a number of reasons: external economies arising from learning-by-doing and other spillovers, the partial public good nature of research and development and investment in other intangibles (especially education), information problems and the associated constraints in financial markets, and systematic cognitive biases and excessively myopic decisions. An issue much studied by public finance economists is the significant divergence between the pre-tax return to capital and the post-tax return to savers. As highlighted by Feldstein (1977), this wedge is largely a creation of the tax code and, insofar as the compensated price elasticity of saving is sizable, this divergence may seriously disrupt capital formation and lower welfare. The focus of scholarly research and policy discussions should be on quantifying the effects on consumption and output of these and other unexploited opportunities for aggressive policy action, not on the largely irrelevant saving proxy.

The recent fall in reported saving rates has received much attention and, as already noted, this decline should not necessarily raise concerns. Instead, although interpretations are difficult, this noisy statistic appears to be relaying good news. A recent study based on microdata by Bosworth, Burtless, and Sabelhaus (1991) found that saving rates had declined for all age groups during the 1980s. Given that the market failures previously noted have not changed markedly over this period, and probably would not have affected all age groups similarly if they had, the recent decline seems quite positive—for various reasons households now appear to believe there is less need to defer consumption. Contributing factors might be windfall gains contributing to wealth, public programs mitigating catastrophic losses, or private programs improving access to credit markets. Of course, given the complexity of the saving decision, many other factors may have played a role and, as emphasized already, it is far from clear that understanding these intricacies is of first-order importance for policy deliberations. Much more careful analysis is needed to establish that the declining saving rate in the 1980s is a cause for major concern.

This tentative conclusion is not meant to suggest that policy is optimal nor that market failures and unexploited opportunities should not be addressed by aggressive policy. Potentially serious impediments remain to efficient resource allocation, a manifestation of which may be too little saving. One frequently discussed remedy for eliminating the already mentioned tax wedge is a consumption tax, which, in a number of incarnations, is highly regressive.[8] State-of-the-art evaluations of this tax policy give no consideration to the interactions between the income distribution and macroeconomic stability. Canterbery's provocative chapter, as well as recent events in financial markets, highlights that such interactions may be important and should be considered in assessing tax policy.

Notes

1. See Feldstein (1986) for further discussion of the distinction between various types of supply-siders.

2. The source is the same as that used in table 4–1. See Feldstein (1988) for a discussion of additional caveats on these types of calculations concerning the treatment of corporate pension funds, the automatic effect of corporate tax changes on dividends and retentions, and differences between nominal and real capital income. In analyzing the 1986 Tax Act, he finds that considering business tax changes leads to a marked increase in the taxation of higher-income groups.

3. See Menchik (1991) for some interesting calculations of the distribution of federal expenditures. As noted there, the incidence of changes in social security may be ambiguous in a lifetime context because of the positive correlation between longevity and income.

4. See the survey by Gertler (1988) for references to this expanding literature and further discussion. Kindleberger (1978) and Minsky (1978) have also analyzed financial crises and aggregate fluctuations.

5. The time path of asset values is given by the exponential equations (4–13). A number of notable analyses — Malthus on population, Jevons on coal, and the Club of Rome on nonrenewable resources — have been based on similar ad hoc exponential relations, and experience with these models suggests caution. Deriving the paths of the speculative bubbles from a more formal analysis — perhaps along the lines of Samuelson's well-known multiplier/accelerator model — and identifying those situations where key parameters may imply complex roots and oscillating paths would be quite interesting. See Canterbery's note. 6 for some interesting suggestions.

6. See Chirinko and Schaller (1991) for a discussion of these studies and some econometric evidence.

7. For a further discussion of these measurement issues, see Eisner (1989), who argues that the appropriate definition of saving should reflect the change in a very broadly defined measure of wealth. Also, see the comments by Bradford, Eisner, and Scott in the September 1990 issue of the *Journal of Economic Literature*.

8. When the consumption tax is made less regressive, welfare gains are reduced by 25 percent to 40 percent (Ballard, Scholz, and Shoven, 1987, table 14.3).

References

Anderson, Martin. *Revolution: The Reagan Legacy*. Stanford: Hoover Institution Press, 1990.
Ballard, Charles L., and John Karl Scholz, and John B. Shoven. "The Value-Added Tax: A General Equilibrium Look at Its Efficiency and Incidence." In *The Effects of Taxation on Capital Accumulation*, edited by Martin Feldstein. Chicago: University of Chicago Press (for the NBER), 1987, pp. 445–480.
Bean, Charles, and James Symons. "Ten Years of Mrs. T." In *NBER Macroeconomics Annual 1989*, edited by Olivier J. Blanchard and Stanley Fischer. Cambridge, Mass.; MIT Press, 1989, pp. 13–60.
Borjas, George, Richard Freeman, and Lawrence Katz. "On the Labor Market Effects of Immigration and Trade." NBER Working Paper No. 3761 (1991).
Bosworth, Barry, Gary Burtless, and John Sabelhaus. "The Decline in Saving: Some Microeconomic Evidence." *Brookings Papers on Economic Activity* (1991:1): 183–241.
Chirinko, Robert S., and Huntley Schaller. "Bubbles, Fundamentals, and Investment: A New Multiple Equation Specification Testing Strategy." University of Chicago (December 1991).
Eisner, Robert. *The Total Incomes System of Accounts*. Chicago: University of Chicago Press, 1989.
Feldstein, Martin S. "Imputing Corporate Tax Liabilities to Individual Taxpayers." *National Tax Journal* 41 (March 1988): 37–60.
Feldstein, Martin S. "Supply-Side Economics: Old Truths and New Claims." *American Economic Review* 76 (May 1986): 26–30.
Feldstein, Martin S. "Does the United States Save Too Little?" *American Economic Review* 67 (February 1977): 116–121.
Friedman, Benjamin M. "The Inefficiency of Short-Run Monetary Targets for Monetary Policy." *Brookings Papers on Economic Activity* (1977:2): 293–335.
Gertler, Mark. "Financial Structure and Aggregate Economic Activity: An Overview." *Journal of Money, Credit and Banking* 20 (August 1988, Part 2): 559–588.
Kindleberger, Charles P. *Manias, Panics and Crashes: A History of Financial Crises*. New York: Basic Books, 1978.
Kotlikoff, Laurence J. *What Determines Savings?* Cambridge, Mass.: MIT Press, 1989.
Krueger, Alan B. "How Computers Have Changed the Wage Structure: Evidence from Microdata, 1984–89." Princeton University (August 1991).
Marx, Karl. *Theories of Surplus Value*. Reprinted in *The Marx-Engels Reader*, 2nd ed., edited by Robert C. Tucker. New York: W. W. Norton, 1978, pp. 443–465.
Menchik, Paul L. "The Distribution of Federal Expenditures." *National Tax Journal* 44 (September 1991): 269–276.

Minsky, Hyman P. *Stabilizing an Unstable Economy*. New Haven: Yale University Press, 1978.

Murphy, Kevin, and Finis Welch. "Wage Differentials in the 1980s: The Role of International Trade." University of Chicago (May 1989).

Skinner, Jonathan. "Precautionary Saving, Wealth Accumulation, and the Saving Downturn of the 1980s." *National Tax Journal* 43 (September 1990): 247–257.

The White House. *America's New Beginning: A Program for Economic Recovery*. Washington, D.C.: The White House, February 18, 1981.

Commentary by R. Jeffery Green
Indiana University

Ray Canterbery has written a provocative and interesting critique of macroeconomic policy in the 1980s. After identifying Reagan policy with supply-side economics, he analyzes the personal tax cuts contained in the Economic Recovery Tax Act of 1981. He finds that both the tax cuts and the resulting deficits produced only small benefits from increases in saving, investment, and output, and these benefits were outweighed by a sharp increase in the inequality of the distribution of income and wealth. Further, these changes, combined with financial deregulation, led to a speculative bubble that he terms the Casino Economy. The effects of the Reagan policies are important to understand because some of the economic problems that produced those policies are still with us as are the results of those policies. Canterbery has identified crucial problems, but some of his conclusions are as yet unproved and a few may be false. Unfortunately, the analysis of supply-side economics brings us face to face with some of the most difficult issues in empirical macroeconomics.

Supply-side economics means different things to different people. The term has been used to describe the economic agenda of the first Reagan administration. It has also been used to identify a body of policy prescriptions and even a basic approach to policy analysis much as the terms *monetarism* and *Keynesianism* were used earlier (Von Furstenberg and Green, 1986). Finally, supply-side economics has been identified with a set of macroeconomic principles capable of being tested.

One supply-side proposition is that a reduction in marginal personal tax rates would stimulate output and productivity. More extreme forms of this proposition, associated with Arthur Laffer, suggested that the increases in output and income would more than offset the effects of lower tax rates and so produce an increase in tax revenues in either nominal or real terms. Situations in which this proposition would hold are very unlikely, as can be seen from the following example.

Suppose tax revenues are proportional to total income as is approximately the case in the United States. Then, for a decrease in the tax rate to produce an increase in revenues, the elasticity of income with respect to the tax rate must exceed one, which is not likely. The Reagan tax cuts reduced the average tax rate by 11.9 percent from its peak in the third quarter of 1981 to its trough in the first quarter of 1984. At the same time, real income rose only 5.8 percent producing a decline of over 6 percent in real tax revenues. Nominal tax revenues did rise during this period, but to believe that the tax cut produced a rise in nominal tax revenues, one would have to believe that, in the absence of the tax cut, nominal income would have risen by less than 6.3 percent over a two and a half year period characterized by relatively high inflation rates. Not many would subscribe to that proposition. Tax revenues grew much less rapidly than expected after the tax cuts, and the federal deficit shot up from $78.9 billion in 1981 to $207.8 billion in 1983 and averaged in excess of $200 billion through 1986. Another hope of some supply-side economists was that the tax reductions would lead to spending reductions that would limit the deficit, even though that had not happened before (Von Furstenberg, Green, and Jeong, 1986). More than anything else the enormous deficits of the 1980s damaged the credibility of supply-side policies.

The fact that tax rate reductions do not necessarily lead to increases in tax revenues does not imply that such cuts are bad policy. Indeed, many economists who were not sympathetic to supply-side economics supported the Reagan tax plan as a method of improving macroeconomic performance. Both supply-siders and Keynesians expected an increase in income and employment but for different reasons. Supply-siders believed that the tax decrease would stimulate output and productivity by raising the price of leisure relative to work. Those from a more Keynesian tradition believed that the tax cut would stimulate demand and raise output. The difference in these two explanations, apart from one focusing on a relative price effect and the other on an income effect, is that supply-siders believed the tax cut would increase potential GNP whereas Keynesians believed the tax cut would increase capacity utilization but not potential GNP.

The timing of the tax reductions was almost perfect. The economy was in a recession in 1981 when the first reductions took place and did not start to grow until late 1982. The first tax rate cuts occurred in 1981 and the last in 1983. Thus the stimulus came at a time of considerable slack in the economy and helped moderate the length and severity of the downturn. Was the stimulus due to a supply-side relative price effect or a Keynesian income effect? The final word on that question is not in, but there were no detectable changes in labor force participation rates or productivity growth that one would expect from a relative price effect. However, the recovery was characterized by declining inflation rates, that might imply that aggregate supply was growing more rapidly. The difficulty is that other factors affect inflation, including energy price inflation, which was declining, and the exchange rate, which was appreciating. All this suggests that we do not yet know the effect of the tax cuts on the rate of growth of potential GNP, so that there certainly was an income effect and there may or may not have been a relative price effect.

Did the Reagan tax cuts increase saving? Yes, the stimulus to demand led to increases in aggregate income and saving. Beyond that, Canterbery argues that the tax cuts increased income inequality so that the highest income groups received the largest increases in income. Then, because higher income households have higher average propensities to save, the change in the distribution of income leads to an increase in the overall saving rate.

While this is a plausible theoretical proposition, and has received some empirical support (Menchik and David, 1983), Canterbery's attempt to measure changes in the marginal propensity to save (MPS) by income level runs into problems. Sufficient details are not given to reproduce his results, but the measures reported in his chapter are extremely volatile across income groups and years. The lowest income group has by far the highest MPS, though this might reflect a data problem. For the other income groups, there are several cases in which the MPS doubles or is cut in half in just a year or two. If one ignores the lowest two income groups, representing incomes less than $10,000, and averages the MPSs for each income group across years, the resulting average MPSs range between 0.33 and 0.40, with four of the five income groups averaging either 0.39 or 0.40. None of this suggests that the MPs is significantly higher at higher levels of income, and consequently there is no indication that the Reagan tax cuts, even if they altered the distribution of income, increased the overall saving rate.

There is another problem with the estimated MPSs for low-income groups. If saving is measured as income minus consumption, and if income is limited to money income, then saving may be understated. This results from nonmoney transfers, such as food stamps, rent subsidies, and medicaid, that would raise consumption without raising money income. A low-income household might be able to save some of its money income and still have total consumption exceed its money income. This also partly explains why the average propensity to save for low-income groups is such a large negative number.

Canterbery argues that an appropriate way to measure real saving is by measuring real investment and then notes that the share of real net investment in NNP dropped during the 1980s, implying Reaganomics did not stimulate savings. However, as Canterbery notes, the share of gross investment in GNP did not fall. The major feature of investment spending in the 1980s was investment in computers and other information processing equipment. The rapid rate of technological change in this sector has made it difficult to calculate depreciation rates and price indexes, and so which ratio is the better indicator of the investment share in the 1980s is an open question.

Shifting the focus from saving to investment introduces a number of other complications. The Reagan tax cuts had large investment incentives in the form of accelerated depreciation, which not only lowered the cost of new investment but may have encouraged the sale of existing capital (Kotlikoff and Auerbach, 1989). Thus disentangling the effects of tax changes on saving from those on investment is a difficult business.

Equating changes in personal and business saving to changes in investment is appropriate only in a closed economy context. Over extended periods of time this was a reasonable approximation (Kotlikoff, 1984), but in 1980s financing domestic investment through capital inflows became important. The current account moved from a small surplus in 1981 to deficit of over $160 billion in 1986. Here again most economists will give the Reagan tax cuts a central role in creating the deficit, but supply-siders and Keynesians differ in the mechanism. Keynesians prefer to focus on the increase in demand stemming from the tax cuts, which, combined with a restrictive monetary policy, led to an increase both in imports and interest rates, leading to an appreciation of the dollar and a fall in exports. The combination of rising imports and falling exports caused the trade balance and the current account deficit to rise dramatically.

An alternate explanation, more in tune with supply-side principles, centers on the effects of the tax cuts on productivity. By raising productivity and potential output, the marginal product of capital was increased, which led to a large inflow of foreign investment and an appreciation of the dollar. The appreciation of the dollar produced the rise in imports and decline in exports that is reflected in the large current account deficit.

Which explanation is more accurate again turns on the size of income and relative price — that is, exchange rate, effects — and as yet a definitive answer is not available. Likewise, it is not certain whether it was rising domestic interest rates coming from expanding demand and tight monetary policy that produced the dollar appreciation of the early 1980s or whether it was improved capital productivity. My guess is that any increases in productivity flowing from the tax cuts were small, but given the problems of both measuring productivity change and tracing the causes of changes in productivity growth, the question is still open.

The reason Keynesians tend to concentrate on the income effects of policy changes whereas supply-siders tend to focus on the relative price effects of policy is, of course, because they are using different models. Keynesians are using disequilibrium models in which income effects dominate, and supply-siders usually use equilibrium models in which relative price effects dominate. That means that in at least one sense the two groups are asking different questions. Keynesians are looking at the short-term effects of policy on the economy as it moves toward equilibrium, while supply-siders are really looking at the characteristics of an eventual equilibrium. The situation is confused when extreme supply-siders assume that long-run equilibrium effects will show up almost immediately.

Given Canterbery's results and the previous commentary, what are we to make of Reaganomics after all? The strongest evidence is that the Reagan tax cuts helped saving, income, and employment grow in the early 1980s, most likely through stimulating aggregate demand. The evidence is also strong that the tax cuts led to an appreciation of the dollar, although whether through productivity effects or monetary effects is less certain. Canterbery's evidence that the tax cuts increased the inequality of income is persuasive, but it is not clear that this had a large effect on savings. Whether the investment incentives in the original 1981 ERTA tax act had a large impact is not certain. Finally, whether the relative price effects counted on by supply-siders materialized—that is, whether reductions in marginal tax rates increased labor and capital productivity—remains unproved.

Canterbery's other main conclusion, besides the tax effects on income inequality of the Reagan tax cuts, is that Reaganomics led to the speculative excesses of the late 1980s that he calls the Casino Economy. I doubt it. The two main ingredients that produced the financial excesses of the 1980s were financial deregulation and the existence of deposit insurance. Neither of these was a product of the Reagan administration. A case can be made that an administration more sympathetic to the need for some regulation would have detected the emerging problems earlier and reduced excesses and the costs generated by them, but there were few, if any, voices who predicted at the time of financial deregulation late in the Carter administration that the S&L industry would evolve as it did.

Macroeconomic policy analysis is always difficult. Analyzing Reaganomics is particularly difficult because the policies were complex and because the economy was simultaneously being buffeted by other factors such as major monetary policy changes, energy price changes, and financial deregulation. The fact that we were operating in a world of floating exchange rates also added difficulties. Deciding whether increases in savings or the appreciation of the dollar were more the result of income effects or relative price effects is even more difficult. Canterbery has added to the debate surrounding Reaganomics by drawing attention to the effects of tax changes on income distribution, but it will be a long while before we fully understand the impacts of the Reagan initiatives of the early 1980s.

References

Kotlikoff, Laurence J. "Taxation and Savings: A Neoclassical Perspective." *Journal of Economic Literature* 22 (1984): 1576–1629.

Kotlikoff, Laurence J., and Alan J. Auerbach. "Investment Versus Savings Incentives: The Size of the Bang for the Buck and the Potential for Self-Financing Business Tax Cuts." In *What Determines Savings?* edited by L. J. Kotlikoff. Cambridge, Mass.: MIT Press, 1989.

Menchik, Paul L., and Martin David. "Income Distribution, Lifetime Savings, and Bequests." *American Economic Review* 73, no. 4 (1983): 672–690.

Von Furstenberg, George M. and R. Jeffery Green. "Supply-Side Modeling from Bits and Pieces." *American Economic Review* 76, no. 2 (1986): 37–42.

Von Furstenberg, George M., R. Jeffery Green, and Jin-Ho Jeong. "Tax and Spend, or Spend and Tax?" *The Review of Economics and Statistics* 68, no. 2 (1986): 179–188.

5 SAVING AND DISTRIBUTION

Gian S. Sahota
Vanderbilt University

Until the 1930s parsimony was considered a virtue. In the standard Keynesian system, saving became a socially undesirable activity in industrial countries. In recent years saving has, once again, become a highly desirable national objective. Notwithstanding these ups and downs in attitudes toward saving, the theory of saving remains one of the less-developed areas in economics.[1] Saving's relationship with the distribution of income and wealth is even more hazy. The main reason for the absence of a well-developed theory of saving is the intertemporal nature of multiple, interrelated choices involved for saving and the difficulty in finding the right kinds of data for empirical tests.[2] The problems in the development of a dependable relationship between saving and distribution are created, in addition, by a parallel lack of a coherent general theory of personal distribution of income (Sahota, 1978; Sahota and Rocca, 1985) and a relative inattention to this topic among economists.

With a view to gleaning from the existing literature the threads of the relationship between saving and distribution, the chapter first presents a brief annotated review of the main *theories of saving* to see whether any consensus is emerging from the recently enkindled debate on competing theories (section 1). Section 2 then annotates the *theories of distribution*. From the two short annotations, an attempt is made to identify possible *interrelationships between the two concepts*. The ramifications of the behavioral relations are such that the treatment will not be complete without a discussion of the *impacts of policies and institutions* on saving and distribution. Those aspects of the topic are surveyed in a relatively long discussion (section 3). Conclusions round out the exposition (section 4).

1. Main Theories of Saving

Treating saving as a dual of consumption, two postwar debates may be distinguished: the early postwar debate between permanent and current-income hypotheses of consumption and the more recent debate between the life cycle and bequest hypotheses of saving. We will discuss the latter debate first.

1.1. Recent Debate: Focus on Intertemporal Theories of Saving

The Bequest Motive of Saving. Two versions of the bequest model can be distinguished, the first of which involves an altruistic motive toward children. Among its different versions, the following may be mentioned: (1) Consumers derive utility from their consumption and from the size of bequest (Abel, 1984; Fischer, 1973; Menchik, 1979; Drazen, 1978; Sheshinski and Weis, 1981; and others). (2) They derive utility from their consumption and the utility of their heirs (Barro, 1974; Becker and Tomes, 1979; Drazen, 1978). (3) They derive utility from their consumption and the utility of their parents (Buiter, 1979; Carmichael, 1982). (4) Consumers derive utility from their own consumption and the utility of their parents and heirs; that is, the model recognizes two-sided altruism (Kimball, 1987; Weil, 1987; Abel, 1987; Burbidge, 1983, 1984; Buiter and Carmichael, 1984). The last mentioned model determines saving whereby individuals earn a wage income, receive income from property, receive bequests from parents, receive gifts from their heirs, desire to leave bequests to their heirs, and provide gifts to their parents.

Insofar as saving magnitudes are concerned (i.e., abstracting from distribution effects), the bequest motive leads each generation to desire to augment its inheritance for bequest. As such, in a stationary economy, ordinarily savings are not expected to decline. Growth of incomes and population will augment saving. The negative bequest motive — for example, net gift to parents — has the opposite effect. As such, the implications for saving are not necessarily identical in the different versions just stated. We shall return to these implications.

The second type of bequest model involves a nonaltruistic motive toward children. Among its variants may be mentioned (1) the model in which parents use the prospect of their bequests to induce their children to behave in ways desirable to the parents (Bernheim, Shleifer, and Summers, 1985, and others) and (2) the model in which parents use the prospect of their bequests as an implicit contract in exchange for their care in old age by their children, creating a kind of within-family private annuity (Kotlikoff and Spivak, 1981; Kotlikoff, Shoven, and Spivak, 1989; Davies, 1981; Eckstein, Eichenbaum, and Peled, 1983; Hubbard, 1984; Abel, 1985; and others).

In this model, bequests can be explained within the framework of the life cycle hypothesis (see the next section). Savings will be lower and national wealth smaller under the nonaltruistic motive than under altruistic motive because of the quid pro quo element between parents and progeny. To a large extent, social security, pension schemes, and similar annuity insurances have replaced implicit family annuities through nonaltruistic bequests.

Life Cycle Hypothesis (LCH) of Saving. The core of the LCH is that households desire to achieve a pattern of lifetime consumption that is typically different from lifetime earnings. As a guide to interpreting saving behavior, the hypothesis has been a landmark. But as a measure of the relative importance of the savings of living persons and inheritance, the results remain controversial. When the hypothesis was first proposed by its authors (Modigliani, 1949; Modigliani and Brumberg, 1954; Modigliani and Ando, 1957; Ando and Modigliani, 1963; Ando and Kennickell, 1987), the absence of bequests was "for convenience only," by way of formulating "a strong simple special case from which powerful conclusions would follow" (Solow, 1987).

More recently, however, the authors of this concept in particular and some other researchers as well have tended to defend the hypothesis on the premise that almost all saving was hump-shaped and bequests were insignificant. The empirical findings by the advocates of the LCH are often referred to as the 80−20 law, according to which approximately 80 percent of U.S. wealth comes from the savings of living persons and only 20 percent from inheritance. The law has been turned upside down in recent studies, to the ratio of 20−80 (Kotlikoff and Summers, 1978, 1981, 1988). Support for the latter finding comes from a number of studies by Kotlikoff and co-authors as well as several others (e.g., Auerbach and Kotlikoff, 1985; Atkinson, 1971; Oulton, 1976). When investment in human capital of children is defined as bequest, the weight of inheritance goes up substantially (Becker and Tomes, 1979; Sahota and Rocca, 1985; Tinbergen, 1975).

Many studies based on cross-sectional data have found that wealth increases with age even among retirees (Projector, 1968; Mirer, 1979; Blinder, Gordon, and Wise, 1983; Menchik and David, 1983). Additionally, the elderly hold about 35 percent of the net property and financial wealth of households (Hurd, 1990). The results obtained from panel data (more appropriate for validating the theory), however, suggest that the elderly gradually decumulate wealth, thus tending to support the LCH (Hurd, 1990). The bequest motive is there, but much of bequest takes place in the form of human capital formation in the early life of the younger generation (Sahota and Rocca, 1985).

The LCH remains as controversial today as it was a decade ago when this author published a survey of the theories of the distribution of personal income (Sahota, 1978), the main reason being the lack of appropriate data to estimate the parameters more precisely. Further research is in order.

The Precautionary Motive for Saving. Containing elements from both the bequest and the life cycle hypotheses as well as being a distinct hypothesis in itself is the precautionary motive for saving, due to the uncertainty of life span, health, unemployment, natural disasters, and the like, resulting in unintended or unplanned bequests (Yaari, 1965; Fischer, 1973; Barro and Friedman, 1977; Levhari and Mirman, 1977; Kotlikoff and Spivak, 1981; Abel, 1985; Solow, 1987; Hurd, 1990; Kessler and Masson, 1986; Lydall, 1955; and others).

There is little disagreement on the existence of precautionary saving and accidental bequests due to uncertainty. The differences concern the magnitudes of saving resulting from this motive. Thus Modigliani and his associates estimate that a large part of bequests is due to the precautionary motive (see, e.g., Modigliani, 1988, 1989; Ando and Modigliani, 1963). Even Kotlikoff and his co-authors, who otherwise turn Modigliani's 80–20 law on its head to the 20–80 law of inheritance find precautionary saving tremendously important (see Kotlikoff, 1989, chs. 4, 5, and 6, the summary on p. 28, and the studies by Davies, 1981; Barsky et al., 1987; and Zeldes, 1986). On the other hand, wealthy families, for whom saving for the rainy day hardly matters, do most of society's saving and make bequests (Atkinson, 1971, 1980, 1981; Oulton, 1976). More research is in order on this issue also.[3]

1.2. Early Postwar Debate: Intragenerational Theories

Saving Theory as a Dual of the Permanent Income Hypothesis (PIH) of Consumption (Friedman, 1957). Consumption is related to permanent income, and saving is a residual factor and thus is closely related to transitory income. In the PIH, long-run $e_s = 1$ and $de_s/dy = 0$, where e_s is the income (y) elasticity of saving.

Several scholars, for instance Ferber (1973) and Barro (1978), treat the LCH and the PIH as one class. Both hypotheses treat income in two components, permanent and transitory, in which the income stream may have little linear relationship with the consumption stream. However, permanent income calculated from the mean of recent past (say five years') incomes or generated by applying geometrically declining weights to distant incomes fits quite well to the consumption data. Also, the hypothesis has little problem with bequests. In the LCH, savings vary with age, whereas the PIH is more general. Rather its rival is the current income hypothesis of consumption.

Current Income Hypothesis of Saving. Two versions of this hypothesis may be distinguished. The first is the current or absolute income hypothesis of Keynes (1936), whereby long-run $e_s > 1$ and long-run $de_s/dy < 1$. In the Keynesian or the Cambridge school model, the marginal propensity to consume out of earnings is close to unity and that out of wealth approaches zero. This hypothesis has critical implications for saving and fiscal policy. A vast literature exists on the tests of the rival theories. The Keynesian theory scarcely squared with facts. For instance, aggregate average propensity to consume in the United States has remained almost constant since 1870 (Goldsmith, 1955; Kuznets, 1955). Keynesians, however, explain that golden ratio by adding the influence of wealth to that of income (Tobin, 1951, 1967). On the whole, the permanent income hypothesis has withstood empirical tests robustly and, as already seen, is also consistent with the LCH.

The second kind of current income hypothesis is the relative income hypothesis. According to this hypothesis, households are concerned with community consumption standards and their savings therefore depend essentially on relative (rather than absolute) income, income relative to some prior level (as tested in time series data) and to that of the community (as tested in cross-sectional data) (Duesenbery, 1949; Modigliani, 1949). Thus people tend to emulate their neighbors. Once a higher level of consumption is attained, people become habituated to it and seek to maintain it even when incomes go down. Therefore, saving rate is an increasing function of one's position in the reference group. In technical language, the saving rate depends on the ratio of current income to the earlier peak income (or peak consumption). Besides the empirical evidence for the dependence of savings in general on relative incomes, support has also been found for the dependence of bequests on relative incomes (see Modigliani, 1986; Menchik and David, 1983; David and Menchik, 1985).

The reader might be struck by the similarity of the relative-income consumption curve to the Keynesian absolute income consumption curve and the Friedmanian permanent income consumption curve, when the horizontal axis is appropriately relabelled! Some argue, however, that the relative income hypothesis does not consider the ceteris paribus factors, as Tobin (1967) has shown by introducing the assets variable, which can explain the constancy of the saving ratio in the United States as due to offsetting of the positive absolute income effect by the negative wealth effect on saving over time.

2. Income Distribution Theories

About half a dozen theories may be distinguished for both functional income distribution and personal income distribution. The former have been surveyed by Brown (1968), Howard (1979), and Asimakopulos (1987), among others, and are fairly well documented.[4] Sahota (1978) conducted a comprehensive survey of the latter. Both sets of theories will be briefly annotated next. It must be understood at the outset, however, that each theory may play an important role at a particular stage of development and in some process of adjustment. All theories may be at work together at any time. The question is which theory predominates.

2.1. Functional Income Distribution Theories

The Bargaining Theory. According to the bargaining theory, factor incomes depend not on marginal products but on the bargaining power of interest groups, such as trade unions and lobbies. Bargaining power does differentiate between employers and employees, at least in the short run and especially in determining working conditions, as does the political clout of parties. Whether bargaining power is a predominant factor in determining functional shares in the long run remains very doubtful. Most empirical tests have not supported this hypothesis.

The Residual Element Theory. Classical economists regarded income of factor capital as the residual after payment to workers at subsistence wage, determined in Malthus's analysis by population pressures and in Marx's analysis by the reserve army of unemployeds. Post-Keynesian theories determine investment exogenously. Profits follow from the widow's cruse theory (see the Cambridge school theory). Therefore, nonlabor income or profit is determined endogenously by the exogenously determined capital accumulation. Consequently, the wage share is residual.

Neo-Ricardians, although following the classical residual concept, often tend to reverse the causes of wage and profit rates of the classical theory. In the tradition of Sraffa's *Production of Commodities by Means of Commodities* (1960), the notion of a subsistence wage is abandoned. One of the distributive variables, usually the profit rate, is assumed to be exogenously determined, either by the requirements of full employment (Pasinetti, 1962) or by reference to a causal relationship between the rates of profit and interest, and the wage is determined residually as an endogenous variable (Roncaglia, 1978).

Most economists would agree that the time of this theory has passed.

Monopolistic Pricing Theory. Another theory of functional shares is based on the pricing policies of big firms. The higher is the nonwage share, the higher is the degree of monopoly (or the lower is the elasticity of demand) (Kalecki, 1954). To a limit, the theory makes sense and is consistent with the one-time popular Galbraithian theme. But because this theory concerns the monopolistic firm, it cannot explain aggregate factor shares.

Even at the firm level, the evidence is conflicting. In recent years, some tests of this theory have come from studies of the wealthiest households of America. Most of these households rule over large enterprises, which can wield varying degrees of monopolistic power but which can also be highly competitive. For instance, Comanor and Smiley (1975) find that monopoly has increased the share of household wealth held by the wealthiest American families by about 40 percent.

A study based on relatively improved data on the Forbes 400 wealthiest individuals for 1986 has come out with opposite findings. According to that study, large fortunes have been made essentially in competitively rather than monopolistically structured industries in the Schumpeterian environment (Blitz and Siegfried, 1990).

Overall, then, the basis of this theory as an explanation of factor shares seems to be rather weak.

The Cambridge School Theory. Traceable to Keynes (1930), the theory is interchangeably called the post-Keynesian theory or the widow's cruse theory (Kaldor, 1956; Pasinetti, 1962). According to this theory, savings are attached to sources of income (Kaldor, 1956) or classes of income groups (actually only capitalists) (Pasinetti, 1974) or are proportional to profits (Kalecki, 1954). At best only a paltry proportion of wages are saved. Wage and profit shares are governed by the requirement that income and profit will grow enough so that saving will equal entrepreneurial investment done independently of saving. Widow's cruse remains always undepleted. Hence, inequalities of income continue growing, checked, however, by various demographic, production, and market forces built into the capitalist system and regressed toward the mean as influenced by the corresponding regression toward the mean of abilities.

Several of the assumptions and conclusions of this theory, however, have not been sustained by empirical tests. For instance, little evidence has been found for the causal flow from investment to saving (Keynesianism) to refute the neoclassical case of the causal flow from saving (supply) to investment (demand). It remains true, however, that the saving rates earned by high-income families are substantially higher than those realized by laboring classes, even when education and similar expenditures are treated as a form of saving. The theory remains a strong competitor to the neoclassical theory, which claims predominance.

Factor Pricing (neoclassical) Theory of Distribution. The neoclassical theory of factor pricing is derived from the supplies and demands for each factor. A standard exposition of this theory may be read in Friedman (1962). In the competitive long-period equilibrium, there is no residual. Profits are zero. Entrepreneurs earn on the same footing as workers. When the allocation of factors can be varied freely, the demands for them can be derived from their marginal products. If the production function is homogeneous of degree one, all product is exhausted by payments to factors according to their marginal products. Individuals optimize, prices are flexible, and markets clear. In the overall Walrasian system, if $n-1$ markets are in equilibrium, the nth market will be also. By contrast, in the Keynesian theory an equality of $n-1$ aggregates does not necessarily imply that demand and supply are equal in the (nth) labor market. In the Keynesian system, prices and wages are inflexible, and equilibrium at the aggregate level—for example, that of saving and investment—does not depend on micro optimization.

In short, in the neoclassical theory, functional distribution is derived from the optimization actions of individual decision makers. Factor incomes are determined in the same process as factor prices. The theory is elegant and takes full account of technological change and growth. It fits reasonably well with historical data. Nevertheless, strong objections question the assumption of competitive equilibrium, the measurement of capital, the nature of the production function, the microeconomic foundation of the theory, the optimization behavior, and indeed the entire neoclassical framework. But the theory remains all-powerful.

2.2. Personal Income Distribution Theories

The following seven theories of personal income distribution were identified in this author's survey article a dozen years ago (Sahota, 1978) and will be briefly annotated but not critically examined here:

1. The ability theory
2. The stochastic theory
3. The inheritance theory
4. The individual choice theory
5. The human capital theory, which includes the theories of educational inequalities
6. The life cycle theory
7. Public income distribution theories

Major ideological contestants for dominance are the inheritance school and the human capital school. The life cycle school is a competitor mainly of the inheritance school and on theoretical grounds only. It coexists with the human capital theory. Since Sahota's 1978 survey article two developments have occurred in distribution theories: First, significant reconciliation has occurred between the two dominant theories of distribution: the human capital theory and the inheritance theory (see Sahota and Rocca, 1980, 1985). The main factors underlying reconciliation are the recognition of inheritance (albeit mainly, though not merely, the inheritance of human capital) by human capitalists (a landmark study being that by Becker and Tomes, 1979) and the acknowledgment of the role of education (acquired, as distinguished from inherited, human capital) by the adherents of the inheritance school.[5] But the reconciliation does not seem to have dawned on the profession as yet. Second, with that controversy having waned, the research interest in the 1980s seems to have shifted to verifying the validity of life cycle versus inheritance theories. As discussed in the preceding section, however, the focus is more on the profiles and magnitudes of saving and wealth than on distributional consequences. On this topic, the standoff continues.

Of the remaining theories, the individual choice theory has all but been subsumed by the human capital theory. Stochastic or luck elements are recognized by all the three schools.[6] While the role of ability is recognized by all the three schools, there is a tendency to minimize its importance. In the human capital studies, the influence of basic ability works not directly on income but indirectly through acquired human capital. The partisans of the inheritance school emphasize material assets more than abilities. The latter are believed to be normally distributed. They are also believed to be subject to a regression toward the mean, prevented only by genetic luck. Regarding public income distribution (which falls in the policy parlance and to which we will return), the steady decline in inequalities over a century until the mid-1940s, a phenomenon heralded by Kuznets (1955) as the "incomes revolution," seems to have come to an end, as no change was witnessed after that until the early 1970s (Schultz, 1975; Reynolds and Smolensky, 1978; Thurow, 1980).[7] A reverse trend is believed to have started, however, with the Reaganomic policies of the 1980s.

Accordingly, for identifying a possible interrelationship between saving and distribution, the next section will concentrate on three theories of personal income distribution: the human capital theory, the inheritance theory, and the life cycle theory.

3. Relationship Between Saving and Income Distribution and the Impact of Policies

For studying the relationship between saving and distribution and the effect of policies, this discussion will focus mainly on those theories considered to be dominant.

Table 5–1 gives a combination of saving and distribution theories. The relevant cells to study are those marked by X. The remaining cells represent, more or less, conforming pairs of theories and have noncontroversial interrelationships—for instance, the life cycle theory of saving versus the life cycle theory of distribution and the bequest theory of saving versus the inheritance theory of distribution. The precautionary theory of saving is consistent with all four theories of distribution in the array, as is the stochastic or luck theory of distribution consistent with all four theories of saving. Therefore, the discussion will turn to rival theories.

Table 5-1. Combinations of Saving Theories and Distribution Theories

Distribution Theory	Saving Theory			
	1 Permanent Income Theory	*2* Bequest Theory	*3* Life Cycle Theory	*4* Precautionary Motive Theory
Human capital theory		X		
Inheritance theory	X		X	
Life cycle theory		X		
Stochastic theory				

A bit later, the effects of three major policies—taxes (income, lump sum), public debt, and social security—will be analyzed.

3.1. Rival Theories of Saving and Distribution

In theory, bequests and similar asset transfers from parents to heirs can buttress, mitigate, or neutrally affect inequalities, as is brought out by the studies collected by Kessler and Masson (1986). However, most results are sensitive to assumptions about various ingredients of the models. In general, bequests reinforce inequalities, according to the inheritance school, and lessen inequalities, according to the human capital school. An elaboration follows.

The Inheritance School and Saving and Distribution. To cite from a representative study of the inheritance school, insofar as material wealth is concerned, "the greater ability of the rich to save a high proportion of their income and to obtain a high yield on what property they do save ... cause great inequalities in capital accumulation (and incomes)." Intergenerationally, there is "a strong tendency in society for good or bad fortune to be handed on to the next generation in associated parcels of genes, income, property and social contacts" (Meade, 1976, pp. 175–176). According to Thurow (1975), Blinder (1974, 1976), and several other scholars, the elasticity of bequests with respect to lifetime resources is greater than unity (bequests are a luxury good). In other studies, this elasticity is high but less than unity: approximately 0.7 in the United States and in the United Kingdom (see, e.g., Kotlikoff, 1989, p. 15;

Harbury, 1962; Menchik, 1979; Wolfson, 1980; Behrman and Taubman, 1990; and Kotlikoff, 1989).[8] According to Thurow (1975), most fortunes are made almost instantly by random walk in the context of a prevailing disequilibrium in real capital markets and equilibrium in financial markets. Those instant wealths, which are capitalized, then tend to grow exponentially. From an analysis of the Forbes 400 wealthiest households of America for 1982, Canterbery and Nosari (1985) find support for Canterbery's vita theory of inequalities where wealth inheritance plays the central role and where wealth once created is largely preserved à la Thurow (Canterbery, 1979). However, using the same data source for a more recent year when the Forbes 400 figures are supposedly improved in quality, Blitz and Siegfried (1990) find opposite results.

The observed high proportions of self-made fortunes in America are not matched anywhere else in the world, as documented in the survey article of Sahota (1978). In the United Kingdom, for instance, the mobility among rich families is about half that in the United States. The evidence about the relative magnitudes of self-made fortunes and inherited fortunes thus remains rather inconclusive. In general, large bequests are confined mainly to wealthy families, who augment their saving even during retirement. The bequests of middle-class families, if any, consist mainly of houses and durable goods (whose lives in general are not longer than those of individuals), and the poor may leave zero or even negative bequests (negative in the form of passing on a poverty culture to their children) (Johnson, 1965).

The Human Capital School and Saving and Distribution. The studies by Becker (1974), Becker and Tomes (1976, 1979), and Ghez and Becker (1975) suggest that bequests atenuate inequalities. By making unequal bequests of material assets to counterbalance unequal endowments, parents try to attain both efficiency and equity among their children. Unequal bequests of material wealth in that sense are equalizing among siblings as well as among families.[9] Another reason for the equalizing force of bequests is their dampening of the stochastic shocks to income, through sharing of luck across the generations of a family (Stiglitz, 1978, Atkinson, 1980; Loannides, 1983; Davies and Kuhn, 1986).

There is no dearth of studies that point out perverse possibilities of bequests (see several papers in Kessler and Masson, 1986; Stiglitz, 1978). Surprising though it may appear, a number of studies find that bequests may be equalizing on the whole.

This finding is contested by several other writers, for instance Menchik (1979, 1980a, 1988) and Menchik and David (1983), who produce substantive evidence to show that equal sharing of transfers even if heirs are unequal is the rule.[10] Equal division of bequests among heirs reduces inequalities (Wolfson, 1980). Furthermore, as wealth distribution is highly skewed and earnings are correlated across generations (Taubman, 1978), even when the Becker model may apply, bequests will still be disequalizing (Menchik, 1979). Inequalities may be widened under several other motives of bequests. For instance, the promise of bequest to children in exchange for support in old age (Kotlikoff and Spivak, 1981) will be disequalizing if heirs exhibit declining absolute risk aversion, as the child with higher earnings is likely to provide more care and receive larger bequests (Kessler and Masson, 1986). The model of the use of prospective bequest as a carrot to manipulate the behavior of heirs (Thurow, 1975; Becker, 1981) implies unequal bequests where siblings are not alike in all respects (Bernheim, Shleifer, and Summers, 1986). In other words, contrary to the Becker-Tomes simulation, unequal bequests may reinforce unequal wealth. Thus the effect of bequests may be positive, negative, or neutral to inequalities. Only empirical tests can settle the controversy, but these are not easy given the present state of data.

The Life Cycle Theory and Saving and Distribution. A consensus concerning the life cycle theory of distribution exists only with regard to the age at which the hump occurs, at about the mid-50s (Mincer, 1976; Heckman, 1976 for the U.S.; Heckman, 1987 for Panama; Creedy and Hart, 1979 for the U.K.; with minor age variations due to various factors discussed by Heckman, 1976). No agreement has so far emerged on the degree to which life cycle elements explain overall inequalities of income and wealth. In general, human capitalists (e.g., Ghez and Becker, 1975) and life cyclists (particularly Modigliani, 1989) attribute the bulk of income inequalities measured at a point in time to an individual's own lifetime factors. Support for this view also comes from nonpartisans, such as Blinder (1974), Bronfenbrenner (1977), and Blitz and Siegfried (1990). Of the two theories, whatever little role is assigned to inheritance in creating inequalities, the human capital theory recognizes the altruistic bequest motive including the bequest of human capital through parental interaction and the like (see the discussion in Sahota and Rocca, 1985), whereas the life cycle theory gives more prominence to the precautionary motive. Asset inheritance theories tend to minimize the role of age in explaining inequalities (see, e.g., Britain, 1977, 1978 for the U.S.; Atkinson, 1975, for the U.K.; Kotlikoff et al., 1989).

A majority of participants tend to believe that those who own large fortunes have much greater ability to save and obtain a high yield on whatever they save as well as greater propensity to bequeath. That ability causes great inequalities in capital accumulation. Life cycle theory seems to apply to a vast section of the remaining population. Thus wealth represented by social security benefits and private pensions, but not necessarily homes and durable assets, is consumed in old age. Likewise, as was discussed earlier, little consensus concerning the theory of life cycle saving has emerged. In this situation, most economists would tend to agree with Solow: "Life cycle theory [is] a guide to interpreting behavior ... households may wish to achieve a pattern of lifetime expenditures rather different from earnings ... there are planned bequests. ... There are also unplanned bequests ... then why all this fuss about bequests?" (Solow, 1987, pp. 224, 228). Empirical research on the relative magnitudes of wealth due to inheritance, on the one hand, and net accumulation by living householders, on the other hand, remain in order for different types of societies.

3.2. Impact of Policies

How do policies affect the relationship between saving and distribution? We will take up three policies: public debt (or simply debt), social security system (SSS) payments, and taxation (income, IT, and lump sum, LT). Since most SSSs operate on the pay-as-you-go basis (are not fully funded) and are publicly managed, they are often defined as hidden or quasi-public debt (Barro, 1990*a*; Flowers, 1986; Boskin, 1986). Hence a clarification of the theoretical relationship of the one will, to a large extent, also serve the same purpose for the other. There are important differences between the two, however. SSS payments are supposed to come out of earmarked SS taxes, while debt service comes out of the general budget. For an individual, the SS payment is a life cycle phenomenon. Interest payment on debt begins in the very year of the loan, so current taxpayers cannot escape the cost entirely. Because the principal is almost never paid, however, future generations have to carry on paying the interest. Therefore, separate treatment of the two policies will serve some purpose.

Debt and the Social Security System. Whether the burden of public debt is borne by future generations (a redistribution from the future to the present generation) has been a controversial topic among public finance economists since the prewar period. Keynesians, with whom fiscal policy was a potent remedy for unemployment, did not see significant difference between tax financing and debt financing or believe public debt could get out of hand (recall the theory of functional finance by Lerner, 1943).[11] A host of public finance and growth economists subscribed to the useful role of a deficit budget to increase effective demand and minimize the fears of debt service swamping national revenue (e.g., Domar, 1944; Musgrave, 1959). Among the dissenting voices, two were louder: Buchanan (1958, 1986), who for all practical purposes associates burden with tax (indeed any involuntary) payment, the deadweight loss apart, and Modigliani (1961), according to whom burden transfer results from a smaller stock of capital for future generations. (For a critique of this view, see Tobin, 1965, 1975).

A more recent controversy echoing the same line started by Feldstein's study (1974), in which the traditional assumption of taxes being paid predominantly out of consumption and public borrowing largely out of saving, becomes a bit more subtle. If the burden of debt were borne by future generations, the present generation would consume more, a logical inference from which seemed to be that government bonds were net wealth. According to Feldstein's (1974, 1982) estimates, the prevailing U.S. social security system depressed private saving by about a quarter.[12] That result emerged despite the fact that during the study period the budget deficits of the magnitudes of the 1980s were absent (see the data in Barro, 1990*b*, table 10.4). According to Boskin (1986, p. xxiv), deficits offset about three quarters of private saving in the United States.

Rather than the SSS per se, several other factors may account for the estimated decline of U.S. saving. For instance, the average retirement annuity under the U.S. SSS (for those who retired in 1970 at age 65) was 70 percent higher than could have been available from alternative investment of payroll taxes (Parsons and Munro, 1978). Similar results are revealed by the estimated "transfer component" to retirees from their contributions to SSS (Burkhauser and Warlick, 1981; Wolff, 1987; and others). Outside the United States, to report from Panama, the transfer–equity ratio of SSS in 1983 was 3.76 for size-class $1–$75, 0.52 for size-class $1001–1500, and 0.69 for the overall aggregate of retirees (Sahota, 1990, ch. 14). These conditions are apt to discourage saving.

Another factor behind the decline of U.S. saving is the average net rate of return on investment: It was over three times higher than the average growth rate of national income during 1948–1973 (Feldstein, 1977). As Flowers (1986) has shown, when the rate of growth is lower than the rate of return on investment, saving will tend to decline. Moreover, since social security stimulates investment in the human capital of children, which has had a higher return than physical capital, it indirectly discourages saving as conventionally defined (Drazen, 1978). Perhaps the main source of the decline in national saving in the United States during the 1980s is public deficits inasmuch as the estimates by saving components reflect no weakening of the private saving rate (Bosworth, 1986). Along the same line, it might be noted that the evidence from the OECD countries in general does not support Feldstein's findings for the United States (OECD, 1983).

A refutation of Feldstein's hypothesis has come from the celebrated study by Barro (1974). According to Barro, if capital markets are perfect, taxes are lump sum and all individuals have operative altruistic bequest motives, then tax finance and debt finance are equivalent. This so-called Ricardian Equivalence Theorem is consistent with Lernerian functional finance. Barro recognized that finitely lived individuals could be viewed to have infinite horizons if they care about their progenies' utility. In that situation, government bonds would not be considered net wealth because public debt creates future tax liabilities of equivalent present value, for which altruistic parents will save. Therefore, saving will not fall, rate of interest will not rise, and investment will not be crowded out. Looked at from a different angle, Barro at once performed a marriage between the classical (Ricardian) view and the Lernerian-Keynesian view, inasmuch as the Ricardian Equivalence Theorem echoes functional finance, and he provided a theoretical rejection of both schools. On the one hand, fiscal policy is impotent because deficit finance is not expansionary—so Keynesians are discredited. On the other hand, fiscal policy is innocuous because it does not stint saving, crowd out investment, or cause inflation—so neoclassical fiscal conservatives are disarmed.

The same applies to the social security system as well. When voluntary intergenerational transfers are recognized—such as gifts from children to parents, retired parents living with children, corner solutions, and similar factors—the governmentally imposed social security system may simply replace such transfers (Barro, 1978; Munnell, 1974). Accordingly, "the hypotheses that can be derived from currently available theory do not support the view that social security depresses private saving" (Barro, 1978, p. 4).[13]

The saving behavior of the Barro-Ricardo Equivalence Theorem, too, has been rejected on various grounds:[14] (1) It assumes perfect foresight of even children's consumption and full employment, the imputation of which "degree of rationality to consumers strains credulity" (Summers, 1986, p. 72; also Summers, 1981). (2) Younger generations will, in general, be better off than older generations; therefore transfers from children to parents rather than vice versa are more consistent with equity (Tobin,

1980; Tobin and Buiter, 1980; Drazen, 1978). (3) Capital markets are imperfect (Tobin and Buiter, 1980; Barsky et al., 1986). (4) Taxes are assumed to be lump sum, and the deadweight losses and future uncertainties of incomes and income taxes are ignored (Tobin and Buiter, 1980; Barsky et al., 1986). (5) Deficit spending may absorb saving, and the supply of bonds may not generate its own demand (Tobin, 1980). (6) People may face liquidity constraints (Flavin, 1981; Hubbard and Judd, 1986). (7) Some may die childless (Tobin and Buiter, 1980). (8) Future incomes and taxes are characterized by uncertainty (Boyer and Kihlstrom, 1984; Grossman and Weiss, 1984; Hahn, 1970; Kessler and Masson, 1986). (9) The typical individual's real discount rate exceeds that of the government, and therefore the present value of future liabilities is lower than the value of debt (see Barsky et al., 1986; and Hayashi, 1982, for empirical evidence and Yaari, 1965; and Blanchard, 1985, for theoretical rationale). Finally, (10) the life cycle hypothesis may operate rather than the altruistic bequest motive (Modigliani, Jappelli, and Paggano, 1987).

All these arguments favor treating debt as net wealth, implying that deficits offset private saving (Tobin and Buiter, 1980; Drazen, 1978; Barsky, Mankiw, and Zeldes, 1986; Abel, 1984; Fischer, 1973; Boskin, 1986; Haque and Montiel, 1989). According to research, fiscal policy does affect aggregate demand, and deficits are harmful to the economy through lower saving, higher rates of interest, relatively cheaper imports, short-term foreign capital inflows, inflation, and crowding out of investment and net exports. However, rejection of the Ricardian Theorem does not necessarily imply acceptance of the Keynesian expansionary effect of deficit; it may simply raise the rate of interest and attract foreign capital with no effect on saving (Feldstein and Elmendorf, 1989; Summers, 1989). The decline in the saving rate during the bulging deficits of the 1980s in America, despite saving incentives such as the individual retirement accounts (which are estimated to have induced net savings) and positive real rates of interest (Wise, 1987; Venti and Wise, 1990), tend to discredit the Barro-Ricardo theorem. Barro nevertheless continues strongly defending it (Barro, 1990a, 1990b).[15]

What has come out of this debate? Viewed in historical perspective, two highly intellectual developments about public policies of the past two decades may be distinguished: the rational expectations hypothesis, particularly focusing on monetary policy, and the Ricardian Equivalence Theorem, addressed mainly to fiscal policy. Both may be said to have originated, not coincidentally, from the University of Chicago by Lucas (1972) along with others at other centers and Barro (1974), who has since moved to Harvard. Both notions destabilized mainstream macroeconomic thought for quite some time and portended the prospects of revolutionary changes in macroeconomics. Both were elegant. Both seemed to sound an apparent death knell to discretionary public policies. Both created bandwagons of research and generated stimulating controversies. Yet the emerging opinion among economists seems to be that both are petering out, yielding place to mainstream economics, though not without leaving a lasting impact on economics, specifically an awareness of how expectations are formed and ought to be modeled.[16]

3.3. Uncertainty, Taxation, and Saving and Distribution

How does *taxation* affect *saving* decisions and *distribution* under increased *uncertainty* about the future? This question has been widely discussed since Marshall's days. To answer it, one may follow Sandmo's (1970) distinction between Marshallian uncertainty and Bouldingian uncertainty. By the former, in the present context we mean uncertainty relating to nonhuman capital (Marshall, 1920). Bouldingian uncertainty refers to income from human capital (Boulding, 1966). The point may be made by reference to grandmother's allegorical riddle and the answer to it. Question: What is it that fire cannot burn, water cannot wash, and robber cannot rob? Answer: Knowledge (or human capital). Nonhuman capital is subject to all these uncertainties. We must recognize, however, that human capital, too, is subject to uncertainty: the uncertainty of life and health and hence income from work, which is Boulding's case of income uncertainty.

Regarding income uncertainty, under increasing temporal risk aversion, individuals make more provision for the future the more uncertain is future income (Hahn, 1970). The income and the substitution effects reinforce each other (Dreze and Modigliani, 1969). Therefore, the theory has an unambiguous prediction sign. For capital risk, however, the substitution effect on present consumption is positive because of the increased Marshallian risk of loss of capital. The income effect of increased uncertainty of future income from capital on present consumption is negative. The two effects are conflicting. As such, theory does not help to predict the direction of the net joint effect.

Under certain plausible assumptions, Levhari and Srinivasan (1969) and Sandmo (1970) derive the following conclusions for capital uncertainty: Given a constant elasticity of marginal utility, a, increased capital risk will reduce, leave unchanged, or increase saving accordingly as $a \lesseqgtr 1$, where $a < 1$ means that the substitution effect dominates. For instance, because

SAVING AND DISTRIBUTION

self-employed people (whose future incomes may depend more on how much they save today) have greater ex ante uncertainty (judging from ex post variability), they are expected to save more than steady-job wage earners; this assumption seems to conform to facts.

Do any of the preceding results change under a tax cut? A lump sum tax, as discussed earlier, will have only an income effect, as it changes only the level and not the variance of future income, whose consequences were discussed in connection with the Barro-Ricardo Equivalence Theorem. In the case of the income tax, however, the substitution effect also becomes relevant; it will reduce the Barro effect, if any, and increase consumption. The reason is the increase in wealth under the tax cut and the reduction in the variance of after-tax future income (Varian, 1980; Barsky et al., 1987). In the uncertain world, therefore, a redistributive tax can provide a "social insurance," whose benefits must be weighed against the deadweight loss of taxation (Varian, 1980; Kimball and Mankiw, 1987). Redistributive taxation induces saving—a happy world!

To the extent higher capital uncertainty causes substitution of human for nonhuman capital, factor prices may change and in turn may alter functional distribution. Similar changes in total wealth can be caused by taxes and tariffs through income distribution between tangible and intangible assets (Engel and Kletzer, 1990).

3.4. Relationship of LDC's Domestic Saving to the Inflow of Foreign Saving and Distribution

In evaluating the relationship between saving and distribution, the experience of developing countries should be enlightening, inasmuch as there has been a perennial net inflow of exogenously determined foreign saving into these countries. We shall look at the saving of these countries in relation to aid and trade.

Trade and Saving. Free trade was viewed by some of the early postwar development theorists to lead to the immiserization of developing countries, as they foresaw worsening terms of trade for primary producer poor countries in relation to industrial countries (Prebisch, 1949). Guided by these first-generation development theories, a vast majority of developing countries followed inward-looking policies of import substitution and self-sufficiency.

Although support for this view has not disappeared (e.g., the study by Kravis, 1984), it has gradually become evident that the reverse of the early postwar policies is, indeed, growth promoting. Even the Machlup-Metzler hypothesis that fast-growing economies would suffer from negative balance of payments squared ill with the experiences of several countries, including contemporary Japan and Germany. The support for liberalized trade (constrained by a lingering, though so far disappointing, faith in the infant industry argument) as being an engine of growth in development is increasing (Balassa, 1988). According to Caves (1970), rapid export expansion is a necessary and perhaps sufficient condition for growth. Immiserization of a poor country could in fact take place due to distorting tariffs rather than free trade (Johnson, 1967). The double to triple rates of growth with bulging exports and high rates of saving without necessarily a worsening of income distribution among the outward-looking, export-promoting East Asian Tigers have discredited both the early postwar Prebisch-Mahalanobis immiserization theories as well as the Machlup-Metzler hypotheses of negative foreign saving from rapid growth (*Economic Development and Cultural Change, Supplement*, 1988).

In the early postwar years of rising interest in development, saving was viewed to form the necessary condition of growth for developing countries (e.g., Rosenstein-Rodan, 1961; Chenery and Strout, 1966). Apart from its advantages as a carrier of technology and a filler of the foreign exchange gap (and disadvantages due to strings), foreign aid was recognized as an augmentation to domestic saving. Feldstein's "habitat" view of the supply of saving creating its own demand (for investment) within the country (Feldstein and Horioka, 1980; Feldstein, 1982)[17] is consistent with the view of development economists who, though ordinarily trained in Keynesianism, assumed developing countries as a classical world, where saving was regarded as a constraint on investment. In general, the high-growth countries are also high-saving countries—for instance, Japan, Hong Kong, Indonesia, Malaysia, and Singapore with savings of approximately one-third of GDP and Korea, Taiwan, the Philippines, and Thailand with saving rates of approximately one-quarter of GDP, as against far lower saving rates for industrial countries and for the rest of the world.

Foreign Aid and Saving. The effect of *aid* on *saving* has ranged from being ambiguous or indeterminate—either because of statistical difficulties, as in Papanek (1972), or because theory does not yield clear-cut results, as in Snyder (1990)—to persistently negative (as in Griffin, 1970; Wasow, 1979; Singh, 1971). Even those economists who find that foreign aid indirectly raises saving through increasing growth admit to foreign aid's negative direct effect on saving (Bhagwati, 1968; Grinols and Bhagwati, 1976).

Among possible explanations for the widely estimated negative effect of aid on domestic saving is the "psychological," hypothesis according to which foreign aid becomes a substitute for domestic saving and causes a relaxation of government saving (Bauer, 1977; Rahman, 1968) and/or private saving (Quibria, 1986; Fry and Mason, 1982). Aid often may result in the immiserization of a developing country due to distortions (Bhagwati, 1968; Grinols and Bhagwati, 1976). In Quibria's (1986) two-country model — a capital-exporting country with a neoclassical (flexible wage) labor market and a capital-importing country with a classical (fixed wage) labor market — immiserization may result from the absence of optimal saving plans, caused in part by the inflow of foreign saving, even when there are no distortions. Eckaus (1988) reports India's experience of healthier domestic saving during the 1970s when foreign aid/saving had dropped to the lowest ebb of the postwar period, thereby emphasizing a stimulus to self-help and private and public saving in the face of reduced dependence on foreign aid.[18] Not infrequently, the bulk of the matching local resources insisted on by donor agencies entail pre-existing costs of buildings, services, wages of persons already employed, repair and maintenance costs budgeted but never incurred, and so forth. For instance, the World Bank and other donors required that Bangladesh match as little as 13 percent of local resources to foreign aid amounting to about 10 percent of the country's GDP in 1989. Even with the indicated probable padding, Bangladesh could not come up with even 10 percent matching (Sahota, 1991), such is the state of her saving effort, where saving as a percentage of GDP has averaged 1.95 during the 1980s (World Bank, 1990). Large foreign funds cause downward pressure on the rate of interest faced by local savers, thereby providing a disincentive to saving.[19]

3.5. Any Estimate of Net Causal Relationship Between Saving and Distribution?

Having surveyed the existing literature, we finally carry out a rather simple test of the final (in the sense of the reduced-form) relationship between saving and distribution, allowing the Kuznets (1955) effect, if any, to be held constant. The test involves a regression of the saving ratio on the distribution parameter as measured by the Gini coefficient, on per capita income in quadratic form to allow for the Kuznets inverted U-shape curve, and on dummy variables to remove cultural and habit effects. The data cover 65 countries for 1975, and the results appear in table 5–2.

Table 5-2. Regression of Saving on Income Distribution

Variable	Coefficient	t-Statistic
C	−1.030	−0.118
G	0.187	1.778
Y	4.872	2.599
YS	−0.334	−2.317
D1	3.434	0.465
D2	1.518	0.188
D3	13.108	1.881
D4	4.094	0.687
D5	13.684	2.175
D6	5.839	0.984

Notes: Adjusted R-squared = 0.3393. Dependent variable S = Saving/GDP in percentages from the World Bank (1990). C = the constant, and G = the Gini coefficient in hundreds of U.S. dollars from Jain (1975). Y = per capita income in thousands of 1975 U.S. dollars from the World Bank (1990). $YS = Y$ squared. Di ($i = 1, \ldots, 6$) = dummies for the respective regions Sub-Sahara, S. Asia, E. Asia and the Pacific, Latin America, Middle East and N. Africa, E. Europe and Mediterranean, with OECD, N. America, Japan, and Oceania as the base.

The coefficient of Gini may be seen as positive and significant at the 10 percent level. The coefficients of Kuznets' inverted parabola have the right signs and are significant at the 1 percent level. The dummy that acquires a positive coefficient with statistical significance, with the OECD countries as the base, is for the Middle East oil-rich countries. In short, the positive effect of inequalities on saving is not rejected.

These cross-sectional regression results are consistent with two pieces of temporal experience of developed versus developing countries. The latter countries attained "a higher propensity to save in 1980 than in 1960, while many of the developed countries had a slightly reduced saving propensity between the two years" (Klein, 1986, p. 201). Simultaneously, inequalities between developed and developing countries probably worsened somewhat (Summers, Kravis, and Heston, 1984).

The reduced form results from a single cross-section, however, do not tell us about the direction of the causal flow or the feedback nexus of the variables involved, which only the structural relationships or theories can reveal. Moreover, a cross-sectional sample cannot account for such dynamic variables as high growth rates and their effects on both saving and distribution, as has been the case in East Asian countries in the past two decades.

4. Conclusions

With a view to discerning probable relationships between saving and income distribution, short surveys of literature on four topics were done: theories of functional distribution of income, theories of personal distribution of income, theories of saving, and a discussion of possible impacts of policies and institutions on saving and distribution. The heightened interest of the 1970s in theorizing about the personal distribution of income (see Sahota, 1978) has been overshadowed by the debate in the 1980s on competing hypotheses of saving. In the latter area, the early postwar controversy between permanent income and current income hypotheses of consumption (alternatively saving) has ceded place to the bequest motive versus the life cycle hypothesis of saving. Within the framework of the bequest motive, much research has been done to test hypotheses based on the altruistic and nonaltruistic motives toward children. The life cycle hypothesis takes a longer view of permanent income. Then there is the precautionary motive for saving, which contains elements from both the bequest and the life cycle hypotheses while being a distinct hypothesis by itself.

On the other side are a half-dozen competing theories of the personal distribution of income, even if we ignore about an equal number of theories of functional income distribution that lie behind the former. Among the dominant theories of the personal distribution of income are the ability theory, the stochastic theory, the individual choice theory, the human capital theory, the life cycle theory, and public income distribution theories.

Although there is some convergence of the rival theories of income distribution (a marriage of the human capital and the inheritance theories; see Sahota and Rocca, 1985), the controversy about the competing theories of the personal distribution of income has not quite been settled yet. The debate about and the empirical tests of various theories of saving are still hot as these lines are being written (see, e.g., Kessler and Masson, 1988). As such, it is apparent that a reliable, definitive relationship between saving and distribution is difficult to identify. In this situation, using broad judgment about the dominance of theories, discussion concentrated on possible interrelationships among the human capital, the inheritance, the life cycle, and the stochastic theories, in the income distribution dimension, and the theories of permanent income, bequest, life cycle, and precautionary motive for saving. Of the 16 cells formed by the cross-tabulation of these theories, most cells are conformable to and consistent with each other. For instance, if the bequest theory of saving causes equalization of incomes because parents tend to bequeathe more to the less-gifted child to counterbalance unequal endowments (as according to human capitalists, e.g., Becker and Tomes, 1979, and others), so will the inheritance theory of income distribution cause equalization (e.g., Wolfson, 1980). On the other hand, if bequests are shared equally even when heirs are unequal, because parents either make equal bequests but rich parents make bigger bequests (Menchik, 1988, and others) or because the child with higher earnings is likely to provide more care and receive larger bequests (Kessler and Masson, 1988, and others), the inheritance theory of distribution will exacerbate income inequalities (Meade, 1976, and others). Thus the effect of bequests may be positive, negative, or neutral with respect to inequalities, depending on which theory(ies) is(are) dominant. Similar conclusions apply to the other conforming theories.

There are at least four cells (interrelationships) crossing rival theories (those marked by X in table 5−1). A definitive relationship in these cases is even less likely to emerge. The current interest in the topic may bring about convergence. It has to be seen.

While the experience of East Asian countries vis-à-vis South Asian countries in the past quarter century has thrown a good deal of light on the role of policies on income distribution, and the positive relationship between growth and equalization has become transparent, the picture remains hazy with regard to the effects of policies and institutions, such as tax, debt, and social security, on saving. Whether tax finance and debt finance are equivalent with regard to saving; whether bonds are net wealth, (whether deficits offset private saving); whether the Ricardian Equivalence Theorem, echoing functional finance, is valid; whether fiscal policy is potent or impotent in influencing private consumption and saving; whether social security depresses private saving—the controversy over these and similar issues has been clarified but not settled.

Consider the two saving theories so extensively discussed during the past decade or so; the bequest and the life cycle theories of saving. What has come out of this debate? Viewed in historical perspective, two highly intellectual developments about public policies of the reference period may be distinguished: the rational expectations hypothesis, particularly focusing on monetary policy, and the Ricardian Equivalence Theorem, addressed mainly to fiscal policy. Both destabilized the mainstream macroeconomic thought for quite some time during these years and seemed to portend the prospects of revolutionary changes in macroeconomics. Both were elegant. Both seemed to sound an apparent death knell to discretionary public policies. Both created bandwagons of research and generated stimulating controversies. The emerging opinion among economists, however, seems to be that both are petering out, though not without leaving a lasting impact on mainstream economics, specifically an awareness of how critical expectations are, how expectations are formed, and how they ought to be modeled.

One reason for the haziness in this area is a lack of long-run, longitudinal data across generations. But considering all the research surveyed here, coupled with the empirical evidence of the 1980s, in which saving rates have declined during the bulging budget deficits, despite saving incentives and positive real rates of interest, one tends to give credence to the result that debt finance is different from tax finance and that fiscal policy does matter in influencing private expenditure and saving, though not as much as it was believed to be during the early postwar years.

The introduction of additional complications in the saving–distribution models—for example, different types of tax cuts and saving (and distribution); uncertainty, taxation, and saving (and distribution); foreign flow of resources and domestic saving (and distribution), also reviewed in this chapter—throws some more light on the issues under investigation, but the picture is still not clear. A lot more empirical research on the relative magnitudes of wealth due to inheritance, on the one hand, and the acquisition of earning capacities and net accumulation of wealth by living householders, on the other hand, remains in order for different types of societies.

Notes

1. Without implying that the existence of saving theory must be judged by saving's relationship with rate of interest alone, it is interesting to note that the U.S. saving rate declined by some 40 percent in the 1970s when the real rate of interest was negative (while saving rates increased in the OECD countries under the same circumstances) and it slumped to an all time low during the 1980s when the real rate of interest in the United States had become significantly positive, tax incentives (which were already generous) had become enhanced, and income inequalities had increased (Walters, 1986; Scitovsky, 1986).

2. Summarizing the findings of 11 conference papers by economic specialists on saving, the rapporteurs conclude: "The theoretical constructs are far developed, if not always realistic in the eyes of some observers, but the empirical information—the surveys and household records of saving and assets holdings—leave much to be desired" (Adams and Wachter, 1986, p. 208). Even the national accounts measures of saving are less than satisfactory. For scarcely in any country is saving measured directly. Traditionally, saving is measured indirectly either by taking the difference between national income and consumption or by adding current account surplus to gross domestic investment (by itself weakly measured, especially in LDCs). The right measures in the form of series of multiyear earnings histories along with bequests and inheritance (and in the sense of net worth, i.e., assets minus liabilities, as distinguished from income minus expenditure) are scarcely available. (See Blinder, 1976; Barro, 1978, p. 3; Avery, Elliehausen, and Gustafson, 1986, p. 155; Klein,

1986; Lipsey and Tice, 1989; Scitovsky, 1986; and Smith, 1980). On LDCs, see Arrieta (1988, pp. 592–593).

3. The list is not exhaustive. The informed reader may have noted the failure to discuss corporate saving behavior and public saving behavior. Both will appear in one form or another in the later discussion of policies and institutions. Also not discussed are the aggregate generation size theories, such as "the bust of the baby boom" (Welch, 1979) or "the generation-size theory of fortunes" (Easterlin, 1980). Once the stationary population theories are understood, the generation-size theories can be easily incorporated.

4. For larger treatments of functional distribution theories, see Bronfenbrenner (1971) and Johnson (1973).

5. The breakthrough came in the model of Becker and Tomes (1979).

6. See the discussion in Sahota and Rocca (1985) and Sahota (1990). The explicit treatment of stochastic and luck elements in their respective distribution theories may be perceived from the studies—for instance, by Friedman (1953) and Becker and Tomes (1979) on the neoclassical side and by Thurow (1975) and Shorrocks (1975) on the opposite side.

7. See, however, Danziger, Haveman, and Plotnick (1981), who suggest that the effect of the current U.S. transfer programs is to reduce labor supply by 4.8 percent, private saving by 0–20 percent, income poverty by 75 percent, and income inequality by 19 percent. Possibly, the fortunes of particular groups are materially affected, yet aggregate indices, like the Gini coefficient, hardly change.

8. The median elasticity of children's earnings with respect to parents' income from about a dozen cross-sectional samples is 0.17 in Becker and Tomes (1986) and is conjectured to fall as parental incomes shift upward. According to the estimates from a panel data by Behrman and Taubman (1990), the same elasticity is 0.80 and increases as parents' incomes increase.

9. In a recent article, however, Tomes (1988) tempers the results of his model co-authored with Becker by relaxing several assumptions of the previous model.

10. Naturally, intergenerational transfer of property by issueless decedents will be redistributive, as property may pass on to government or nonprofit organizations. In the cases of primogeniture and one-heir families, transfers will reinforce inequalities.

11. The central idea of functional finance, which rejected completely the doctrine of sound finance, was that spending and taxing, borrowing and repayment of loans, and issuing of new money and its withdrawal all amount to leaving more or less purchasing power in the hands of the public and should be judged by no other criterion than their effects on employment and inflation. Keynes was intrigued by and accepted Lerner's concept of functional finance as being impeccable, but cautioned against its being made the conduct of policy (Keynes, 1943). See the discussion in Colander (1984).

12. Feldstein's initial results suffered from a statistical error that overstated the effect. However, even after correcting the flaw, the negative saving effect of SSS, as reported in the text, was significant.

13. Irrespective of whether SSS discourages saving à la Feldstein or is neutral à la Barro, the American SSS is, on the whole, redistributive. Insofar as the developed world is concerned, two of its effects have been widely corroborated: (1) It is redistributive from the young to the old, at least until now, in the sense that retirees receive more than they pay into it, and (2) it is redistributive within cohorts, it favors workers with low earnings (Wolff, 1987). Because social security wealth amounts to about half of total household wealth in America, its weight in overall distribution must be substantial. In developing countries (e.g., in Latin America), for all practical purposes the foregoing conclusions apply only to the covered workers, meaning formal sector employees. The informal sector workers and the

poor are left out by the system. As such, for the overall population, the system is probably unequalizing. See Sahota (1990, pp. 303–18) and Burkhauser (1986).

14. It may be noted that Ricardo presented as a theoretical curiosum what has now come to be known as Ricardian Equivalence Theorem but rejected it as of little practical significance.

15. While Barro has not spelled it out himself, it is clear that his rehabilitation of public expenditure also reconciles self-interest with the public sector. Through sheer self-interest, infinitely lived individuals allocate their resources to human and nonhuman capital so as to increase the earning capacity of future generations (where Becker's altruism will augment capital formation even more). On the other side, in Barro's framework, public capital assets have large externalities and thus enhance growth of per capita income and consumption (Barro, 1990*b*).

16. For the latest state of the rational expectations theory, see the survey article by Mankiw (1990).

17. Feldstein's findings were based on regressions of simple saving and investment ratios across a score countries. These findings are subject to the problem of simultaneity (Leff and Sato, 1975): The saving and investment covariation does not necessarily indicate international capital immobility (Finn, 1990) and depend importantly on the nontraded goods sector (Wong, 1990). Other studies have found international capital movements quite prevalent (Hamada and Iwata, 1989). Further support can be found in Harberger (1980).

18. For a survey of the pre-1973 literature on saving functions in developing countries, see Mikessell and Zinser (1973).

19. On the effect of foreign aid on growth, the experience has been mixed. Even when in the form of subsidies, as distinguished from loans, foreign aid has not been necessarily all gain. Indirect evidence may be found in the recent debt crisis (Lal and Wijnbergen, 1986). As direct evidence, several researchers have found aid to be detrimental to growth (e.g., Griffin and Enos, 1970; Rahman, 1968; Weisskopf, 1972; Areskoug, 1969). Surprising as the finding is to the present author, investment is negatively correlated with foreign aid for one of the highest aid recipient countries of the world, namely, Bangladesh (Sahota, 1991). In many other studies, however, foreign aid has been found, as predicted by theory and common sense, to enhance economic growth (Grinols and Bhagwati, 1976, Papanek, 1972, and others).

References

Abel, A. B. "Capital Accumulation and Uncertain Lifetimes with Adverse Selection." Harvard University, 1984. Mimeo.
———. "Bequests and Social Security with Uncertain Lifetime." *American Economic Review* 75 (4) (1985): 777–791.
———. "Operative Gift and Bequest Motives." *American Economic Review* 77 (5) (December 1987): 1037–1047.
Adams, Gerard F., and Susan M. Wachter. *Savings and Capital Formation.* Lexington, Mass.: Lexington Books/D.C. Heath & Co, 1986.
Ando, Albert, and Arthur B. Kennickell. "How Much (or Little) Life Cycle Is There in Micro Data? The Cases of the United States and Japan." In *Essays in Honor of Franco Modigliani*, edited by Rudiger Dornbusch et al. 1987.

Ando, Albert, and Franco Modigliani. "The Life Cycle Hypothesis of Saving: Aggregate Implications and Tests." *American Economic Review* 53 (1) (1963): 55–84.

Areskoug, Kaj. *External Borrowing: Its Role in Economic Development.* New York: Praeger, 1969.

Arrieta, G. M. G. "Interest Rates, Savings, and Growth in LDCs: An Assessment of Recent Empirical Research." *World Development* 16 (5) (1988): 589–605.

Asimakopulos, Athanasios. *Theories of Income Distribution.* Boston: Kluwer Academic Publishers, 1987.

Atkinson, Anthony. "The Distribution of Wealth and the Individual Life Cycle." *Oxford Economic Papers* 23 (1971).

———. *The Economics of Inequality.* Oxford: Oxford University Press, 1975.

———. "Inheritance and the Redistribution of Wealth." In *Public Policy and the Tax System*, edited by G. M. Heal and G. A. Hughes. London: Allen and Unwin, 1980.

———. "On Intergenerational Income Mobility in Britain." *Journal of Post Keynesian Economics* 3 (1981): 194–218.

Auerbach, A. J., and L. J. Kotlikoff. "National Savings, Economic Welfare, and the Structure of Taxation." In *Behavioral Simulation Methods in Tax Policy Analysis*, edited by Martin Feldstein. Chicago: University of Chicago Press, 1983, pp. 459–498.

Avery, Robert B., Gregory E. Elliehausen, and Thomas A. Gustafson. "Pensions and Social Security in Household Portfolios: Evidence from the 1983 Survey of Consumer Finances." In Adams and Wachter (1986), pp. 127–162.

Balassa, Bela. "The Lessons of East Asian Development: An Overview." *Economic Development and Cultural Change. Supplement: Why Does Overcrowded, Resource-Poor East Asia Succeed—Lessons for the LDCs?* 36 (3) (April 1988): S273–S290.

Barro, Robert J. "Are Government Bonds Net Wealth?" *Journal of Political Economy* (November-December 1974): 1095–1118.

———. *The Impact of Social Security and Private Saving: Evidence from the U.S. Time Series.* Washington, DC: American Enterprise Institute, 1978.

———. *Macroeconomic Policy.* Cambridge, Mass.: Harvard University Press, ch. 9, 1990*a*.

———. "Letters: Barro and Ricardo." *The Economist* 317 (7685) (1990*b*): 6–8.

Barro, Robert J., and J. W. Friedman. "On Uncertain Lifetimes." *Journal of Political Economy* 85 (1977): 843–849.

Barsky, R., G. N. Mankiw, and S. P. Zeldes. "Ricardian Consumers with Keynesian Propensities." *American Economic Review* 76 (1986): 676–691.

Bauer, Peter T. *Two Essays on Income Distribution and the Open Society.* Ottawa, IL.: Distributed by Green Hill, 1977.

Becker, Gary S. "A Theory of Social Interactions." *Journal of Political Economy* 82 (1974): 1063–1093.

———. *A Treatise on the Family.* Cambridge, Mass.: Harvard University Press, 1981.

Becker, Gary S., and Nigel Tomes. "Child Endowments and the Quantity and Quality of Children." *Journal Political Economy* 84 (1976): S143–S162.

———. "An Equilibrium Theory of the Distribution of Income and Intergenerational Mobility." *Journal of Political Economy* 87 (6) (June 1979): 1153–1189.

———. "Human Capital and the Rise and Fall of Families." *Journal of Labor Economics* 4 (2), Part 2 (July 1986): S1–S39.

Behrman, Jere R., Robert Pollak, and Paul Taubman. "Family Resources, Family Size, and Access to Financing for College Education." *Journal of Political Economy* 97 (2) (1980): 398–419.

Behrman, Jere R., and Paul Taubman. "The Intergenerational Correlation Between Children's Adult Earnings and Their Parents' Income: Results from the Michigan Panel Survey of Income Dynamics." *Review of Income and Wealth* 36 (2) (1990): 115–128.

Bernheim, B. D., A. Shleifer, and Lawrence Summers. "The Strategic Bequest Motive." *Journal of Political Economy* 93 (1985): 1045–1076.

———. "Bequests As a Means of Payment." *Journal of Political Economy* 93 (6) (1986): 1045–1076.

Bhagwati, Jagdish N. "Distortions and Immiserizing Growth: A Generalization." *Review of Economic Studies* 35 (1968): 481–485.

———. "Substitution Between Foreign Capital and Domestic Saving." In *Dependence and Interdependence: Essays in Development Economics*. Series, Vol. 2, edited by Gene Grossman. Cambridge, Mass.: MIT Press (1985), pp. 244–252.

Blanchard, O. J. "Debt, Deficits and Finite Horizons." *Journal of Political Economy* 93 (1985): 223–247.

Blinder, Alan. *Toward an Economic Theory of Income Distribution*. Cambridge, Mass.: MIT Press, 1974.

———. "Intergenerational Transfers and Life Cycle Consumption." *Papers and Proceedings of the American Economic Association* 66 No. 2 (1974): 87–93.

Blinder, Alan, A. R. Gordon, and D. Wise. "Social Security, Bequests and the Life Cycle Theory of Saving: Cross-Sectional Tests." In *The Determinants of National Saving and Wealth*, edited by Franco Modigliani and R. Hemming. New York: St. Martin's Press, 1983, pp. 89–122.

Blitz, Rudolph C., and John J. Siegfried. "How Did the Wealthiest Americans Get So Rich?" Vanderbilt University, Department of Economics. Mimeo, 1990.

Boskin, Michael J. "Theoretical and Empirical Issues in the Measurement, Evaluation, and Interpretation of Postwar U.S. Saving. In Adams and Wachter (1986), 11–44.

Bosworth, Barry P. "Savings and Government Policy." In Adams and Wachter (1986), 173–188.

Boulding, K. E. *Economic Analysis, Volume I: Microeconomics*. 4th ed. New York: Harper and Row, 1966.

Boyer, Marcel, and Richard E. Kihlstrom. "Introduction." In *Bayesian Models in Economic Theory*. Amsterdam: North-Holland, 1984.

Brittain, John A. *Inheritance of Economic Status*. Washington, D.C.: Brookings Institution, 1977.
———. *Inheritance and the Inequality of Material Wealth*. Washington, D.C.: Brookings Institution, 1978.
Bronfenbrenner, Martin. *Income Distribution Theory*. Chicago: Aldine, 1971.
———. "Ten Issues in Distribution Theory." In *Modern Economic Thought*, edited by Sidney Weintraub. Philadelphia: University of Pennsylvania Press, 1977.
Brown, Phelps, Henry. *Functional Income Distribution*. Oxford: Clarendon Press, 1968.
Buchanan, James. *Public Principles of Public Debt*. Homewood, Ill.: Richard Irwin, 1958.
———. "Public Debt and Capital Formation." In Lee (1986), 177–194.
Buiter, Willem. "Government Finance in an Overlapping-Generations Model with Gifts and Bequests." In *Social Security Versus Private Saving*, edited by George M. von Furstenberg. Cambridge, Mass.: Ballinger, 1979.
Buiter, Willem, and Jeffrey Carmichael. "Government Debt: Comment." *American Economic Review* 74 (September 1984): 762–765.
Burbidge, John B. "Government Debt in an Overlapping-Generations Model with Bequests and Gifts." *American Economic Review* 73 (March 1983): 222–227.
———. "Government Debt: Reply." *American Economic Review* 74 (September 1984): 766–767.
Burkhauser, Richard V. "Social Security in Panama: A Multiperiod Analysis of Income Distribution." *Journal of Development Economics* 20 (1986): 53–64.
Burkhauser, Richard V., and Jennifer L. Warlick. "Disentangling the Annuity from the Redistributive Aspects of Social Security in the United States." *Review of Income and Wealth* 27 (December 1981): 401–421.
Canterbery, E. Ray. "A Vita Theory of the Personal Income Distribution." *Southern Economic Journal* (July 1979): 12–48.
Canterbery, E. Ray, and E. Joe Nosari. "The Forbes Four Hundred: The Determinants of Super-Wealth." *Southern Economic Journal* 51, no. 4 (April 1985): 1073–1083.
Carmichael, Jeffrey. "On Barro's Theorem of Debt Neutrality: The Irrelevance of Net Wealth." *American Economic Review* 72 (March 1982): 202–213.
Caves, Richard E. "Export-Led Growth: The Postwar Industrial Setting." In *Induction, Growth and Trade: Essays in Honor of Roy Harrod*, edited by W. A. Eltis, M. FG. Scotto, and J. N. Wolfe. Oxford: Oxford University Press, 1970.
Chenery, Hollis B., and A. M. Strout. "Foreign Assistance and Economic Development." *American Economic Review* 56 (September 1966): 679–733.
Cohen, Jon S., and G. C. Harcourt. *International Monetary Problems and Supply-Side Economics*. London: Macmillan Press, 1986.
Colander, D. "Was Keynes a Keynesian or a Lernerian?" *Journal of Economic Literature* 22 (1984): 1572–1575.

Comanor, William S., and Robert H. Smiley. "Monopoly and the Distribution of Wealth." *Quarterly Journal of Economics* (May 1975): 1771–1794.
Creedy, J., and P. E. Hart. "Age and the Distribution of Earnings." *Economic Journal* 89 (354) (June 1979): 280–293.
Danziger, Sheldon, Robert Haveman, and Robert Plotnick. "How Income Transfer Programs Affect Work, Savings, and the Income Distribution: A Critical Review." *Journal of Economic Literature* 19, no. 3 (September 1981): 975–1028.
David, M., and P. L. Menchik. "The Effect of Social Security on Lifetime Wealth Accumulation and Bequests." *Economica* 52 (1985): 421–434.
Davies, James B. "Uncertain Lifetime, Consumption, and Dissaving in Retirement." *Journal of Political Economy* 89 (1981).
Davies, James B., and Peter Kuhn. "Redistribution, Inheritance, and Inequality: An Analysis of Transition." In Kessler and Masson (1988), 123–143.
Domar, Evsey. "The 'Burden of Debt' and National Income." *American Economic Review* 34 (1944): 798–827.
Drazen, Allan. "Government Debt, Human Capital and Bequests in a Life Cycle Model." *Journal of Political Economy* 86 (June 1978): 505–516.
Dreze, J., and Franco Modigliani. "Consumption Decisions Under Uncertainty." *CORE Discussion Paper 6906*, Louvain, 1969.
Duesenberry, J. S. *Income, Saving, and the Theory of Consumer Behavior*. Cambridge, Mass.: Harvard University Press, 1949.
Easterlin, Richard. *Births and Fortunes: The Impact of Numbers on Personal Welfare*. New York: Basic Books, 1980.
Eckaus, Richard S. "Prospects for Development Finance in India." In *Financing Asian Development 2: China and India*, edited by Robert F. Dernberger and Richard S. Eckaus. New York: University Press of America, 1988.
Eckstein, Z., M. Eichenbaum, and D. Peled. "Uncertain Lifetimes and the Welfare Enhancing Properties of Annuity Markets and Social Security." Mimeo, 1983.
Economic Development and Cultural Change, Supplement: *Why Does Overcrowded, Resource-Poor East Asia Succeed—Lessons for the LDCs?* 36 (3) (April 1988): Supplement.
Engel, Charles, and Kenneth Kletzer. "Tariffs and Saving in a Model with New Generations." *Journal of International Economics* 28 (February 1990): 71–92.
Feldstein, Martin S. "Social Security, Induced Retirement and Aggregate Capital Accumulation." *Journal of Political Economy* 82, no. 5 (September/October 1974): 905–926.
———. "Social Security and Private Savings: International Evidence in an Extended Life-Cycle Model." In *The Economics of Public Services*, edited by M. Feldstein and R. Inman. London: Macmillan, 1977.
———. "Social Security and Private Saving: Reply." *Journal of Political Economy* 90 (1982): 630–642.

———. *Taxation and Capital Formation*. Chicago: University of Chicago Press, 1987.

Feldstein, Martin S., and Douglas W. Elmendorf. "Budget Deficits, Tax Incentives, and Inflation: A Surprising Lesson from the 1983–84 Recovery." In Summers (1989), 1–24.

Feldstein, Martin S., and C. Horioka. "Domestic Saving and International Capital Flows." *Economic Journal* 90 (June 1980): 314–329.

Ferber, Robert. "Consumer Economics, A Survey." *Journal of Economic Literature* 11, no. 4 (December 1973): 1303–1342.

Finn, Mary G. "On Saving and Investment Dynamics in a Small Open Economy." *Journal of International Economics* 29 (1990): 1–21.

Fischer, Stanley. "A Life Cycle Model of Life Insurance Purchases." *International Economic Review* 14 (February 1973): 132–152.

Flavin, M. A. "The Adjustment of Consumption to Changing Expectations About Future Income." *Journal of Political Economy* 89 (1981): 974–1009.

Flowers, Marilyn R. "Social Security, Saving, and Our Legacy to the Future." In Lee (1986), 195–224.

Friedman, Milton. "Choice, Chance, and the Personal Distribution of Income." *Journal of Political Economy* 61, no. 4 (August 1953): 277–290.

———. *A Theory of the Consumption Function*. Princeton, N.J.: Princeton University Press, 1957.

———. *Price Theory*. Chicago: Aldine, 1962.

Fry, Maxwell J., and Andrew Mason. "The Variable Rate-of-Growth Effect in the Life-Cycle Saving Model." *Economic Inquiry* 20, no. 3 (July 1982): 426–442.

Ghez, Gilbert R., and Gary S. Becker. *The Allocation of Time and Goods Over the Life Cycle*. New York: NBER, distributed by Columbia University Press, New York, 1975.

Goldsmith, R. W. *A Study of Saving in the United States*. Vols. 1 and 2. Princeton, N.J.: Princeton University Press, 1955.

Griffin, Keith. "Foreign Capital, Domestic Savings, and Economic Development." *Oxford Bulletin of Economics and Statistics* 32 (1970): 99–112.

Griffin, Keith, and John Enos. "Foreign Assistance: Objectives and Consequences." *Economic Development and Cultural Change* 18 (1970): 313–337.

Grinols, Earl, and Jagdish Bhagwati. "Foreign Capital, Saving and Dependence." *Review of Economics and Statistics* 58 (November 1976): 416–424.

Grossman, Sanford J., and Laurence Weiss. "Saving and Insurance." In *Bayesian Models in Economic Theory*, edited by M. Boyer and R. E. Kihlstrom. New York: Elsevier, ch. 16, 1984.

Hahn, F. G. "Savings and Uncertainty." *Review of Economic Studies* 37, no. 1 (January 1970): 21–24.

Hakansson, N. H. "Optimal Investment and Consumption Strategies for a Class of Utility Functions." Working Paper No. 101. University of California, Los Angeles, 1966.

Hamada, Koichi, and Kazumasa Iwata. "On the International Capital Ownership Pattern at the Turn of the Twenty-First Century." *European Economic Review* 33 (1989): 1055–1085.

Haque, Nadeem U., and Peter Montiel. "Consumption in Developing Countries: Tests for Liquidity Constraints and Finite Horizons." *Review of Economics and Statistics* 71, no. 3 (1989): 408–415.

Harberger, A. C. "Vignettes on the World Capital Market." *American Economic Review* 70 (1980): 331–307.

Harbury, C. D. "Inheritance and the Distribution of Personal Wealth in Britain." *Economic Journal* 72, no. 288 (December 1962): 845–868.

Hayashi, F. "The Effects of Liquidity Constraints on Consumption: A Cross-Sectional Analysis." NBER Working Paper 882. Cambridge, Mass., 1982.

Heckman, James J. "A Life Cycle Model of Earnings, Learning, and Consumption." *Journal of Political Economy* 84, no. 4, part 2, (August 1976): S11–S44.

———. "The Labor Market Earnings of Panamanian Males." *Journal of Human Resources* 21 (4) (1987): 507–542.

Howard, Michael C. *Modern Theories of Income Distribution*. New York: St. Martin's Press, 1979.

Hubbard, R. Glenn. "Precautionary Saving Revisited: Social Security, Individual Welfare, and the Capital Stock." NBER Working Paper 1430, August, 1984.

Hubbard, R. Glenn, and Kenneth L. Judd. "Liquidity Constraints, Fiscal Policy, and Consumption." *Brookings Papers on Economic Activity* 1 (1986): 1–50.

Hurd, Michael D. "Research on the Elderly: Economic Status, Retirement, and Consumption and Saving." *Journal of Economic Literature* 28 (June 1990): 565–637.

Jain, Shail. *Size Distribution of Income: A Compilation of Data*. Washington, D.C.: World Bank, 1975.

Johnson, Harry G. "Poverty and Unemployment." In *The Economics of Poverty*, edited by Burton Weisbrod. Englewood Cliffs, N.J.: Prentice Hall, 1965, 166–170.

———. "The Possibility of Income Losses from Increased Efficiency or Factor Accumulation in the Presence of Tariffs." *Economic Journal* 77 (1967): 151–154.

———. *The Theory of Income Distribution*. London: Gray-Mills, 1973.

Kaldor, Nicholas. "Alternative Theories of Distribution." *Review of Economic Studies* 23, no. 2 (1956): 83–100.

Kalecki, M. *Theory of Economic Dynamics*. London: Allen & Unwin, 1954.

Kessler, Denis and Andre Masson. *Keynes's General Theory: Fifty Years On*. London: Institute of Economic Affairs, 1986.

———. *Modelling the Accumulation and Distribution of Wealth*. Oxford: Clarendon Press, 1988.

Keynes, John Maynard. *A Treatise on Money*. London: Macmillan, 1930.

———. *General Theory of Employment, Interest and Money*. New York: Harcourt, Brace & World, 1936.

———. *The Collected Writings of John Maynard Keynes* 27 (1943): p. 320. Letter to J. E. Meade April 25, 1943.
Kimball, M. S. "Making Sense of Two-Sided Altruism." *Journal of Monetary Economics* 20 (1987): 301–326.
Kimball, M. S., and N. G. Mankiw. "Precautionary Saving and the Timing of Taxes." Harvard University. Mimeo, 1987.
Klein, Lawrence R. "International Aspects of Saving." In Adams and Wachter (1986), ch. 10.
Kotlikoff, Laurence J. *What Determines Savings?* Cambridge, Mass.: MIT Press, 1989.
Kotlikoff, Laurence J., and A. Spivak. "The Family as an Incomplete Annuities Market." *Journal of Political Economy* 89 (1981): 372–391.
Kotlikoff, Laurence J., and Lawrence Summers. "Long Run Tax Incidence and Variable Labor Supply Revisited." Working Paper 111. Los Angeles: University of California, 1978.
———. "The Role of Intergenerational Transfers in Aggregate Capital Accumulation." *Journal of Political Economy* 90 (August 1981): 706–732.
———. "The Contribution of Intergenerational Transfers to Total Wealth: A Reply." In Kessler and Masson (1988), 53–67.
Kotlikoff, Laurence J., John Shoven, and Avia Spivak. "Annuity Insurance, Savings, and Inequality (1986–87)." In Kotlikoff (1989), ch. 5.
Kravis, Irving B. "Comparative Studies of National Income and Prices." *Journal of Economic Literature* 22, no. 1 (March 1984): 1–39.
Kuznets, Simon. "Economic Growth and Income Inequality." *American Economic Review* 89, no. 1 (1955): 1–28.
Lal, Deepak, J. G. Sweder, and Van Wijn Bergen. "Government Deficit, the Real Interest Rate, and LDC Debt: On Global Crowding Out." In Lal and Wolf (1986), 182–238.
Lal, Deepak, and Martin Wolf. *Stagflation, Savings, and the State*. Oxford: Oxford University Press, 1986.
Lee, Dwight R., ed. *Taxation and the Deficit Economy*. San Francisco: Pacific Research Institute for Public Policy, 1986.
Leff, N., and K. Sato. "A Simultaneous Equations Model of Savings in Developing Countries." *Journal of Political Economy* 83, no. 6 (December 1975): 1217–1228.
Lerner, Abba P. "Functional Finance and the Federal Debt." *Social Research* 10 (1943): 38–51.
Levhari, D., and J. Mirman. "Savings and Consumption with an Uncertain Horizon." *Journal of Political Economy* 85 (1977): 265–282.
Levhari, D., and T. N. Srinivasan. "Optimal Savings Under Uncertainty." *Review of Economic Studies* 36 (1969): 153–163.
Lipsey, Robert, E., and Helen S. Tice, eds. *The Measurement of Saving, Investment, and Wealth*. NBER Studies in Income and Wealth. Vol. 52. Chicago: University of Chicago Press, 1989.

Loannides, Y. M. "Heritability of Ability, Intergenerational Transfers and the Distribution of Wealth." School of Management, Boston University. Mimeo, February 1983.

Lucas, Jr., Robert E. "Expectations and the Neutrality of Money." *Journal of Economic Theory* 4, no. 2 (1972): 103–124.

Lydall, H. "The Life Cycle of Income, Saving and Asset Ownership." *Econometrica* 23 (1955): 131–150.

Mankiw, Gregory N. "A Quick Refresher Course in Macroeconomics." *Journal of Economic Literature* 28, no. 4 (December 1990): 1645–1660.

Marshall, Alfred. *Principles of Economics*. 8th ed. London: Macmillan, 1920.

Meade, James E. *The Just Economy*. Vol 4: *Principles of Political Economy*. Albany, N.Y.: State University of New York Press, 1976.

Menchik, Paul L. "Intergenerational Transmission of Inequality: An Empirical Study of Wealth Mobility." *Economica* 46 (1972): 346–362.

———. "Primogeniture, Equal Sharing, and the U.S. Distribution of Wealth." *Quarterly Journal of Economics* 94, no. 2 (1980a): 299–316.

———. "The Importance of Material Inheritance: The Financial Link between Generations." In Smith (1980b). ch. 4.

———. "Unequal Estate Division: Is It Altruism, Reverse Bequest, or Simply Noise?" In Kessler and Masson (1988), 105–116.

Menchik, Paul L., and M. David. "Income Distribution, Lifetime Savings, and Bequests." *American Economic Review* 73 (1983): 672–690.

Mikessell, Raymond F., and James E. Zinser. "The Nature of the Savings Function in Developing Countries: A Survey of the Theoretical and Empirical Literature." *Journal of Economic Literature* 2 (March 1973): 1–26.

Mincer, Jacob. "Progress in Human Capital Analyses of the Distribution of Earnings." In *The Personal Distribution of Incomes*, edited by Tony Atkinson. London: Allen & Unwin, 1976.

Mirer, T. "The Wealth-Age Relationship Among the Aged." *American Economic Review* 69 (1979): 435–443.

Modigliani, Franco. "Fluctuations in the Saving-Income Ratio: A Problem in Economic Forecasting." *Studies in Income and Wealth* 11 (1949). New York: NBER.

———. "Long-Run Implications of Alternative Fiscal Policies and the Burden of the National Debt." *Economic Journal* 71 (1961): 730–755.

———. "Life Cycle, Individual Thrift and the Wealth of Nations." *American Economic Review* 76 (3) (1986): 197–313.

———. "Measuring the Contribution of Intergenerational Transfers to Total Wealth: Conceptual Issues and Empirical Findings." In Kessler and Masson (1988), 21–52.

———. "Life Cycle, Individual Thrift, and the Wealth of Nations." *American Economic Review* 76 (June 1989): 297–313. Nobel Lecture, 1985. First published in *American Economic Review*, 1986. Reprinted in *Essays in Honor of Franco Modigliani*, 1987, pp. 1–28.

Modigliano, Franco, and A. K. Ando. "Tests of the Life Cycle Hypothesis of Savings." *Bulletin of the Oxford University Institute of Economy and Statistics* 19 (1957): 99–124.

Modigliano, Franco, and R. Brumberg. "Utility Analysis and the Consumption Function: An Interpretation of Cross-Section Data." In *Post-Keynesian Economics*, edited by K. K. Kurihara. New Brunswick, N.J.: Rutgers University Press, 1954.

Modigliani, Franco, T. Jappelli, and M. Paggano. "Fiscal Policy and Saving in Italy Since 1860." In Boskin, Flemming, and Gorini (1987). ch. 6.

Munnel, Alicia H. "The Impact of Social Security on Personal Savings." *National Tax Journal* 27 (December 1974): 553–567.

Musgrave, Richard A. *The Theory of Public Finance*. New York: McGraw-Hill, 1959.

OECD. *OECD Economic Outlook*. Paris: OECD. No. 1 (Autumn 1983).

Oulton, N. "Inheritance and the Distribution of Wealth." *Oxford Economic Papers* 28 (1976): 86–101.

Papanek, Gustav. "The Effect of Aid and Other Resource Transfers on Savings and Growth in Less Developed Countries." *Economic Journal* 82 (September 1972): 934–950.

Parsons, Donald O., and Douglas R. Munro. "Intergenerational Transfers in Social Security." In *The Crisis in Social Security: Problems and Prospects*, edited by Michael Boskin. San Francisco: Institute for Contemporary Studies, 1978.

Pasinetti, Luigi L. "Rate of Profit and Income Distribution in Relation to the Rate of Economic Growth." *Review of Economic Studies* 24, no. 4 (October 1962): 267–279.

———. *Growth and Income Distribution*. Cambridge: Cambridge University Press, 1974.

Prebisch, Rhaul. *El Desarollo Economico de la America-Latina y Algunos de Sus Problemas*. Santiago: U.N. Commission for L.A., 1949.

Projector, D. *Survey of Changes in Family Finances*. Washington, D.C.: Board of Governors of the Federal Reserve System, 1968.

Quibria, M. G. "A Note on Foreign Investment, The Savings Function and Immiserization of National Welfare." *Journal of Developmental Economics* 21 no. 2 (1986): 361–372.

Rahman, Anisur. "Foreign Capital and Domestic Savings: A Test of Haavelmo's Hypothesis with Cross-Country Data." *Review of Economics and Statistics* (February 1968): 137–138.

Reynolds, Morgan, and Eugene Smolensky. "Why Changing the Size Distribution of Income Through the FISC Is Now More Difficult." In Horst Claus Recktenwald, *Secular Trends of the Public Sector*. Proceedings of the 32nd Congress of the International Institute of Public Finance, Cujas, Paris, 1978, pp. 69–80.

Roncaglia, A. *Sraffa and the Theory of Prices*. New York: Wiley, 1978.

Rosenstein-Rodan. "International Aid for Underdeveloped Countries." *Review of Economics and Statistics* (May 1961).

Sahota, Gian S. "Theories of Personal Income Distribution: A Survey." *Journal of Economic Literature* 16, no. 1 (March 1978): 1–55.
———. *Poverty: Theory and Policy: A Study of Panama*. Baltimore and London: The Johns Hopkins University Press, 1990.
———. "An Assessment of the Impact of Industrial Policies in Bangladesh." *Bangladesh Development Studies: Special Issue*. (1991).
Sahota, Gian S., and Carlos A. Rocca. "Survey of Latest Developments: A General Model of Family Income Distribution: Chicago and Cambridge Reconciled." *Journal of Policy Modeling* 2 (2) (1980): 75–78.
———. *Income Distribution: Theory, Modeling, and Case Study of Brazil*. Ames, Iowa: Iowa State University Press, 1985.
Sandmo, A. "The Effect of Uncertainty on Saving Decisions." *Review of Economic Studies* 37, no. 2 (July 1970): 353–360.
Schultz, T. Paul. "Long-Term Change in Personal Income Distribution: Theoretical Approach, Evidence, and Explanations." In *The Inequality Controversy: Schooling and Distributive Justice*, edited by Donald M. Levine and Mary Jo Bane. New York: Basic Books, 1975, 147–169.
Scitovsky, Tibor. "Why the US Saving Rate Is Low—A Conflict Between the National Accountant's and the Individual Saver's Perceptions." In Cohen and Harcourt (1986), ch. 7.
Sheshinski, E., and Yoram Weiss. "Uncertainty and Optimal Social Security Systems." *Quarterly Journal of Economics* 96 (1981): 189–206.
Shorrocks, Anthony. "The Age-Wealth Relationship: A Cross-Section and Cohort Analysis." *Review of Economics and Statistics* 57 (1975): 1551–163.
Singh, S. K. "The Determinants of Aggregate Savings." Washington, D.C.: World Bank, 1971.
Smith, James D., ed. *Modeling the Distribution and Intergenerational Transmission of Wealth*. Chicago: University of Chicago Press, 1980.
Snyder, Donald. "Foreign Aid and Domestic Savings: A Spurious Correlation?" *Economic Development and Cultural Change* 39, no. 1 (1990): 175–182.
Solow, Robert M. "Comments on 'How Much (Or Little) Life Cycle Is There in Micro Data?' The Case of the United States and Japan." In Dornbusch, Rudiger et al. eds. *Essays in Honor of Franco Modigliani*, 1987, ch. 7.
Sraffa, P. *Production of Commodities by Means of Commodities*. Cambridge: Cambridge University Press, 1960.
Stiglitz, J. E. "Equality, Taxation and Inheritance." In *Personal Income Distribution*, edited by W. Krelle and A. F. Shorrocks. Amsterdam: North-Holland, 1978.
Summers, Lawrence H. "Capital Taxation and Accumulation in a Life Cycle Growth Model." *American Economic Review* (September 1981): 533–544.
———. "Issues in National Savings Policy." In Adams and Wachter (1986), ch. 4.
———. *Tax Policy and the Economy 3*. Cambridge, Mass.: MIT Press, 1989.
Summers, Lawrence H., Irving B. Kravis, and Alan Heston. "Changes in the World Income Distribution." *Journal of Policy Modeling* 6 (2) (1984): 237–269.

Taubman, Paul. *Income Distribution and Redistribution*. Reading, Mass.: Addison-Wesley, 1978.
Thurow, Lester. *Generating Inequality: Mechanics of Distribution in the U.S. Economy*. New York: Basic Books, 1975.
———. *The Zero-Sum Society*. New York: Basic Books, 1980.
Tinbergen, Jan. *Income Distribution: Analysis and Policies*. Amsterdam: North-Holland, 1975.
Tobin, James. "Relative Income, Absolute Income, and Saving." Previously published: 1951. Reprint in James Tobin, *Essays in Economics, Vol. 2: Consumption and Econometrics*. Cambridge, Mass.: MIT Press, 1987, 91–114.
———. "The Burden of the Public Debt: A Review Article." *Journal of Finance* 20, no. 4 (December 1965): 679–682.
———. "Life Cycle Saving and Balanced Growth." In *Ten Economic Studies in the Tradition of Irving Fisher*, edited by William Fellner et al. New York: Wiley, 1967, 231–236.
———. "Does Fiscal Policy Matter." In James Tobin (P. M. Jackson, ed.). *Policies for Prosperity: Essays in a Keynesian Mode*. Cambridge, MIT Press, 1975.
———. *Asset Accumulation and Economic Activity: Reflections on Contemporary Macroeconomic Theory*. Oxford: Blackwell, 1980.
Tobin, James, and W. Buiter. "Fiscal and Monetary Policies, Capital Formation, and Economic Activity." In *The Government and Capital Formation*, edited by G. M. von Furstenberg. Cambridge, Mass.: Ballinger Press, 1980, 73–151.
Tomes, Nigel. "Inheritance and Inequality Within the Family: Equal Division Among Unequals or Do the Poor Get More?" In Kessler and Masson (1988), 79–104.
Varian, Hal R. "Redistributive Taxation as Social Insurance." *Journal of Public Economy* 14 (1980): 49–68.
Venti, Steven F., and David A. Wise. "Have IRAs Increased U.S. Savings: Evidence from Consumer Expenditure Surveys." *Quarterly Journal of Economics* CV (3) (August 1990): 661–698.
Walters, Alan. "Consumption, Savings and the Multiplier." In Cohen and Harcourt (1986), 89–100.
Wasow, Bernard. "Saving and Dependence with Externally Financed Growth." *Review of Economics and Statistics* 61, no. 1 (February 1979): 150–156.
Weil, P. "Love Thy Children: Reflections on the Barro Debt Neutrality Theorem." *Journal of Monetary Economics* 19 (1987): 377–391.
Weisskopf, Thomas. "The Impact of Foreign Capital Inflow on Domestic Saving in Underdeveloped Countries." *Journal of International Economics* 2 (February 1972): 21–38.
Welch, Finis. "Effects of Cohort Size on Earnings: The Baby Boom Babies' Financial Bust." *Journal of Political Economy* 87 (5), Part II (October 1979): S65–S98.
Wise, David A. "Individual Retirement Accounts and Saving." In Feldstein (1987), ch. 1.

Wolff, Nancy. *Income Redistribution and the Social Security Program*. Ann Arbor: U.M.I. Research Press, 1987.

Wolfson, Michael C. "The Bequest Process and the Causes of Inequality in the Distribution of Wealth." In Smith (1980), ch. 5.

Wong, David Y. "What Do Saving-Investment Relationships Tell Us About Capital Mobility?" *Journal of International Money and Finance* 9 (1990): 60–74.

World Bank. *World Tables*. Baltimore: The Johns Hopkins University Press for the World Bank, 1990.

Yaari, Menachem E. "Uncertain Lifetime, Life Insurance, and the Theory of the Consumer." *Review of Economic Studies* 32 (April 1965): 137–150.

Zeldes, S. "Consumption and Liquidity Constraints: An Empirical Investigation." University of Pennsylvania, R. L. White Center for Financial Research, Discussion Paper 24–85, 1986.

Commentary by William A. Darity, Jr.
University of North Carolina at Chapel Hill

Gian Sahota's chapter is useful for a number of reasons. The first is the comprehensiveness of its coverage of two seemingly disparate branches of literature in economics: the literature on savings behavior and the literature on the distribution of income. The second is the detail with which he examines the relevant literature on each topic from the perspective of an applied microeconomist.

But it is vital that the reader understand that Sahota's perspective is that of an applied microeconomist, because that is the central weakness of the chapter as well. Sahota's perspective is necessarily narrow and dismissive of approaches that do not tackle the relationship between saving and distribution from that particular point of view. Indeed the literature in economics written from the approach of applied microeconomics rarely conceives of saving and distribution as themes that form a unified whole.

Thus we find missing from this chapter a discussion of growth theory in the classical tradition that is premised on a regressive redistribution of income toward the capitalists, who possess the higher saving rate by class, which raises the aggregate saving rate and then results in a higher rate of accumulation. This is the essential element of Ricardo's analysis of avenues to delay the approach of the stationary state and Lewis's (1954) much later construction of a model of growth with unlimited supplies of labor.

In the Lewis model the fixity of the real wage ensures that as the modern sector expands, the proportion of national income going to capital increases relative to the proportion going to labor. As long as the laboring class is far more numerous than the capitalist class and as long as the variance in income among members of the laboring class is narrower than that among the capitalists, the shift in the functional distribution of income toward capital will be reflected in an adverse change in the size distribution of income. This means, in turn, that under the classical view in Ricardo-Lewis terms there is an inverse relationship between economic growth and the distribution of income mediated by a rise in the savings rate. The Ricardo-Lewis model is one of savings-cum-distribution-driven economic growth.

It is possible to look at the historical record to assess whether this a realistic model. Lewis's assumption of an unlimited supply of labor to the modern sector aside, one can ask, at minimum, (1) whether a rise in the savings rate correlates with a deterioration in the distribution of income, (2) whether economic growth is driven by savings, and (3) whether a rise in the rate of economic growth correlates with a deterioration in the distribution of income.

These questions lie at the heart of a recent empirical dissertation by Leightner (1989), in which he generally finds less support for the classical view than the more Keynesian view that, on the margin at least, growth and improved equality go hand in hand. Leightner's study examined the cases of Thailand, the United Kingdom, Sweden, South Africa, and Korea, using data from the 1960s through 1980s. He found that only in the Thai case did the classical phenomenon of growth and diminished equality move in tandem. Leightner's results for Korea parallel Rao's (1978) earlier discovery that the period of most rapid growth for Korea also was a period of an equalizing spiral with respect to incomes. Fei et al. (1979) also arrived at similar anticlassical findings in their study of growth and distribution in post–World War II Taiwan.

But Lewis (1955, pp. 225–226) was inspired in part by a stylized fact he detected in the growth experiences of countries drawn from a considerably earlier historical epoch, that of the eighteenth, nineteenth, and early twentieth centuries. Lewis observed that in stagnant economies during that era the saving rate typically was 4 to 5 percent, but in growing economies it was 12 percent or more. He attributed this alteration in the saving rate to class transformation and income distribution (Lewis, 1955, pp. 225–226): "the essential change ... is the emergence of the a new class in society—the profit-making entrepreneurs—which is more thrifty than all the other classes ... and whose share of national income increases relatively to all others."

Perhaps the connection between saving and growth was stronger in earlier times. The connection may be weaker after the development of a complex financial apparatus that can provide credit without necessarily awaiting a new act of private saving. Investment can move independently of saving to such an extent that by the time he wrote *The General Theory*, Keynes already was treating saving as the passive actor in the macroeconomic game.

Sahota only borders on addressing these grand historical questions explicitly at the end of his chapter, where he finally introduces the Kuznets U-curve hypothesis and provides his own new estimates of the Kuznets relationship. And his estimates are very interesting, broadly consistent with the findings of a host of World Bank affiliated researchers in the mid-1970s (e.g., Ahluwalia, 1974, and Jain, 1975) that such a U-relationship exists between the level of per capita income and various measures of the distribution of income in cross-sectional data sets for a large sample of countries.

Unfortunately, the hypothesis really seems to concern the dynamics of growth for individual countries, and very little work has been done (since Kuznets' initial efforts) to explore the relationship between economic development and income distribution with secular time series data nation-by-nation. A rare exception is Soltow's (1965, 1968) work on a limited number of countries for which he could find data suggestive of long-run patterns.

One potential explanation for the downward sloping portion of the Kuznets U-curve is the presence of a Ricardo-Lewis growth dynamic for low-income countries experiencing a rise in per capita income. The turning point in the U-curve could correspond to the turning point in the Lewis model where additional employment can be purchased only with increased wages. Thereafter, arguably, the functional distribution of income shifts in favor of labor and the size distribution also improves. Without an interest in these "grand" questions of the dynamics of growth, Sahota does not even address these potential theoretical explanations for the existence of the U-curve.

Indeed, the Cambridge school tradition, which is based on the classical approach to growth and distribution, receives very brief notice in Sahota's chapter and is set aside with the tart observation that "most economists would agree that the time of this theory has passed." Perhaps most economists would agree, but this one is not in that putative majority. If the time of grand dynamics is past, with what are we left? Fiscal policy, bequests and inheritances, and human capital — a yawning chasm of options, pun intended. The more interesting question, which certainly remains relevant to the poorer nations of the world and the societies of Eastern Europe that are dismantling "actually existing socialism" is, to achieve growth, must they necessarily make a Faustian pact with the devil and institute a worsening distribution of income? Fiscal policy, bequests and inheritances, and human capital potentially are subordinate aspects of this larger theme.

The Cambridge school tradition certainly is not dead. The Pasinetti approach, which associates different saving rates with different heritable classes of savers (workers and capitalists or rentiers), and the Kaldor approach, which associates different savings rates with types of income (wages and profits), have a wide range of applications in both theoretical and empirical economics today. For example, the neo-neo political economy literature represented by Alesina and Tabellini's (1989) recent attempt to theorize about capital flight from LDCs has at its base, without acknowledgment of the source, Pasinetti's (1962) macrodistribution framework. The work that Findlay (1981) and I (Darity, 1990) have done on the fundamental determinants of the terms of trade also has utilized the Anglo-Italian approach to saving and distribution. Macroeconometric models in the Kaleckian tradition combine Cambridge distribution theory with markup pricing; that work has been summarized nicely by Reynolds (1987).

I suspect that the basis for Sahota's dismissal of the Cambridge (England, not Massachusetts!) tradition goes to the heart of the philosophical gulf that separates the applied microeconomist's view of the world from the Anglo-Italian school. For in the Cambridge tradition there is always a residual portion of the national product that does not constitute a factor return. It is a pure surplus, and it is the ultimate source of profits and rents, the income of the capitalist-cum-rentier class. The surplus approach to economics is borne of Sraffa's (1960) interpretation of classical economics as an integrated theory of pricing and distribution where equilibrium is dictated by fulfillment of complete intersectoral equalization of profit rates. The profit rate is derived from the allocation of the surplus among capitalists and is not vested with the connotations of time preference, a reward for waiting, or any of the other apologetic niceties for extraction of surplus labor time that characterize neoclassicism.

That neoclassicists react to the notion of a pure surplus as if it were an oxymoron is not surprising. Their mode of thought leads them to view all income as necessarily a factor payment. But if the neoclassicists embrace marginal product factor pricing as the foundation of their approach to distribution, their belief that all income must be some type of factor reward is sustainable and logically consistent only under conditions of constant returns to scale. Even on the terrain of neoclassical economics, there must be a pure surplus if marginal product factor pricing coexists with decreasing returns to scale. Under increasing returns, thoroughgoing marginal product factor pricing cannot be maintained because there will be a shortfall in aggregate income relative to the factor shares.

These anomalies do not even arise in the Cambridge surplus approach; the Sraffa system's configuration is independent of any specific assumption about returns to scale. The Cambridge tradition actually offers a more general approach to saving and distribution than the neoclassical approach that undergirds applied microeconomics. Indeed, the interesting theoretical questions for those researchers using the surplus approach are quite different. They include the following: What mechanisms assure that there is a tendency toward profit rate equalization? What is the nature of prices and distribution under conditions when profit rate equalization is incomplete? If capital flows are invoked as the means of bringing about profit rate equalization, are the relevant flows primarily movements of physical or financial capital? Does such a tendency toward equalization exist on a subnational, national, or international scale, if at all? This research agenda with respect to saving and distribution is wholly distinct from that emerging from applied microeconomics.

Sahota's discussion of the Keynesian theory of saving and distribution — which reverses the relationship between growth and equality from the one posited by the classicals (excepting Adam Smith and Thomas Malthus, who both posited a key role for effectual demand) — also is unsatisfactory. In the Ricardo-Lewis variant of the classical approach, growth is savings driven. In the Keynesian theory growth is demand-driven, so that higher consumption and hence a distribution of income that favors groups or classes with lower propensities to save is more conducive to growth. Thus Leightner has aptly dubbed the Ricardo-Lewis view as an anti-equality approach to economic growth while he labels the Keynesian view as pro-equality.

Sahota bemoans the absence of research on saving functions comparable to that undertaken on the consumption function. But if saving is merely the dual of consumption, to the extent that there is a well-developed body of research on the latter, then there is a well-developed implicit body of research on the former. Certainly I see no great research benefit from sending waves of dissertation students out to estimate aggregate saving functions instead of aggregate consumption functions.

To the extent that distribution is viewed as prior to saving and indeed as a critical determinant of saving, then any of the factors that influence the distribution of income also can influence saving (and consumption). Omitted from Sahota's discussion is the literature linking racial and ethnic inequalities in societies to income distribution. This is an especially important consideration in nations that are ethnically plural. Lewis (1983) began to systematize this discussion, and more recently, Henry (1989) has argued that the position and shape of country-specific U-curves will be altered by the nature of their racial and ethnic makeup and the degree of inequality among these groups of the population.

Disaggregation of the population into subgroups with different saving rates, an impulse prompted by the Cambridge tradition, often yields rich insights. For example, Bunting (1991) recently has argued that the fall in the U.S. saving rate—a fall that has been the object of much attention lately—can be best explained by disaggregating the U.S. population into income classes. Bunting demonstrates that if the U.S. population is partitioned by quintile income share recipients, the fall in the aggregate saving rate can be shown to be due in direct fashion to the combination of a redistribution of income between 1972 and 1986 that favored the topmost quintile and a decline in saving rates for all quintiles. Bunting argues that the fall in the saving rates for the lowest three quintiles, all of whom were engaged in net dissavings in 1986, can be explained in large measure by the adverse effects on their income position of the regressive redistribution of income that occurred during the Carter and especially the Reagan administration years. Bunting suggests a complex set of interdependencies whereby changes in the distribution of income lead to changes in subgroup saving rates, which in turn influence the aggregate saving rate and volume of savings out of the prevailing level of income.

Finally, I would note that the analysis of saving and distribution can be conducted at the international level. The distribution of income between countries can affect which nations are net savers and hence potential lenders versus which nations are net borrowers. The reallocation of international savings coupled with the analysis of the international distribution of income can lead to fruitful analyses of the external debt crisis of LDCs, capital flows between nations, and the like. Recent empirical work (see, e.g., Arndt, 1991) on the intercountry correlations between saving and investment activity is an entry point to these issues.

Much, much theoretical and empirical work has to be done on the linkage between saving and distribution that returns to the subject that prompted the emergence of economics as a field; the subject of economic growth. But the subject will not flower before our eyes in the same way if our eyes are covered by the lenses of applied microeconomics.

References

Ahluwalia, Montek. "Income Inequality: Some Dimensions of the Problem." In *Redistribution with Growth*, edited by Holis Chenery et al. Oxford: Oxford University Press, 1974.

Alesina, Alberto, and Guido Tabellini. "External Debt, Capital Flight, and Political Risk." *Journal of International Economics* 27 (November 1989): 199–220.

Arndt, H. W. "Saving, Investment and Growth: Recent Asian Experience." *Banca Nazionale Del Lavoro Quarterly Review* 177 (June 1991): 151–64.

Bunting, David. "Saving and the Distribution of Income." *Journal of Post-Keynesian Economics* 14, no. 1 (Fall 1991): 3–22.

Darity, William, Jr. "The Fundamental Determinants of the Terms of Trade Reconsidered." *American Economic Review* (September 1990): 816–828.

Fei, J. C., D. Ranis, and S. Kuo. *Growth and Equity: The Taiwan Case*. Oxford: Oxford University Press, 1979.

Findlay, Ronald. "The Fundamental Determinants of the Terms of Trade." In *The World Economic Order: Past and Prospects*, edited by Sven Grassman and Erik Lundberg. London, 1981, 425–457.

Henry, Ralph. "Inequality in Plural Societies: An Exploration." *Social and Economic Studies* 38, no. 2 (1989): 69–110.

Jain, Shail. *Size Distribution of Income: A Compilation of Data*. Washington, D.C.: The World Bank, 1975.

Kaldor, Nicholas. "Alternative Theories of Distribution." *Review of Economic Studies* 23, no. 2 (1955–56): 83–100.

Kuznets, Simon. "Economic Growth and Income Inequality." *American Economic Review* (1955): 1–28.

Leightner, Jonathan. *Essays on the Compatibility of Increased Equality and Growth and on Technology Transfer to Japan*. Unpublished Ph.D. dissertation, University of North Carolina at Chapel Hill, 1989.

Lewis, W. Arthur. "Economic Development with Unlimited Supplies of Labour." *The Manchester School* 28 (1954): 139–191.

Lewis, W. Arthur. *The Theory of Economic Growth*. London: George Allen & Unwin, 1955.

Lewis, W. Arthur. *Racial Conflict and Economic Development*. Cambridge: Harvard University Press, 1983.

Pasinetti, Luigi. "Rate of Profit and Income Distribution." *Review of Economic Studies* 29, no. 4 (October 1962): 267–279.

Rao, D. C. "Economic Growth and Equity in the Republic of Korea." *World Development* 6, no. 3 (1978): 383–396.

Reynolds, Peter. *Political Economy: A Synthesis of Kaleckian and Post Keynesian Economics*. New York: St. Martin's Press, 1987.

Ricardo, David. *Principles of Political Economy and Taxation*, edited by P. Sraffa and M. Dobb. Cambridge: Cambridge University Press 1951.

Soltow, Lee. *Toward Income Equality in Norway*. Madison: University of Wisconsin Press, 1965.

Soltow, Lee. "Long Run Changes in British Income Inequality." *Economic History Review* (April 1968): 17–29.

Sraffa, Piero. *Production of Commodities by means of Commodities*. Cambridge: Cambridge University Press, 1960.

Commentary by Paul J. Taubman
University of Pennsylvania

On the whole Dr. Sahota has done an excellent expository job on a difficult topic. Nevertheless, I feel obliged to make a few points. First, the material on taxes might have been expanded and better integrated. The dead weight loss from a proportional income tax may be more or less than that from an equal revenue yield consumption or wage tax. The income tax distorts both saving and labor-leisure choices, whereas the other two taxes distort only the saving choice. However, the income tax rate needed to provide equal revenues is smaller.

Second, a progressive tax rate means that in all utility functions other than a Leontief, the tangencies of indifference curves and the after-tax budget line imply that consumption–income elasticities calculated from cross-sectional data with no inclusion of after-tax interest rates should be greater than one. Elaboration of this point can be found in Taubman (1975).

Third, there is no discussion of interest rate elasticities or of the role of saving for a fixed goal, such as children's college tuition. Here increased interest rates reduce the amount needed to be set aside.

Fourth, Sahota should be more cautious about the Becker-Tomes results on equity and efficiency in parental provision of education and bequests. Their results only necessarily hold if parents are wealthy enough to provide all siblings with bequests. Behrman, Pollak, and Taubman (1982) provide an alternative conclusion about education and bequests in an altruistic model where bequests and education are in separable parts of the utility function.

Finally, the discussion relating wealth to age should be qualified. Currently much of the elderly's wealth is invested in pension and social security assets, which are dissaved but which are not included in the calculations of most of the cited items. Also although only half of the elderly receive pensions, the dollar amounts exceed social security benefits. They should be mentioned as should the strange difference of treatment in the National Income Accounts; that is, social security taxes are deducted from personal income whereas social security benefits are added, but pension contributions (and the fund's earnings) are added to personal income whereas pension benefits are *not* added.

References

Behrman, Jere R., Robert A. Pollak, and Paul Taubman. "Parental Preferences and Provision for Progeny." *Journal of Political Economy* 90 (February 1982): 52–73.

Taubman, Paul J. "The Interest Elasticity of Savings, Income Taxes, and the Permanent-Income Hypothesis." *Journal of Political Economy* 83 (February 1975): 215–218.

6 INCREASING THE SAVING RATE: AN ANALYSIS OF THE TRANSITION PATH

Laurence S. Seidman and Kenneth A. Lewis

University of Delaware

Suppose an economy permanently raises its saving rate. In the neoclassical growth model of the late 1950s, the economy attains an attractive new steady-state with higher per capita output and, provided the new saving rate does not exceed Phelps's golden rule rate, higher per capita consumption. The early steady-state papers tempted readers to look longingly at the final steady-state and ignore the discomforts of the journey that might be required to reach it.

Classroom experience has shown, however, that even an undergraduate of modest interest and ability will suspect a trap. If insufficiently polite, the student will invariably ask. "How long will it take to get there,' and won't we lose in the short run?" Unfortunately, a simple authoritarian suppression of the question seldom succeeds. The question is irrepressible. In fact, our profession itself took only several years to go beyond steady-state analysis and confront this central question.

1. The Sato Controversy Revisited

The issue was joined in the 1960s by R. Sato and K. Sato and the aftermath of their papers cast a dark shadow over the proposal to raise the national saving rate — a shadow that lingers to this day. R. Sato (1963, p. 23) struck first, jolting analysts who had contented themselves with steady-state analysis: "In our example, it takes from 50 to 150 years to achieve 90 per cent of the total adjustment."

In a brave rescue attempt, K. Sato (1966, pp. 263, 265) responded that it's not that bad:

> Indeed, the adjustment time responds very sensitively to realistic modifications of the neoclassical model. These modifications refer to explicit recognition of depreciation of capital and of technical improvements embodied in new investment and the saving behavior underlying the model. Then, the adjustment time at issue may be reduced by as much as three-quarters. ... If it takes 100 years to cover 90 per cent of the displacement in the model of [R. Sato], we can expect it to be between 25 and 37.5 years in our model.

But with a friend like this, who needs an enemy? Despite K. Sato's noble attempt to make an increase in the saving rate seem bearable, his reference to a quarter of a century did little to dispel the gloom.

In reacting to the Sato controversy, it was natural for economists to focus on how the Satos differed. Yet we want to argue that, on the contrary, it is crucial to grasp that the Satos agreed on two fundamental points. First, they concentrated on the capital–output ratio or its reciprocal. Second, they concentrated on what we will call "the epsilon-(ε)-time"—the time required for their key variable to close the fraction ε of the gap between its initial value and its final steady-state value in response to an increase in the saving rate.

Virtually all analysts accepted their decision to focus on ε-time. For example, ε-time is the only measure Burmeister and Dobell (1970) consider in their treatment of the transition phase of a neoclassical growth model, citing R. Sato and K. Sato. It is the measure used by Conlisk (1966), Williams and Crouch (1972), and Ramanathan (1975, 1982) in their adjustment time studies. R. Sato (1980) and Gapinski (1981) also use ε-time to evaluate the transition path of a growth model. Yet we believe that the Satos' use of the ε-time of the capital–output variable (or its reciprocal) has been extremely misleading.

In its place, we offer three alternative measures of the transition path: (1) *the sacrifice time* τ—the time that elapses until the new consumption path overtakes the path consumption would have traversed at the initial saving rate, (2) *the T-year gain* (of consumption or output)—the percentage gap in year T between the path a variable traverses under the new saving rate and the path that variable would have traversed under the initial saving rate, and (3) *the saving rate return*—the discount rate required to make the present value of the post-τ consumption gains equal to the present value of the pre-τ consumption losses. It turns out that our three measures generate a much more optimistic impression concerning the response of the economy to an increase in the saving rate.

In a paper on the Sato controversy (Lewis and Seidman, 1991a) we use the same growth model as K. Sato, one based on Solow (1959). The model includes both embodied and disembodied technical progress and concentrates on consumption and output. By contrast, K. Sato focused exclusively on an adjusted-capital−output ratio (adjusted for embodied technical progress), and R. Sato focused exclusively on the output−capital ratio. Phelps (1962) and K. Sato (1966) showed that if the saving rate is fixed, then the model converges to steady-state values for consumption per effective labor, output per effective labor, and the adjusted-capital−output ratio or its reciprocal (where effective labor grows faster than labor due to technical progress).

Consider this result for plausible parameter values. For an $\varepsilon = 90$ percent—the closing of 90 percent of the gap between the initial and final steady-state values—the ε-time for K. Sato's capital−output ratio is 31.2 years—gloomy indeed. But now consider our three measures. The sacrifice time is only 6.5 years, the decade gain in consumption is 1.3 percent, the decade gain in output is 5.0 percent, and the saving rate return is 15.0 percent.

How can this be? The ε-time measure, in fact, has a serious weakness. It tells the time required to close the fraction ε of the gap between the initial and final steady-states without indicating whether that gap is large or small. If the gap is large, as in this example, then the ε-time (with a high value of ε) may be long, yet the sacrifice time may be short, the decade gains significant, and the saving rate return high.

Thus, in this example, the Sato measure of three decades will no doubt seem gloomy to the average citizen. But when the same citizen is told that consumption will be permanently greater after roughly half a decade of sacrifice, that within a decade consumption will be more than 1 percent higher and output 5 percent higher, and that a comparison of future gains and short-run losses yields a rate of return of 15 percent, our citizen likely will be considerably cheered up about raising the saving rate.

2. Empirical Analysis: A Continuous Time Model

Although we can conveniently provide transition path estimates using "plausible" parameter values, "plausible" will not do if we want to get serious about an actual experiment with the U.S. economy. In a recent paper (Lewis and Seidman, 1991b), we analyze the quantitative consequences of a permanent unphased increase in the U.S. gross saving rate.

Following Solow (1959), Phelps (1962), and K. Sato (1966), we bravely assume that the U.S. economy can be tolerably approximated by a closed one-sector neoclassical growth model with a constant-returns-to-scale Cobb-Douglas production function (where gross output is a function of the factors) with technical progress (disembodied and/or embodied) and that there is constant utilization of factors along the transition path. We adopt the model of K. Sato (1966), which is similar to Phelps's (1962) and is based on the putty-putty vintage capital model of Solow (1959). In such a model a permanent increase in the gross saving rate causes the economy to move gradually from one steady-state to another.

We focus on the transition path. How long does it take before the new consumption path overtakes the control path? How long is this *sacrifice time* for the U.S. economy? What is the percentage change in consumption or output relative to its control path after T years—the T-*year gain*? What is the *saving rate return*—the internal rate of return on a permanent increase in the saving rate?

We readily admit that certain features of our model—in particular, constant returns to scale, Cobb-Douglas, putty-putty, closed economy, constant utilization of factors along the transition path, and the use of gross rather than net output and saving—can each be questioned. We do not attempt to refute arguments for increasing returns to scale (Romer, 1987), CES or translog, putty-clay (Gapinski, 1981), open economy (Ribe and Beeman, 1986), inclusion of human and government capital (Eisner, 1989), transition path underutilization of factors (Conlisk, 1966), or a net model (Gramlich, 1984) because we find some of these arguments plausible.

Instead, we offer a different defense of these features. The advantage of the Solow-Phelps-Sato vintage capital model (where gross investment embodying current technology is a fraction of gross output), with its Cobb-Douglas functional form and constant factor utilization, is that it generates a differential equation that yields formulas for the sacrifice time and T-year gains for an unphased increase in the saving rate, assuming the economy is initially in a steady-state. This mathematical tractability explains its frequent adoption in the growth model literature. For example, the sacrifice time is given by

$$\ln \left[\Delta_s/(1 + \Delta_s - \psi^{-\beta/\alpha}) \right]/\theta, \qquad (6-1)$$

where Δ_s is the percentage increase in the saving rate, ψ is a function of the saving rate, α and β are the Cobb-Douglas exponents, and θ is a function of the rates of embodied and disembodied technical progress, the deterioration rate, and the labor growth rate.

Our study tries to give an up-to-date empirical treatment of their model. A benchmark is useful for comparing studies that make alternative assumptions or cannot be solved analytically. Moreover, some of these features may be acceptable approximations. For example, in their investigation based on the two-input translog function with the constant returns to scale constraint, Jorgenson, Gollop, and Fraumeni (1987) write:

> Our overall conclusion is that the aggregate production function can be represented in the form proposed by Cobb and Douglas (1928). Aggregate technical change can be regarded, equivalently, as Hicks neutral, Harrod neutral, or Solow neutral." [p. 336]

Experimenting with a two-input CES function with the vintage capital data described later, we found evidence that the estimated elasticity of substitution may not differ significantly from 1.

Also, as Feldstein-Horoika (1980) and Feldstein-Bacchetta (1989) contend, an increase in U.S. saving could result in an increase in U.S. investment that is almost as great, despite the openness of the U.S. economy. Moreover, we performed a calculation that shows that it is at least possible that the sacrifice time may not be very sensitive to whether an increase in U.S. saving flows abroad or "stays home."

Finally, we concede the difficulty of maintaining full employment in the initial stage of the transition path if the increase in the saving rate is unphased. However, it is not obvious that a phase-in necessary to maintain constant utilization of factors would significantly lengthen the sacrifice time. We will consider a more realistic phased increase in the saving rate in the section 3.

Our econometric estimation with embodied technical progress builds on work by Solow (1962, 1963) and Intriligator (1965) with the Cobb-Douglas vintage model. Using BEA data on gross investment, we construct vintage capital series for equipment, plant, and residential structures and then aggregate using the BLS data on rental income shares. We construct effective capital series for alternative values of embodied technical progress. We also check our results against two other data sets (Jorgenson, Gollop, and Fraumeni [JGF], 1987; and Bureau of Labor Statistics [BLS], 1988), where all technical progress is disembodied.

Although there is a substantial theoretical literature on the adjustment time in a growth model (for example, K. Sato, 1966), and a large empirical literature on production functions (for example, JGF, 1987), there are few recent papers that try to assess the impact of a change in the U.S. saving rate on the U.S. consumption path.

What do we find? First, the "sacrifice time" is roughly six years. Across alternative specifications and data sets, the sacrifice time varies within a band of a third of a decade to a decade. Second, the sacrifice time is insensitive to the percentage increase in the saving rate. An increase in that percentage steepens the time profile of the change in consumption around a relatively fixed sacrifice time: The immediate loss in consumption is greater, but so is the steady-state gain, whereas the sacrifice time remains roughly constant. Third, the "saving rate return"—the internal rate of return on a permanent increase in the saving rate—is roughly 16 percent and is insensitive to the percentage increase in the saving rate.

In one example with parameter values supported by econometric analysis, in response to an increase in the U.S. gross saving rate from 15 percent to 18 percent: the sacrifice time would be 5.8 years; at the end of a decade, output would be 5.5 percent higher and consumption would be 1.7 percent higher; in the long-run, output would be 10.6 percent higher and consumption would be 6.7 percent higher; and the saving rate return would be 16.5 percent.

3. Empirical Analysis: A Discrete Period Simulation Model

The continuous time model of the preceding section has the seductive allure of mathematical tractability, permitting the derivation of formulas for the sacrifice time, the T-year gains of output and consumption, and the steady-state gains of these variables. However, these advantages have a price. We are compelled to assume the production function is Cobb-Douglas, the economy begins at a steady-state, and the increase in the saving rate is unphased.

In another paper (Lewis and Seidman, 1991c) we have dispensed with the advantages of tractability in order to relax these three restrictions. Being cautious by nature, we retain the rest of the framework. We assume that the U.S. economy can be tolerably approximated by a closed one-sector neoclassical growth model with a constant-returns-to-scale translog production function with technical progress (disembodied and/or embodied).

We retain the putty-putty vintage-capital approach of Solow (1959), which includes embodied technical progress. We utilize our own vintage capital series from Bureau of Economic Analysis (1987) gross investment data following Solow (1962, 1963) and Intriligator (1965). We jointly estimate a two-factor translog production function and a capital income share equation using three-stage least squares with a correction for first-order serial correlation.

Our objective is to obtain empirically based estimates of transition paths generated by alternative phase-in periods, using a more flexible production function. We therefore adopt a discrete time version of the model and perform computer simulations based on our translog production function estimates.

The analysis of an abrupt significant increase in the saving rate using a Cobb-Douglas continuous time model (described in section 2) is an extremely useful first step in providing a benchmark. However, it is necessary to go beyond this framework for two reasons. First, the actual economy may be unable to immediately shift substantial resources from the consumption sector to the investment sector while maintaining full employment, contrary to the assumption of the neoclassical model. The neoclassical assumption is more likely to be valid if the phase-in is gradual rather than abrupt.

Second, if the intent of policy is to raise the saving rate, a gradual phase-in is probably more desirable. Under an abrupt increase in the saving rate, consumption per labor will most likely decline initially, so that there will be a literal fall in the standard of living in the short run. By contrast, under a sufficiently gradual phase-in, consumption per labor will grow more slowly than it otherwise would have in the short-run, but a literal fall in the standard of living can be avoided.

The key equation in the simulation model is

$$J = (1 - \delta)J_{-1} + (1 + \mu)^{t-1} (s_{-1} Q_{-1}). \qquad (6-2)$$

It says that this period's effective capital J equals last period's (reduced by deterioration) plus last period's investment (adjusted for embodied technical progress), where I_{-1} equals last period's saving rate times output, $s_{-1}Q_{-1}$. Labor L is assumed to grow at a constant rate. Given this period's J and L, the translog production function yields this period's Q, and so the simulation continues, period by period.

How much difference does it make to use a more flexible function for production, allow the economy to begin not at a steady-state, and gradually phase-in the increase in the saving rate? It turns out: Not much.

With three-year phasing of a 20 percent increase in the saving rate, the sacrifice time is roughly eight years, compared to six years with an unphased increase and ten years for a six-year phasing. With three-year phasing, the decade gain is roughly 4 percent for output and 1 percent for consumption; the five-decade gain is roughly 10 percent for output and 6 percent for consumption; and the saving rate return is roughly 15 percent. These magnitudes are quite close to those reported for the continuous time model in the preceding section.

It strains credulity to believe that constant utilization of factors can be maintained in the face of an abrupt increase in the saving rate from 15 percent to 18 percent. However, with proper monetary policy, it might be possible to achieve this goal under three- or six-year phasing. Fortunately, our estimates are changed only modestly when we allow for more realistic, gradual phasing.

4. The Impact on the Wage of Low-Educated Labor

Thus far all of the analysis has focused on the consequence for consumption and output. What about the wage of low-educated labor? Controversy continues over whether capital accumulation has an antipoverty dividend. For example, in a recent article, Danziger and Gottschalk (1989, pp. 182–183) write:

> Incentives to increase the rate of capital formation may increase both growth and poverty. The increased demand for capital will be accompanied by an increase in demand for high-skilled workers and a decrease in demand for low-skilled workers if capital is complementary with high-skilled workers and substitutable for low-skilled workers. Poverty will increase unless the labor-upgrading response to the resulting increase in the wages for high-skilled workers more than offsets the decreased wages for those who remain unskilled.

If capital and low-educated labor are "q-substitutes," then the wage of low-educated labor indeed will be reduced by capital accumulation. However, if capital and low-educated labor are "q-complements," then an increase in investment will raise the wage of low-educated labor.[1]

In a recent paper (Lewis and Seidman, 1991d), we seek to estimate the quantitative impact of an increase in the U.S. investment rate on the wage of low-educated labor. A two-factor production function will not do. We estimate a three-factor constant-returns-to-scale translog production function with capital, high-educated labor and low-educated labor, with technical progress (disembodied or embodied). "High-educated labor" is labor with at least some college, while "low-educated labor" is labor with at most a high-school degree. Using the estimated production function, we simulate the impact of an increase in the U.S. gross investment rate on the marginal product and thus on the wage of low-educated labor. In the simulations, we assume that the U.S. economy can be tolerably approximated by a closed one-sector neoclassical growth model.

We assume that each factor is paid its marginal product, which is a function of the factor ratios. If the United States phases in an increase in its investment rate, the wage (marginal product) of each type of labor will in general change due to the change in the factor ratios. A three-factor model does not guarantee a priori that both marginal products will increase. The wage of a particular type of labor will increase if and only if that labor and capital are q-complements. We estimate the percentage change in each wage relative to its control path after T years—the "T-year gain (loss)."

Not surprisingly, we adopt the putty-putty vintage-capital approach of Solow (1959), which includes embodied technical progress utilizing our own vintage capital series. The production function contains two labor inputs: low-educated labor (high school or less) and high-educated labor (more than high school). Each of the labor inputs is a Divisia index of labor hours. For each education level, we aggregate over part time and full time, male and female workers for seven age categories. We jointly estimate the production function and two factor income share equations using three alternative techniques: seemingly unrelated regression, three-stage least squares, and three-stage least squares with a correction for first-order serial correlation. The latter technique uses generalized differences to estimate the three-equation model, allowing for both our own and cross-equation autocorrelation. Our estimation shows that capital and low-educated labor are indeed q-complements: Capital accumulation does raise the marginal product of low-educated labor.

Using the estimated production function, we simulate the impact of an increase in the U.S. gross investment rate on the marginal product and thus on the wage of low-educated labor. What do we find? A three-year phase-in of a 20 percent increase in the U.S. gross investment rate would raise the wage of low-educated labor roughly 1 percent in five years, 3 percent in ten years, 4 percent in fifteen years, and nearly 4.5 percent in twenty years. Capital accumulation does indeed have a significant anti-poverty dividend.

5. Conclusion

Our research has made us feel more optimistic about the transition than we felt when we read the earlier growth model literature, especially the papers by R. Sato and even K. Sato. We must temper our enthusiasm by recognizing that we have not considered a more realistic putty-clay framework (Gapinski, 1981) or the risk of transitional unemployment (Conlisk, 1966), as well as several other issues noted earlier. Nevertheless, here's why we feel better about raising the U.S. saving rate.

First, we believe we have better measures of the transition path than the traditional ε-time—the time required to close the fraction ε of the gap between the initial and final steady-state values. In one example with "plausible" parameter values, 31 years are required to close 90 percent of the gap. But "the sacrifice time τ"—the time that elapses before the new consumption overtakes the control path—is only 6.5 years; the decade gain in consumption (above its control path) is 1.3 percent, the decade gain in output is 5.0 percent, and the saving rate return—the discount rate required to make the present value of the post-τ consumption gains equal to the present value of the pre-τ consumption losses—is a healthy 15.0 percent.

Second, using a continuous time Cobb-Douglas model that yields convenient formulas for the sacrifice time and T-year gains, we estimate that the U.S. sacrifice time is roughly six years for an unphased increase in the saving rate, and the "saving rate return"—the internal rate of return on a permanent increase in the saving rate—is roughly 16 percent. In one example with parameter values supported by econometric analysis, in response to an increase in the U.S. gross saving rate from 15 percent to 18 percent, the sacrifice time would be 5.8 years; at the end of a decade, output would be 5.5 percent higher and consumption would be 1.7 percent higher; in the long run, output would be 10.6 percent higher and consumption would be 6.7 percent higher; and the saving rate return would be 16.5 percent.

Third, how much difference does it make to use a more flexible translog function for production, allow the economy to begin not at a steady-state, and gradually phase-in the increase in the saving rate so that there is a possibility, with proper monetary policy, of avoiding transitional unemployment? We estimate: Not much. With three-year phasing of a 20 percent increase in the saving rate, the sacrifice time is roughly eight years, compared to six years with an unphased increase, and ten years for a six-year phasing. With three-year phasing, the decade gain is roughly 4 percent for output and 1 percent for consumption; the five-decade gain is roughly 10 percent for output and 6 percent for consumption; and the saving rate return is roughly 15 percent. These magnitudes are quite close to those reported for the continuous time Cobb-Douglas model.

Finally, does capital accumulation have an antipoverty dividend? Our estimation shows that capital and low-educated labor are indeed q-complements: Capital accumulation does raise the marginal product of low-educated labor. A three-year phase-in of a 20 percent increase in the U.S. gross investment rate would raise the wage of low-educated labor roughly 1 percent in five years, 3 percent in ten years, 4 percent in fifteen years, and nearly 4.5 percent in twenty years. Capital accumulation does indeed appear to have a significant antipoverty dividend.

Despite the limitations and constraints of our research, we cannot help feeling better about raising the saving rate than when we began our investigations.

Note

1. Seidman (1989) clarifies why it is the "q" concept of complements and substitutes, not the "p" concept, that is relevant for this question.

References

Atkinson, A. "The Timescale of Economic Models: How Long Is the Long Run?" *Review of Economic Studies* 36 (1969): 137–52.
Bureau of Economic Analysis. *Fixed Reproducible Tangible Wealth in the United States, 1925–85* (1987).
Bureau of Labor Statistics. Data (Print-Out), 1988.
Burmeister, E., and R. Dobell. *Mathematical Theories of Economic Growth*. New York: Macmillan, 1970.
Conlisk, J. "Unemployment in a Neoclassical Growth Model: The Effect on Speed of Adjustment." *Economic Journal* 76 (1966): 550–566.
Danzinger, S., and P. Gottschalk. "Increasing Inequality in the United States: What We Know and What We Don't." *Journal of Post Keynesian Economics* (Winter 1989): 182–183.
Eisner, R. *The Total Incomes System of Accounts*. Chicago: University of Chicago Press, 1989.
Feldstein, M., and P. Bacchetta. "National Saving and International Investment." National Bureau of Economic Research, Working Paper No. 3164, 1989.
Feldstein, M., and C. Horioka. "Domestic Saving and International Capital Flows." *Economic Journal* 90 (1980): 314–329.
Gapinski, J. "Steady Growth, Policy Shocks, and Speed of Adjustment under Embodiment and Putty-Clay." *Journal of Macroeconomics* 3 (1981): 147–176.
Gramlich, E. "How Bad Are the 'Out-Year' Deficits?" In *Federal Budget Policy in the 1980's*, edited by J. Palmer and Q. Mills. Washington: Urban Institute, 1984.
Intriligator, M. "Embodied Technical Change and Productivity in the United States 1929–1958." *Review of Economics and Statistics* (1965): 65–70.
Jorgenson, D., F. Gollop, and B. Fraumeni. *Productivity and U.S. Economic Growth*. Cambridge: Harvard University Press, 1987.
Lewis, K., and L. Seidman. "The Transition Path in a Growth Model: The Sato Controversy Revisited." *Journal of Macroeconomics* 13 (Summer 1991*a*): 553–562.

Lewis, K., and L. Seidman. "The Quantitative Consequences of Raising the U.S. Saving Rate." *Review of Economics and Statistics* 73 (August 1991*b*): 471–479.

Lewis, K., and L. Seidman. "A Phased Increase in the U.S. Saving Rate: Sacrifice Times, *T*-Year Gains, and Saving Rate Returns." University of Delaware Department of Economics Working Paper, 1991*c*.

Lewis, K., and L. Seidman. "The Impact of Raising the U.S. Investment Rate on the Wage of Low-Educated Labor." University of Delaware Department of Economics Working Paper, 1991*d*.

Phelps, E. "The New View of Investment: A Neoclassical Analysis." *Quarterly Journal of Economics* 76 (1962): 548–567.

Ramanathan, R. "The Elasticity of Substitution and the Speed of Convergence in Growth Models." *Economic Journal*. 85 (1975): 612–613.

Ramanathan, R. *Introduction to the Theory of Economic Growth*, Berlin: Springer-Verlag, 1982.

Ribe, F., and W. Beeman. "The Monetary-Fiscal Mix and Long-Run Growth in an Open Economy." *American Economic Review Papers and Proceedings* 76 (1986): 209–212.

Romer, P. "Crazy Explanations for the Productivity Slowdown." In *NBER Macroeconomics Annual 1987*, edited by S. Fischer. Cambridge, Mass.: MIT Press, 1987.

Sato, K. "On the Adjustment Time in Neoclassical Growth Models." *Review of Economic Studies* 33 (1966): 263–268.

Sato, R. "Fiscal Policy in a Neoclassical Growth Model: An Analysis of Time Required for Equilibrating Adjustment." *Review of Economic Studies* 30 (1963): 16–23.

Sato, R. "Adjustment Time and Economic Growth Revisited." *Journal of Macroeconomics* 2 (1980): 239–246.

Seidman, L. "Complements and Substitutes: The Importance of Minding p's and q's." *Southern Economic Journal* 56 (1989): 183–190.

Solow, R. "Investment and Technical Change." In *Mathematical Methods in the Social Sciences*, edited by K. Arrow, S. Karlin, and P. Suppes. Palo Alto: Stanford University Press, 1959.

Solow, R. "Technical Progress, Capital Formation, and Economic Growth." *American Economic Review Papers and Proceedings* 52 (1962): 76–86.

Solow, R. *Capital Theory and the Rate of Return*. Chicago: Rand McNally & Company, 1963.

Williams, R., and R. Crouch. "The Adjustment Speed of Neo-classical Growth Models." *Journal of Economic Theory* 4 (1972): 552–556.

Commentary by Winston W. Chang
State University of New York at Buffalo

1. General Observations

When a nation's saving rate is permanently raised, the economy will adjust from an old equilibrium to a new one in the neoclassical growth framework. Of special interest is the adjustment time required for a variable to move a certain percentage from its initial state to the new steady-state equilibrium. Using a neoclassical one-sector growth model, R. Sato (1963) concluded that it would take 50 to 150 years to achieve 90 percent of the adjustment in the output–capital ratio. K. Sato (1966) showed that by realistically modifying the neoclassical model, the adjustment time may be reduced to as little as 25 years. Numerous studies have subsequently shown that the adjustment time depends crucially on model specification. Ramanathan (1973) even showed that in a two-sector model with fixed coefficients, the time to complete 90 percent of the adjustment is less than six years.

In their chapter Seidman and Lewis summarize the main results of their recent work on the analysis of the transition path. They have rekindled the Sato controversy and provided alternative new measures to characterize the transition path. As a result, they claim to have found a more optimistic picture of the impact of raising the saving rate. Instead of focusing on the adjustment time, they have provided three alternative measures: (1) the sacrifice time — the time needed for the new consumption path to catch up with the old one, which would have been traversed with the initial saving rate; (2) the T-year gain — the percentage gain in output or consumption in year T of the new path over the old one; and (3) the saving rate return — the internal rate of return that equates the present discounted values of the new and old consumption paths. In one example with parameter values obtained from econometric estimation, they found that if the U.S. gross saving rate is raised from 15 percent to 18 percent, the sacrifice time would be 5.8 years, the saving rate return would be 16.5 percent, and at the end of a decade output would be 5.5 percent higher and consumption 1.7 percent higher. They also considered a simulation model with the increase in saving rate gradually phased in over a number of years. The results did not differ significantly from those obtained when the increase was not phased in. They have also investigated the effect of capital accumulation on the wage rate of the low-skilled labor. Their estimation has shown that capital accumulation has a significant antipoverty dividend.

Seidman and Lewis have introduced interesting new measures in characterizing the transition path. Their empirical analyses have provided useful information for judging the desirability of raising the saving rate. By revisiting the original Sato controversy, they have carried the analysis of the transition path into new dimensions.

As Seidman and Lewis have already noted, their model, though a standard neoclassical one, has well-known limitations. For example, a putty-clay framework (Gapinski, 1981) and allowance of transitional unemployment (Conlisk, 1966) may be more realistic. The one-sector specification and restriction to a closed economy are also limitations. Many new growth models that incorporate features such as endogenous technical change, accumulation in human capital, and spillover of knowledge from one sector to the other further reveal the oversimplifying framework of the present model. In light of these limitations, their empirical results must be used with caution. But their new alternative measures are welcome additions to the literature and are applicable for future research in models with different specifications.

With this overall view, one can begin examining Seidman and Lewis's current work by summarizing some of their key variables and basic relations. Let the output in period t, $Q(t)$, be a function of aggregate capital $J(t)$ and labor $L(t)$, $Q(t) = Ae^{\gamma t}J(t)^{\alpha}L(t)^{\beta}$, where A is a constant, $\alpha + \beta = 1$, and $J(t) = \int_{-\infty}^{t} e^{\mu v}I(v)e^{-\delta(t-v)}dv$. $I(v)$ is investment in vintage v, δ is the rate of capital depreciation, and μ and γ are the rates of embodied and disembodied technical progress. With the assumption of a constant saving rate s, gross investment $I(t)$ and consumption $C(t)$ in period t can be written as $I(t) = sQ(t)$ and $C(t) = (1-s)Q(t)$. It can be shown that $\dot{J}(t) = -\delta J(t) + sQ(t)$, where $\dot{J}(t) \equiv dJ/dt$. Let η be K. Sato's "adjusted capital/output ratio," $\eta \equiv e^{-\mu t}J/Q$. Assume that labor grows at a constant rate, $\dot{L}(t)/L(t) = n$. Then the preceding $\dot{J}$ differential equation can be transformed into $\dot{\eta} = -\theta\eta + \beta s$, which yields the solution

$$\eta(t) = [\eta(0) - \beta s/\theta]e^{-\theta t} + \beta s/\theta, \qquad (6C-1)$$

where $\theta \equiv \beta(g + \mu + \delta)$ and $g \equiv n + \beta^{-1}(\gamma + \alpha\mu) \equiv n + \lambda$. Clearly, as time goes to infinity, $\eta(t)$ converges to the steady-state value $\eta^* = \beta s/\theta$. The higher the s, the higher the steady-state value η^*.

2. The Adjustment Time Problem

To study the adjustment time in this neoclassical model, it is convenient to assume that the economy starts from an initial steady-state equilibrium. Therefore, as s increases, the economy moves toward a new steady-state equilibrium. Because the new equilibrium is reached asymptotically, the original Sato problem is to examine the adjustment time for a variable to cover the ε percent of its total disturbance between the two steady-state equilibria. R. Sato originally chose to examine the adjustment time of the output-capital ratio, ρ. K. Sato, on the other hand, chose η to study its adjustment time. These two variables are reciprocals.

To formulate the adjustment time problem, assume that s increases from s_0 to s_1. Let x_0^* be the initial steady-state value of x and x_1^* the new steady-state value after the saving rate is permanently changed. We will treat the original steady-state value of η to be $\eta_0^* = \eta(0) = \beta s_0/\theta$, and the new steady-state value, $\eta_1^* = \eta^* = \beta s_1/\theta$. Then (6C–1) can be written as

$$\eta(t)/\eta_0^* = [1 - (s_1/s_0)]e^{-\theta t} + s_1/s_0. \qquad (6C-1)$$

Letting $\tilde{x}$ be the percentage change in the variable x ($\tilde{x} \equiv x_1/x_0 - 1$), one can rewrite (6C–1) as

$$\tilde{\eta} = \omega(t)\tilde{s}, \qquad (6C-1)$$

where $\omega(t) \equiv 1 - e^{-\theta t}$. As $\rho/\rho_0^* = \eta_0^*/\eta$, we have $\tilde{\rho} = (1 + \tilde{\eta})^{-1} - 1$. Thus the percentage change of R. Sato's variable is

$$\tilde{\rho} = [1 + \omega(t)\tilde{s}]^{-1} - 1. \qquad (6C-2)$$

Let $\tilde{x}^* \equiv x_1^*/x_0^* - 1$. Then from (6C–1) and (6C–2), we have $\tilde{\eta}^* = \tilde{s}$ and $\tilde{\rho}^* = -\tilde{s}/(1 + \tilde{s})$. The percentage of adjustment of a variable x can now be written as $\varepsilon_x(t) \equiv [x_1(t) - x_1(0)]/(x_1^* - x_0^*) = \tilde{x}/\tilde{x}^*$, where $x_1(0) = x_0^*$. Denote the time needed to achieve the ε percent of adjustment in x by t_x.

From (6C−1), (6C−2), and the definitions of ε_η and ε_ρ, one can obtain K. Sato's and R. Sato's adjustment times as follows:

$$t_\eta = \theta^{-1} \ln[1/(1 - \varepsilon_\eta)] \tag{6C-3}$$

$$t_\rho = \theta^{-1} \ln[(1 + \varepsilon_\rho \tilde{\rho}^*)/(1 - \varepsilon_\rho)]. \tag{6C-4}$$

It is important to note that the ε adjustment time is dependent on which variable is chosen. If we set $\varepsilon_\eta = \varepsilon_\rho$, the two Satos' adjustment times are different. Given that $\tilde{s} > 0$, we have $\tilde{\rho}^* < 0$; therefore, if $\varepsilon_\eta = \varepsilon_\rho$, we have $t_\rho < t_\eta$. Thus R. Sato's adjustment time is less than K. Sato's, given the same percentage of adjustment of their respective variables.[1] As an example, if $\varepsilon_\eta = \varepsilon_\rho = 0.9$, $\mu = .03$, $\delta = .05$, $g = .03$, $\beta = .67$, and $\tilde{s} = .2$, then $\theta = .0737$ and we have $t_\eta = 31.2$ and $t_\rho = 28.9$.

On the other hand, if t_η is set to equal t_ρ, then (6C−3) and (6C−4) imply

$$\varepsilon_\rho = \varepsilon_\eta (1 + \tilde{\eta}^*)/(1 + \tilde{\eta}^* \varepsilon_\eta) = \varepsilon_\eta (1 + \tilde{s})/(1 + \tilde{s}\varepsilon_\eta). \tag{6C-5}$$

Given $\tilde{s} > 0$, we see that $\varepsilon_\eta < \varepsilon_\rho$.

3. Seidman and Lewis's Alternative Measures

Although Seidman and Lewis reexamined the Sato controversy (see, e.g., Lewis and Seidman, 1991), they have focused mainly on the analysis of adjusted per capita consumption $[c \equiv C/(e^{\lambda t}L)]$ and occasionally on the adjusted per capita output $[q \equiv Q/(e^{\lambda t}L)]$, where $\lambda \equiv (\gamma + \alpha\mu)/\beta$. Because $C(t) = (1 - s) q(t)$ and $q(t) = A^{1/\beta}\eta(t)^{\alpha/\beta}$, we see that both c and q are constant in a steady-state equilibrium. The comparative rate of growth of c between the two dynamic paths (one being the original steady-state path with s_0 and the new one being the transition path with s_1) is defined as $\tilde{c} \equiv [c_1(t) - c_0^*]/c_0^*$. Because $c(t)/c_0^* = \varphi(\eta/\eta_0^*)^{\alpha/\beta}$, where $\varphi \equiv (1 - s_1)/(1 - s_0) = [1 - s_0(1 + \tilde{s})]/(1 - s_0)$, we have

$$\tilde{c}(t) = \varphi(1 + \omega(t)\tilde{s})^{\alpha/\beta} - 1. \tag{6C-6}$$

Clearly, $\tilde{c}^* \equiv \tilde{c}(\infty) = \varphi (1 + \tilde{s})^{\alpha/\beta} - 1$.

The three alternative measures of Seidman and Lewis can now be conveniently expressed as follows: (1) The sacrifice time, τ, is that t such that $\tilde{c}(\tau) = 0$. (2) The T-year gain is $\tilde{c}(T)$. (3) The saving rate return, R_c, is that R_c such that $\int_0^\infty [C(t) - C_0^*]e^{-R_c t}dt = 0$.[2]

In a broad sense, Seidman and Lewis's three new measures are, like the Sato problem, designed to analyze the transition path. Their first measure, the sacrifice time, can be regarded as a special case of the ε adjustment time. If we define $\varepsilon_c(t) \equiv (c_1(t) - c_0^*)/(c_1^* - c_0^*)$, then the sacrifice time is the time τ_c such that $\varepsilon_c(\tau_c) = 0$.[3] Thus it can be regarded as a special case of the ε adjustment time with ε being set to be zero percent. Their second measure, the T-year gain, fixes a time period T and measures the percentage gain in c of the new path over the old one. Both measures have the virtue of simplicity. Their third measure, the saving rate return, shows the return of raising the saving rate by forgoing some of the early consumptions in exchange for higher later consumptions. This is theoretically sound and interesting for measuring the desirability of raising the saving rate. Seidman and Lewis have thus established new ways of examining the transition path. Their characterization of it has enabled them to address the desirability question of raising the saving rate. From this perspective, their analysis is quite different from the original Sato problem.

The measure of sacrifice time is certainly an interesting concept. However, it does not reveal the magnitude of losses and gains, nor the trade-off between them. The same remarks also apply to the T-year gain. On the other hand, the saving rate return provides the measure of trade-off between the losses during the sacrifice periods and the gains afterward. Thus the sacrifice time and T-year gain, though empirically interesting, paint only a partial picture of the transition path. The third measure gives more relevant information when addressing the question of the desirability of raising the saving rate. However, whether a saving rate return is high enough to generate an optimistic impression on the impact of raising the saving rate is still unclear. To be optimistic, the saving rate return must be considered high. But what is the basis for comparison? Is it compared with some market interest rate or with some social rate of discount set by a policy maker, or perhaps some other index? Without specifying a meaningful figure for comparison, it would be difficult to draw stronger conclusions.

4. The Overtaking Time

To gain more information on the transition path, I would like to introduce an added measure called the overtaking time. It is the minimum time needed for the new consumption stream to overtake the old one when each instantaneous consumption is weighed by a given discount rate. Suppose that the policy maker is concerned with the variable, per capita consumption (C/L), which could serve as a proxy for a welfare indicator of a nation. To study the time paths of per capita consumption with different saving rates, the policy maker uses a discount rate r to discount future consumptions. For a given r, the new path $C(t)/L(t)$ is said to "overtake" the original one $C_0^*(t)/L(t)$ from time period y on if $\int_0^y [C(t)/L(t) - C_0^*(t)/L(t)]e^{-rt}dt \geq 0$ for all $t \geq y$. Thus at y, we have

$$\int_0^y [C(t)/L(t) - C_0^*(t)/L(t)]e^{-rt}dt = 0. \tag{6C-7}$$

As $c \equiv C/(e^{\lambda t}L)$ and $c_0^*(t)$ $(= c_0^*)$ is constant for all t, (6C–7) is equivalent to $\int_0^y [c(t) - c_0^*(t)]e^{-(r-\lambda)t}dt = c_0^* \int_0^y \tilde{c}(t)e^{-(r-\lambda)t}dt = 0$. Therefore, we obtain the following condition:

$$F(r, y) \equiv \int_0^y [\varphi(1 + \tilde{s}\omega(t))^{\alpha/\beta} - 1]e^{-(r-\lambda)t}dt = 0. \tag{6C-8}$$

The F function provides the relation between the discount rate and the overtaking time.

Although the underlying model is a descriptive and not an optimizing one, the overtaking time gives added information in comparing the two consumption streams. It is positively related to the discount rate. The higher the discount rate, the longer it is for the new consumption path with a higher saving rate to overtake the old one with a lower saving rate. If the discount rate is very high, the future gains after the sacrifice time will be weighed very lightly in comparison with the losses in the early periods. Then, even if the sacrifice time is considered "short," the overtaking time will be "long," and the new path may not be so attractive at all. With the overtaking time in mind, Seidman and Lewis's sacrifice time must be applied with caution.

Seidman and Lewis's second alternative measure, the T-year gain, provides information for only a given point in time. Although it helps to characterize the transition path, its application must also be used with caution. A high decade gain may look appealing on the surface but may weigh very little in terms of its present discounted value if the discount rate is high. On the other hand, a low decade gain may still be very appealing if the discount rate is very low.

Seidman and Lewis's third measure is a useful one for considering the desirability of raising the saving rate. In fact, their saving rate return is maximum discount rate when the overtaking time is infinite. For practical purposes, however, an infinite horizon will most likely not be the concern of a policy maker. It would be useful to know the minimum number of years for the new path to overtake the old, given a particular discount rate. Alternatively, it would be useful to know the saving rate return given a fixed finite horizon.

To gain some idea about the relation between r and y for plausible parameter values, consider the following example: Assume that $s_0 = .15$, $s_1 = .18$, $\alpha = .33$, $\beta = .67$, $g = .03$, $\mu = .03$, $\delta = .05$, and $n = .01$. It follows that $\tilde{s} = .2$, $\varphi = .9647$, $\theta = .0737$, and $\lambda = g - n = .02$. With these parameter values, the value of y for each r can be solved from equation (6C–8). For each specified value of r that ranges from 0 percent to 14 percent the approximate values of y are shown in the following table:

r	y	r	y
0%	13.5	8%	17.9
1%	13.8	9%	19.0
2%	14.2	10%	20.4
3%	14.6	11%	22.2
4%	15.1	12%	25.0
5%	15.7	13%	30.3
6%	16.3	14%	138.6
7%	17.0		

Note that as r approaches 15 percent, the value of y increases very rapidly toward infinity. The table shows that if there is no discounting of gains or losses, it will take 13.5 years for the new path to overtake the old. As the discount rate is increased from 5 percent to 10 percent, the overtaking time is increased from 15.7 years to 20.4 years. If the discount rate is further increased to 14 percent, the overtaking time would have reached 138.6 years. A higher discount rate above 14 percent will reduce the gains in later periods to virtually no weight at all in the present value calculation. The overtaking time is therefore extremely sensitive to small increases in r when the latter is close to its maximum.

The relation between r and y is affected by the percentage change in the saving rate. For the same value of s_0 but a higher value of $\tilde{s}$ (hence a higher value of s_1), the overtaking time is increased for a given discount rate. To illustrate, if $\tilde{s}$ is changed to .3 in the previous example, then for $r = 0$ percent, $y = 14$ years; for $r = 5$ percent, $y = 16.5$ years; for $r = 10$ percent, $y = 22.1$ years; and for $r = 12$ percent, $y = 28.7$ years.

The overtaking time allows for more realistic intertemporal comparisons of the two consumption paths. However, an appropriate value for the discount rate is still left to be determined by a policy maker or an economic agent. And criteria for deciding whether an overtaking time is "long" are also left to individual judgment. With a descriptive model like this, the power of inferring the desirability of raising the saving rate is unfortunately quite limited.

In conclusion, Seidman and Lewis have proposed three new measures to characterize the transition path and have obtained interesting econometric estimates for these measures. Instead of the adjustment time analysis, their focus has shifted to the analysis of the desirability of raising the saving rate. Their first two measures, the sacrifice time and the T-year gain, provide simple and useful information for a policy maker, although caution should be given in practical applications. Their third measure, the saving rate return, is conceptually sound and useful in addressing the desirability question of raising the saving rate. However, it may not be practical for use by a decision maker who normally would base decisions on a finite horizon. In light of this, the overtaking time can be a useful added measure. It provides a more complete picture of intertemporal comparisons between the new and old consumption paths and is therefore better suited for a decision maker in considering the desirability of raising the saving rate.

Notes

1. In general, a variable and its reciprocal will not have the same adjustment time, given the same ε, because they do not have a linear relationship. This can be easily proved by plotting the two variables on a two-dimensional space. The resulting graph is a rectangular hyperbola. Let two points on the rectangular hyperbola represent two steady-state equilibria, each with a different saving rate. After an increase in the saving rate, the economy moves from the initial equilibrium toward the new one *along* the curve. This must generate different ε's for the two variables at any given point in time before reaching the new equilibrium. However, a point on the chord formed by joining the two equilibrium points will give the same ε's for the two variables. These geometric properties can be used to prove the stated results.

2. They have also shown that the sacrifice time of c is equal to that of C and is also equal to that of C/L. In addition, the T-year gain of c is equal to that of C and is also equal to that of C/L. Furthermore, they have shown that the saving rate return for c is $R_c - g$ and the saving rate return for C/L is $R_c - n$.

3. Note that at $t = 0$, $\tilde{\eta}$ and $\tilde{\rho}$ are both zero but $\tilde{c}(0) = \varphi - 1$. So c falls below c_0^* at the instant $t = 0$ when s is raised to s_1. Here in defining ε_c, the initial value of c is regarded as c_0^*.

References

Conlisk, J. "Unemployment in a Neoclassical Growth Model: The Effect on Speed of Adjustment." *Economic Journal* 76 (1966): 550–566.

Gapinski, J. "Steady Growth, Policy Shocks, and Speed of Adjustment Under Embodiment and Putty-Clay." *Journal of Macroeconomics* 3 (1981): 147–176.

Lewis, K., and L. Seidman. "The Transition Path in a Growth Model: The Sato Controversy Revisited." *Journal of Macroeconomics* 13 (Summer 1991).

Ramanathan, R. "Adjustment Time in the Two-Sector Growth Model with Fixed Coefficients." *Economic Journal* 83 (1973): 1236–1244.

Sato, K. "On the Adjustment time in Neoclassical Growth Models." *Review of Economic Studies* 33 (1966): 263–268.

Sato, R. "Fiscal Policy in a Neoclassical Growth Model: An Analysis of Time Required for Equilibrating Adjustment." *Review of Economic Studies* 30 (1963): 16–23.

Commentary by John Conlisk
University of California at San Diego

Seidman and Lewis review a series of papers in which they have investigated the effects on aggregate consumption and other variables of a change in the saving rate. The central question is whether an increase in the saving rate is desirable. Do the later benefits justify the intervening costs? The question is addressed through neoclassical growth models. Most of my comments concern the sensitivity of their results to alternative technical change specifications (section 3). First, however, I would like to set aside what I think are some false issues (sections 1 and 2). Comments are summarized at the end (section 4).

1. The Controversy with the Satos

Seidman and Lewis package their chapter as a controversy between themselves on one side and R. Sato (1963) and K. Sato (1966) on the other. Seidman and Lewis state that R. Sato (1963) "cast a dark shadow over the proposal to raise the national saving rate" and that K. Sato (1966) "did little to dispel the gloom." On the basis of their own analyses, however, Seidman and Lewis "cannot help feeling better about raising the saving rate." It appears to me that Seidman and Lewis have misinterpreted what the Satos demonstrated and thus have packaged their own interesting work as a false controversy.

As I have understood their work, the Satos demonstrated that, due to speed of adjustment considerations, steady-state approximations from a neoclassical growth model are doubtful approximations for investigating the effects of parameter changes, such as a change in the saving rate. Like any other comparative statics exercise in economics, steady-state comparison can provide a good or a bad approximation, depending on the importance of the transition between the old and the new static equilibrium. If the transition takes a long time, transitional effects are more likely to be important. It seems perfectly reasonable to address the speed of adjustment question as the Satos did—by asking how long it takes to complete most of a transition. When the Satos found that 10 percent of the transition might still remain after 25 to 150 years, economists were justified in questioning steady-state approximations.

The inadequacy of a steady-state approximation certainly casts a dark shadow over naive reliance on steady-state methods. However, it tells us nothing about the desirability of an increase in the saving rate. Given that steady-state approximation is doubtful, a saving rate increase needs to be studied by measures that take transitions into account. Seidman and Lewis propose such measures. In doing so, it seems to me, they have taken exactly the approach called for by the Satos' work. Their work and the Satos' work are complementary. I can find no conflict. (Incidentally, the adequacy or inadequacy of steady-state approximations also tells us nothing about the value of neoclassical growth models, despite the phrasing of conclusions in R. Sato 1963 and K. Sato 1966.)

Seidman and Lewis criticize the speed of adjustment measure used by the Satos. They note that the Satos' measure does not provide a reasonable measure of the desirability of an increase in the saving rate. The statement is certainly correct, but it seems beside the point. The Satos were asking a speed of adjustment question, not a desirability of adjustment question. Their measure was appropriate to their purpose.

2. The Three Seidman and Lewis Summary Measures

Following Seidman and Lewis, it is convenient to view an increase in the saving rate as an investment project that alters society's consumption path. Relative to the original path, the new path will involve lower consumption levels for a while. These are the costs. Under usual assumptions, a time will come at which consumption levels on the new path rise above levels on the original path. These are the benefits. The question is whether the benefits outweigh the costs. To answer that question, Lewis and Seidman propose three measures of the desirability of an increase in the saving rate. Only one of the three measures seems sensible to me.

Let consumption at time t without and with an increase in the saving rate be denoted $C(t)$ and $C^+(t)$, and let $t=0$ be the date of the increase. Graphed against time, $C^+(t) - C(t)$ will initially lie below the time axis, but will at some date cross the axis and lie above it thereafter. The graph tells the whole the story of the aggregate consumption effects — the costs, the benefits, and their timing. How might we reduce the graph to a scalar summary measure of the desirability of the increase in the saving rate? An obvious candidate is the internal rate of return, call it ρ, of the project. It is defined implicitly by the usual zero present value equation:

$$\text{(Rate of return } \rho) = \left\{ \text{solution for } \rho \text{ of } \int_0^\infty e^{-\rho t}[C^+(t) - C(t)]dt = 0 \right\}. \tag{6C-1}$$

The internal rate of return ρ is one of Seidman and Lewis's summary measures. I will use it repeatedly hereafter.

Seidman and Lewis consider two other measures. One is the "sacrifice time," defined as the length of time that society suffers costs before the benefits begin.

$$\text{(Sacrifice time } \tau) = [\text{solution for } \tau \text{ of } C^+(\tau) = C(\tau)].$$

This crossing date is certainly one prominent feature of the graph of $C^+(t) - C(t)$. Nonetheless, the sacrifice time does not seem to be a good summary measure. In their discussion, Seidman and Lewis seem to use the sacrifice time partly as a measure of speed of adjustment and partly as a measure of desirability of adjustment. Because these are distinct questions, the sacrifice time surely cannot answer both. I suspect that it does not help much with either. The speed of adjustment question might be broken into two pieces. How long do the costs take, and how long do the benefits take? The sacrifice time answers the first question exactly, but neglects the second question completely. Regarding the desirability of adjustment question, the sacrifice time says nothing about the magnitude, as opposed to the duration, of costs and says nothing whatever about benefits.

The remaining measure discussed by Lewis and Seidman is the "T-year gain," defined as the undiscounted net benefit from 0 to T:

$$(T\text{-year gain}) = \int_0^T [C^+(t) - C(t)]dt.$$

Though this measure may have some appeal for some contexts, it is problematic as an overall summary measure. If T is set small, the T-year gain will make a saving increase look unduly bad because the costs precede the benefits. Conversely, if T is set large, the T-year gain may make a saving increase look unduly good because distant benefits will enter the gain with no discounting. The T-year gain can be viewed as a net present value with strange discounting — a zero discount rate for $t \leq T$ and an infinite discount rate for $t > T$. One could overcome the arbitrariness of choosing a particular T by plotting the T-year gain against T. However, this plot would simply display in less digestible form the same information as a plot of $C^+(t) - C(t)$ itself.

3. The Treatment of Technical Change

Now turn to what (in my view) is the heart of the Seidman and Lewis work, the computation of rates of return to saving rate increases. Such computations require a model for predicting the effects of the increase. To evaluate Seidman and Lewis's results, we have to ask how well we trust the neoclassical growth models they use. I suspect that economists do not trust them very well.

A central message of the growth literature has been that technical change is the primary engine of growth. However, the growth model literature has made little progress in modeling the determinants of technical change. Treating technical change as exogenous, as Seidman and Lewis do, is standard practice. Nonetheless, the practice seems to beg the central question of explaining growth. The issue is of great potential importance to the work of Seidman and Lewis. Suppose, in contrast to their assumptions, that economies that save more generate greater technical change as well as more capital. Then an increase in the saving rate will have greater beneficial effects than Seidman and Lewis account for. To investigate this potential misspecification, I made a number of rate-of-return calculations. They are like the calculations of Seidman and Lewis, but they use several alternative models of technical change. Consistent with Seidman and Lewis, I considered only models from the mainstream growth literature (although I tend to think that the nonmainstream approach of Nelson and Winter 1982 is more promising).

Seven models follow. The first is a benchmark model with exogenous technical change. The remaining six models embody various endogenous technical change specifications. For each model, I have computed the rate of return ρ corresponding to a particular numerical specification. The specifications are intended to be the same across models on all dimensions except the technical change dimension. The calculations are intended to suggest how much higher or lower the rate of return would be if technical change took one form rather than another, all else equal (though "all else equal" can be a problematic condition). The models are simpler than the Seidman and Lewis models on several dimensions. For example, the models neglect vintage effects. Nonetheless, the comparisons suggest the importance of technical change considerations.

3.1. Benchmark Model — Exogenous Technical Change

Consider a standard Solow-Swan model with exogenous technical change. It is a prototype for the models considered by Seidman and Lewis. It will serve as a benchmark for the models to follow.

$$Y = AK^\alpha L^{1-\alpha}, \quad DK = sY - \delta K, \quad L = zN, \quad N = 1,$$
$$Dz/z = \lambda, \quad C = (1 - s)Y. \tag{6C-2}$$

The first equation is an aggregate production function giving output Y as a constant returns function of capital K and "effective labor" L. For simplicity, the production function is assumed to be Cobb-Douglas. In the second equation and throughout, D denotes a time derivative; so $DK \equiv dK/dt$. The parameters s and δ are the saving rate and the depreciation rate, respectively. The third equation states that the effective labor force equals raw labor N multiplied by a labor-augmenting technology multiplier z. N and z are determined, in turn, by the fourth and fifth equations. For simplicity, raw labor is held fixed and normalized at $N = 1$. The technology multiplier z is assumed to grow at an exogenously given rate λ. The last equation defines consumption C. The variables of the model are Y, K, L, N, z, and C. A time index will be added to the variables when helpful. The other magnitudes A, α, s, δ, and λ are constant parameters. The fixed population assumption ($N = 1$) is an innocent simplification in the majority of the models to be discussed. When the assumption is not innocent, that fact will be noted.

For a given setting of the parameters and initial conditions, the model will generate a time path $C(t)$ for consumption. Then the computation can be repeated with a higher saving rate, but with initial conditions and other parameters the same. The second path is $C^+(t)$. Finally, the rate of return ρ defined by equation (6C-1) can be computed. This exercise was carried out for the specification:

$$\alpha = .3, \quad \delta = .05, \quad \lambda = .01, \quad s = .15, \quad s^+ = .20,$$
$$Y(0)/K(0) = .4. \tag{6C-3}$$

The time unit is assumed to be a year. The two saving rates s and s^+ are the ones used to generate the $C(t)$ and $C^+(t)$ paths, respectively. A verbal interpretation of specification (6C−3) is this: $\alpha = .3$ is capital's share of output under marginal productivity factor pricing; $\delta = .05$ is roughly the fraction of the capital stock that wears out in a year; $\lambda = .01$ is the equilibrium growth rate of output; $s = .15$ and $s^+ = .20$ are the fractions of output devoted to capital accumulation, without and with a saving increase; and the initial condition $Y(0)/K(0) = (\lambda + \delta)/s = .4$ assures that the model is in steady-state equilibrium at $t = 0$ for the original saving rate s. No further assumptions are needed to determine the saving rate of return ρ. (Settings for A and for other initial values do not influence ρ.)

For computational simplicity, the model (6C−2)−(6C−3) was put into discrete time form before beginning the computations. The same is true for the other models that follow. The appendix describes the discrete time analogs. Continuous time specifications are presented in the text because they are more conventional and are easier to absorb.

For specification (6C−3), the rate of return is $\rho = .0607$. This is a benchmark value for what follows. Specification (6C−3) is roughly representative of values used by Seidman and Lewis. They used a more optimistic equilibrium growth rate ($\lambda = .03$) and a slightly large α-value ($\alpha = .33$). Because computed ρ-values are very sensitive to λ and α, the ρ-values presented in this comment run substantially smaller than the Seidman and Lewis ρ-values. This fact is not important for what follows, however. The issue will be the relative sizes of ρ for different technical change specifications, not the absolute levels of ρ.

3.2. Human Capital Model

Growth in human capital is one possible source of technical change. Consider a Solow-Swan model with a second capital input, to be interpreted as human capital.

$$Y = AK^\alpha H^\beta N^{1-\alpha-\beta}, \quad DK = sY - \delta K, \quad DH = hY - \gamma H, \quad N = 1.$$
(6C−4)

Here human capital H enters the model the same way that physical capital K does; h and γ are saving and depreciation rates for human capital. The labor-augmenting technology multiplier z from the benchmark model is now gone.

To use (6C−4) as a model of sustained per capita growth, we must depart completely from steady-state analysis. By standard growth model reasoning, the asymptotic growth rate of model (6C−4) is zero; the two endogenously accumulating inputs K and H cannot grow indefinitely faster than the limiting input N, which does not grow.

Therefore, using model (6C–4) to explain a long period of per capita growth requires that the model be in disequilibrium and that the disequilibrium persist for a long time. In particular, if per capita growth is to be attributed to human capital H, then H must lie below its equilibrium value so that, as it rises toward that equilibrium value, it will generate growth. In a model like (6C–4), a period of disequilibrium growth can indeed be long. The speed at which models like (6C–2) and (6C–4) adjust to their equilibria is positively related to, and very sensitive to, the size of the exponent on the limiting population input. In the benchmark model (6C–2), the critical population exponent is $1 - \alpha$, which is generally taken to be well above one half. In model (6C–4), however, the critical population exponent is $1 - \alpha - \beta$, which is likely to lie well below one half. Thus model (6C–4) may adjust to equilibrium quite slowly and may generate disequilibrium growth for a long time. Model (6C–4) provides a potential explanation of endogenous technical change.

Consider a numerical specification.

$$\alpha = .3, \quad \beta = .5, \quad \delta = .05, \quad \gamma = .025, \quad s = .15,$$
$$s^+ = .20, \quad h = .05, \quad DK(0)/K(0) = DH(0)/H(0) = .01^{1/(\alpha + \beta)}. \tag{6C–5}$$

Here, to promote comparability, α, δ, s, and s^+ are set the same as for the benchmark model. The new setting $\beta = .5$, together with $\alpha = .3$, supposes that, under marginal productivity factor pricing, physical capital gets a fraction .3 of output; human capital gets a fraction .5 of output; and raw labor gets a fraction .2 of output. The new setting $\gamma = .025$ supposes that human capital depreciates at half the rate of physical capital. The new setting $h = .05$ supposes that saving for human capital accumulation is 5 percent of total output. The initial condition $DK(0)/K(0) = DH(0)/H(0)$ supposes that growth is initially balanced between the two types of capital. Setting $DK(0)/K(0)$ and $DH(0)/H(0)$ both equal to $.01^{1/(\alpha + \beta)}$ assures that the initial growth rate of output itself is .01, as in the specification of the benchmark model.

Specifications (6C–5) are adequate to simulate the model. For the growth path corresponding to $s = .15$, the output growth rate, which is initially .01, has dropped by only half after 100 years, indicating that a disequilibrium path can generate long-term growth. Comparing the consumption paths for $s = .15$ and $s^+ = .20$ yields the saving rate of return $\rho = .0849$. This is substantially larger than the benchmark value $\rho = .0607$ computed under exogenous technical change. The numerical specifications for the two models were chosen to be comparable. Thus the primary cause of the difference in ρ-values is the differing treatment of technical change. In both models, an increase in saving stimulates output growth by stimulating capital growth. In the benchmark model, this is the only effect. In the human capital model, the stimulus to output in turn stimulates human capital growth. As a result, the saving increase results in a larger and longer lasting effect. The comparison suggests that Seidman and Lewis's treatment of technical change as exogenous may cause them to understate the effect of a saving rate increase.

3.3. Technical Change as an Endogenous Labor-Augmenting Effect—the SEJ Model

In the benchmark model, technical change takes an exogenous labor-augmenting form. Consider a model in which the labor augmentation is endogenous. Let the model be identical to the benchmark model except that the exogenous technical change assumption $Dz/z = \lambda$ is replaced by

$$Dz = bY/N - \mu z. \tag{6C-6}$$

The interpretation is this. Suppose the economy devotes a fraction q of its output to innovation. Then qY/N is the innovation expenditure per worker. Suppose that the labor-augmenting multiplier increases in proportion to this expenditure per worker—that is, suppose $Dz = \theta q Y/N$ for some parameter θ. Then add the assumption that the innovation effect is partly a training effect that dissipates as old workers retire. Therefore, add on a dissipation term $-\mu z$, where μ is the dissipation rate. The equation becomes $Dz = \theta q Y/N - \mu z$. Letting $b \equiv \theta q$ then yields (6C-6). Because N is here normalized at one, the N on the right of (6C-6) has no effect. In a model with a growing population, however, the N on the right of (6C-6) would be important in assuring a well-behaved steady-state.

Consider then the model consisting of the benchmark equations (6C-2) with $Dz/z = \lambda$ replaced by (6C-6). It is possible to eliminate N and z from this model and to restate it in the form

$$Y = AK^\alpha L^{1-\alpha}, \quad DK = sY - \delta K, \quad DL = bY - \mu L,$$
$$C = (1 - s)Y. \tag{6C-7}$$

In this form, the model displays a symmetric treatment of the two inputs K and L, although the DL equation originates from assumptions about factor-augmenting technical change whereas the DK equation does not. Model (6C-7) will be called the "SEJ model" because it was discussed in the *Southern Economic Journal* by Conlisk (1967).

Like the benchmark model, the SEJ model has a steady-state in which Y, K, and L all grow at the same rate. Unlike the benchmark model, however, the SEJ model generates steady-state growth through endogenous, rather than exogenous, technical change. Further, whereas the steady-state growth rate in the benchmark model equals λ and thus depends on one parameter only, the steady-state growth rate in the SEJ model depends on all parameters. In particular, an increase in the saving rate s will increase the steady-state growth rate. Thus a saving rate increase is a more potent stimulus in the SEJ model than in the benchmark model; we expect the SEJ model to display a larger saving rate of return ρ.

Consider the numerical specification:

$$\alpha = .3, \quad \delta = .05, \quad \mu = .025, \quad s = .15, \quad s^+ = .20,$$
$$b = 0.8859, \quad A = .3921, \quad K(0)/L(0) = 1. \quad (6C-8)$$

Here α, δ, s, and s^+ are as in the preceding models. The dissipation rate μ of the labor-augmentation multiplier z is akin to the depreciation rate γ of human capital in the human capital model; both are human longevity effects. Hence $\mu = .025$ was set the same as $\gamma = .025$. The specifications of b, A, and $K(0)/L(0)$ were set to assure an equilibrium growth rate of .01 under saving rate s and to assure that the model was initially in that equilibrium.

The saving rate of return for this specification is $\rho = .0940$. As expected, this rate is substantially higher than in the benchmark model ($\rho = .0607$), again suggesting that Seidman and Lewis's treatment of technical change as exogenous may cause them to understate the effect of a saving rate increase.

3.4. Learning by Doing—Arrow Version

In the type of learning-by-doing model associated with Arrow, the labor-augmenting multiplier z increases with the cumulative experience of the economy. People learn by doing. In a common version of the idea, the creation of new capital is viewed as the relevant learning experience because that is where technological decisions are primarily made. Thus cumulative gross investment is taken as the measure of cumulative experience. But cumulative gross investment behaves much like cumulative net investment, which is just K itself. Thus we can capture the spirit and much of the letter of a standard learning-by-doing model by viewing K as the measure of cumulative experience and by assuming that z is an increasing function of K. The usual functional relationship is $z = K^\sigma$, where σ is a parameter obeying $0 < \sigma < 1$. Therefore, a simplified version of a standard learning-by-doing model consists of the equations of the benchmark model, but with $z = K^\sigma$ in place of $Dz/z = \lambda$:

$$Y = AK^\alpha L^{1-\alpha}, \quad DK = sY - \delta K, \quad L = zN, \quad N = 1,$$
$$z = K^\sigma, \quad C = (1-s)Y. \tag{6C-9}$$

This model has the difficulty that its asymptotic growth rate is zero. (If population were growing, this would not be true, but the difficulty would persist in another guise, as discussed in Conlisk 1989, pp. 792–793.) Thus in this model as in the preceding human capital model, sustained growth must be explained as a disequilibrium phenomenon in which capital slowly rises toward its asymptotic value.

Consider the numerical specification

$$\alpha = .3, \quad \delta = .05, \quad s = .15, \quad s^+ = .20, \quad DY(0)/Y(0) = .01. \tag{6C-10}$$

The values of α, δ, s, and s^+ are as in preceding models, and the specification $DY(0)/Y(0) = .01$ assures that the model's initial growth rate is the same as in preceding models. ρ was computed for several values of σ:

σ-value	.3	.5	.7	.9
ρ-value	.1685	.2342	.3000	.3670

For the σ-values considered, the rates of return ρ are much larger than for the benchmark model. In a learning-by-doing model, a saving increase stimulates faster experience growth and thus faster technical change as well as faster capital growth.

3.5. Learning by Doing in the Spirit of Romer

The learning-by-doing specification $z = K^\sigma$ displays diminishing returns ($\sigma < 1$) to cumulative experience. We might instead suppose that diminishing returns apply to incremental experience. Consider the specification $Dz/z = g(sY)$, where g is a nonnegative increasing function with the strong diminishing returns property that $g'' < 0$ and that $g(.)$ has a finite upper bound $g(\infty)$. The increment to experience in building new capital is measured by sY; hence $Dz/z = g(sY)$ states that the proportional increment in the technology multiplier increases with the increment to experience. This specification is very much in the spirit of Romer (1986).

Inserting this specification in place of the $z = K^\sigma$ equation in the learning-by-doing model (6C−9) yields:

$$Y = AK^\alpha L^{1-\alpha}, \quad DK = sY - \delta K, \quad L = zN, \quad N = 1,$$
$$Dz/z = g(sY), \quad C = (1-s)Y. \quad (6C-11)$$

In this model, output growth will be driven by $Dz/z = g(sY)$, which will grow over time as sY grows. In the long run, both DY/Y and Dz/z will approach the growth rate limit $g(\infty)$. Romer argues the plausibility of a rising growth rate during economic development.

Consider the numerical specification

$$\alpha = .3, \quad \delta = .05, \quad s = .15, \quad s^+ = .20,$$
$$Y(0)/K(0) = .4, \quad g(x) = .015x/(75+x), \quad Y(0) = 1000. \quad (6C-12)$$

The values of α, δ, s, and s^+ are as in previous examples. Given them, the specifications for $Y(0)/K(0)$, $g(x)$, and $Y(0)$ assure that the growth rates of K, z, and Y are all .01 initially and .015 asymptotically. Specifications (6C−12) imply the saving rate of return $\rho = .0862$. As in the previous models with endogenous technical change, the ρ-value is larger than for the benchmark model because more saving stimulates faster technical change as well as faster capital growth.

3.6. The SEJ Model with a Romer Effect

Consider a somewhat different algebraic development of Romer's idea that the technology increment Dz depends on the experience increment sY. Let the exact specification be $Dz = \eta sY/N$, where η is a positive parameter. This specification states that the labor-augmenting multiplier z increases in proportion to the incremental experience per worker. Substituting this equation in place of $Dz/z = \lambda$ in the benchmark model (6C−2) and then substituting out N and z yield the model

$$Y = AK^\alpha L^{1-\alpha}, \quad DK = sY - \delta K, \quad DL = \eta sY, \quad C = (1-s)Y. \quad (6C-13)$$

This model has nearly the same algebraic structure as the SEJ model (6C−7). However, because of the Romer effect, the saving parameter now enters the model in the DL equation as well as the DK equation. We might therefore expect the saving rate of return to be higher than in the SEJ model.

Consider the numerical specification

$$\alpha = .3, \quad \delta = .05, \quad s = .15, \quad s^+ = .20, \quad \eta = .1709,$$
$$A = .3921, \quad K(0)/L(0) = 1. \quad (6C-14)$$

Here α, δ, s, and s^+ are as in the preceding models. The settings of η, A, and $K(0)/L(0)$ then assure that the model is initially in steady-state equilibrium (for saving rate s) with steady-state growth rate .01.

The saving rate of return under specification (6C-14) is $\rho = .1362$. As expected, this is substantially higher than in the earlier SEJ model ($\rho = .0849$) and still higher than in the benchmark model ($\rho = .0607$).

3.7. Very Old and Very New Theories

A typical Harrod-Domar model from the late 1940s and early 1950s might be written

$$Y = A \min(K, N), \quad DK = sY - \delta K, \quad N = 1.$$

The production function displays fixed factor proportions. If the first branch of the production function applies (so $Y = AK$), the model implies the so-called "warranted" rate of growth

$$DY/Y = As - \delta. \quad (6C-15)$$

This strong dependence of DY/Y on s clearly will make a difference to saving rate of return calculations. However, when the second branch of the production applies (so $Y = AN$), the growth rate is zero. Nonetheless, numerous papers used the warranted rate (6C-15) as a complete growth theory. Solow (1956) and Swan (1956) discredited this use of (6C-15) by replacing fixed factor proportions with smooth substitutability in production and by showing that the equilibrium growth rate is then independent of the saving rate. The speed of adjustment paper by Sato (1963) can be read as an argument that the discrediting of (6C-15) was overdone because DY/Y may show a sensitivity to s over a sustained period of time.

Consider a second theoretical route for getting to equation (6C-15). Set $\sigma = 1$ in the learning-by-doing model (6C-9). Then the first, second, third, and fifth equations of the model imply

$$DY/Y = AsN - \delta. \quad (6C-16)$$

For a fixed population, with N normalized at $N = 1$, (6C-16) is the same as (6C-15). So the learning-by-doing model can generate (6C-15). However, fixing the population is not an innocent simplification here. Equation (6C-16) carries the implication that, in a country with a growing population, DY/Y will grow steadily with population. Indeed, for plausible settings of DY/Y and δ, the elasticity of DY/Y with respect to N implied by (6C−16) is well above one. (For $DY/Y = .01$ and $\delta = .05$, the elasticity of DY/Y with respect to N is 6.) The empirical implausibility of such a prediction was the literature's rationale for assuming $\sigma < 1$ and for rejecting (6C−12).

Throughout the boom in growth modeling from the late 1950s through the middle 1970s, and throughout the bust in growth modeling from the middle 1970s to the middle 1980s, there was little interest in growth rate expressions like (6C−15) and (6C−16). However, in the revival of growth modeling that began in the middle 1980s, expressions like (6C−15) and (6C−16) began to reappear (often camouflaged in assorted microfoundations). For example, Romer (1987), Prescott and Boyd (1987), Barro (1990), Grossman and Helpman (1990), Romer (1990), and Rebelo (1991) all present models whose underlying technical change specifications are essentially like (6C−16).

Thus we have the curious fact that the 40 years of growth modeling begun by Solow and Swan have led economists back to the warranted rate equation which Solow and Swan set out to improve upon. The encouraging feature of this revival of the warranted rate is its motivation. Recent authors have been very sensitive to the idea that growth theory should treat technical change as endogenous rather than exogenous; equation (6C−16) can do that. The discouraging feature of the recent revival is that simple plausibility checks, such as the compatibility of a specification with a growing population, are often neglected. Such plausibility checks were routine in the "old growth theory" but seem to need rediscovery in the "new growth theory."

In the fixed population case with N normalized at one, equation (6C−16) allows explicit solution for the saving rate of return. It is $\rho = A - \delta$. Consider the numerical specification

$$\delta = .05, \quad s = .15, \quad s^+ = .20, \quad DY(0)/Y(0) = .01.$$

These settings are the same as for previous examples; they imply $A = .4$ and thus $\rho = A - \delta = .35$. This ρ-value, derived for continuous time, is not directly comparable to the discrete time rates previously computed. A comparable rate of return, computed for the discrete analog of model (6C−16), is $\rho = .4011$ (see the appendix). This is the largest ρ-value of all the examples, far above the benchmark value $\rho = .0607$.

4. Conclusions

Seidman and Lewis's main goal is to measure the desirability of a saving rate increase using various neoclassical growth models. They have packaged their results as a dispute with the Satos about speed of adjustment to steady state. In my view, this dispute is artificial. Knowing whether adjustment is fast or slow (the Satos' concern) tells us essentially nothing about the desirability of a saving rate increase (Seidman and Lewis's concern).

Confounding of the speed of adjustment question and the desirability question carries over to two of Seidman and Lewis's three measures of the saving rate effect. Two of the measures seem partly designed to answer the speed question and partly designed to answer the desirability question. In my view, they fail to do either job. Seidman and Lewis's third measure, the internal rate of return from the additional investment generated by an increase in the saving rate, is a sensible indicator of the desirability of a saving increase.

The best way to read the Seidman and Lewis chapter is perhaps to ignore the claimed dispute with the Satos and to ignore two of their three measures of saving rate effect. Then we can focus on what is a genuinely interesting and important issue — the magnitude of the saving rate of return. Seidman and Lewis have done a number of interesting calculations regarding this rate.

The growth theory of the last decade or so is sometimes called the "new growth theory" to distinguish it from the "old growth theory" that began with Solow-Swan and that fell out of fashion by the early 1970s. The Seidman and Lewis work is old-fashioned in the sense that it would be right at home in the old growth literature. I like that. The main difference between the old and the new growth theory is the new theory's adherence to the fashion that models must have microfoundations. The trouble with this seemingly worthy fashion is that economists are unable to handle serious microfoundations (a diversity of agents facing changing circumstances) and still prove theorems. We might (and probably should) resort to simulations, as in the growth work of Nelson and Winter (1982); but simulation is not fashionable. Instead we create a parody of serious microfoundations through identical agent assumptions, thus allowing theorems. Identical agent assumptions achieve microfoundations essentially by eliminating the distinction between micro and macro. The aggregation question is handled by refusing to ask it. The new growth theory tends to take this parody direction.

From the viewpoint of the new growth theory, Seidman and Lewis's treatment of the saving rate as exogenous is unacceptable. Instead, the new growth theory would let the saving rate emerge as the endogenous outcome of an intertemporal utility maximization by the representative agent. Seidman and Lewis would be forced to ask questions in terms of a change in a "deep" parameter such as a tax rate or subjective discount rate. I like Seidman and Lewis's old-fashioned approach better. Given a suspicion that our economy is not saving enough, we would like to know (1) how to increase the saving rate and (2) what the effect would be. The new growth theory would pretend to answer both questions at once by investigating, say, a tax rate change; but, without good microfoundations, it is not clear why the new growth theory would give a good answer to either question. Seidman and Lewis, by splitting off the second question, have a better chance of getting a sensible answer.

Liking the old growth theory better than the new is not the same as trusting it, however. Most of the preceding comments concern the sensitivity of saving rate of return calculations to the specification of technical change. In fairness to Seidman and Lewis', it should be noted that they do investigate a number of different models and that, no matter how many models they try, one can always name others they have not tried. However, all their models assume exogenous technical change, whereas technical change is widely thought to be endogenous. The alternative models discussed here suggest that a false assumption of exogenous technical change will lead to an understatement of the saving rate of return. If an increase in the saving rate induces faster technical change as well as faster capital accumulation, the benefits of a saving increase will be understated, as will be saving rate of return. The numerical exercises suggest that the understatement may be sizable. As the wide range of computed values suggests, however, we know far too little about the determinants of technical change to get a plausible fix on magnitudes.

References

Arrow, Kenneth J. "The Economic Implications of Learning by Doing." *Review of Economic Studies* 29 (1962): 155–173.

Barro, Robert J. "Government Spending in a Simple Model of Endogenous Growth. *Journal of Political Economy* 98 (1990): S103–S125.

Conlisk, John. "A Modified Neoclassical Growth Model with Endogenous Technical Change." *Southern Economic Journal* 34 (1967): 199–208.

Conlisk, John. "An Aggregate Model of Technical Change." *Quarterly Journal of Economics* 104 (1989): 787–821.

Grossman, Gene M., and Elhanan Helpman. "Trade, Innovation, and Growth." *American Economic Review Papers and Proceedings* 80 (1990): 86–91.

Nelson, Richard R., and Sidney G. Winter. *An Evolutionary Theory of Economic Change.* Cambridge, Mass.: Harvard University Press, 1982.

Prescott, Edward C., and John H. Boyd. "Dynamic Coalitions: Engines of Growth." *American Economic Review Papers and Proceedings* 77 (1987): 63–67.

Rebelo, Sergio. "Long-Run Policy Analysis and Long-Run Growth." *Journal of Political Economy* 99 (1991): 500–521.
Romer, Paul M. "Increasing Returns and Long-Run Growth." *Journal of Political Economy* 94 (1986): 1002–1037.
Romer, Paul M. "Growth Based on Increasing Returns Due to Specialization." *American Economic Review Papers and Proceedings* 77 (1987): 56–62.
Romer, Paul M. "Endogenous Technical Change." *Journal of Political Economy* 98 (1990): S71–S102.
Sato, Kazuo. "On the Adjustment Time in Neoclassical Growth Models." *Review of Economic Studies* 33 (1966): 263–268.
Sato, Ryuzo. "Fiscal Policy in a Neoclassical Growth Model: An analysis of Time Required for Equilibrating Adjustment. *Review of Economic Studies* 30 (1963): 16–23.
Solow, Robert M. "A Contribution to the Theory of Economic Growth." *Quarterly Journal of Economics* 70 (1956): 65–94.
Swan, T.W. "Economic Growth and Capital Accumulation." *Economic Record* 32 (1956): 334–343.

Appendix: Discrete Time Analogs

The discrete time analog of equation (6C–1) is

(Rate of return ρ) = $\left\{ \text{solution for } \rho \text{ of } \sum_{t=1}^{\infty} e^{-\rho t}[C^{+}(t) - C(t)]dt = 0 \right\}$.

The following table displays continuous time equations and corresponding discrete time analogs. The discrete time analog of a particular model was derived by replacing each continuous equation with its discrete analog.

Continuous time equation	*Discrete time analog*
$Y = AK^{\alpha}L^{1-\alpha}$	$Y(t) = AK(t)^{\alpha}L(t)^{1-\alpha}$
$DK = sY - \delta K$	$K(t+1) = e^{-\delta}K(t) + sY(t)$
$L = zN$	$L(t) = z(t)N(t)$
$N = 1$	$N(t) = 1$
$Dz/z = \lambda$	$z(t+1) = e^{\lambda}z(t)$
$C = (1-s)Y$	$C(t) = (1-s)Y(t)$
$Y = AK^{\alpha}H^{\beta}N^{1-\alpha-\beta}$	$Y(t) = AK(t)^{\alpha}H(t)^{\beta}N(t)^{1-\alpha-\beta}$
$DH = hY - \gamma H$	$H(t+1) = e^{-\gamma}H(t) + hY(t)$
$Dz = bY/N - \mu z$	$z(t+1) = e^{-\mu}z(t) + bY(t)/N(t)$
$DL = bY - \mu L$	$L(t+1) = e^{-\mu}L(t) + bY(t)$
$z = K^{\sigma}$	$z(t) = K(t)^{\sigma}$
$Dz/z = g(sY)$	$z(t+1) = e^{g(sY(t))}z(t)$
$DL = \eta sY$	$L(t+1) = L(t) + \eta sY(t)$
$Y = A \min(K, N)$	$Y(t) = A \min[K(t), N(t)]$
$DY/Y = As - \delta$	$Y(t+1) = (As + e^{-\delta})Y(t)$

For the warranted rate model (6C–15), explicit solution for the rate of return ρ is possible. For continuous time, the solution is $\rho = A - \delta$. For discrete time, the analogous solution is (the log of)

$$e^\rho = (s^+ - s)gg^+/[(1 - s)g - (1 - s^+)g^+],$$

where $g = As + e^{-\delta}$ and $g^+ = As^+ + e^{-\delta}$.

7 SAVING IN THE DEVELOPMENT PROCESS

T. N. Srinivasan
Yale University

1. Introduction

The importance of domestic saving in the process of economic development has been stressed by a long line of distinguished economists from Adam Smith on. Two recent, excellent surveys (Gersovitz, 1988; Deaton, 1989) of the theory of and empirical evidence on saving from developing countries are available. An earlier survey by King (1985), though not devoted to development per se, is also useful. This section attempts to highlight some relatively neglected if not altogether ignored aspects, though some overlap with the earlier surveys is unavoidable. In particular, discussion begins with the severe problems of measurement errors and biases in the available data on income and saving from developing countries, using Indian data for illustration. The section then explores the implications of the absence and imperfect functioning of credit and insurance markets in developing countries, drawing on some recent theoretical developments and empirical studies.

The late Sir Arthur Lewis, in his celebrated paper on economic development with unlimited supplies of labor, argued that the "central problem of economic development is to understand the process by which a community which was previously saving and investing 4 or 5 percent of its national income or less converts itself into an economy where voluntary saving is running at about 12 to 15 percent of national income or more. This is the central problem because the central fact of economic development is rapid capital accumulation (including knowledge and skills with capital)" (Lewis, 1954, p. 155). If published international data are reliable, *the process* of conversion must be complete already! According to the IMF, the developing countries saved (and invested at home) 23.7 percent of their GDP during 1983–1990 (IMF, 1991, table 12). Assuming capital consumption allowances of 10 percent, the implied net saving rate (i.e., ratio of net saving to net domestic product) is 15.3 percent. On the other hand, although the average annual rate of growth of GDP per capita in developing countries accelerated from about 2 percent in the 1950s to roughly 3.5 percent in the 1960s, since the oil shock of 1973, according to the World Bank data, the record is one of deceleration from 3.9 percent during 1965–1973 to 2.5 percent during 1975–1980 and 1.6 percent during 1980–1989 (World Bank, 1991, table 1). This deceleration in per capita growth was not because of any acceleration in the rate of growth of population; on the contrary, there is some evidence of a *decline* in the latter from about 2.5 percent per annum during 1965–1973 to about 2.1 percent during 1973–1980. Thus the increasing rate of saving (and of investment, not including accumulation of human capital) has not resulted in any increase in the rate of growth of income. Of course, in a neoclassical model with *indefinitely* diminishing marginal returns to capital as capital accumulates relative to labor, the *steady-state growth* rate is independent of the investment rate. But even in that model during the transition to the steady-state, the investment rate influences the growth rate. As no developing country is likely to be in a steady-state by definition, either the link between increasing saving and development that Lewis postulated was not operative or the data on saving as well as income growth are unreliable, or both!

In Lewis's model the primary force that brought about an increase in the saving rate was the redistribution of income in favor of the classes that saved (which he viewed as the top decile of the income distribution) rather than growth of per capita incomes per se. The data on distribution of income are unavailable for many countries, and even where available, their conceptual basis, coverage, and reliability are known to be problematic. These problems notwithstanding, there is no evidence of a massive shift in the distribution of income in favor of the rich that would account for the observed increase in aggregate saving rates. Another influential strand in the early development literature placed the state at the center stage of the development process. The state in the paradigm, among other things, was to acquire an increasing share of national output (through taxation and surpluses of public enterprises) and to save and invest a substantial portion of what it acquired. Of course, if what has come to be known as Ricardian Equivalence holds, then the private sector in its saving decisions would take into account and offset the saving of the public sector, leaving the aggregate rate at the same level regardless of the extent of public sector activity. But even if one were to ignore Ricardian Equivalence for the reason that there is little empirical support for it in the data from developing countries (Haque and Montiel, 1989), public sector saving, if anything, does not appear to have increased significantly in the last four decades. In either case, one has to look for an explanation in the behavior of the private sector for the measured rise in aggregate saving rates.

Within the private sector, saving by households is usually distinguished from the saving (i.e., retained earnings) by corporate and unincorporated enterprises. If the analogue of Ricardian Equivalence holds, that the enterprise is merely a veil, then once again any changes in enterprise saving would be offset by household saving so that the aggregate saving in the private sector as a whole would remain unchanged. If capital markets are active and efficient with extensive financial intermediation taking place, an enterprise would have no incentive to retain and invest in itself a part of its earnings unless, of course, the returns to such investment are comparable to the best available in the market. The same applies to a household—its savings need not be invested in household enterprises (e.g., farm, household production of nonfarm products or service for the market, and the like). In particular, a household would not have to accumulate savings prior to investing in its enterprise or buying a house or consumer durable or any investment activity that is lumpy. It would instead borrow from the market and service the debt from future earnings. Thus the existence and efficiency of financial markets affect the saving and investment process.

The complete absence of a market for claims or resources available at different dates in the future, claims that can be traded for one another and for claims on current resources through arm's-length transactions among anonymous agents, is an extreme. Equally extreme is the assumption of a complete set of markets for all such claims from here on for all dates into the indefinite future, the markets being competitive and efficient so that no opportunity for arbitrage remains in equilibrium. The real world is at neither extreme, the situation in the less developed countries perhaps being closer to the former extreme and that in the industrialized world to the latter. This makes the analysis of saving in less developed countries somewhat complex not only in theory but more so empirically. One has to account for the imperfect functioning of credit markets and allow for the possibility that intertemporal transactions such as saving, lending, and borrowing may involve agents known to each other and be combined with other transactions between the same two agents. The limited availability of financial intermediation means that the saving and investment decisions have to be considered jointly. For example, in the absence of a mortgage market, a decision to buy a house means a decision to accumulate the purchase price through prior savings. Also, given limited financial intermediation, household production opportunities through farm and nonfarm activities and transactions across generations within the same household, and so on, are likely to be much more important in household saving and investment decisions than in developed countries.

In the absence of opportunities to provide for one's retirement through the market for annuities and through nonmarket arrangements such as state organized social security, individuals have to rely in part on their progeny or kin for old-age support. This means that fertility decisions would be made jointly with saving and investment decisions. This is not to imply that intergenerational transfers and implicit contracts are not important in developed countries. Indeed, the works of Kotlikoff and Summers (1981) on the bequest motive for savings among U.S. households and the phenomenon of retired Japanese parents inviting one of their adult offspring to live with them and inherit their house in exchange for taking care of them (Dekle, 1990; Ando et al., 1991) suggest that old-age provisions through markets, employers, and the government are not adequate even in developed countries.

Besides markets for dated claims on resources, the existence and the functioning of markets for risk is relevant for saving decisions. Indeed, one of the major motives for saving is the precautionary motive; households save and accumulate some assets that can be sold to maintain consumption in the future when there are adverse shocks to income. If insurance markets exist and function effectively, a household can smooth its consumption even though incomes are subject to random shocks by buying an insurance contract. Even if insurance markets do not exist, if the credit markets function well and a household has access to such markets, it can maintain consumption and tide over a temporary adverse shock in income by borrowing and expect to repay the debt when it experiences a favorable shock. The absence or imperfect functioning of credit markets will tend to reinforce the precautionary motive: The anticipated inability to borrow whenever an income fall is experienced in the future is an argument for accumulating assets when times are good. The absence of well-functioning credit markets thus affects the ability of a household to transfer resources over time as well as across uncertain states of nature relating to its income. Whether greater uncertainty about income, in a well-defined sense, leads to greater precautionary saving and analogously whether greater uncertainty about returns to investment increases saving are issues discussed in the literature. A large proportion of households in less developed countries earn their incomes from agriculture directly or indirectly. Because agriculture is an inherently uncertain activity, the role of uncertainty in saving and investment decisions of households is particularly important in such countries.

Any credit transaction by definition involves an exchange separated by time. The possibility is real that the agent obligated to pay at a future date may renege, either because he did not put the resources received earlier to such use as would have generated the wherewithal to repay or because he willfully defaults in spite of having the ability to repay. Thus default risk and moral hazard have to be taken into account by a lender who cannot observe and monitor the actions of a borrower. Whether a creditor can get a loan contract enforced against a borrower and a borrower can ensure that he is left with some means of survival in the event of his inability to meet his obligations to the creditor depend on the legal system, particularly the laws relating to bankruptcy and limited liability. Also laws against usury or even charging of any interest would constrain the operation of credit markets. The legal system for enforcement of contracts is likely to be weak in the early stages of development. This weakness can inhibit saving because such savings lent to others are not safe.

Households in the aggregate would save if those who save actually save enough to offset the dissavings of other households. For example, if the population of households is stationary in number and age structure, and each household experiences the same income profile over its lifetime and optimally chooses a constant consumption stream whose present value equals that of its income at the market rate of interest, then in the aggregate there will be no net saving. Depending on the income profile, allowing the number of households to change or income profile to shift exogenously over time would generate saving. The simplest version of a model describing the optimal saving decision of an individual is one in which the individual lives for just two periods ($t = 1, 2$) and receives an exogenous income y_t in period t. His preference over consumption c_t ($t = 1, 2$) in the two periods is described by a concave utility function u (c_1, c_2). He faces an exogenous interest rate r at which he can invest his savings (or borrow for financing his dissavings) in the first period. Thus his problem is to maximize $u(c_1, c_2)$ subject to the constraint $c_1 + Rc_2 = y_1 + Ry_2 \equiv w$, where $R = 1/(1 + r)$ and w is wealth or the present value of the income stream. Saving in the first period is $(y_1 - c_1)$. At an optimum in which the individual consumes a positive amount in each period, the marginal rate of substitution—that is, the ratio u_2/u_1 of the marginal utilities $u_t(t=1, 2)$—will equal R.

R is the price of future consumption relative to present consumption. It is also the present value (in terms of present income or consumption) of a unit of future income or the wealth per unit of future income. Thus an increase in the interest r, by decreasing R, makes future consumption c_2 cheaper relative to c_1. Thus, for given wealth, c_2 will go up. On the other hand, a decrease in R reduces wealth and thus would reduce c_2 as long as future consumption is normal. The net effect on c_2 of an increase in r is therefore ambiguous. If c_2 goes down, then clearly c_2R goes down, as R decreases with an increase in r. Even if c_2 goes up, if the elasticity of c_2 with respect to R is less than unity, the product c_2R will go down as r increases. Thus if c_2R goes down by more than the fall in wealth, then $c_1 = w - c_2R$ will go up and hence saving, $s_1 = y_1 - c_1$, will fall. If c_2R goes down by less than the fall in wealth or if it goes up, then c_1 will fall and saving will rise. All these events are well known. Leaving aside for a moment the facts that for a two-period model saving of period 1 is dissaved in period 2 and that whether there is net saving in the aggregate depends on whether there is growth in the population, its implications for policy, particularly in developing countries, are important for several reasons.

First, a very influential strand of the literature going back to Gurley and Shaw (1967), McKinnon (1973), and more recently Fry (1987) has argued that in many developing countries a policy of financial repression through ceilings on interest rates and requirements that commercial banks hold a specified proportion of their investment portfolio in the form of public debt and soon, discourages saving and that financial liberalization would increase saving. Such liberalization would almost certainly raise the *return* on saving but, as is clear from the two-period model, it is not certain in *theory* that it would raise the *volume* of saving. Whether the elasticity of saving with respect to the real interest rate is positive is an *empirical* question.

Second, if one moves away from the unrealistic assumption that the financial markets are well integrated, then the issue becomes even more complex. Lack of integration means that there would be a *distribution* of interest rates corresponding to different segments of the market. Once again, in theory, integrating and unifying such markets through policy may raise or lower the return to saving as compared to its mean value prior to integration, and even if it does go up, the aggregate volume of savings need not go up. One has to look to empirical analysis for answers.

Third, a feature of credit markets in developed as well as developing countries is the problem arising from information asymmetry between borrowers and lenders; the moral hazard in the use of borrowed funds and adverse selection of projects proposed to lenders for financing. A basic insight of the literature (Stiglitz and Weiss, 1981) on this problem is that equilibrium in such markets may well be characterized by quantitative rationing of credit rather than one of the interest rate adjusting to equate demand and supply. In developing countries, the rationing equilibrium arises both for reasons of moral hazard and adverse selection but also because the interest rate charged by formal institutions is often fixed by the government at a level below the market clearing level. However, informal credit arrangements, which in some countries are sufficiently extensive and organized to be termed *informed credit markets*, coexist with the formal institutions. Those who are denied credit altogether or are not given as much credit as they would like to have at the fixed formal sector interest rate turn to informal credit. Clearly, given this market segmentation, the spillover of demand from the formal to the informal market, and the possibility that informal credit transactions may be tied to transactions in other markets between the same agents, public policy intervention in the credit market, say for encouraging saving, might fail to do so or have other unintended and even deleterious consequences. This is just another illustration of the theory of the second best: If an initial equilibrium is characterized by distortions in several markets, intervening to remove one distortion while leaving others in place can be welfare worsening.

An implication of the possibility of an individual's being denied or rationed credit is that she cannot smooth consumption in the face of fluctuating income to the desired extent. In turn her consumption (and savings) would be more responsive to (responsive only to) current income (responsive in the case of her having no access to credit at all). A growing macroeconometric literature in the developed countries is testing the significance of liquidity constraints to smoothing of aggregate consumption. The simplistic assumption of these models, that the population of agents consists of two groups, one set of identical agents (the so-called "life cycle" or permanent income consumers) who are not liquidity constrained and another set, again of identical agents (the so-called "Keynesian" or current income consumers) who are constrained, is laughably extreme. Given the heterogeneity of agents and the range of possibilities of self-financing through purchases and sales of physical assets (land, farm animals, jewelry, and the like) that they have, it is unlikely that the popular but simplistic macroeconometric model would be appropriate for the analysis of aggregate saving behavior of households in developing countries.

Finally, in an economy open to foreign capital inflows, domestic investment can be financed in part by such inflows and, equally, part of domestic savings can be invested abroad. If the world capital market is well integrated and efficient so that investable capital freely moves across national boundaries seeking the highest return, there should be no correlation between domestic saving and domestic investment. Yet, puzzlingly, Feldstein and Horioka (1980) found such a correlation in their study of 21 countries over the period 1960–1974. Since then, others have tried to reexamine and explain why the Feldstein-Horioka puzzle may not be a puzzle after all! The role of foreign capital in the context of development has been recognized from the early days of development economics. The then popular two-gap model (Chenery and Bruno, 1962) revolved around the twin roles of external capital, for example, in supplementing domestic savings in financing investment and in adding to export earnings in paying for imports. An issue that generated controversy and some empirical analysis in an attempt to resolve it was whether domestic saving was exogenous to foreign capital inflow so that a unit of inflow was translated into a unit of additional investment or whether it was endogenous so that a unit of inflow generated less (respectively more) than a unit of additional investment if it was a substitute (respectively complement) for domestic savings.

More recently the problem of capital flight from developing economies has been the focus of attention. Such flight is induced by public policies such as taxation and threats of expropriation that depress returns to domestic investment and make the returns riskier as well. Whether capital once flown out of a country can be induced to come back would depend on the credibility of policy reform. Credibility of proposed policy reform is achieved, of course, by definition if the government can (credibly!) precommit to pursuing reforms even when an incentive to deviate arises in the future. But such precommitment comes at the cost of flexibility to respond to unforeseen future events that might call for revising the reform program. The problem is the private sector's difficulty in distinguishing between flexibility and flip-flops in adherence to a reform program. At the very least, the private sector may take considerable time to be convinced of the seriousness of the government's intention to implement reforms and until then would have little or no response to reform. Thus flight capital might return, if at all, only after the credibility of the reform is established. Thus an empirical analysis that does not allow for this lag might wrongly conclude that private saving and portfolio choices do not respond to incentives.

To sum up, first, there are serious conceptual problems as well as measurement errors and biases in the data on saving, investment, and income of developing countries. These problems are discussed in some detail in section 2. Second, although aggregate savings and investment rates seem to have increased significantly, the link between them and growth of income appears to be more complex than was originally thought. It was noted also that the interaction between household, corporate, and public saving depends on the extent to which households, in making their own saving decisions, allow for corporate decisions regarding earnings retention and the future tax implications of public decisions to accumulate (or retire) public debt. Also whether household saving responds positively to an increase in the rate of interest (or more generally to an increase in the rate of return to assets in which savings are invested) and whether households are constrained in their ability to smooth their consumption in the face of fluctuating income are primarily empirical issues, the former depending on certain elasticity parameters and the latter on the existence and efficient functioning of the markets for credit and insurance. Section 3 summarizes the available empirical evidence from developing countries on trends in saving and investment as well as on the determinants of saving. Section 4 is devoted to a discussion of informal credit and insurance markets in developing countries. Section 5 concludes the chapter with some observations on policy implications.

2. Saving and Income in Developing Countries: Data Problems

Statistical agencies in different countries, developed and developing, do not follow uniform procedures in measuring income and savings, even though the System of National Accounts (SNA) promoted by the United Nations Statistical Office attempts to bring about such uniformity. An example of diverse practice is the assessment of depreciation of capital. It is not necessarily the case that diversity is in itself to be deplored. Given the enormous variance across countries and over time in economic and social development and heterogeneity in market and nonmarket institutions (legal systems, custom, and usage) through which economic exchanges take place, forcing a uniform structure on developing and developed countries for data collection, tabulation, and reporting could be counterproductive. Still that diversity in statistical practice calls for caution in the interpretation and use of published data. A major cause of the diversity in practice is the difficulty in moving from more or less well defined concepts to their acceptable empirical counterparts.

An act of saving by definition involves abstaining from consuming all currently available resources or current "income." Translating this concept into an empirical measure involves, first, defining consumption and income and then finding the empirical counterparts to each. In gathering data from households in a survey or in putting together aggregate data from national income accounts, the definition of consumption that is used is often a matter of more or less arbitrary accounting conventions rather than one of consistency with some well-specified economic theory. A seemingly clear notion that consumption yields immediate welfare while saving-investment yields future welfare by augmenting the capacity to generate future income runs into several problems in its empirical implementation. For example, the use of current resources on education (conventionally included under consumption in the aggregate data) yields (hopefully) current welfare through the pleasure derived from being educated as well as enhances future earnings capacity through its role as investment in human capital. Further, depending on the length of the time period, the same expenditure could be deemed as saving-investment or as purchase of current inputs. For a farmer who spends on an irrigation facility that stores water from one crop season to the next within a year but that ceases to function at the end of the year, the expenditure would be investment in the first season if data are compiled on a seasonal basis but would be deemed expenditure on a current input that is used up in production if the data are compiled on an annual basis. Even if the irrigation facility were to last for more than a year so that the resources spent on it would be deemed conceptually as saving cum investment, it may not be recorded as such in household surveys and national income accounts if the farm household constructs the facility with its own labor and uses no purchased materials but only earth, stones, and other material that it gathers. In most national accounts data, such production cum investment activity within the household would not enter income and investment flows. It should be noted that the fact that the exclusion of such flows understates true investment and income by the *same* amount does not mean it is innocuous: Investment and saving *rates* are understated as well.

More generally the treatment of different goods and services that are produced and wholly used (for consumption or investment) *within* households in national accounts is far from consistent or uniform. The time spent by a household member in preparing a meal for home consumption is not part of the value added in national accounts. But the value of, say, the rice the same member produces in the family plot of land is often included in national income even if the entire rice harvest is consumed by the household and not a grain is sold in the market! This differential treatment of the value added in a home-cooked meal and home-produced grain is not due to any greater difficulty of imputation of value but merely to an arbitrary convention. Using the prevailing market price for cooked meals in food shops or restaurants for arriving at a value for a home-cooked meal is just as easy or difficult as valuing home-produced-and-consumed grain using farm harvest prices.

In the national accounts of some developing countries the data on domestic investment, saving, and their decomposition into household, corporate, and government components are not based on direct observation but arrived at through indirect estimation. In India total *domestic* gross *investment* in physical capital is estimated by the so-called commodity flow method: Domestic investment is the sum of additions to construction, machinery and equipment, and inventories. These additions equal the value of all commodities (e.g., equipment, steel, cement) that can be used for investment. The quantities used for investment are obtained by adding imports to the domestic production of each such commodity in the relevant period and then subtracting from the total the sum of exports and the amount used for noninvestment purposes. The commodity vector so obtained is then valued at producer's prices, and to this value a trade and transportation margin and indirect taxes are added to arrive at an estimate of the value of investment at purchaser's prices.

Clearly at each step there could be measurement errors: in estimating domestic availability, in the norms used to split investment and noninvestment uses of a commodity, in valuing the commodity flow through a set of prices that are not necessarily the prices at which the goods were bought or sold, in the trade and transport margin, which is often derived from some ancient benchmark survey, and so on. Indeed, a government committee that looked into the estimates of capital formation and saving in India pointed out that "while it is relatively simple to compute the available quantities each year of the main commodities that go into fixed capital formation, there can be large margins of errors in estimating the total capital outlay with which they are associated since they would depend on the correctness of a variety of norms used for this purpose ... the possible errors in estimation of aggregate investment in the economy are not only sizable but, in the present state of our statistical data base, quite indeterminate" (Reserve Bank of India, 1982, p. 3). Gross investment in the public and private corporate sectors are independently estimated from their published accounts. Gross investment of the rest of the economy—that is, the household sector inclusive of unincorporated enterprises—is obtained as the difference between aggregate gross investment in the economy and that in the public and private corporate sectors. Being a residual, this estimate of gross investment of the household sector in physical assets incorporates estimation errors of the two magnitudes of which it is the difference.

One estimate of aggregate *domestic saving* is obtained by subtracting net external resource inflow (after allowing for changes in the holdings of external financial assets) from estimated aggregate investment. Measuring resource inflow is also subject to errors and biases. In India there are two often wildly differing estimates of foreign trade deficit financing, which is a large component of the inflow. One estimate is based on the flow of imports and exports through customs checkposts. The other is based on foreign exchange receipts from exports and payments for imports that go through the banking system. Even after adjusting for time lags between shipments and payments and for other accountable factors, the difference between the two estimates has been large. Further, neither estimate takes (or indeed can ever take) into account illegal underinvoicing of exports and overinvoicing of imports that in part enable capital flight and in part finance smuggled imports of gold and other commodities whose domestic price far exceeds the world price converted at the official exchange rate. Given the incentives that the exchange control system in India created for smuggling, capital flight, and evasion of high tariffs, it is likely that both estimates based on officially recorded data are wide of the mark. It goes without saying that if some exchanges are in principle covered by the statistical system and others, particularly the transactions in the black markets, are not only not covered but also take place at prices substantially different from recorded prices in the official data, income and saving data would be distorted. India is not unique in this respect among developing countries.

Estimates of public sector saving are obtained from the accounts of central, state, and local authorities. Although these estimates should in principle be free of error, in practice the coverage often is not complete and the classification of expenditures (into capital and current expenditures) can be arbitrary. It is a matter of record that among developed countries the United States has the distinction of not separating capital and current expenditures in the government budget! Be that as it may, in India corporate saving is derived from balance sheets and to the extent there is some "creative" accounting in the income statement and balance sheet, savings estimates would be biased. The household sector's financial savings — that is, additions to its holdings of financial assets (currency, bank deposits, insurance and provident funds, and shares and debentures) — are estimated once again as a residual — that is, the difference between additions to the financial assets of the economy as a whole and the additions to the holdings of such assets by the public and corporate sectors. Adding the estimated additions to physical assets by the household sector (which as mentioned earlier is a residual) to the sector's financial savings, total savings of the household sector are obtained. Finally the sum of the savings of public, corporate, and household sectors provide a *second* estimate of the aggregate gross savings in the economy.

The two estimates of aggregate saving have differed to a considerable extent in some years. The statistical authorities appear to treat the second estimate of savings as more reliable so that their estimate of aggregate investment is obtained by adding external capital flow to the second "more" reliable estimate of domestic savings. The difference between this investment estimate and that based on the commodity flow method is treated as "errors and omissions." It should be noted that the household sector's investment in physical assets, which is residually estimated and hence incorporates the errors in measures and biases in the variables of which it is the difference, is a component of the estimate of aggregate savings. It is not an insignificant component — it accounted for about 39 percent of aggregate savings and 49 percent of household sector's savings in 1987–88, and these figures were much higher in the fifties and sixties. Because India is one of a few developing countries with a well-developed statistical system, the fact that Indian estimates of household sector and aggregate saving are subject to possibly serious biases and estimation errors suggests that the saving estimates for other countries with less well developed statistical systems would be even worse. The measurement problems and biases in nominal magnitudes get compounded by similar problems in the deflators used to convert them into constant-price series.

Many countries, developed and developing, collect economic data on a regular basis through household surveys. Such surveys often include information on household income, consumption, and saving. It is extremely rare to find instances of a close agreement between survey-based estimates and those derived from national accounts data. Deaton (1989) eloquently describes the problems in estimating income in developing countries through a survey as follows:

> The concept of income is itself extraordinarily complex, and most people in developing countries have little reason to distinguish between business and personal cash transactions. A farmer who buys seeds and food in the same market at the same time may not appreciate that, when computing income, he

should only deduct the expenditure on seeds from his receipts. Nor is a seller of street food likely to distinguish accurately between what is eaten by his customers and what by his family. A subsistence farmer, whose outgoings approximately equal his incomes, is quite likely to report that his income is zero. (Even in developed countries the measurement of self-employment income is notoriously inaccurate.) The problems are not entirely solved even by the detailed questioning of more sophisticated surveys, in which the surveyor, not the respondent, calculates income. And the national accounts data for household saving are not themselves reliable enough to provide a good cross-check that will show what sort of surveys do best or how they should be redesigned to do better. [P. 63]

It is worth noting that in countries such as India, self-employment (rather than wage and salary employment or being an employer) is the dominant mode of employment. In agriculture, on which nearly two thirds of the labor force depends for employment, cultivators form the major group. It is unlikely that a self-employed artisan, a street vendor, or a cultivator who is likely to have engaged in many transactions in kind rather than for cash would be able to say what his or her income (in the economic sense) in the previous week, month, or year was! Besides, the upper-income groups, particularly in urban areas, such as lawyers, doctors, and other self-employed professionals, often do not respond in surveys or are likely to understate their incomes if they do. For all these reasons in India the National Sample Survey (NSS) collects data on consumption, rather than income, of households. Ever since the NSS was established in the early fifties, several attempts were made (see Minhas, 1988, and references cited by him) to compare the levels and time trends in national income account-based and survey-based estimates of household consumption in the aggregate as well as of individual commodity groups. This literature forcefully makes the point that a simplistic belief that national accounts-based estimates are more reliable and less biased is not necessarily true. Several adjustments for differences in coverage, period, valuation, imputation, and so forth have to be made before the two estimates are compared. The difference between the two, in levels and in trends, appears to narrow in the Indian data once the adjustments are made.

3. Saving and Investment: Empirical Evidence on Trends and Determinants

Turning to the available empirical knowledge about saving behavior and its implications for growth and development, table 7−1 presents the

Table 7-1. Trends in Investment and Savings in Selected Developing Countries

Country	GNP per Capita U.S.$ 1989	Gross Domestic Investment (% of GNP) 1965–1973	Gross Domestic Investment (% of GNP) 1973–1980	Gross Domestic Investment (% of GNP) 1980–1989	Gross National Savings (% of GNP) 1965–1973	Gross National Savings (% of GNP) 1973–1980	Gross National Savings (% of GNP) 1980–1989	Gross Domestic Investment (% of GDP) 1965–1989	Gross Domestic Investment (% of GDP) 1965–1989	Gross Domestic Savings (% of GDP) 1965–1989	Gross Domestic Savings (% of GDP) 1965–1989
Latin America & the Caribbean											
Argentina	2,160	19.7	23.4	15.5	20.1	...	15.5	19	12	22	19
Bolivia	620	25.4	24.9	12.2	21.3	18.5	12.2	22	13	17	9
Brazil	2,540	21.3	24.0	21.5	19.1	19.3	21.5	20	22	22	26
Mexico	2,010	20.6	24.2	23.1	14.9	20.2	23.1	20	17	19	18
Uruguay	2,620	12.0	15.7	12.3	12.0	11.3	12.3	11	9	18	15
Sub-Saharan Africa											
Ethiopia	120	12.8	9.5	12.8	11.0	6.9	12.8	13	13	12	−5
Ghana	390	12.3	8.7	...	8.7	6.9	...	18	12	8	6
Kenya	360	22.6	26.0	25.4	17.2	16.3	25.4	14	25	15	20
Nigeria	250	16.3	22.8	13.8	11.8	24.4	13.8	14	13	12	21
Tanzania	130	19.9	23.9	...	17.1	14.1	...	15	21	16	5
East Asia											
Indonesia	500	15.8	24.5	30.4	13.7	24.6	30.4	8	35	8	37
Korea, Rep.	4,400	23.9	31.2	31.2	17.6	25.9	31.2	15	35	8	37
Philippines	710	20.6	29.1	21.7	19.7	24.3	21.7	21	19	21	18
South Asia											
India	340	17.2	21.3	23.9	15.8	21.0	23.9	17	24	15	21
Pakistan	370	16.1	17.5	18.8	...	11.7	18.8	21	18	13	11
Sri Lanka	430	15.8	20.6	25.8	11.2	13.4	25.8	12	21	13	12
Middle East											
Egypt	640	14.0	29.3	27.9	9.3	18.2	27.9	18	24	14	7
Turkey	1,370	18.5	21.8	22.8	16.0	18.1	22.8	15	22	13	21

Source: The World Bank, *World Development Report 1991* (Tables A.5, 1, and 9) (Oxford University Press, 1991).

trends in aggregate saving for a number of countries. Keeping in mind the numerous problems with the data discussed in section 2, and hoping that these problems do not completely offset and reverse the trends seen in table 7−1, one would draw the conclusion that, broadly speaking, average saving and investment rates have been high in most countries since the mid-sixties and have increased in some. However, in the eighties, a period of recession and recovery in the industrialized countries and of relatively high real interest rates and crisis of debt service in some highly indebted countries, there was a decline in savings, investment, and growth rates in some countries, particularly in Sub-Saharan Africa and Latin America.

As mentioned earlier, the early development economists saw a close link between increased saving and investment on the one hand and growth of national income on the other, although they stressed the effect of saving and investment on growth rather than the effect going the other way. Maddison (1991) analyzed long-run saving, investment, and growth in a sample of 11 countries of which Australia, Canada, France, Germany, the Netherlands, the United Kingdom, and the United States might be termed high-income countries throughout the period 1870−1989, while India, Japan, Korea, and Taiwan might be termed as developing for part or whole of the period. He concluded that there is a general positive relationship between the faster growth in output per head since World War II and the acceleration in the saving rate and a slowdown in both saving and growth rates after the 1973 oil shock. Interestingly, the United States had the smallest acceleration in postwar growth in per capita income and it was also the country with the least change in long-run saving habits.

Deaton (1989) rightly argues that "the fundamental problem is the direction of causality: from growth to saving (the life-cycle explanation) or from saving to growth." He dismisses as unconvincing, once again rightly, attempts at a purely econometric resolution of the problem of causality through the use of instrumental variables because these are not backed by an adequate theory of growth. His own admittedly crude graphical analysis of the relations between gross savings ratio (in 1986) and the growth rate of GDP (during 1980−1986) in 106 countries suggests a positive relationship between the two, with the saving rate increasing 1−1.5 percentage points for every percentage increase in growth rate. The relationship, though statistically significant by conventional statistical standards, is not particularly close.

The life cycle model of consumption and saving in its simplest form would predict that given an economy in which incomes grow faster than in another economy, the age–consumption profile should be relatively higher among the younger cohorts in the former. Summers and Carroll (1989) found the profiles in Japan, the United States, and Canada to be virtually the same despite differences in growth rates. Deaton analyzed profiles in five countries, with Cote d'Ivoire at one extreme with a GNP per capita that at an average annual rate of 1.2 percent during 1965–1986, with Hong Kong and Korea at the other extreme with growth rates of 6.2 percent and 6.7 percent, respectively, and Indonesia and Thailand in the middle with growth rates of 4.6 percent and 4.0 percent, respectively. He concludes that the standard life cycle model explanation of growth effects, namely that "younger cohorts are saving and spending on a larger scale simply does not work" (Deaton, 1989, p. 81).

Turning to causality in the other direction, that between saving rates (more precisely investment rates) and growth rates, Scott (1989) argues that conventional growth theories are fundamentally wrong in neglecting to allow for changes in relative price of capital. The fact that relative price changes in the aggregate (at least in developed countries) reduced capital values has the effect of understanding the contribution of investment to growth by a large amount. He regressed the growth rate of output on the share of gross investment in output, rate of growth of quality-adjusted employment, and a host of other variables meant to capture the efficiency of investment. His data were 26 observations relating to different countries (the United Kingdom, the United States, Japan, Belgium, Denmark, France, Germany, the Netherlands, Norway, and Italy) and different periods. For the United States, Japan, and the United Kingdom, the data went back to the eighteenth century; for the remaining countries the relevant period was 1955–1962. The investment share variable was statistically highly significant. Put another way, roughly 45 percent of the weighted average of the 26 observations on the growth rate was accounted for by investment and another 45 percent by the growth in quality adjusted labor force. Thus unlike in the celebrated Solow model, in the Scott model growth of inputs rather than the residual explained an overwhelming share of the growth of output in the developed countries. However, because investment is endogenous and because Scott used ordinary least squares in estimating his regression, the estimated parameters and hence the contribution of investment to growth are biased.

Solow-type models, when estimated with data from developing countries, suggest that a proportion ranging from 58 percent to 73 percent of the growth in output during 1960–1987 was accounted for by growth in capital and a proportion ranging from 14 percent to 30 percent was accounted for by the growth in labor input (World Bank, 1991, table 2–

3). As contrasted with this cross-sectional evidence, within-country time series data point to a considerably different picture. Using an implicit constant returns to scale Cobb-Douglas model of production (with an elasticity of output with respect to capital of 0.4), Fry (1991, table 1) finds that contribution of the growth of capital to output growth ranges from a low of about 2 percent in Sri Lanka for the period 1961–1967 to a high of 92 percent in Indonesia during 1982–1988. The latter is an outlier, however, as it relates to a period when employment fell. In fact, 29 of the 31 estimated proportions were less than 50 percent, with as many as 11 being less than 30 percent. Indeed, this time series evidence supports the assertion made in section 1 that the link between investment and growth is less strong than it was believed to be by early development economists. It should be noted, however, that if the Solow residual is viewed as the contribution of total factor productivity growth induced by technical progress, it follows that the greater the contribution of the growth of inputs, including capital to output growth, the less is the contribution of productivity growth. But this conventional interpretation of the residual is not the only possible one. The residual could be due to the productivity increases that arise solely from shifts in the composition of aggregate output and relative price changes and not from any changes in the technology of production in any sector.

Fry (1991) also estimates a regression of national saving rate to assess the real income growth effects given life cycle behavior and the effects of lagged income, population growth, terms of trade changes, real deposit rate, and of several variables to represent the terms of access external capital. Data from ten Asian countries for the period 1961–1988 were used in the estimation. Although the coefficients representing income growth (positive), population depending ratio (negative), real deposit rate (positive), lagged income (positive), and foreign debt to GNP ratio (negative) are statistically significant, the fact that it is a single-equation model in which several of the explanatory variables could be rightly viewed as *endogenous* raises serious doubts about the econometric validity of inferences made from it.

Section 1 pointed out that in theory the response of saving to an increase in the real interest rate is ambiguous. Empirical evidence, such as it is, seems to be consistent with theory, in that positive as well as negative responses were found. Yet an overwhelming majority of responses appear to be positive, though many of them are not significantly different from zero. A survey of a number of studies based on aggregate data from developed and developing countries is available in Balassa (1990). He reports that in a study of Williamson (1968) the (real) interest elasticity of saving was found to be negative in five out of six Asian countries, although apart from that for Japan the others were not significantly different from zero. Another study by Gupta (1970) found a positive interest elasticity for India. Balassa also cites a study of Brown (1973) in which the real interest rate and, alternatively, the nominal interest rate and inflation rate were used as explanatory variables with personal saving as the dependent variable. The regression coefficient of the real interest rate was statistically significant and positive. In the alternative regression the coefficient of nominal interest rate was positive and that of the inflation rate negative. Brown's result were confirmed in a subsequent study of Yasuf and Peters (1984). The other studies cited by Balassa include Fry (1977, 1979) for Portugal and Turkey, with *positive* response of savings to interest rate; DeMelo and Tybout (1986) for Uruguay, with positive but weak effect for the period 1962–1983 but stronger effect for the subperiod 1962–1973; McDonald (1983) for twelve Latin American countries, with positive interest rate effects for most countries; and Gupta (1984) for twelve Asian countries in which financial saving and saving in physical assets were distinguished. For the ten countries for which the nominal interest rate was available, nine showed a positive relationship between financial saving and the interest rate, though in only five of them was the relation statistically significant. The interest rate had a generally negative effect on physical savings, though again significant effects were found only in four cases.

The last study cited by Balassa is by Giovannini (1985), who analyzed the effect of the real interest rate on the growth of consumption in a year compared to the previous year for 18 developing countries. Such a regression can be derived as the first-order condition (Euler equation) of intertemporal utility maximization subject to a lifetime budget constraint. Under certain assumptions (in particular that lifetime utility is time separable, utility in each period is the logarithm of consumption in that period, and the utility discount rate is the same as the interest rate on investment of savings), it translates into the hypothesis that the logarithm of consumption follows a random walk with drift if interest rates vary. Except for some equations for Brazil, India, and Malaysia the real interest rate had a positive coefficient, thus implying a *positive* response of savings.

Besides the time series studies, Balassa also reports on several time series cum cross-sectional regressions. These include Fry (1978, 1980, 1987), Fry and Masar (1982), Giovannini (1983), Gupta (1987), and Leite and Makonnen (1986). The countries covered developing countries around the world. Most showed a positive response of savings to real interest rates. None of the time series and time series cum cross-sectional regressions allowed for the possibility that some consumers may be liquidity constrained. The only study to allow for it is that by Rossi (1988), who used pooled time series and cross-sectional data for six developing country regions. He found a clear evidence for a positive effect of the interest rate on the rate of growth of per capita consumption. Finally, Balassa refers to the work of Cuddington (1987) who found that in Mexico and Venezuela, capital flight responds positively to foreign interest rates.

Subsequent to Balassa's survey, Raut and Virmani (1989) analyzed the determinants of consumption and saving decisions using aggregate data from 23 developing countries. They, like Giovannini (1985), test the random walk implication of optimal consumption choice given a lifetime budget constraint. It turns out that this hypothesis is rejected if the interest rate is assumed to be constant over time and is not rejected if it varies. They also find a *positive* effect of the real interest rate on the growth of consumption, also implying a positive response of saving to the real interest rate. However, if the nominal interest rate and the inflation rate are separately entered in the regression, both have significantly *negative* coefficients, with that of the latter being larger in absolute value. This effect suggests that inflation has an additional role besides reducing the real value of a given nominal interest rate. It affects growth of consumption negatively perhaps because it signals greater uncertainty about future real income prospects.

One of the controversial themes in the literature is the relationship between saving rates and the age structure of the population. If young children and the old in a household are assumed to consume more than they contribute to household income, then higher dependency (i.e., larger proportion of young and old in households) implies a lower saving rate, given the same level of household income. Also, if the population is growing rapidly, the age structure will show a larger proportion of children than in a slowly growing population. Unless incomes also grow rapidly, this dependency effect would tend to lower savings. Rossi (1989) points out that most empirical studies following the influential paper of Leff (1969) were not based on an adequately specified consistent theoretical framework. He provides such a framework in the form of a model of stochastic dynamic utility maximization by a household subject to a lifetime budget constraint. The dependency feature is introduced in two alternative ways: In one the household's intertemporal preferences are expressed in terms of consumption per "equivalent" adult, assuming that each child in the age group 1−14 is equivalent to a fraction of an adult. In the other, preferences are expressed in terms of per capita consumption net of the "overhead" cost of children. The two alternatives have different implications: The first implies the traditional view of a negative relationship between dependency and the growth rate of consumption. In the second the direction of the relationship is ambiguous, depending on the strength of the elasticity of the intertemporal substitution and the share of committed child "overhead" costs in consumption. With pooled time series and cross-sectional data from a sample of 11 low-income and 38 middle-income countries for the period from 1973 to 1980, 1981, 1982, or 1983, depending on the country, Rossi estimates his model and finds that with the exception of his sample countries from southern Europe, "the estimates linking the rate of growth of consumption to the expected change in the dependency rate are highly imprecise. ..." The proxies for liquidity constraints turn out to be significant except in the case of countries of Central America and the Caribbean.

Lahiri (1989) also addressed in part the dependency issue in his study of savings in eight Asian countries. He uses a general framework that distinguishes private and public saving and incorporates the effects of growth, dependency, inflation, terms of trade changes, and the importance of exports in GNP. Three hypotheses are nested in the framework: H_1, the extreme rational expectation PIH with no liquidity constraints, in which only unanticipated changes in income would affect consumption; H_2, the hypothesis that liquidity constraints bind and current income matters so that anticipated and unanticipated changes in income have the *same* effect on consumption; and finally, H_3, current income matters, but the consumption–income ratio adjusts to its long-run constant value with lags that have a procyclical structure. H_1 is rejected. H_2 is rejected (at a 5 percent level of significance) only in the case of Sri Lanka, though this rejection has to be viewed with caution in light of the abnormally high (about 3) long-run income elasticities of consumption. Except for Indonesia, the Philippines, and Thailand, H_3 and its implication that the long-run elasticity of consumption is unity is not rejected. Growth unambiguously leads to increased private savings in all countries with a long-run elasticity of about one. On an average, a one-point increase in the percentage of population in the age group 15–64 leads to a 1.6 percentage point rise in average propensity to save in the long run except in Indonesia and the Philippines, where no lasting effect of the age composition on saving was found. However, Lahiri is cautious about attributing too much significance to this result, as the data on age composition are available only in intercensal intervals of ten years or so. Annual values in between are interpolated, inducing a correlation between age composition and the time trend. On average inflation and adverse terms of trade changes tend to depress private savings.

Before turning to the evidence from household surveys, it is worth remarking that almost all of the studies based on aggregate data derive their estimating equations from a theoretical framework based on the behavior of a household, in many cases, an infinitely-lived household! Barring the ridiculous notion that a whole society can be viewed as replication of a single representative household, strong assumptions about the *distribution* of households with respect to the relevant characteristics, including the household-specific error terms, would be needed if estimating equations are to represent consistent aggregation of the behavior of heterogeneous households. Few of the studies previously discussed seem to be aware of, let alone address, this aggregation problem. As such, the inferences drawn from them have to be used with extreme caution and circumspection.

It was pointed out earlier that the difficulty of eliciting an economically meaningful response to questions about income in household surveys has meant that most surveys concentrate on household consumption expenditure. There is an enormous literature on the estimation of consumer demand systems based on such surveys. The literature on household saving behavior that is based on surveys is much sparser. Bhalla (1979, 1980) tested the Friedman permanent income hypothesis (PIH) using three-year (1969–1971) panel survey data from rural India. This survey, unlike India's National Sample Survey, collected data on income and consumption as well as assets and liabilities of households so that savings could be estimated alternatively as the difference between income and consumption of a period or the change in value of net assets between adjacent periods. He defines permanent income and tests the hypothesis in alternative ways. His general results are robust with respect to changes in the definition of permanent income and methods of testing. Although the marginal propensity to save out of transitory income is higher than that out of permanent income, the latter is not zero as the PIH would suggest. Nor is the positive saving rate out of permanent income independent of the level of permanent income. However, for households that can be classified as subsistence households on the basis of an exogenously specified income level, the marginal propensity to consume out of permanent income appears to be unity, leading to the conclusion that a redistribution of income in favor of such households would reduce aggregate savings.

Musgrove (1979) tests the PIH with household budget data collected in 1967–1969 from four principal cities in Colombia, two in Ecuador, and one in Peru. He finds that pure transitory variation in income is quite small and much of the residual income unexplained by factors associated with permanent income is best regarded as measurement error. He, like

Bhalla, found the average elasticity of consumption with respect to permanent income to be clearly less than one, thus rejecting the PIH.

Paxson (1988) compares estimates of income and saving based on household survey and national income−accounts data in Thailand in 1975−76 and 1981. Although she finds the survey-based income estimate to be lower (by 24 percent in 1975−76 and 32−39 percent in 1981), she is rightly cautious in noting that national accounts estimates are subject to error and cover nonprofit institutions besides households. Her analysis of saving using the survey data is supportive of the PIH in that the marginal propensity to save (MPS) out of transitory income is not significantly different from unity. But the MPS out of permanent incomes (though considerably lower than the MPS out of transitory income) is positive and significantly different from zero.

Paxson (1991) presents a model of consumption and saving of rural households that face seasonal fluctuations in incomes and prices and whose preferences may also exhibit seasonal shifts. Her model tests two alternative theories: (1) a perfect smoothing theory in which only seasonal variations in prices and preferences matter and income fluctuations are smoothed and (2) one in which there is no smoothing with seasonal expenditure patterns driven solely by income variations. She tests the model with household survey data from Thailand for three years; 1975−76, 1981, and 1986. Most of her tests favor the perfect smoothing hypothesis so that timing of income receipts affects seasonal savings patterns but has little effect on expenditure patterns. She draws the strong policy implication that policies that attempt to reduce seasonal variations in income may be misguided.

Deaton (1991) analyzes survey data from Cote d'Ivoire, Ghana, and Thailand. The data on household borrowing and lending in the first two countries suggest that very few loans carry interest payments or regime collateral. Most loans do not even prespecify regular payments. All these features strongly suggest the functioning of informal credit markets (to be discussed in the next section). The loans are too small relative to the needs of consumption smoothing even though their seasonal pattern is consistent with it. All in all, the data do not support the hypothesis of a strong consumption smoothing role for loans. The age−consumption profiles in Cote d'Ivoire and Thailand are the opposite of the tipping toward the young predicted by the life cycle model, so that "hump" saving, so familiar from the model, is unlikely to be a very important source of saving in these two countries. Finally, the test of the PIH for Cote d'Ivoire suggests that even though farmers do behave in a forward-looking way, the data do not support either the strong version of PIH or its liquidity-constrained version.

4. Informal Credit and Insurance Markets

The role of informal credit markets in the generation of savings and in the provision of insurance is a complex one. As Hoff and Stiglitz point out in their introduction to a symposium on imperfect information and rural credit markets, such markets have been the focus of policy attention in developing countries, an attention that derives from viewing informal lenders as monopolistic usurers who exploit poor peasants. Policies to provide cheap credit through the extension of formal credit institutions were instituted. However, the results of such policies have been disappointing. Hoff and Stiglitz (1990) argue that the view that rural credit markets are neither perfectly competitive nor monopolized by informal money lenders seems to address several features of these markets such as:

> The formal and informal sectors coexist, despite the fact that formal interest rates are substantially below those charged in the informal sector.
>
> Interest rates may not equilibrate credit supply and demand: there may be credit rationing, and in periods of bad harvests, lending may be unavailable at any price.
>
> Credit markets are segmented. Interest rates of lenders in different areas vary by more than plausibly can be accounted for by differences in the likelihood of default; and local events — a failure of a harvest in one area — seem to have significant impacts on the availability of credit in local markets.
>
> There is a limited number of commercial lenders in the informal sector, despite the high rates charged.
>
> In the informal sector interlinkages between credit transactions and transactions in other markets are common.
>
> Formal lenders tend to specialize in areas where farmers have land titles. [pp. 236–237]

The Asian Development Bank studied the informal financial sector in five Asian Countries (Bangladesh, India, Indonesia, the Philippines, and Thailand). The report on the findings from this research (Ghate, 1990) covers a number of aspects of the functioning and role of informal financial institutions. While rightly pointing out that the significance of the informal sector in mobilizing saving in the aggregate is extremely difficult to assess in theory and in quantitative terms, it highlights its role in deposit mobilization, direct lending from lender to the user of credit, and financial intermediation. Traditionally, informal lenders, particularly rural moneylenders, do not engage in intermediation by accepting deposits for lending to others. The reason, in part, is that the usual synchronization of agricultural operations often dictates that potential depositors would want to withdraw their deposits at about the same time as others would want to borrow from the lender and also that the incomes of depositors and borrowers would be highly correlated. Another reason is that the depositors could engage in direct lending to borrowers without going through the lenders and earn a better return on their resources. Still, in some areas of India (rural Kerala), the study found a substantial volume of deposit taking, not by individual moneylenders, but by finance companies, trusts, and banks that, though significant in the size of their operation, are not part of the formal financial system. Also in Bangladesh as well as India, traders in agricultural commodities who extend credit to farmers for their working capital needs accept deposits from others. These deposits are more like equities than deposits bearing fixed interest, in that the depositor and the trader share the profits of the trader.

In urban India, major informal financial intermediaries such as hire-purchase companies, finance companies, and indigenous bankers extended about 12 percent of informal credit, Chit Funds (an old Indian institution similar to the rotating savings and credit institutions (ROSCAs) in other parts of the world) accounted for another 18 percent, and the remaining 70 percent came from direct lenders such as friends and relatives. ROSCAs in various forms, as well as nonrotating mutual financial institutions, are very active in India, Indonesia, the Philippines, and Thailand. A typical ROSCA is formed by a number of people well known to one another. Each contributes a fixed sum to a kitty each period, say, a month. The monthly kitty is assigned to a member either by random drawing or by auction. If auctioned, the bidders offer to pay a sum for the access to the kitty. The successful bidder is excluded from subsequent auctions but is required to continue contributing each month until the end of the period of the association's existence (equal to as many months as there are members). The familiarity of members with one another and the inevitable social sanction that will ensue if members fail to contribute after successfully obtaining the kitty assure the success of ROSCAs.

There is considerable evidence from the study that ROSCAs — variously known as Chit Funds in India, *Arisans* in Indonesia, *Paluwagans* in the Philippines, *Kye* in Korea, *Pia Hueys* in Thailand — are very popular. Called *tontines*, they have a long history in some African countries as well. They are in some ways like "Christmas clubs" and in other ways like the pension institutions of developed countries in that once a decision is made to join, there is an element of compulsion in having to save and contribute. They provide a relatively easy and speedy access to credit with no collateral requirements and formalities of any kind. The credit obtained is used for a variety of purposes from purchase of durables to working capital. Although it is hard to provide a quantitative estimate of the contribution of ROSCAs and their nonrotating counterparts in urban areas in mobilizing saving, the study suggests that the contribution could be significant.

One could argue that in village societies in which the same families and kinship groups have lived for generations in a slowly changing, if not completely stationary, economic environment, the information asymmetries and monitoring problems that result in moral hazard and adverse selection should not be significant. If this is the case, the informal credit markets should function well even without collateral or interlinking of credit contracts with exchanges in other markets. Udry (1990) indeed finds this to be the case in rural northern Nigeria. Credit transactions apparently pool risk among households so that repayment owed on a loan depends on the realization of random production shocks by both the borrower and the lender.

According to Siamwalla et al. (1990), informal rural lenders in Thailand incur costs that need not be particularly high given that lenders and borrowers live in the same village and know one another well enough so that nearly complete information can be acquired regarding the borrowers. A resident lender can also completely monitor and regulate the borrower's behavior, including enforcing exclusivity, that is, that the lender alone is the source of credit to the borrower. The informal sector is competitive, and the interest rates charged reflect information costs. A formal institution, an agricultural bank, was created in 1966 to lend only to farmers. Since 1970 the commercials have been required to lend heavily to the rural sector. By confining itself to working capital loans only and using group lending cum peer monitoring, the agricultural bank has been largely successful in avoiding excessive overdues. However, it remains unsuccessful in expanding its scope of activities beyond financing working capital and enlarging its clientele to include poor farmers or farmers in riskier areas. The overall impact of extending formal credit seems to have been modest, leaving a large segment of the market to be served by informal lenders.

In India the informal lenders, particularly the professional moneylender, occupied a dominant position as a source of finance in the early 1950s. A public policy of establishing a system of cooperative credit institutions was instituted "to provide a positive institutional alternative to the money lender himself, something which will compete with him, remove him from the forefront and put him in his place" (Reserve Bank of India as quoted in Bell, 1990). In 1969 all the major commercial banks were nationalized and were expressly required to extend the banking system and credit to areas and sectors, particularly rural areas and agriculture, perceived to be neglected by them until then. A system of specialized banks was also established to extend credit to the farm sector. Official data suggest that the share of informal lenders (other than friends and relatives) in rural debt fell from 80 percent in 1951 to a mere 24 percent in 1981 and that of formal institutions rose from 7 percent to 61 percent. However, Bell (1990) points to other evidence that shows not only that the informal lender is far more active but also that the progressive commercialization of agriculture in areas such as the Punjab, where the Green Revolution made substantial progress, has led to the rise of the interlinking of product and credit markets through the trader cum lender. Bell reports survey data from four states (Andhrapradesh, Bihar, Punjab, and Tamil Nadu) that show that trade and money lending not only flourish with advancing commercialization but are also fairly competitive. In the meantime the formal institutions, including cooperatives, have been plagued with defaults—overdue agricultural loans were on the order of 40 percent to 50 percent of scheduled repayment in the mid-1980s, a situation that got worse since the farm lobby succeeded in persuading the government to write off a significant proportion of overdue loans. Even in Punjab, where cooperatives are healthy, a tie with the trader is very useful for a farmer. Econometric estimates by Bell et al. (1991) suggest that, ceteris paribus, accepting a tied-loan contract enabled a farmer to obtain additional private credit of Rs. 8450 in 1980−81. By taking the minimum of Rs. 8450 and the amount actually transacted in the private market for each of the households having tied loans, Bell and co-workers found that private credit advanced to cultivators would fall by over 70 percent and the volume of credit would fall by 35 percent, were tying arrangements to be banned in the mistaken perception that they exploit the poor farmer.

Aleem (1990) presents survey data from rural Pakistan that appear to be consistent with a monopolistic competition credit model for the large group (à la Chamberlin). His estimates of costs of screening, chasing delinquent loans, overhead costs, and capital suggest that informal lenders' charges equal their average costs (i.e., a zero profit, free-entry equilibrium) but exceed their marginal costs (i.e., monopolistic behavior).

As noted earlier, among households living in a high-risk (but stationary) environment in which problems of informational asymmetry are minimal, informal institutions could potentially insure them against income fluctuations. As also noted, Udry (1990) found that lending and borrowing transactions among households in northern Nigerian villages appear to provide such insurance. Townsend (1991) tested an implication of village-risk pooling—that the consumption of an individual household would vary with average consumption of all households in the village rather than with its own income — using panel data from households in three villages from a semi-arid part of India. Although complete insurance against idiosyncratic risks is rejected by the data, only a few variables (other than average village consumption) affect an individual household's consumption and even their influence is rather weak. Deaton (1991, p. 3) finds that "the village risk-pooling story is not decisively rejected by our data (from Cote d'Ivoire), but neither does it provide predictions that cannot be explained by other, possibly more plausible stories."

To sum up, in rural areas of the developing countries, where a majority of the world's poor live and eke out their livelihood from risky agriculture, a plethora of informal arrangements provide opportunities for consumption smoothing and insurance, largely because formal credit and insurance institutions are either absent or ill-equipped to overcome the information problems at reasonable costs.

5. Conclusions and Policy Implications

Briefly stated, although the aggregate data on saving, investment, and income from developing countries are subject to serious problems of biases and measurement error that undoubtedly differ in their severity across countries and over time, it would appear that saving and investment rates have increased significantly in the last four decades. However, the simplistic belief that such an increase in investment rates would result not only in increased aggregate growth rates but also in sustained growth has proved to be overly optimistic.

Econometric analysis with aggregate data of the determinants of consumption and saving has shown some limited support for the rational expectation — permanent income — life cycle model, particularly when the model is modified to recognize liquidity constraints. Theory suggests that because the income and substitution effects move in opposite directions, the sign of the interest elasticity of saving is ambiguous. The empirical evidence bears this out, although the net effect seem to be positive (whether or not significantly different from zero) in more studies. However, the aggregate econometric models are often simplistic analogs of micro behavior of an individual or household. That the assumptions needed for the analogs to be valid descriptions are rarely specified let alone tested and that the data used to test the model are subject to serious biases and measurement errors are facts that should temper the inferences drawn.

Gathering information about income and saving from household surveys in developing countries is extraordinarily difficult in view of the fact that the notion of income in the economic sense is hard to convey to self-employed farmers, traders, and artisans. For this and other reasons, relatively few surveys collect and report income data. These data also provide some support for the hypothesis of forward-looking rational behavior of individuals, though again as in aggregate models, the extreme versions of rational expectations—permanent income hypothesis is rejected by most survey data. Also the age—consumption profiles from the data do not quite correspond to the tilting toward the young that a life cycle model would suggest.

The existence and efficient functioning of credit and insurance markets is presumed in the standard models of saving based on a model intertemporal welfare maximization subject to a lifetime budget constraint by an infinitely lived individual. Yet, even for developed countries this assumption is extreme. But for developing countries it is completely inappropriate. Market structure is incomplete, and formal and informal markets coexist in such countries. The problems of moral hazard and adverse selection that lead to equilibria with quantity rationing, which are by now staples of the literature on credit markets in developed countries, are attenuated to some extent by the long-term economic and social relationships and linkages across a spectrum of transactions including credit between pairs of agents living in the same villages of developing countries. The available evidence suggests that informal lenders, far from being the usurers that the early development literature portrayed them to be, happen to be competitive (albeit monopolistically competitive in some cases) and that their higher interest charges often reflect the costs of information acquisition and default risk. Besides, to observe no interest charges at all in the data is not uncommon, particularly when the loan transactions involve interlinking with other transactions.

From a policy perspective, the fact that the interest elasticity of saving does not appear to be high even when it is positive suggests that policies of financial liberalization, even if they raise the return to saving, may not generate much additional savings. Fiscal incentives for promoting saving, merely change the composition of assets in which the savings are invested without affecting the volume of saving. In any case, given that equilibria in credit markets involve rationing, liberalization may reduce the severity of the rationing without affecting the interest rate charged. The policy problem becomes much more complex once the coexistence of formal and informal markets for credit is recognized. Policy-induced expansion of formal credit may simply end up at best substituting informal credit one-for-one and at worst, by driving out informal lenders from the market, remove the only source of credit for those who would not have access to formal credit. In particular, policies that restrict the operations of trader-lender or more generally the interlinking of credit with other transactions can be counterproductive. Instead, policies that exploit the valuable knowledge of informal lenders by employing them as agents for the disbursal of formal credit and its recovery should be considered seriously. However, because rigorous theoretical and empirical analysis of the coexistence and functioning (in particular, the role of interlinking) of informal and formal credit markets is in its infancy, much research needs to be done before firm policy conclusions can be drawn.

References

Aleem, I. "Imperfect Information, Screening, and the Costs of Informal Lending: A Study of a Rural Credit Market in Pakistan." *The World Bank Economic Review* 4, no. 3 (September 1990): 329–349.

Ando, Albert, L. Guiso, D. Terlizzese, and D. Dorsainvil. "Saving, Demographic Structure and Productivity Growth: The Case of Japan." Paper presented at the Conference on Saving, Behaviour: Theory, International Evidence and Policy Implications, Finnish Savings Banks Research Foundation, Helsinki, 1991.

Balassa, Bela. "The Effects of Interest Rates on Savings in Developing Countries." *Banca Nazionale Del Lavoro Quarterly Review*, no. 172 (March 1990): 101–118.

Bell, C. "Interactions Between Institutional and Informal Credit Agencies in Rural India." *The World Bank Economic Review* 4, no. 3 (September 1990): 297–327.

Bell, C., T. N. Srinivasan, and C. Udry. "Segmentation, Rationing and Spillover in Credit Markets: The Case of Rural Punjab." Mimeo, 1991.

Bhalla, S. S. "Measurement Errors and the Permanent Income Hypothesis: Evidence from Rural India." *American Economic Review* 69 (1979): 295–307.

———. "The Measurement of Permanent Income and Its Application to Saving Behavior." *Journal of Political Economy* 88 (1980): 722–743.

Brown, G. T. *Korean Pricing Policies and Economic Development in the 1960s*. Baltimore, Md.: Johns Hopkins University Press, 1973.

Chenery, Hollis, and Michael Bruno. "Development Alternatives in an Open Economy." *Economic Journal* 72 (1962): 79–103.

Cuddington, John T. "Macroeconomic Determinants of Capital Flight: An Econometric Investigation." In Donald R. Lessard and John Williamson, eds., *Capital Flight and the Third World Debt*, Washington, D.C., Institute for International Economics, 1987, pp. 88–102.

Deaton, Angus. "Saving in Developing Countries: Theory and Review." *Proceed-

ings of the World Bank Annual Conference on Development Economics, Supplement to the *World Bank Economic Review*, 1989, pp. 61–96.

———. "Household Saving in LDC's: Credit Markets, Insurance and Welfare." Paper presented at the Conference on Saving Behaviour: Theory, International Evidence and Policy Implications, Finnish Savings Banks Research Foundation, Helsinki, 1991.

Dekle, R. "Do the Japanese Elderly Reduce Their Total Wealth? A New Look with Different Data." *Journal of Japanese International Economies* 4, no. 3 (September 1990): 309–317.

DeMelo, J., and J. Tybout. "The Effects of Financial Liberalization on Savings and Investment in Uruguay." *Economic Development and Cultural Change* 34 (April 1986): 561–588.

Feldstein, M. S., and C. Horioka. "Domestic Saving and International Capital Flows." *Economic Journal* 90 (June 1980): 314–329.

Fry, M. J. "Financial Instruments and Markets." In *Conferencia International sobre Economia Portuguesa*, Lisbon, German Marshall Fund and Fundacao Calouste Gulbenkian, vol. II, 1977, pp. 191–208.

———. "Money and Capital or Financial Deepening in Economic Development?" *Journal of Money, Credit and Banking* 10 (November 1978): 474–475.

———. "The Cost of Financial Repression in Turkey." *Savings and Development* 3 (2) (1979): 127–135.

———. "Savings, Investment, Growth and the Cost of Financial Repression." *World Development* 8 (April 1980): 317–328.

———. *Money, Interest, and Banking in Economic Development*. Baltimore, Md.: Johns Hopkins University Press, 1987.

———. "Domestic Resource Mobilization in Developing Asia: Four Policy Issues." *Asian Development Review* 9, No. 1 (1991): 15–39.

Fry, M. J., and Andrew Masar. "The Variable Rate-of-Growth Effect in the Life-Cycle Saving Model: Children, Capital Inflows, Interest and Growth in a New Specification of the Life-Cycle Model Applied to Seven Asian Developing Countries." *Economic Inquiry* 20 (July 1982): 426–442.

Gersovitz, M. "Saving and Development." In *Handbook of Development Economics*, vol. 1, edited by H. Chenery and T. N. Srinivasan. Amsterdam: North-Holland, 1988, pp. 381–424.

Ghate, P. *Informal Finance: Some Findings from Asia*. Manila, the Philippines, Asian Development Bank, 1990.

Giovannini, A. "The Interest Elasticity of Savings in Developing Countries: The Existing Evidence." *World Development* 11 (July 1983): 601–608.

———. "Saving and the Real Interest Rate in LDCs." *Journal of Development Economics* 18 (August 1985): 197–210.

Gupta, K. L. "Personal Saving in Developing Nations: Further Evidence." *The Economic Record* 46 (1970): 243–249.

———. "Financial Intermediation, Interest Rate and the Structure of Savings: Evidence from Asia." *Journal of Economic Development* 60 (July 1984): 7–24.

———. "Aggregate Savings, Financial Intermediation, and Interest Rate." *Review of Economics and Statistics* 69 (May 1987): 303–311.

Gurley, J. G., and E. S. Shaw. "Financial Development and Economic Development." *Economic Development and Cultural Change* 15, no. 3 (April 1967): 257–265, 267–268.
Haque, Nadeem U., and P. Montiel. "Consumption in Developing Countries: Tests for Liquidity Constraints and Finite Horizons." *Review of Economic Statistics* 71 (3) (August 1989): 408–415.
Hoff, K., and Stiglitz, J. E. "Introduction: Imperfect Information and Rural Credit Markets—Puzzles and Policy Perspectives." *The World Bank Economic Review* 4, no. 3 (September 1990): 235–250.
IMF. *World Economic Outlook, May 1991*. Washington, D.C., 1991.
King, M. "The Economics of Saving: A Survey of Recent Contributions." In *Frontiers in Economics*, edited by K. Arrow and S. Honkapohja. Oxford: Basil Blackwell, 1985, pp. 227–294.
Kotlikoff, L. J., and L. H. Summers. "The Role of Intergenerational Transfer in Aggregate Capital Accumulation." *Journal of Political Economy*, 89 (1981): 706–732.
Lahiri, A. "Dynamics of Asian Savings." *IMF Staff Papers* 36 (1) (1989): 228–261.
Leff, N. "Dependency Rates and Savings Rates." *American Economic Review* (1969): 886–896.
Leite, S. P., and D. Makonnen. "Saving and Interest Rates in the BCEA Countries: An Empirical Analysis." *Savings and Development* (July-September 1986).
Lewis, W. A. "Economic Development with Unlimited Supplies of Labour." *The Manchester School* 22 (1954): 139–191.
Maddison, A. "A Long Run Perspective on Saving." Paper presented at the Conference on Saving Behaviour: Theory, International Evidence and Policy Implications, Helsinki, 1991.
McDonald, D. "The Determinants of Saving Behavior in Latin America." Washington, D.C.: International Monetary Fund, mimeo, 1983.
McKinnon, R. I. *Money and Capital in Economic Development*. Washington, D.C.: Brookings Institution, 1973.
Minhas, B. S. "Validation of Large Scale Sample Survey Data: Case of NSS Estimates of Household Consumption Expenditure." *Sankhya: The Indian Journal of Statistics* 50, Series B, Pt. 3, Supplement (1988): 1–63.
Musgrove, P. "Permanent Household Income and Consumption in Urban South America." *The American Economic Review* 69, no. 3 (June 1979): 355–368.
Paxson, Christina H. "Household Savings in Thailand: Responses to Income Shocks." Woodrow Wilson School Discussion Paper No. 137, Princeton University, mimeo, 1988.
———. "Consumption and Income Seasonality in Thailand." Woodrow Wilson School Discussion Paper No. 150, Princeton University, mimeo, 1991.
Raut, L., and A. Virmani. "Determinants of Consumption and Savings Behavior in Developing Countries." *The World Bank Economic Review* 3, No. 3 (September 1989): 379–393.

Reserve Bank of India. *Capital Formation and Saving in India 1950–51 to 1979–80*. Reserve Bank of India, February 1982.
Rossi, N. "Government Spending, the Real Interest Rate, and the Behavior of Liquidity-Constrained Consumers in Developing Countries." *IMF Staff Papers* 35 (March 1988): 204–240.
———. "Dependency Rates and Private Savings." *IMF Staff Papers* 36 (1) (1989): 166–181.
Scott, M. F. G. *A New View of Economic Growth*. Oxford: Clarendon Press, 1989.
Siamwalla, A., et al. "The Thai Rural Credit System: Public Subsidies, Private Information, and Segmented Markets." *The World Bank Economic Review* 4, no. 3 (September 1990): 271–295.
Stiglitz, J. E., and A. Weiss. "Credit Rationing with Imperfect Information." *American Economic Review* 71, no. 3 (1981): 393–410.
Summers, L. H., and C. Carroll. "The Growth-Saving Nexus." Paper presented to National Bureau of Economic Research Conference on Savings, Maui, Hawaii, January 1989.
Townsend, R. "Risk and Insurance in Village India." Mimeo, 1991.
Udry, C. "Credit Markets in Northern Nigeria: Credit as Insurance in a Rural Economy." *The World Bank Economic Review* 4, no. 3 (September 1990): 251–269.
Williamson, Jeffrey G. "Personal Saving in Developing Nations: An Intertemporal Cross-Section Estimate for Asia." *The Economic Record* 44 (1968): 194–210.
World Bank. *World Development Report*. New York: Oxford University Press, 1991.
Yusuf, S., and R. K. Peters. "Savings Behavior and Its Implications for Domestic Resource Mobilization. The Case of the Republic of Korea." *World Bank Staff Working Papers* 628, Washington, D.C., World Bank, April 1984.

Commentary by Mark Gersovitz
University of Michigan

Saving and development is a broad and important topic that has recently been the subject of some really excellent research. T. N. Srinivasan has discussed the findings of this work in the context of earlier thinking on the subject. His chapter should be of use to researchers on saving, for whom he has particular strictures, and to those who want to learn about this aspect of economic behavior. Two broad and related, but distinct, classes of questions are worth emphasizing.

First, how do individuals decide how much of their income to save? In particular, is this process well represented by the simplest model of intertemporal consumption by a utility-maximizing individual faced with a fixed interest rate at which the individual can either borrow or lend? Potential additional influences on the saving decision would include (1) various uncertainties in income, rates of return, survival, and health status and the availability and conditions of the corresponding insurance; (2) complications in the opportunities for borrowing or lending, often termed credit constraints; (3) expenditures on consumer durables, education, and health for which the distinction between consumption and saving is blurred; and (4) familial and other relationships among individuals including that of prospective heirs, meaning that individuals' decisions are interdependent.

We have some evidence on these questions. On the one hand, Paxson (1991) shows that Thai savers seem able to smooth their consumption relative to seasonal variation in incomes, and Paxson (1992) shows that they also seem able to smooth their consumption relative to annual shocks to income from climatic sources. On the other hand, evidence shows that saving up may be an important motivation in poor countries, a notion most naturally tied to ideas of credit constraints. Bhalla (1978) presents some evidence that Indian farmers with the potential for adopting high-yielding varieties may have to save to realize these opportunities. Besley and co-workers (1990) argue that the ubiquitous institution of rotating savings and credit associations (ROSCA) may be designed to improve the circumstances of individuals who would otherwise have to save in isolation. So the picture is a mixed one, with some evidence suggesting that consumers can smooth their consumption and other evidence suggesting that this situation does not prevail.

Rather than view the whole picture as confusing and contradictory, it may be possible to make sense of it by thinking about the frequency of the variation in income that the consumer may want to transform into smooth consumption via saving and borrowing. The available evidence seems to suggest that individuals can smooth high-frequency variation in their incomes, although it may be beyond their capabilities to smooth medium-frequency variation. Finally, there is a suspicion that individuals in developing countries also may be well situated to smooth the lowest frequencies of variation, namely, life cycle variation, via the use of the extended family to deal with consumption in old age. But it is only a suspicion; almost nothing is known about bequests in poor countries, a subject about which relatively little information is available even in the United States and the United Kingdom.

What is needed is a model of intertemporal consumption subject to all sorts of income variation to see whether an integrated picture along these lines can emerge. Indeed, problems at one frequency may ease smoothing of higher frequencies. For instance, if one is already saving over a multiyear horizon, smoothing consumption over the seasons will be much less difficult. So it seems that research is making progress in understanding how people in poor countries save, but, of course, more must be done, including replicating findings from a very few countries for others.

Answers to the second class of questions, about the determinants of saving at the aggregate level, seem as elusive as ever. Nonetheless, it is clear that one ultimate goal of research on saving has to be an accounting for the great apparent differences in saving behavior across countries and across time that Srinivasan highlights. How we will realize this accounting is somewhat of a mystery, but some temptations must be avoided. For one thing, no researcher on saving behavior and perhaps no one at all knows very much about how the aggregate data are constructed and what the differences are in procedures among countries. What little is known, as Srinivasan points out, makes clear that the measurement of saving involves a complicated series of approximations. The temptation to continue to take these data at face value would seem to be a bad one.

Furthermore, it should always be kept in mind that most purported empirical explanations of aggregate saving behavior across countries are instead associations among clusters of jointly determined endogenous variables. There is very little scope for finding and using exogenous variables in this type of analysis.

References

Besley, T., et al. "The Economics of Rotating Savings and Credit Associations." Research Program in Development Studies Discussion Paper No. 149, Princeton University, 1990.

Bhalla, S. S. "The Role of Sources of Income and Investment Opportunities in Rural Savings." *Journal of Development Economics* 5 (1978): 259–281.

Paxson, C. H. "Household Savings in Thailand: Responses to Income Shocks." Mimeo, Princeton, 1990.

Paxson, C. H. "Using Weather Variability to Estimate the Response of Savings to Transitory Income in Thailand." *American Economic Review* 82 (March 1992): 15–33.

Commentary by Christina H. Paxson
Princeton University

T. N. Srinivasan's chapter covers a wide variety of interesting and important topics. These comments will expand on one issue: the role of household saving in consumption smoothing. The use of saving to buffer consumption from random income fluctuations may well be one of the most important uses of saving in developing countries. In economies where incomes are both low and variable, and formal social security systems are weak or nonexistent, households that do *not* take measures to smooth consumption may face extremely adverse welfare consequences. Further, many important policy issues hinge on how well households do or do not smooth consumption.

As Srinivasan points out, despite the importance of the topic, relatively few household-level empirical studies have investigated issues of saving and consumption smoothing. The lack of research cannot be attributed to a lack of data on household income and saving (or income and expenditure). Many countries conduct cross-sectional income and expenditure surveys. Visaria (1980) documents a number of these surveys for a set of Asian countries, several of which have information on asset changes in addition to information on income and expenditure. Similar data exist for a number of African and Latin American countries. Short panel data sets, in which households are interviewed for at least two consecutive years, are available from a growing handful of countries. Srinivasan has discussed the problems of obtaining reliable information from household surveys. This commentary will focus on some methodological issues, namely, how these data can be used to estimate and test models of saving and consumption smoothing.

The major problem that confronts researchers in this area is that cross-sectional data, and even short panels, are not designed for the study of saving and consumption smoothing. Cross-sectional data provide a snapshot of a household at a single period in time; all but the simplest models of saving behavior are dynamic. For example, most of the existing research in this area is couched in terms of the familiar permanent income model. Testing this model entails identifying what part of observed income is permanent and what part is transitory; the former should largely determine consumption, and the latter should determine saving. This decomposition of current income is difficult when past and expected future incomes are unknown to the researcher. Unfortunately, the ideal data for examining saving behavior — long panels on the income and consumption of individual households — are not likely to be widely available for some time. The key question, then, is whether the type of data that are currently available can be usefully exploited to yield information on consumption smoothing.

Many of the studies that use cross-sectional data estimate propensities to consume out of permanent income. See, for example, Musgrove (1979) and Wolpin (1982). Others are cited by Gersovitz (1988). The basic and well-known approach of these studies is as follows. First, actual income is assumed to be composed of two unknown components: permanent and transitory income. If a permanent income model is correct, the propensity to consume out of the former component should equal 1, and the propensity to consume out of the latter component should be close to 0. Because measured income is the sum of these two types of income (and is likely to contain measurement error as well), regressions of consumption on income will typically yield consumption propensities between 0 and 1. Formally, the problem is one of errors in variables: Reported income is an error-ridden measure of permanent income, and so the coefficient on income will suffer from attenuation bias. To estimate the true propensity to consume out of permanent income, one must find a set of instrumental variables that are correlated with permanent income but not with transitory income. A regression of consumption on instrumented income should yield the correct propensity to consume out of permanent income.

This standard approach has several problems. First, suitable instruments are difficult to find. Musgrove used age, education, and occupation measures for his study of urban households in three Latin American countries. These measures could be correlated with transitory income if individuals in various age/occupation/education categories received common transitory shocks to income in the survey year. Wolpin (1982) used historic regional rainfall, which is far less likely to be correlated with current transitory income.

A more serious problem with the preceding procedure is that it may not be useful for distinguishing between a permanent income model, in which consumption equals permanent income, and a very different model in which consumption simply tracks income. This can be shown by the following simple example. Let measured income Y be composed as the sum of permanent income Y^P, transitory income Y^T, and a measurement error ε:

$$Y = Y^P + Y^T + \varepsilon. \tag{7C-1}$$

A general consumption equation is specified as:

$$C = Y^P\beta_1 + Y^T\beta_2 + u. \tag{7C-2}$$

For simplicity, an intercept is omitted from the consumption equation. (One could think of all variables as having been transformed into deviations from sample means.) Assume also that the error terms in equations (7C-1) and (7C-2) are uncorrelated (although such a correlation is likely to exist in practice). If a permanent income model is correct, β_1 should equal 1 and β_2 should be close to 0. Conversely, if a consumption-tracks-income model is right, both β_1 and β_2 should equal 1.

Consider the results one would obtain if consumption C is regressed on measured income Y:

$$C = Y\beta + \text{error}. \tag{7C-3}$$

Under *either* the permanent income model or the consumption-tracks-income model, one would expect the estimate of β to be less than 1. In both cases, this result is due to attenuation bias. In the first model, Y is an error-ridden measure of Y^P. In the second model, Y is an error-ridden measure of true income $(Y^P + Y^T)$. If the second model is correct, the estimated propensity to consume may be quite low if the variance in the measurement error of income (ε) is large. And, as Srinivasan points out, measures of income from household surveys *are* likely to be quite noisy.

Now, consider the results under each model if the consumption equation is estimated using instrumental variables. For simplicity, suppose a scalar variable X is the instrument in a first-stage income equation. The estimate of β can be expressed as:

$$\widehat{\beta} = \text{cov}(X,C)/\text{cov}(X,Y). \tag{7C-4}$$

If a permanent income model is correct ($\beta_1 = 1$ and $\beta_2 = 0$), and X is orthogonal to Y^T, ε, and μ, then the probability limit of $\widehat{\beta}$ will equal 1. However, if a consumption-tracks-income model is correct ($\beta_1 = \beta_2 = 1$), and X is orthogonal to ε and μ (although not necessarily to Y^T), the probability limit of $\widehat{\beta}$ will also equal 1. In other words, one gets the same results regardless of whether a permanent income model or a model in which consumers do not use saving to smooth consumption is correct.

This is not to say that the procedure is without merit: It does distinguish between a permanent income model of consumption and a static Keynesian model, in which the consumption propensity is much less than unity. However, if one wants to know whether households use savings to buffer consumption from income shocks, this research strategy is not useful.

A more fruitful research strategy is to measure, explicitly, both permanent and transitory income and examine whether the consumption propensities out of each differ. As previously noted, it is difficult to measure both permanent and transitory income using cross-sectional data. One approach, in Paxson (1992), is to make use of time series information on regional determinants of income to construct variables that are correlated with transitory but not permanent income. For the sample of Thai rice farmers used in the analysis, measures of the deviation in regional rainfall in the survey year from average regional values were constructed and matched to households according to their region of residence. The basic idea was that these rainfall shocks would produce transitory shocks to farm incomes, without altering permanent incomes. Income was then regressed on the measures of rainfall shocks, as well as a set of variables that were assumed to be determinants of permanent income. The results of this first-stage income regression were used to construct measures of *both* transitory and permanent income. Propensities to save out of these two income measures were then estimated. The results imply that farm households in Thailand do use saving to buffer consumption from shocks in income due to weather.

This empirical strategy may have limited applicability because the data requirements are more onerous than they might at first appear to be. First, the method requires time series information at a regional level on a set of variables that are determinants of income. For farm households, weather is a natural choice, and many countries collect regional rainfall data over time. For nonfarm households, however, it is less obvious what variables qualify as determinants of transitory income. Likely candidates, such as wages or other prices, may not have been collected regionally for long time periods and may have little true variation across regions. Second, implementation of this approach requires more than one cross section of household data. The reason is that the region of residence is likely to be a determinant of permanent income, and so a region-specific intercept should be included in the first-stage income equation. With only one cross section (i.e., one year) of household data, the measures of transitory income (which are region-specific) will be colinear with the region-specific intercepts.

A growing number of countries have collected panel data on households, whereby households are interviewed for more than one year, and a small number of saving studies use these data. For example, Bhalla (1979, 1980) used a three-year panel from India. Deaton (1992) used a two-year panel from Cote d'Ivoire. Can short panel data sets be used to overcome the problems inherent in cross sections? Although panels do provide more information on movements in household income, applying models of saving behavior to these data typically requires strong assumptions about the stochastic process that governs income. Bhalla (1980), for example, constructed a measure of transitory income equal to the deviation in current income from its three-year average. The implicit assumption is that incomes are identically and independently distributed for each household over time. If, instead, incomes are serially correlated, a permanent income model could be incorrectly rejected.

Deaton's approach differs from that of Bhalla. He tested a basic implication of a permanent income model: The change in consumption between two periods (t and $t-1$) should be orthogonal to information known (by the household) at time $t-1$. If a permanent income model is correct, a regression of consumption in t on consumption and income in $t-1$ should yield (1) a unit coefficient on lagged consumption and (2) a coefficient of 0 on lagged income. A required assumption is that each household's income follows a stationary process. Unfortunately (as Deaton points out) heterogeneity across households in the unconditional mean of income can make the results difficult to interpret. Deaton shows that if the permanent income model is correct, the parameter estimates will be consistent regardless of whether heterogeneity exists. However, if households only partially smooth consumption, heterogeneity will result in inconsistent parameter estimates. Thus, although the method is useful for testing a permanent income model, it may not provide good information on how much households smooth consumption given that they do not smooth perfectly. It would be interesting to use Deaton's techniques on Bhalla's three-year panel, given that with three years of data household-specific heterogeneity can be properly accounted for.

In summary, although there is no lack of data from developing countries on household income and savings, testing and estimating models of saving with these data is difficult. There are problems of data accuracy as well as methodological problems. Despite these problems, the overall results indicate that households in developing countries do smooth consumption, at least partially. As Srinivasan points out, however, most studies reject a strong version of the permanent income model. It should be kept in mind that rejection of the permanent income model does not necessarily imply that credit markets function imperfectly. The standard permanent income model (which says that consumption equals the annuity value of expected lifetime wealth) hinges on *two* assumptions: that credit markets are perfect and that utility functions are quadratic, with linear marginal utility. Recent work (for example, Zeldes, 1989) has explored the implications of convex marginal utility, which results in a "precautionary" motive for saving. An interesting empirical implication of this work is that precautionary motives for saving can result in consumption patterns that have similarities to those that would be expected with borrowing constraints. We simply do not know, at this time, whether failures of permanent income models are due to credit market imperfections or to a misspecification of preferences. More research on the extent of credit market imperfections and their implications for consumption needs to be done.

References

Bhalla, Surjit S. "Measurement Errors and the Permanent Income Hypothesis: Evidence from Rural India." *American Economic Review* 63 (June 1979): 295–307.

Bhalla, Surjit, S. "The Measurement of Permanent Income and its Application to Savings Behavior." *Journal of Political Economy* 88 (June 1980): 722–743.

Deaton, Angus. "Household Saving in LDC's: Credit Markets, Insurance and Welfare." *Scandinavian Journal of Economics* 94 (1992): 253–273.

Gersovitz, Mark. "Saving and Development." In *Handbook of Development Economics*, edited by H. B. Chenery and T. N. Srinivasan. Amsterdam: North-Holland, 1987.

Musgrove, Philip. "Permanent Income and Consumption in Urban South America." *American Economic Review* 69 (June 1979): 355–368.

Paxson, Christina H. "Using Weather Variability to Estimate the Response of Savings to Transitory Income in Thailand." *American Economic Review* 82 (March 1992): 15–33.

Visaria, Pravin. "Poverty and Living Standards in Asia: An Overview of the Main Results and Lessons of Selected Household Surveys." Living Standards Measurement Study Working Paper No. 2. Washington: D.C.: World Bank, 1980.

Wolpin, Kenneth I. "A New Test of the Permanent Income Hypothesis: *The Impact of Weather on the Income and Consumption of Farm Households in India.*" *International Economic Review* 23 (October 1982): 583–594.

Zeldes, Stephen P. "Optimal Consumption with Stochastic Income: Deviations from Certainty Equivalence." *Quarterly Journal of Economics* 104 (1989): 275–298.

ABOUT THE AUTHORS

Besides their interest in the economics of saving, the authors contributing chapters to this volume have other attributes in common. They are respected academicians, they are acknowledged researchers, and they are energetic publishers. They have many accomplishments, only some of which can be noted in the ensuing paragraphs.

E. RAY CANTERBERY received the Ph.D. from Washington University (St. Louis). Before coming to Florida State University, where he is Professor of Economics, he was Assistant Professor at the University of Maryland (College Park), which conferred on him an Excellence in Teaching Award. At Texas Christian University he held the position of Cecil and Ida Green Honors Professor, and earlier at Simon Fraser University he held that of Visiting Associate Professor.

Canterbery is an elected member of the New York Academy of Sciences and lifetime emeritus member of the Board of Directors of the Eastern Economic Association, having served the EEA as its President, President-elect, and Vice President.

He has served as a member of the Board of Directors of the World Academy of Development and Cooperation. During the early 1980s Canterbery was a consultant to the United Nations in Vienna, where he helped to develop and draft UNIDO's first (of an annual) *Global Report*. A veteran grantsperson, Canterbery has received funding from the National Science Foundation, the Rockefeller Foundation, the U.S. Agency for International Development, and the U.S. Bureau of Mines.

While publishing 50 articles and eight books including *The Making of Economics* (now in a third edition at Wadsworth), Canterbery has found the time to be guest editor for a Symposium on Galbraith and American Economics for the *Journal of Post Keynesian Economics* and co-editor with the legendary Harry G. Johnson of the Symposium on Justice, Nozick and Rawls for the *Eastern Economic Journal*.

Presently, Canterbery is editing a Symposium on the Financial Fragility of American Capitalism for the *Journal of Post Keynesian Economics* and publishing a new book, *Economists in Their Times*, Bristlecone Books, 1993. Meanwhile, he has written op-ed style for the *New York Times Magazine*, *Challenge*, and newspapers and makes frequent appearances on radio and television.

ROBERT EISNER is William R. Kenan Professor of Economics at Northwestern University, where he has taught since 1952. Past President of the American Economic Association and also of the Midwest Economic Association, he is a Fellow of the American Academy of Arts and Sciences and of the Econometric Society. He has been a Guggenheim Fellow and a Fellow at the Center for Advanced Studies in the Behavioral Sciences. Eisner has also served on the Board of Directors of the Social Science Research Council and on its Executive Committee. He is an Associate Editor of the *Review of Economics and Statistics* and is on the editorial or advisory boards of the *Journal of Economic Education* and the *Journal of Economic Perspectives*. His previous editorial board posts include those of the *American Economic Review* and the *Journal of Economic Literature*. He has testified frequently before congressional committees on a variety of issues of economic policy.

Eisner has devoted major portions of his career to the study of business investment and to the development of extended measures of income and output. He has published extensively in the leading journals of the profession. His books include *Factors in Business Investment*, Ballinger (1978); *How Real Is the Federal Deficit?*, The Free Press, Macmillan (1986); and *The Total Incomes System of Accounts*, the University of Chicago Press (1989). Eisner received his Master's degree from Columbia University and his doctorate from Johns Hopkins University.

JAMES H. GAPINSKI earned his Ph.D. degree from the State University of New York at Buffalo. A Phi Beta Kappa member and a Summa Cum Laude graduate, he is Professor of Economics at Florida State University. For his research work he received the University's Developing Scholar Award, and for his classroom activity, he received its Teaching Award. Additionally, he was granted membership in the University's Council for Excellence in Teaching. As Brookings Economic

Policy Fellow in Washington, Gapinski held the post of economist with the U.S. Department of Commerce. Afterward he completed two tours of duty at the University's Study Center in London, where he later spent part of a sabbatical leave as Academic Visitor with the London School of Economics and with Queen Mary College. He published *Macroeconomic Theory: Statics, Dynamics, and Policy* with McGraw-Hill, co-authored *Modeling the Economic Performance of Yugoslavia* for Praeger, and co-edited *Essays in Post-Keynesian Inflation* for Ballinger. Gapinski has also published more than 45 articles in journals and contributed works.

An Amherst College alumnus having Cum Laude status, **KENNETH A. LEWIS** took his Ph.D. from Princeton University. He spent his Assistant Professor years at Boston College before moving to the University of Delaware, where he advanced through rank to Professor, his present position. Along the way, he received the University's Excellence in Teaching Award and three other tributes for meritorious teaching. Since the dawn of the eighties, Lewis accepted six separate appointments as Acting Chairperson and one as Domestic Policy Coordinator for Governor Pierre du Pont. Besides being a dedicated teacher and a willing University and community servant, Lewis maintains an active research program. His published articles, which number more than 20, cover a wide range of topics from saving to baseball, while his grant work centers on an econometric model of Delaware. The U.S. Department of Justice, the Delaware Transportation Authority, and the Bell Telephone Company have been just some of his consultantships.

PAUL J. PIEPER, a Ph.D. graduate from Northwestern University, is presently Associate Professor of Economics at the University of Illinois, Chicago. Besides his previous positions as Lecturer and Assistant Professor at Illinois, Pieper held the posts of Consultant for the Argnonne National Laboratory and Visiting Economist with the Bureau of Economic Analysis. A member of the Conference on Research in Income and Wealth sponsored by the National Bureau of Economic Research, he has been the recipient of grants from the National Science Foundation. His publications include more than a dozen articles, some of which have been translated into foreign languages.

GIAN S. SAHOTA received his Master's degrees from Panjab University and Leeds University and earned the doctorate from the University of Chicago. He then moved through all three academic ranks at Vanderbilt University, where he enjoys emeritus status. Sahota has been much in demand. He was Visiting Professor at the University of Colorado, the University of Sao Paulo, the Institute of Economic Growth in Delhi, the University of Hawaii, and has had visiting assignments at the Harvard

International Tax Program, London School of Economics, National Institute of Public Finance and Policy, and the Delhi School of Economics. Moreover, he served as Simon Senior Fellow at the University of Manchester and as economic adviser to the governments of Brazil and Singapore and to international agencies such as the United Nations and the World Bank. Presently he is Project Associate at the Harvard Institute for International Development and the P. K. Seidman Distinguished Visiting Professor at Rhodes College. Besides publishing armfuls of articles, Sahota has published five books, including *Brazilian Economic Policy: An Optimal Control Theory Analysis* for Praeger, *Income Distribution: Theory, Modeling and Case Study of Brazil* for Iowa State University Press, and *Poverty: Theory and Policy: A Study of Panama* for Johns Hopkins University Press.

After graduating Magna Cum Laude from Harvard University and obtaining the Ph.D. from the University of California at Berkeley, **LAURENCE S. SEIDMAN** accepted positions at the University of Pennsylvania, Swarthmore College, and the University of Delaware, where he is Professor of Economics. In addition, he became a member of the Brookings Panel on Economic Activity and a consultant to the Federal Reserve Bank of Philadelphia. A frequent publisher, Seidman has more than 40 papers to his credit. His *Challenge* pieces cover topics ranging from incomes policy to health insurance, and his op-ed columns appear in leading newspapers such as the *New York Times*. His books include *Saving America's Economic Future: Parables and Policies* for Sharpe and *Macroeconomics* for Harcourt, Brace, Jovanovich. *The Design of Federal Employment Programs* for Lexington Books is the published version of his doctoral dissertation.

DAVID J. SMYTH is the LSU Foundation Distinguished Professor of Economics at Louisiana State University. Previously he held academic posts at the University of Queensland (Australia), the University of Birmingham (England), the State University of New York at Buffalo, the Claremont Graduate School, and Wayne State University. At Wayne State he chaired the Department of Economics for nine years, received the University's Faculty Recognition Award, and was elected to the institution's Academy of Scholars. Visiting posts held by Smyth include an S. W. Brooks Professorship at the University of Queensland and an Erskine Fellowship at the University of Canterbury (New Zealand) and research posts at the United Kingdom Department of Economic Affairs, the Central Bank of Ireland, and the OECD. Smyth is the founder and editor of the *Journal of Macroeconomics*. A prolific publisher, Smyth is the author of 125 articles and five books, including the co-authored

Forecasting the United Kingdom Economy for D. C. Heath and *Size, Growth, Profits and Executive Compensation in the Large Corporation* for Macmillan and a solo effort, *Macroeconomics*, forthcoming with West Publishing.

T. N. SRINIVASAN earned his Master's and Ph.D. degrees from Yale University, where he presently is Samuel C. Park, Jr. Professor of Economics and Director of the Economic Growth Center. Internationally acclaimed, he held the position of Visiting Professor at Stanford University, the Massachusetts Institute of Technology, and the University of Minnesota as well as the post of Research Associate at the International Institute for Applied Systems Analysis in Laxenburg, Austria. Moreover, he was appointed Research Professor at the Indian Statistical Institute in New Delhi. Srinivasan was elected Fellow of the Econometric Society, Fellow of the American Academy of Arts and Sciences, and Honorary Member of the American Economic Association. His list of honors also includes the Mahalanobis Memorial Medal, of which he was co-recipient. A founding co-editor of the *Journal of Development Economics*, he served as associate editor of the *International Economic Review* and the *Journal of International Economics*. Srinivasan also co-edited *Econometrica* and *Economics and Politics*. His own publications include ten books, five being edited volumes, over 140 journal-type articles, 12 book reviews, and two biographies. Currently he is a consultant to the World Bank.

Name Index

Akaike, H., 137
Aleem, I., 305
Alesina, A., 235
Anderson, M., 178
Ando, A., 7, 70, 74, 75, 195, 196, 282
Arrow, K. J., 270
Aschauer, D., 129n
Auerbach, A. J., 190

Bacchetta, P., 245
Bailey, M. J., 11
Baillie, R. T., 70, 81
Balassa, B., 212, 297
Ball, R. J., 7, 14
Ballard, C. L., 184n
Barro, R. J.
  on bequests, 194, 196
  on fiscal deficits, 207
  on measurement, 217n
  on permanent income hypothesis, 197
  on quasi-public debt, 206, 218n
  on Ricardian Equivalence, 11, 23, 208–210, 211, 219n
  on technical progress, 274
Bartlett, B., 154
Batten, D. S., 135
Bean, C., 179
Becker, G.
  on income distribution, 196, 201, 204, 205, 216, 218n, 219n, 239
  on productivity, 129n

Beeman, W., 244
Behrman, J. R., 204, 239
Bell, C., 304–305
Bernheim, B. D., 12, 25, 195, 205
Besley, T., 313
Bhagwati, J. N., 213
Bhalla, S. S., 300, 301, 312, 319
Blecker, R., 174n, 161t
Blinder, A., 103, 196, 203, 205, 217n
Blitz, R., C., 199, 204, 205
Block, F., 160, 174n
Bloomfield, M. A., 142n
Borjas, G., 179
Boskin, M. J., 134, 206, 207, 209
Bosworth, B. P., 5, 42n, 183, 208
Boulding, K., 174n, 210
Boyd, J. H., 274
Bradford, D., 103
Brady, D., 89n
Breusch, T. S., 83
Brown, G. T., 297
Brown, T. M., 6
Brumberg, R., 7, 70, 195
Bruno, M., 286
Buchanan, J. M., 11, 207
Buiter, W., 209
Bunting, D., 43n, 237
Burmeister, E., 242
Burtless, G., 183

Canterbery, E. R., 204
Carroll, C., 23, 25, 295

327

Caves, R. E., 212
Chenery, H., 286
Chirinko, R. S., 184n
Clark, C., 54, 55, 64
Colander, D., 218n
Comanor, W. S., 199
Conlisk, J., 242, 244, 249, 254, 269, 271
Cooley, T. F., 137
Crouch, R., 242

Danziger, S., 248
Darity, W., Jr., 235
Darrat, A. F., 142n
David, M., 189, 196, 198, 204
Davidson, J. E. H., 82
Davis, T. E., 6
Deaton, A. S.
  on consumption, 103, 105, 106
  on income calculation, 291
  on informal credit markets, 301, 306
  on money illusion, 87
  on saving in developing countries, 279, 294–295, 319
Dekle, R., 282
DeMelo, J., 297
Dickey, D. A., 136–137
Dobell, R., 242
Domar, E., 207, 273
Drake, P. S., 7, 14
Duesenberry, J. S., 6, 57–60, 197

Eckaus, R. S., 213
Eisner, R.
  on fiscal deficits, saving, and investment, 11, 114, 128, 130n
  on measurement, 126, 129n, 130n
  on Ricardian Equivalence, 11, 25
  on saving rate, 112
  on total incomes system of accounts, 6, 112, 184, 244
Elmendorf, D. W., 209
Evans, P., 42n

Fackler, J. S., 135
Fei, J. C., 233

Feldstein, M. S.
  on fiscal deficits, 209
  on saving and investment, 212, 219n, 245, 286
  on social security, 207, 212, 218n
  on tax code, 183, 184n
Ferber, R., 89n
Findlay, R., 235
Flavin, M. A., 7, 78, 85, 104, 209
Flowers, M. R., 206, 207
Fraumeni, B. M., 6, 245
Freeman, R., 179
Friedman, B. M., 149, 182
Friedman, J. W., 196
Friedman, M.
  on correlations, 64, 65
  on empirical tests, 67–69, 70
  on factor pricing, 200
  on income distribution, 218n
  on longsightedness, 7
  on permanent income, 63
  permanent income hypothesis of, 57, 62, 84, 300
Fry, M. J., 284, 296, 297
Fuller, W. A., 136–137

Gali, J., 106
Gapinski, J. H., 43n, 89n, 242, 244, 249, 254
Genberg, J., 137
Gersovitz, M., 279, 316
Gertler, M., 184n
Ghate, P., 302
Gilder, G., 154, 163
Giovannini, A., 297
Goldsmith, R., 54, 55t, 57, 197
Gollop, F., 245
Gordon, A. R., 196
Gottschalk, P., 248
Gowland, D., 87
Gramlich, E., 244
Green, R. J., 188
Greider, W., 174n
Grossman, G. M., 274
Grossman, S. J., 100
Gupta, K. L., 297
Gurley, J. G., 284

NAME INDEX

Haan, J. de, 136
Hafer, R. W., 135
Hall, R. E., 7, 77–78, 83, 84, 85, 104
Hamberg, D., 43n
Haque, N. U., 281
Harrod, R. F., 7, 32–33, 245, 273
Harvey, A. C., 83
Hayashi, F., 85
Helpman, E., 274
Hendershott, P. H., 5
Henry, R., 236
Heston, A., 214
Hoff, K., 302
Holloway, T. M., 5, 130
Holmes, J. M., 68–69
Horioka, C., 212, 245, 286
Hsiao, C., 137

Intriligator, M., 245, 246

Jackson, J. D., 57, 59–60, 69, 77, 89n
Jeong, J.-H., 188
Johnson, H. G., 212, 218n
Johnson, M. H., 134
Jorgenson, D. W., 6, 70, 245

Kaldor, N., 28, 200,235
Kalecki, M., 199, 200, 235
Katz, L., 179
Kawai, M., 137
Kennickell, A. B., 195
Kessler, D., 203, 204, 209, 215, 216
Keynes, J. M.
  absolute income hypothesis of, 6, 7, 47, 48–54, 64, 70, 74, 80–81, 87, 93, 102, 104, 105, 197, 198, 285, 318
  aggregate demand view of, 154, 164, 188, 190, 236
  depression view of, 146
  disequilibrium model of, 191, 200
  on fiscal deficits, 157, 206–207, 216
  on functional finance, 218n
  The General Theory of, 47–50, 233
  on habit persistence, 6, 49, 89n
  income distribution theory of, 200, 233
  policy prescriptions of, 187, 208
  saving response view of, 23, 27, 40, 147, 148, 160–162, 173, 233, 236
  Say's law and, 154
Kindleberger, C. P., 184n
King, M., 279
Klein, L. R., 214, 217n–218n
Kotlikoff, L. J.
  bequest model of, 195, 196, 203–204, 205, 282
  on law of inheritance, 195, 196
  on saving determinants, 182, 190
Kravis, I. B., 214
Krueger, A. B., 179
Kuznets, S., 54, 197, 202, 213, 234

Laffer, A., 154, 187
Lahiri, A., 299
Lange, O., 114, 149
Laroque, G., 100
Lee, T. H., 70
Leff, N., 298
Leightner, J., 233, 236
Leite, S. P., 297
Lerner, A. P., 207, 208, 218n
LeRoy, S. F., 137
Levhari, D., 210
Lewis, K., 243, 246, 248, 256
Lewis, W. A., 232–233, 236, 279–280
Lipsey, R. E., 5, 218n
Lucas, R., 104, 209
Lupoletti, W., 137
Lutkepoh, J., 135
Lydall, H. E., 77

McDonald, D., 297
McKinnon, R. I., 284
McMahon, P. C., 70, 77, 81
Maddison, A., 294
Makonnen, D., 297
Malthus, T., 236
Mansfield, E., 129n
Marshall, A., 210
Masar, A., 297
Masson, A., 203, 204, 209, 215, 216

Meade, J. E., 203, 216
Menchik, P. L., 184n, 189, 196, 198, 204, 216
Minhas, B. S., 292
Minsky, H. P., 184n
Modigliani, F.
　on bequests, 196, 198, 205
　on debt burden, 207
　on empirical tests, 74–75
　on habit persistence, 6
　lift cycle hypothesis of, 70, 195
　on longsightedness, 7
　relative income hypothesis of, 59, 198
Molana, H., 85
Montgomery, E., 103
Montiel, P., 281
Murphy, K., 179
Musgrave, R. A., 207
Musgrove, P., 300, 316

Nagatani, K., 71, 74
Nelson, R. R., 265, 275
Nosari, E. J., 204

O'Driscoll, G. P., Jr., 12

Papanek, G., 212, 219n
Pasinetti, L. L., 29, 199, 200, 235
Paxson, C. H., 301, 312, 318
Peek, J., 5
Peters, R. K., 297
Phelps, E. S., 241, 243, 244
Pieper, P., 11, 114, 129n, 126
Placone, D., 10
Pollak, R. A., 239
Prescott, E. C., 274

Quah, D., 106
Quibria, M. G., 213

Ramanthan, R., 242, 253
Rao, D. C., 233
Raut, L., 298

Reagan, R.
　administration of, 25–26, 27, 28, 157, 160, 172, 176, 177, 178, 187, 191, 237
　election of, 157
　federal deficits under, 2, 157, 188
　income shares under, 169, 177, 237
　Reaganomics and, 28, 153–155, 177–178, 191
Rebelo, S., 274
Reynolds, P., 235
Ribe, F., 244
Ricardo, D., 11–12, 40, 181, 219n, 232, 236
Rocca, C. A., 193, 196, 201, 205, 215, 218n
Romer, P. M., 244, 271–273, 274
Rossi, N., 298–299
Ruggles, N. D. 6
Ruggles, R., 6

Sabelhaus, J., 183
Sahota, G. S., 193, 196, 201, 205, 215, 218n
Salemi, M. K., 137
Sandmo, A., 210
Sato, K., on transitional path, 34, 241–245, 249, 253–257, 262–263, 275
Sato, R., on transitional path, 33, 37, 241–243, 249, 253–257, 262–263, 273, 275
Schaller, H., 184n
Scholz, J. K., 184n
Schumpeter, J. A., 199
Scott, M. F. G., 295
Shaw, E. S., 284
Shleifer, A, 195, 205
Shoven, J. B., 184n, 195
Siamwalla, A., 304
Siedman, L., 243, 246, 248, 251n, 256
Siegfried, J. J., 199, 204, 205
Sims, C. A., 137
Skinner, J., 182
Smiley, R. H., 199
Smith, A.,236, 279
Smithies, A., 55

NAME INDEX

Smyth, D. J., 57, 59–60, 69, 70, 74, 77, 81, 89n
Snyder D., 212
Solow, R. M.
  growth model of, 32, 243, 244, 266, 267, 273–275
  on investment and economic growth, 28, 178, 295–296
  on life cycle hypothesis, 195, 196, 206
  on technical progress, 245, 246, 249
Soltow, L., 234
Spivak, A., 195, 196, 205
Sraffa, P., 12, 199, 235, 236
Srinivasan, T. N., 210
Stiglitz, J. E., 285, 302
Stock, J., 135
Stockman, D., 154, 157
Summers, L.
  on age-consumption profile, 295
  on bequests, 195, 205, 282
  on fiscal deficits, 209
  on law of inheritance, 195
  on Ricardian Equivalence, 208
  on saving equations, 23, 25
  on world income distribution, 214
Swan, T. W., 266, 267, 273–275
Swoboda, A., 137
Symons, J., 179

Tabellini, G., 235
Taubman, P. J., 204, 239
Thorning, M., 142n
Thurow, L., 202, 203, 205, 218n
Tice, H. S., 5, 218n
Tobin, J., 197, 198, 207, 209
Tomes, N., 196, 201, 204, 205, 216, 218n, 239

Townsend, R., 305
Tybout, J., 297

Udry, C., 304, 305
Ulbrich, H., 10

Varian, H. R., 211
Veblen, T., 172
Virmani, A., 298
Visaria, P., 315
Von Furstenberg, G. M., 188

Walker, C. E., 142n
Wallace, M., 10
Wanniski, J., 154
Watson, M., 135
Webb, R. H., 137
Weiss, A., 285
Welch, F., 179
West, K., 106
White, H., 80
Wickens, M. R., 83
Williams, R., 242
Williamson, J. G., 296
Winter, S. G., 265, 275
Wise, D., 196
Wolpin, K. I., 316
Woytinski, W. S., 52, 53–54

Yasuf, S., 297

Zahid, K. H., 13
Zeldes, S. P., 320
Zelhorst, H. D., 136

Subject Index

Absolute income hypothesis, 6, 7, 47, 48–54, 64, 70, 74, 80t, 81, 87, 93, 102, 104, 105, 197, 198, 285, 318
Adaptive expectation, 83
Adaptive rationality, 17
Adjustment time, 33–37, 41–42, 241–251, 253–260, 262–276, 277–278, 280
Antipoverty dividend, 248, 249, 250, 254
Arbitrage, 281

Bonds, *see* Government bonds, as net wealth; Junk bonds

Capital
  effective, equation for, 247, 254
  vintages, series on, 245, 246, 249
  see also Putty–clay capital; Putty–putty capital
Capital asset pricing model, 93–94, 95, 98, 99, 100
Capital flight, 235, 286–287, 290, 298
Capital gains tax, 168
Carter administration
  deregulation under, 157, 172, 191
  income redistribution under, 237
  social-security taxes and, 25–26, 155–156

Casino Economy
  Marx and, 28, 176, 180–181
  net worth in, 170, 171
  Reaganomics and, 153, 169–170, 187, 191
  saving and, 27, 173–174
Casino effect, 169–173, 176, 178, 179, 180–181
Chit funds, 303
Commodity flow method, 289, 291
Consumption–β model, 8, 93–101
Consumption binge, 118
Consumption smoothing, *see* Economic development, consumption smoothing and; Life cycle hypothesis, consumption smoothing and; Liquidity constraints, consumption smoothing and; Permanent income hypothesis, consumption smoothing and
Credit markets, informal, 38, 279, 281–282, 285, 287, 301, 302–306, 307–308
Crowding out hypothesis
  rejection of, 10, 40, 114, 120t, 121, 122, 123t, 128–129, 135, 141, 142, 208
  statement of, 9, 128
  support for, 10, 13, 40, 146, 148, 150, 173, 209

332

Danaid jar, 168
Deficit, fiscal
  interest rate and, 9, 10, 146, 147, 149, 150, 157, 208, 209
  investment and, 114, 116, 118–119, 119–128, 134–142, 145–151, 173, 208; *see also* Crowding out hypothesis
  in Reagan years, 2, 157, 188
  saving and, 8–11, 40–41, 103, 109–129, 134–142, 145–151, 176, 187, 207–210, 216, 217; *see also* Ricardian Equivalence
  state and local surplus and, 110*t*, 112–113, 134, 146, 174
  supply-side economics and, 2, 157, 187–188
  trade deficit and, 13, 40, 109, 115–116, 134, 135, 139–141, 142, 142*n*, 147, 149, 190
Deficit, trade, *see* Deficit, fiscal, trade deficit and
Dependency effect, 298–299
Divisia index, 249

Economic development
  agriculture and, 37, 283, 292, 302–303, 306
  capital flight and, 235, 286–287, 290, 298
  consumption smoothing and, 38–39, 42, 282–283, 285, 287, 301, 306, 312–313, 315–320
  focus of, 37, 279–280
  foreign aid and, 212–213, 219*n*, 286
  immiserization and, 212, 213
  income distribution and, 211–212, 233, 234–235, 292, 300
  informal credit markets and, 38, 279, 281–282, 285, 287, 301, 302–306, 307–308
  infrastructure and, 37
  legal system and, 283, 287
  Machlup-Metzler hypothesis and, 212
  policy in, 284–285, 286–287, 304–305, 307–308

  see also Saving, economic development and
Economic growth
  Classical theory of, 233, 234, 236
  Domar model of, 273
  golden rule and, 241
  Harrod model of, 32, 41, 273
  investment and, 28, 32, 154–155, 232
  natural rate of, 33
  Neoclassical model of, 241–242, 244, 247, 253, 254–256, 262–263, 265, 274–275, 280; *see also* Economic growth, Solow model of
  old theory of vs. new theory of, 273–276
  Solow model of, 32–33, 41, 178, 243, 244, 249, 266, 267, 273, 295–296; *see also* Economic growth, Neoclassical model of
  speed of adjustment and, 33–37, 41–42, 241–251, 253–260, 262–276, 277–278, 280
  warranted rate of, 32, 273, 274, 278
  see also Saving, economic growth and; Supply-side economics, economic growth and; Transitional path
Economic Recovery Tax Act of 1981, 155, 157, 187, 191
Error correction models, 82–83, 89
Euler equation, 83, 84, 95, 97, 98, 104, 297
Euler's Theorem, 30
Excess sensitivity, 7, 84–85, 86*t*, 104–106

Forbes 400, 199, 204
Foreign aid, 212–213, 219*n*, 286
Functional finance, 206–207, 208, 216, 218*n*

Gini coefficient, 31, 43*n*, 213, 218*n*
Government bonds, as net wealth, 11, 14, 17, 21, 40, 207, 208, 209, 216
Granger causality, 137, 139, 140*t*

Green Revolution, 305

Habit persistence school, 6
   Keynesian basis of, 49, 89n

Illiteracy, 119, 128
Immiserization, 212, 213
Income distribution
   Cambridge theory of, 28–29, 31–32, 41, 165, 173, 200, 232–237, 280, 300
   causal link to saving, 213–214, 215, 236, 237, 280
   across countries, 237, 280
   economic development and, 211–212, 233, 234–235, 292, 300
   functional, defined, 31
   functional, theories of, 28–31, 41, 198–201, 215, 218n, 232–237
   Gini coefficient and, 31, 43n, 213, 218n
   marginal productivity theory and, 29, 200–201, 248–249, 250, 266–267, 268; *see also* Income distribution, Neoclassical theory of
   Neoclassical theory of, 29–31, 41, 200–201, 235; *see also* Income distribution, marginal productivity theory and
   Neo-Ricardian theory of, 199
   personal, defined, 31
   personal, theories of, 31, 41, 193, 196, 201–202, 203–206, 215–216, 218n, 280
   Post-keynesian theory of, *see* Income distribution, Cambridge theory of
   technical progress and, 200–201
   during transition, 248–249, 254
   uncertainty and, 210–211
   see also Anti-poverty dividend; Life cycle hypothesis, personal income distribution and; Saving, income distribution and; Supply-side economics, income distribution and

Incomes revolution, 202
Individual retirement accounts, 209
Inflation, real balance effect and, 87
   see also Saving, inflation rate and
Inflation tax, 119–120
Interest rate, *see* Deficit, fiscal, interest rate and; Saving, interest rate and
Investment, *see* Deficit, fiscal, investment and; Economic growth, investment and; Saving, investment and

Junk bonds, 164, 168–169, 171, 172

Kemp-Roth tax bill, 156

Laffer curve, 154
Law of inheritance, 195–196
Learning-by-doing models, 270–273
Life cycle hypothesis, 7, 40, 62, 77, 82, 93, 102, 103, 104, 294–295, 296, 301, 307, 313
   bequests and, 73, 195–196, 206, 215, 126
   consumption smoothing and, 76, 95, 97–98, 285–286
   discussion of, 70–76, 94–95
   liquidity constrains and, 73, 285–286
   personal income distribution and, 75, 201–203, 205–206
   tests of, 73–76, 99, 294–295, 307
   uncertainty and, 73–74
   see also Permanent income hypothesis, life cycle hypothesis and
Liquidity constraints
   consumption smoothing and, 285–286, 312–313
   life cycle hypothesis and, 73, 285–286
   models of, 106, 297–298, 299, 301, 312
   permanent income hypothesis and,

SUBJECT INDEX 335

85, 105–106, 285–286, 301, 306, 319–320
Liquidity transfers, 166–169, 171, 172, 173
Longsightedness hypothesis, 7
Lucas Critique, 104

Marginal productivity theory, *see* Income distribution, marginal productivity theory and
Martingale function, 104
Modern theories, 48, 77, 82
Money illusion, absence of, 87
Moral hazard, 283, 285, 304, 307
Multiplier-accelerator model, 184n

National Income and Product Accounts (NIPA)
  alternatives to, 5–6
  weaknesses of, 5
  see also Saving, NIPA concept of; Saving, as residual
Net worth, in Casino Economy, 170, 171
  see also Saving, as net worth change

Overtaking time
  defined, 36–37, 257–258
  discount rate and, 37, 258
  estimates of, 259
  formula for, 258
  vs. sacrifice time, 37, 257–260

Peace dividend, 147
Permanent income hypothesis, 7, 8, 40, 77, 83, 84, 93, 102–106, 215
  consumption smoothing and, 62, 63, 76, 95, 97–98, 285, 318–320
  discussion of, 60–70, 94–95, 197, 283–284
  life cycle hypothesis and, 40, 62, 76, 82, 93, 94–95, 97–98, 99, 102–104, 197, 215, 285, 306
  liquidity constraints and, 85, 105–106, 285, 301, 306, 319–320

relative income hypothesis and, 198
tests of, 67–70, 80–82, 84–85, 99, 105, 106, 197, 299, 300–301, 306–307, 315–320
uncertainty and, 62–63, 87
Productivity
  supply-side economics and, 28, 187, 188–189, 190
  of total factors, 296
Putty-clay capital
  defined, 33
  speed of adjustment and, 34–35, 249, 254
Putty-putty capital
  defined, 34
  speed of adjustment and, 34–35, 244, 246, 249

q-substitutes, vs. q-complements, 248–249, 250, 251n
quasi public debt, 206

Random walk models, 7, 84, 204, 297, 298
Ratchet models, 59–60, 80–82
Rate of return, *see* Saving, rate of return, on; Transitional path, saving rate return and
Rational expectations
  consumption models and, 82, 83–85, 99, 102–103, 104–105, 299, 306–307
  Lucas Critique and, 104
  Ricardian Equivalence and, 25, 209–210, 216–217
  theory of, 219n
Rational lag model, 70
Reaganomics
  Casino Economy and, 153, 169–170, 187, 191
  federal deficit and, 2, 157, 188
  income shares and, 169, 177, 237
  see also Supply-side economics
Real balance effect
  in consumption, 13, 14, 17, 21
  inflation and, 87

Real estate, valuation of, 99, 168, 170–173, 180, 181
Relative income hypothesis, 7, 40, 57–60, 77, 197–198
  absolute income hypothesis and, 198
  permanent income hypothesis and, 198
Reserve army of unemployeds, 199
Ricardian Equivalence
  conditions necessary for, 12, 25, 208–209, 211
  vs. nonequivalence, 12, 40
  as rational expectations counterpart, 25, 209–210, 216–217
  Ricardo on, 11–12, 40, 219n
  saving and, 11–25, 40–41, 208, 216
  tests of, 8, 13–25, 40–41, 103, 209, 217, 281
  theory of, 11–13, 208, 216–217, 219n, 287
  see also Deficit, fiscal, saving and
Rotating Savings and Credit Institutions (ROSCAS), 303–304, 313

Sacrifice time
  defined, 35–36, 242, 253, 256, 264
  estimate of, 36, 243, 245, 247, 250, 253–254
  formula for, 244, 250, 264
  vs. overtaking time, 37, 257–260
  weaknesses of, 36, 37, 257, 264
  see also Transitional path, sacrifice time and
Sato controversy, 241–243, 253–254, 256, 262–263, 274–275
Saving
  age structure and, 74–76, 298–299, 301, 307
  Casino Economy and, 27, 173–174
  consumer durables and, 5, 38, 39, 57, 77–78, 89, 93, 100–101, 118, 120t, 126, 128–129, 159–160, 312
  as consumption obverse, 6, 48, 93, 194, 236
  consumption smoothing and, see

Consumption smoothing
  economic development and, 37–39, 42, 211–213, 219n, 279–308, 312–314, 315–320
  economic growth and, 32–37, 145–146, 149, 150–151, 154–155, 178, 212, 214, 233, 236, 241–251, 253–260, 262–278, 279–280, 287, 292–296, 299, 306
  endogenous technical progress and, 37, 265, 267–276
  estimated equations for, 21–25, 65–66, 80–82, 87–88, 103, 105–106
  facts of, 1–5, 28, 37–38, 39, 41, 116, 118–119, 129n, 134, 159, 160–161, 162t, 165–166, 173, 182, 183, 189, 207–208, 209, 212, 214, 217, 217n, 233, 237, 279–281, 287, 292–301, 306, 313
  foreign aid and, 212–213, 286
  income distribution and, 28–32, 154, 155, 159, 176, 193–217, 217n, 232–237, 280
  inflation rate and, 8, 85–88, 89, 106, 135, 136–137, 146, 164–165, 296–297, 298, 299
  informal credit markets and, 38, 281–282, 285, 302–306, 307–308
  interest rate and, 38, 60–62, 84, 94–99, 104, 105, 135, 138, 146, 150, 213, 217n, 239, 283–285, 287, 294, 296–298, 306, 307–308
  as intermediate target, 177, 182–183
  investment and, 8–9, 25, 27, 28, 32, 41, 110, 112, 114, 134–135, 136, 145–146, 148–149, 155, 159, 161–162, 165, 168, 173, 178, 190, 200, 233, 237, 245, 263, 280, 281–282, 286, 287, 288, 291, 292–301, 306–307
  measurement error in, 5, 6, 27, 39, 103, 106, 129n, 159, 182, 189, 217n–218n, 279–280, 287–292, 300, 301, 306, 313
  as net worth change, 5–6, 25, 39, 41, 103, 159–160, 164–169, 170–171, 182, 184n, 217n, 300

SUBJECT INDEX

NIPA concept of, 5, 39, 41, 57, 103, 109–112, 116–118, 122, 159, 182, 217n, 240
  rate of return on, 36, 37, 242–251, 253–254, 256, 257, 258–259, 260, 260n, 263–264, 265–278, 284, 287, 312
  as residual, 5, 39, 48, 78–80, 93–94, 103, 113, 159, 166, 189, 217n, 288, 290, 300
  Ricardian Equivalence and, 11–25, 40–41, 208, 216
  supply-side economics and, 25–28, 41, 153–174, 176–184, 189, 191, 217n
  theories of, 6–8, 38, 39–40, 47–89, 93–101, 102–106, 182, 193, 194–198, 215, 216–217, 217n, 219n, 236, 281–282, 283–284, 296–297, 298–299, 300, 301, 306, 312, 313, 316–318
  uncertainty and, 62–63, 73, 87, 210–211, 217, 282–283, 298, 312
  see also Deficit, fiscal, saving and; Transitional path
Say's law, 154–155, 157, 177, 181
Scotch verdict, 28, 177
Second best, theory of, 285
Shortsightedness hypothesis, 7, 42n, 76
Speculative bubbles, 27, 28, 41, 172–174, 176, 180, 181, 184n, 187, 191
Speed of adjustment, 33–37, 41–42, 241–251, 253–260, 262–276, 277–278, 280
Stagflation
  defined, 25
  supply-side economics and, 153, 154
Stationarity, 10, 135, 136–137, 139, 319
Stock market
  assets traded on, 94, 170
  prices in, 157–158, 167, 168, 172, 182
Supply-side economics
  capital gains tax and, 168
  deregulation and, 27, 154, 157–158, 169, 172, 173, 177–178, 187, 191–192

economic growth and, 154–155, 177, 178
fiscal deficits and, 2, 157, 187–188
income distribution and, 25–26, 27, 31, 41, 153, 155–156, 158–159, 160–161, 168, 169, 170, 172, 173, 176, 177, 179–181, 187, 189, 191–192, 202, 217n, 237
productivity and, 28, 187, 188–189, 190
Reagan administration and, 25–26, 27, 28, 157, 160, 172, 176, 177–178, 187, 191, 237
saving and, 25–28, 41, 153–174, 176–184, 189, 191, 217n
speculative bubbles and, 27, 28, 41, 172–174, 176, 180, 181, 187, 191
stagflation and, 153, 154
theory of, 25–26, 154–155, 177–178, 187–188
as trickle-down theory, 157
System of National Accounts (SNA), 287

Tax Reform Act of 1986, 184n
Technical progress
  disembodied, 33, 243–246, 248, 254, 259
  embodied, 33, 146, 243–249, 254, 259
  endogenous, models of, 267–276
  exogenous vs. endogenous, 37, 254, 265–276
  income distribution and, 200–201
  neutrality of, 245
  in the 1980s, 190–191
  speed of adjustment and, 34, 243–251, 253–260, 262–278
  total factor productivity and, 296
Thatcher government, 28, 180
Trade deficit, *see* Deficit, fiscal, trade deficit and
Transitional path, 33–37, 41–42, 241–251, 253–260, 262–276, 277–278, 280
  epsilon time and, 242–243, 249–250, 253, 255–257, 260, 260n

sacrifice time and, 242–251, 253–254, 256–257, 260, 260n, 264
saving rate return and, 242–251, 253–254, 256, 257, 258–259, 260, 260n, 263–264, 265–278
T-year gain and, 242–251, 253–254, 256, 257, 258, 260, 260n, 264–264
Trickle-down theory, 157
Twin deficits, *see* Deficit, fiscal, trade deficit and
T-year gain, *see* Transitional path, T-year gain and

Uncertainty
Boulding and, 210
income distribution and, 210–211
life cycle hypothesis and, 73–74
Marshall and, 210
permanent income hypothesis and, 62–63, 87
saving and, 62–63, 73, 87, 210–211, 217, 282–283, 298, 312
Unit roots, 105, 106, 136–137

Vector autoregressive models, 10, 104, 137–142
Vita theory, 204

Walrasian system, 200
Wealth adjustment hypothesis, 7, 76–77, 81, 87–88
Wealth theoretic school, 6–7
Widow's cruse, 29, 168, 199, 200